Towards Understanding Hindu Myths

Towards

Understanding Hindu Myths

Sadashiv Ambadas Dange

Aryan Books International
New Delhi

Towards Understanding Hindu Myths

ISBN: 978-81-7305-080-0

First Published: 1996

Reprinted: 2022

Published by:

Aryan Books International
Pooja Apartments, 4B, Ansari Road, New Delhi-110 002 (India)
Tel.: 23287589, 23255799; Fax: 91-11-23270385
E-mail: aryanbooks@gmail.com
www.aryanbooks.com

Printed in India

Books That Live!

Aryan Books International was established in 1992. Though it began as a commercial venture, business was only a part of the whole. The primary aim was to bridge the gap between the history taught and the real history of our country, and also to present its lesser known and sometimes deliberately neglected facets. In academia, the legacy of our art, culture and ethos was being undermined to perpetuate a narrative which left us looking weak, soft and lagging behind the so-called progressive West.

It was this narrative that we sought to contest. The journey over the last thirty years has not been an easy one. However, it gives us a sense of satisfaction to have possibly made a small difference by publishing over 750 titles written by the most acclaimed authors in the field. We have specialized in publishing ingenious and outstanding scholarship, both established as also fresh. While we focus on our long forgotten history, we also bring to the fore certain extremely important aspects of Indian art, culture and traditions.

Apart from pioneering content, we also ensure that our production quality remains the best in the business, as we continue with the mission to publish books that **Live Forever**!

We are also aware that this is just the beginning of a long journey. A long road lies ahead. A lot more needs to be said. A lot more needs to be explored. We assure you that we're on it with renewed commitment!

To

Prof. R.N. Dandekar

Whom

I always regard

as

The 'Adhyakṣa' (adhi–akṣa)

of my

Academic endeavour

Contents

Preface

The idea in the present venutre is not to treat all myths that obtain in the Hindu texts, or in the oral tradition and to classify the various motifs that may reveal in such a collective study. That is a stupendous task, which would require another effort. As the title shows, the aim in writing this book is to take a note of, and re-examine, some of the most important theories that evolved in the study of myths, during the present century, and to explore the feasibility of applying them to the understanding of Hindu myths. The conclusion is foregone; for, no one theory can act as the 'Open Sesame' for going to the inner meaning of myths. Yet, it was felt that a review of modern approaches towards the understanding of myths, placed side by side with Hindu myths, would be a welcome venture. This would also help clarify the confusion between the traditional concept behind the term mythology and its expected scientific meaning.

The idea of looking at Hindu myths, both from the Vedic texts and from the post-Vedic ones, from a rather untraditional angle, in the light of wider studies of myths conducted by scholars who were, however, not Sanskrit-based, was pursued by me in my book: *Legends in the Mahābhārata* published as far back as 1969 (Motilal Banarsidass, Delhi). With the same angle other books dealing with Vedic myths, symbols and ritual followed (Bhau Vishnu Ashtekar Vedic Lectures *Pastoral Symbolism from the Ṛgveda*, at the University of Poona, published by that University, 1970; *Vedic concept of 'Field' and the Divine Fructification*, University of Bombay, 1971; *Sexual Symbolism from the Vedic Ritual*, Delhi, 1979; and Acharya Dr. Vishvabandhu Memorial Lecutres, *Vedic Myths in Social Perspective*, Panjab University, Chandigarh-Hosiarpur, published by VVRI, Hoshiarpur, 1982). The strain common to these lectures and publications was that Vedic myths should not be studied in isolation, and that in many myths the reflection of ritual provides the key to its meaning, if another ritual of a similar nature be compared. This is done by internal comparison. This has to be further substantiated, where feasible, by myths not only from the post-Vedic records but also from other sources, with the differences marked. About the myths from the Veda, and Ṛgveda in particular, it could be said, with Gonda, that, "The Ṛgveda is much more varied than it has sometimes been supposed to be" (*Proceedings of the All India Oriental Conference*, Twenty-ninth Session, BORI, Poona, 1980, p.1; this is from his address as the General President). As such, a multi-phased comparative method of study is a necessity.

A pointed effort to present a fresh analysis of Hindu myths on these lines was the result of an invitation, to frame a course of two weeks, and to deliver lectures, from the Central Institute of Languages, Mysore, which conducted an 'International Institute of Semiotics and Structural Studies' from December 17, 1984 through January 12, 1985. During discussions in the class with students—Indian and foreign—who attended my lectures on Hindu myths, and who were teachers in various colleges in India and outside India, the subject ripened. A further stimulus came when Dr. (Mrs.) Sindhu S. Dange, Professor and Head, Department of Sanskrit, University of Bombay, was successful in starting the

Post-graduate Diploma Course in Comparative Mythology in the said Department in 1990 and invited me to deliver lectures on 'The Methodology for the Understanding of Myths'. To the best of my knowledge, no other university in India has such a course, at the time of writing this Preface. In these lectures (since 1990 till date) and in the discussions with mature participants of various disciplines, such as Medicine, Histrionics, Architecture, Dance, Art and Theatrical Direction, the topics of the present book took shape.

Shri Vikas Arya, the publisher, called on me when I happened to be in New Delhi, in the Summer of 1993 and requested me for a book, specially on myths. I agreed.

Prof. (Dr.) Sindhu Dange's request to me to lecture to the students of Comparative Mythology gave me an opportunity to brush up my ideas in the discussions that followed after every lecture, and also during the lecture, for which she deserves my thanks. She also went through the typescript and offered useful suggestions at various stages as the book was being prepared for the press.

Mrs. Vidya Joshi, Lecturer in the J.J. School of Arts, Bombay, did the design and the picture for the flap. Mrs. Vidya Kamat (M.A. Fine Arts), who is a Diploma Holder of the course in Comparative Mythology, and is doing her Ph.D. in the Department of Sanskrit, Bombay University, did the inside pictures. She is also an artist for *The Times of India,* Bombay. I thank both these artists.

I deem it a privilege to dedicate this book to Prof. (Dr.) R.N. Dandekar, with whom my acquaintance goes back to 1955, when my revered *guru,* Professor (late) H.D. Velankar, introduced me to him. I have always felt myself accountable to him in my academic endeavour.

Meaning of a myth is often elusive—like the nature of the Absolute! About the meanings of myths suggested here, in the pages to follow, scholars could say, "No; not thus!" (*neti=na+iti*). Well, I keep the avenue of my satisfaction open even with, "May be as I have suggested"!! (*veti=va+iti*).

BOMBAY **Sadashiv Ambadas Dange**

19th May, 1995

Abbreviations and Sanskrit Texts

Agni P. (Agni-purāṇa), Ed. H.N. Apte, Ānandāśrama, Pune (Poona), 1900

AV (Atharvaveda), Ed. S.D. Santabalekara (Satavlekar) Aundh, Vikrama-Saṁvat 1995, Sālivāhana Śaka, 1860.

Ait. Ār. (Aitareya Āraṇyaka), Ānandāśrama, Pune, 1992

Ait. Br. (Aitareya Brāhmaṇa) Ānandāśrama, Pune, 1992

Ait. (Aitareya Upaniṣad), fr. *Ten Principal Upaniṣads*, with Śāṅkarabhāṣya, Motilal Banarsidass, Delhi, 1978 (1964).

Bhāg. P. (Bhāgavata Purāṇa), Gītā Press, Gorakhpur, Samvat 1997-2018

Bhav.P. (Bhaviṣya-purāṇa), Veṅkaṭeśvara Press, Bombay 1959

Brahma P. (Brahma-Purāṇa), Ed. H.N.Apte, Ānandāśrama, Pune, 1895

Brahmāṇḍa P., Ed. J.L.Shastri, Motilal Banarsidass, Delhi, 1973

Brahmavai.P. (Brahmavaivarta-Purāṇa), Ed. Vasudev Shastri Marathe, Ānandāśrama, Pune, 1935

Bṛahad.Up. (Bṛahadāraṇyaka-upaniṣad), fr.*Ten Principal Upaniṣad*-s, Motilal Banarsidass, Delhi, 1978 (1964).

Chānd.Up. (Chāndogya-upaniṣad), Motilal Banarsidass, Delhi 1978 (1964)

Garuḍa P. (Garuḍa-purāṇa), Ed., Ramshankar Bhattacharya, Caukhamba, Varanasi, 1964

Hari V. (Harivaṁs'a), Gītā Press, Gorakhpur.

Jai. Br.(Jaiminīya-Brāhmaṇa), Ed. Raghuvira and Lokeshchandra, Motilal Banarsidass, Delhi, 1986 (Nagpur, 1954)

Kāth. Sam. (Kāṭhaka-saṁhitā), Ed. Satavlekar, Aundh, 1943

Kau./Kauṣ.Br.(Kauṣītaki-brāhmaṇa=Sāṅkhāyana Br.), H.N. Apte, Ānandāśrama, Pune, 1911

Kūrma P. (Kūrma-purāṇa), Ed. Anandasvarupa Gupta, All India Kashiraja Trust, Varanasi, 1972

Mb. (Mahābhārata), Gītā Press, Gorakhpur, Vikrama-saṁvat, 2013-15

Mait. Sam. (Maitrāyaṇī-Samhitā), Ed. Leopald von Shroeder, 1923

Manu/Manu Sm. (Manusmṛti), Nirṇayasāgara, Bombay, 1946

Mārk. P. (Mārkaṇḍeya-Purāṇa), Ed. Jivanand Vidyasagar, Calcutta, 1879

Matsya P. (Matsya-Purāṇa), Ānandāśrama, Pune, 1981

Padma-P. (Padma-Purāṇa), Ānandāśrama, Pune, 1893-94

Rām. (Śrīmad-Valmīki Rāmāyaṇam), Ed. K. Chinnasvami and V.H. Subrahmanyam Shastris, Mylapur, Madras, 1958

ṚV (Ṛgveda), Vaidika Saṁśodhana Maṇḍaḷa, Pune 1933-1951

Samarāṅgaṇasūtra-dhāra, Gaekwad's Oriental Series, Oriental Institute. Baroda, 1966

Śat. Br. (Śatapatha Brāhmaṇa), Mādhyandina, Ed. Chinnasvami and Pattabhirama Shastris, Chaukhamba, Varanasi

Śiva P. (Śiva-Purāṇa), Ed. Ramtej Shastri, Varanasi, Vikrama-samvat. 2020

Sk.P.(Skanda-Purāṇa), Veṇkaṭeśvara Press, Bombay

Tait.Br.(Taittirīya-brāhmaṇa), Ānandāśrama, Pune, 1979

Vāj. Sam. (Vājasaneyi-saṁhitā),

Vāmana P. (Vāmana-purāṇa), Ed. Anandasvarupa Gupta, Kashiraj Trust, Ramnagar, Varanasi, 1968

Varāha P. (Varāha-Purāṇa), Ed. Hrishikesh Shastri, Calcutta, 1893

Vāyu P. (Vāyu-Purāṇa), Ed. Rajendra Lal Mitra, Calcutta, 1882

Viṣṇu P. (Viṣṇu-Purāṇa), Gītā Press, Gorakhpur, Vikrama Saṁvat, 2045 (1990)

Yājñ.Sm. (Yājñavalkya-Smṛti), Nirṇayasāgara, Bombay, 1936

* * *

ABORI : *Annals of the Bhandarkar Oriental Research Instt.*

Encl. Rel. and Ethics : *Encyclopaedia of Religion and Ethics*

Encl. P.B.P. : *Encyclopaedia of Puranic Beliefs and Practices*

JAOS : *Journal of the American Oriental Society*

VIJ : *Vishveshvarananda Indological Journal.*

Introduction

The study of Hindu myths has a pretty long history. One of the earliest efforts in this direction was of Charles Coleman (1832: *Mythology of the Hindoos*, London), and by about the close of the nineteenth century Wilkins presented his *Hindu Mythology—Vedic and Puranic* (1882: Calcutta). Another book that closely preceded that of Wilkins was that by Cox (1970: *Mythology of the Aryan Nations*) which followed the method of etymology and interpreting these myths as mostly nature-myths. Apart from the efforts of Max Müller, who led the nature-myth school from among the Sanskritists and whose studies on comparative mythology were very well known by the close of the nineteenth century through the beginning of the twentieth, A.A. Macdonell's *Vedic Mythology* (1897, Strassburg) served as a model for E.W. Hopkins (1915: *Epic Mythology*, Strassburg), and was preceded by Fausboll (1903: *Hindu Mythology according to the Mahābhārata*, London). From among the non-Sanskritists who wrote about the myths and legends of the Hindus, Donald Mackenzie's multi-phased researches contain remarks about Hindu gods and their myths. However, when he says that Indra was the "elephant-rider" and that "a later Indian form of Indra was the elephant-god Ganesh, the son of Shiv and Parvati" (no year: *Myths of Pre-Columbian America*, London, pp.30-31) it poses a problem of investigation. He confuses Varuṇa with *vāraṇa* (elephant) and mixes the later image of Indra riding the elephant, named Airāvata. Airāvata is mentioned in Mb. in the context of the churning of the ocean. As the beast comes out of the ocean, it is appropriated by Indra among the gods (Mb. Ādi 18.40). Airāvata does occur in AV(VIII.10.29); but the word refers to a *nāga* (which word has the connotation also as elephant, in addition to 'serpent' in the later period) and has no association with Indra. Etymology has been useful, to a certain extent, in understanding myths; but, beyond a certain limit, it has to be used cautiously. Similar appears to be true, when the Asura Śambara is seen as synonymous with Varuṇa through a very late post-Vedic variation, Śaṁvara (with the interchange of *b* and *v*), arguing that the name Śambara supports the Proto-Māgadhī etymology (Parpola,1988: "The coming of the Aryans to Iran and India and the Cultural and Ethnical Identity of the Dāsas", *Studia Orientalia*, 64: 195-302; also 1992: p. 298). The point is whether the Proto-Māgadhī support could be extended back to the Vedic Śambra, and seeing the Asura, in fact, as Saṁvara ('cover of rain-water'), and another name of Varuṇa, as both could be traced to the root *vṛ*, 'to cover' and thence to 'water', with which the association of Varuṇa is already clear in ṚV. A well attested trait about myths is, that earlier personalities get currency also in later period with added particulars and new garbs. Even in the case of Śambara the trait is seen. He is seen in Mb. not only as an adversary of Indra (Vedic detail) (Mb. Ādi 137. 43; Vana 168.81), but also is said to be son of Kaśyapa and Danu, the traditional parents of demons (Ādi 65.22). A new hero, Sāmba, is credited with his defeat (Vana 120.13). He is also said to have been killed by Kṛṣṇa, through Pradyumna, who is his grandson (Sabhā, Southern reading after the regular 38.29; also the regular version, Udyoga 68.4; Anuś. 14.28). According to Mb. he was an ancient ruler, which statement could be compared with the one from ṚV, where he is said to be the Dāsa chief and son of Kulitara (ṚV IV.30. 14). This would indicate that he was a real person,[1] who became a mythical Asura later on. But, it is certain, that he had nothing to do with Magadha, or with a dialect that could be called Proto-Māgadhī, as Śambara's mountain resort, at the period of the Ṛgveda, and earlier, has to be taken somewhere in the north-western side of present day India. Probably it was Gāndhāra or Kashmir. It is clear, that relying too much on etymology is likely to lead us astray. Yet, the influence of Max Müller's approach of etymology and his theory of the 'disease of language' cast a lasting influence on later Sanskrit scholars. So, Pāṇḍu, the father of the Pāṇḍava brothers was seen as the pale sun (*pāṇḍu*), and Duryodhana ('difficult to fight') was interpreted as the sun in the winter season. So was the blind Dhṛtarāṣṭra the powerless winter sun. Draupadī, called Kṛṣṇā, was understood as the dark (kṛṣṇa) earth, and Draupadī's (Kṛṣṇā's) cloak, that was taken off from her body, was thought to be indicative of the barren earth in the winter season, being unmindful of the seasons in India and the changes as different from those in the West, and also that these are historical persons. According to this view, Mb accounts of war and strife indicated only the mythology of seasons, and that, later, the human element encroached upon this original superhuman central theme.[2] Following the same line of understanding myths, Dahlmann, like Ludwig, believed that the polyandrous marriage of the Pāṇḍava brothers with Draupadī was purely a mythical element.[3] G.J. Held (1935), who took a survey of earlier efforts to reach the inner meaning of the Mahābhārata. cautioned about the excesses of etymology and the naturophobia, as did the newly emerging schools of the study of myths. These new schools, consisting mainly of non-Sanskritists, equipped with the tools of anthropology and ethnology, and also acquainted with Hindu myths, began striking against the theories of the Sanskritists who toed the line of Max Müller. Held's was, avowedly, an ethnological approach (1935, p.39), though restricted to the Mahābhārata, as that was of L. von Schroeder (1908 : *Mysterium und Mimus im Rigveda*, Leipzig) relating to the Ṛgveda in the beginning of the twentieth century. But, this welcome effort of Schroeder was heavily criticized by A.B.Keith (1909 JRAS, pp.207ff; also 1911, pp. 105ff). While the anthropologists and the ethnologists outright nicknamed Max Müller as 'solarist', and even 'sun' (thus, "here comes the Sun"), dubbing his interpretations as 'comic'[4], Held's reaction to Max Müller was rather soft. He says that, if we accept Max Müller's version of mythology as a result of the 'disease of language', we can see in religion at the most a system of irrational aberrations of the human mind, but never religion as such (Held, 1935, p. 102). We may substitute 'religion' by 'myths' and say, that to accept the theory of Max Müller (etymology and nature based, in toto) we might see in myths only irrational aberrations of the mind of the persons to whom myths were suggested and of those who perpetuated them in tradition. But, that is hardly the case. Held rightly suggested, that we must take a myth in its entirety. This is perfectly sound; because, a myth is a point of faith for the people whose tradition nurtured it. Held asks, "What is it that people believed in?"; he answers, "It is not the naturalistic substratum of the myth that the people believed in; but, it is the myth as a whole" (*ibid.* p. 104). However, Held leads myth to the scaffolds of ritual for its meaning when he says, "Myths do not, therefore, transport us into a purely imaginary heaven, but conduct directly or indirectly to the spot where the rites are celebrated" (*ibid*). This very clearly shows that Held goes on the lines of the Ritual-myth theory, or that he is, very probably, influenced by the views of Frazer and those who followed him. This was the line of thought which, at that period, was gaining strength. Held does not show any influence of, or even acqaintance with, the views of Malinowski (1926), who, about the time Held was formulating his views, had forked away from the Ritual-myth theory and had proposed that it is the function that is the crux in a myth.

It is to be noted, that Sanskrit scholars of this period, by and large, western or eastern, remained, practically, aloof from the various schools that proposed various methods for deciding the meaning of myths that were in the purview of their study and investigation, viz. the Hindu myths—Vedic and post-Vedic. The exception is of Max Müller, who had brushes with the anthropologists trying to uncover myths. Later scholars practically followed the lead of Max Müller. Though references to tribal practices were made, they were of a casual nature and for comparison. This continued till pretty long after the first half of the twentieth century rolled off. On the other hand, investigators about the nature and meaning of myths in the wider sphere, who were mostly non-Sanskritists, studied also Hindu myths. This is clear from the passing mention we have made of some names. Further, Andrew Lang, not a Sanskritist by core, refers to Hindu myths and attempts to give their meaning. Thus, for example, he mentions the myth of Prajāpati running after his daughter, giving also the source (Ait. Br.III.33). However, as is expected in such cases where information is taken from translations, he does less justice to the word '*deva*' in the original (that, from the mighty bodies of the various gods a *deva* was produced) by retaining the rendering as "monster" (1884, p. 134). Apart from this harmless detail, he takes only that much portion of the whole myth which has developed into a star-myth, and which is needed for his chapter. This leaves the whole myth, the most essential part being the relationship between the 'father' and the 'daughter'. In this he accepts (through translation, though) the version of the Ait. Br. (and, though not mentioned, that of Śat. Br.). Lang objects to the nature-based interpretation of the myth of Urvaśī and Purūravas and says, that the myth revolves round the custom of married women—more particularly, a nuptial etiquette (*ibid.* p. 68ff). But, even here the whole myth is left out, attention being focused on the departure of Urvaśī as her husband did not abide by the promise he gave her, according to which he was not to see her without clothes on his body in broad daylight. As is very well known, the myth has its roots in ṚV; it is elaborated in the Śat.Br. and takes a new implication in the Puranic period. He also refers to the myth of the primeval boar fishing out the earth from the waters at the beginning of creation and the creation myth involving the cosmic egg (1913, pp. 230ff.). Etymology and ethnology could be worked together; but, even here caution is needed. In the absence of caution, and readiness to present a composite thought some fantastic etymologies might be presented.[5] A balanced use of comparative material is seen with J.Gonda (1954: *Aspects of Early Viṣṇuism*). He saw a Chinese parallel in the Indra-Vṛtra myth, where Indra is said to have roused the 'serpent' (Vṛtra) as the latter lay sleeping (ṚV I.103.7 *sasantam vajreṇābodhayo' him*), for releasing rain. The imagery occurs also at another place (ṚV IV.19.3). About the passage in question Gonda says that, "it strongly reminds us of the Chinese conception of the origin of the annual rain. The dragon who is the giver of rain sleeps during the winter season, hidden deep in the ground; on the second day of the second month, the day of the first thunder-storm, he breaks the earth and ascends to heaven, producing that very thunder" (*ibid.*, 29). This parallelism is perfectly agreeable. However, we may add something. One feels it necessary to examine the motif of the sleep of the Ṛbhus in the house of Agohya and the resultant rain, where sleep gives rise to rain. The same is the case, where Viṣṇu is said to sleep for the four rainy months. The situation presents a contrast, as far as the Hindu tradition is concerned. In the case of Viṣṇu (in the post-Vedic mythical and ritual tradition), and the Ṛbhus (in the Ṛgvedic myth) rain is associated with their sleep. While in the case of the serpent (Vṛtra) and the Chinese dragon (serpent), it is their non-sleep (their being aroused from sleep) ushers rain. Again, it is the rousing up of the frogs (=their non-sleep) that brings rains (ṚV VII.103). What Gonda has said about the dragon, getting up from his earthly abode and rising to heaven to thunder and shower rains, is seen also in the Chinese myth of the Blue Boy.[6] Gonda's approach to the understanding of the myths in connection with the early aspects of Viṣṇuism brings together the ethnological, etymological and the archaeological evidences (p.73) and comes closer to the method of scholars working in the wider field in quest of the meaning of myths.

It should be noted, that Gonda was not particularly satisfied with the approach to the study of Vedic myths even by the last quarter of the twentieth century. This is clear from his remarks as the General President of the twenty-ninth session of the All India Oriental Conference, (Poona, 1978), published later (1980). To quote: 'In the later decades of the 19th century the one-sidedly naturalistic explanations of ancient Indian gods were considered almost self-evident because at that time these interpretations were in vogue, not only in Indo-European mythology but also in the comparative study of religion in general. I am not detracting from the merits of Max Müller (1823-1900), whose works stimulated widespread interest in the study of religion and linguistics, when I say that his naturalistic interpretations of the Indian pantheon, his obsession with etymological explanation of Vedic mythology have too often been accepted and shared by authors who should have known better" (*Proceedings* of the said Conference, Poona, 1980, p.3). As to the study of Vedic mythology he pointed out, that interpretations other than the naturalistic, historical and sociological have not been often attempted; that the new insights into the structure and function of myths in archaic societies gained by scholars outside the field of Sanskrit did not seem to have attracted the attention they deserved (*ibid*., p.6f.). This would show the state of the study of Vedic myths (and we may add, of Hindu myths), according to Gonda, till fairly recent times. (However, see Dange, 1969; 1970; 1971; also 1979).

Study about the types and nature of Hindu myths showed its glimpse as early as the end of the nineteenth century (Cox, 1870; pp. 40ff; Ch. "Sources of Mythical Speech"). Two types were suggested by Cox: (i) Primary myths; and (ii) Secondary myths. According to him a primary myth is the very first story of a particular phenomenon, when the original etymological meaning is lost.The stage for a secondary myth is set when old epithets become new independent names, each giving rise to its own story. It is not difficult to see that in this he relied on Max Müller's concept of 'disease of language.' However, this division is already suggested by Yāska in his Nirukta (I.14;VII.4 and the concept of *māhābhāgya*, which involves various associations and activities giving rise to many names). Extending this principle to myths one could say that an additional exploit may generate a new name and a new myth. If the new myth bases its elaboration on the earlier one, it is the secondary myth. It will be seen, that this division of Cox was based on etymology and nature myths, which is just workable but very preliminary. Possibly, we could classify myths as: (i) Pseudo myths; (ii) Myths; and (iii) Metamyths, looking to the content and formation of the myths. A pseudo myth could be taken as one which is in a very cryptic form, may be just an expression, which could be developed into, or is prone to become, a fuller story, depending on other requirements of a myth, such as acceptance in the particular tradition. A myth, in many cases, has the form of a metaphor. This is seen mainly in nature-myths and, to some extent, when it is tinted with allegory. Let us take an example. This is from ṚV where Uṣas, the goddess of Dawn is described: "Here has arrived the rosy fair damsel along with her tawny calf (the sun at the rise). Lo! Behold; the dark woman (night) has vacated the vaults for her" (ṚV I.113.2), or: "She, the bountiful one (Dawn) leads the beautiful white steed, which is the 'eye' of the gods (the sun)" (VII.77.3). No doubt, these could be taken merely as examples of good poetry; but they have a potential to get transformed into a charming narration. The first may be retold as follows: Once there was a beautiful young girl, who was banished from her abode with many apartments by her sister, who was dark. However, the good fair young woman found, as a helpmate, a white steed, which had an eye in its fore-head (or, a white horse which could get transformed into an eye). The calf followed her emitting light and heat, which drove her dark sister out of the expansive abode she had usurped. Thus could the metaphoric expression be metamorphosed into a myth. And, there is no limit on the length of a myth. However, the point is, that such a myth is not actually told, and, hence, is not current in the tradition. Hence, it could not be called myth. As we shall see later (in the main discussion), a pure myth cannot be artificial; and though it may appear to be made on purpose, the maker of it remains unknown to the tradition which cradles the myth (take the example of the myth of the type of charter, to be discussed later). Hence, the seeming artificiality gets lost in the sanction of the tradition and renders it a natural flow. That is the difference in poetry and a myth. The former may go on the maker's name; the latter has no such 'maker'. As another example of a pseudo myth we may point to the one that tells of Indra killing the ascetics (*yati*-s), or their being offered to the hyenas (*sālāvṛka*-s). This myth does not appear in a complete form at one place, and we do not know if these different parts, as they occur in different contexts, actually formed a whole myth originally. The common part that is seen in all cases is, "Indra offered the *yati*-s to the hyenas"; but each separate part is told to extol a particular item in ritual: the northern part of the altar, the fruits called *karīra (Capparis aphylla)*, or the *kharjura (Phoenix silvestris*; the date-fruits). It is not also quite sure if these *yati*-s were offered to the hyenas by Indra, or they offered themselves (see Ch.Six). Some of the exploits of the twin-gods Aśvins, the Ṛbhus (mortals who are said to have attained divinity) and Indra (the hero and the mortal king who came to be worshipped as a god?), as they are mentioned in ṚV (and later texts, except for the Ṛbhus) are hazy and could be taken as pseudo myths in their form in ṚV. In later texts, they get the status of a full myth, when some details are added to fatten them. Other examples are those of Apālā (ṚV VIII.91), Indra-Indrāṇī-Vṛṣākapi (ṚV X.86), Bhāvayvya (ṚV. I.126.6-7) and Agastya (ṚV I.179). In such cases there are two alternatives open: (i) Full-fledged myths were already popular and the Ṛgvedic seers allude only to fragments; or (ii) They are disconnected fragments, which could be termed 'myths in making' at the Ṛgvedic stage, and myths when they got a fuller form in the later period.

About a regular myth there is no question and no discussion is necessary, as there a regular connected story, though not always normal, obtains. Metamyth is a term which could be applied to such myths as have been fashioned on earlier myths but with a change in the main characters. This condition is different from the one where the same old myth appears with variations and additions, the original main characters remaining practically unchanged. Thus, the myth of the 'father' running after his 'daughter' occurs in ṚV in a cryptic pseudo myth form, their union resulting in the birth of Vāstoṣpati (ṚV X.61.5-7). It gets additions in the Samhitā and the Brāhmaṇa texts. In this later form the original 'father' gets to be Prajāpati, while the daughter gets changed from *kṣmā* (earth, ṚV) to Speech or sky. Further, both get to be a male and female deer, while in the Puranic records, they get to be birds the male flying after the female bird (swallow). Before that she is seen as the daughter who circumambulates the father, Brahmā, who looks lustily at her. In all these variations not only the relationship of father and daughter is maintained, but the pattern is also the same as in the original (at ṚV), viz. pursuit, metamorphoses and the sexual urge of the father. Hence, all these have to be understood as variations of the same myth. As contrasted to this myth, the one involving Manu and Iḍā has only the relationship in common; but, with a difference. While the former myth has no indication of how the daughter was produced, or born, that of Manu–Iḍā states that the daughter (Iḍā) was produced from the offerings of Manu (Śat.Br.I.8.1.7.4.). Further, apart from the mutual relationship between Manu and Iḍā, there is nothing in common with the earlier one. There is no sexual urge on the part of Manu, nor is there any pursuit. However, there is no doubt that the latter myth is formulated on the pattern of the earlier one; but, the characters are changed. It is to be noted that in the earlier case, 'father', Prajāpati, and Brahmā are only variations of the primeval Creator. Brahmā is Prajāpati himself with a new name, and the source of the name Brahmā is *brahman*, which is a term for the composite sacrifice comprising both prayer and ritual. This is clear also in the earliest (ṚV) version, which speaks of the gods creating *brahman*, as the Father rushes towards his daughter and ejects his semen (ṚV X.61.7). This *brahman* is said to create Vāstoṣpati, who is the 'protector of vows' (*vratapā*) and has to be taken as the 'lord of the sacrificial ground', with which Rudra is never associated in the Vedic rituals.[7] The Vāstoṣpati in this context is the very spirit of sacrifice composed of ritual and *mantra* (cf. Sāyaṇa who rightly mentions as such, *vāstospatim yajña-vāstu-svāminam*). As he is the product of the *brahman* (ritual-prayer) of the gods, herein is the source of the later god Brahmadeva, who is described as having a close affinity with sacrifice, and iconographically who is shown as having such sacrificial implements in his hand as the *sruva* and a *kamaṇḍalu*[8] (a jar of waters, representing the jar of the waters called Praṇītā).

Kirk (1970, p.253ff) attempted a classification of myths. According to him myths are, mainly, of three types: (i) Primarily narrative and entertaining. In this type he includes also patriotic myths, which, according to him, are of the nature of legends. They are called 'legendary' by him; (ii) Operative, leterative, and valedictory; and (iii) Speculative and explanatory. In the first type he includes also such myths as deal with the names of places, myths about the reversal of the course of the sun and the beginning and the end of seasons. In the second type he includes accounts of geneology (and we may add, myths that give divine origin to geneologies). When he speaks of these myths being of valedictory nature, we cannot but suspect that he is influenced by the charter type of myths, proposed by the functionalists. The last type of myths, named speculative by him include myths regarding creation, about specially sacred places, about the life after death and such other topics. It will be seen that the classification is too general and overlapping. However, the second type may suit the *arthavāda* type of myths known in the Vedic ritual tradition. The *arthavāda* is a statement, or a narration, that supports a particular ritual, or a detail in a ritual; it is done very often with a story-like narration. Joseph Campbell also has offered a classification of myths, which is : (i) Mystical. Myths of this type dwell on the wonder about the universe and ultimately enter the sphere of the holy; (ii) Cosmological; (iii) Sociological, where myths explain and support the social order; and (iv) Pedagogical, where the aim of the myths appears to be to teach how best to lead the life (Ed. Betty S.Flowers, 1988, p.28f.). A further and a matter-of-fact classification would be as suggested from Kirk, again (1976, Ch.s 6-9): (i) Myths of the gods and the early History of Man; (ii) The Heroes; and such other topics (which could be gathered from the titles of chapters of his book on the nature of Greek myths; which is seen generally in any book on mythology (cf. Edith Hamilton, 1942: *Mythology*, I The Gods; II The two Gods of Earth; III How the World and Mankind were Created and so on). Such a classification restricts myths to Gods' Tales. This is not according to the modern concept of myth, which goes beyond the mere tales of gods and demons, as Kirk has himself made amply clear in his earlier book (1970), while dealing with, and accepting the views of Malinowski and Claude Lévi-Strauss. This raises a question: Is a myth, after all, a tale that should have a god or a hero alone at the centre? If so, what happens to such myths as of the Twins, feet-first born people and others noted by Lévi-Strauss (1978)? Also of other myths mentioned in the present study (*gavhāḷi-mugāḷi,* Poḷā and others)? The impression from the study of Greek myths by Kirk in the late and closing quarter of the twentieth century would be that the Greeks had no myths beyond the tales of gods and heroes. This is an impression like the one from the approach of Edith Hamilton who wrote in the first half of the same century, the nature of critical study in the case of the former (Kirk) notwithstanding. What about the star myths like that of Castor and Pollux, the twin brothers identified as the stars in the constellation Gemini ? They were the sons of Leda and were famous for taming and controlling horses.[9] They have a faint parallel in the Australian Turree and Wanjel who pursued Purra and killed him at the commencement of the hot season. After killing Purra they roasted him. The smoke of the fire wherein they thus roasted him is said to have produced the mirage, called Toorang in their language (Lang, 1884, p. 127f). The same may be said about the Pleiads, comprising the seven daughters of the Giant Atlas. They were seven sisters, but six got changed to stars (cf. the myth of the six stars in the Hindu Kṛttikā constellation, which fed Skanda whereby he was called Kārttikeya). The seventh had a mortal husband; hence she lost her lustre and position (*ibid.*, p.126) Should one say that the Pleiad narration qualifies for being termed myth, because the Giant Atlas figures in it? As a matter fact, any striking tale which got the sanction of, and currency in, the tradition is a myth; and, it need not be restricted to the tale of gods or heroes.

Such a classification as noted above is too general and is of the nature of the five characteristics of a Purāṇa (*purāṇa-pañca-lakṣaṇa*) in the Hindu tradition, namely: Creation, Counter-Creation, dynastic description, various eras and exploits of the persons of various families, which corresponds to the description of cosmogony, cosmology, heroes' exploits and so on. But, this would not exhaust the types of myths; because, myths may be about trees, mountains, rivers, holy and forbidden forests, in addition to those of gods, heroes and demons. They could be about stars and constellations, also about social problems, fertility of land, childbirth, and what not? Even as late as the last quarter of the twentieth century when scholars with the modern equipment are seen, as noted above, to indicate that myths are to be classified in the same old traditional way, what comes to the fore is the grip of the concept of *göttersage*. Another example is of W.D. O'Flaherty (1975: *Hindu Myths*, Penguin) who presents the myths of Prajāpati, Brahmā, Indra, Agni, Rudra, Śiva, Viṣṇu, Devī, gods and demons, though her study is multi-pronged. It is the "tool-box" approach, as she rightly calls it (1981, p.8). The reason for this classification is, probably, that the general readers are used to the concept of myths being (mainly) stories of such sort. It may not be unwarranted if we review some of her views. While one can agree with her when she says that, in the myth about Reṇukā, the cutting of her head (by the son, and not by her husband) is an expression of sexual tension in the husband (1981, p.86), it is difficult to see how, "throughout the myth of Mahiṣa beheading is closely related to castration and intercourse to the devouring of the penis" (*ibid.*, p.84). Further she says, that the Devī "kills Mahiṣa by copulating with him" (*ibid.*, p.116; also p.163) and that "the images of Mahiṣa usually show her as crouching or sqatting on top of him; this is *viparītarata*" (*ibid.*, p.116). This is not attested from such images right from the early Kuṣāṇa period, nor from the description from the Purāṇa texts. The images do show the goddess right on the back of the demon, Mahiṣa; but, there is absolutely no indication of sexual intercourse, let alone of *viparītarata* (or, *puruṣāyita* as is the other name of the position).[10] If such Tantric icons of Mahiṣāsuramardinī are available (of which the present writer accepts ignorance), no supporting proof appears in the present book (1981). As the position of the Devī on the back of the demon does not vouch *viparītarata*, or even sexual intercourse for that matter, there could hardly be any comparison of this position with the goddess (Durgā-Pārvatī) on the top of Śiva, inspite of there being a Śiva-liṅga in the throat of Mahiṣa, which detail, again, does not show Mahiṣa's identification with Śiva but makes him Śiva's devotee (cf. the practice of the Liṅgyata-s, who wear a Śiva-linga in their sacred thread), Moreover, not all myths about Mahiṣa and the Devī mention the detail of the *liṅga* in the throat of the demon. This being the case with the relationship between the Devī and the demon, any parallelism between the position of the Mahiṣī (the eldest queen of the royal sacrificer at the Horse-sacrifice) and the horse, on the one hand, and of the Devī and Mahiṣa, on the other, is unhappy; for, in the case of the horse-and-the queen ritual there is coitus, though symbolic; it is totally absent in the case of the Devī and Mahiṣa. It is not also possible to understand with Devī Mahiṣa the inversion of the position seen at the horse-sacrifice and understand Mahiṣī at the Horse-sacrifice as 'she-buffalo' (mahiṣī) (O'Flaherty, 1981, p.114).

In the myth of the Devī and the demon, Mahiṣa, the central meaning is the fertility of the land. The employment of this myth in the popular theme of the marriage of the goddess with her victim in the southern Indian context, has to be understood as the fusion of the northern Indian myth of Devī-Mahiṣa with the southern Indian Devī-victim-marriage motif in the ritual and myths in southern India. Though regionally unrelated, we may do well to compare a Buffalo myth from among the Blackfoot tribe of the Algonquin Indians of America. The occasion of the myth is the desired fall of the buffaloes from the cliffs (or arrival of the buffaloes) to the plains to serve as food in the winter season. We may review the myth which, in short, is as follows: In the very early period the buffaloes did not fall from the cliffs, though their fall was necessary. One day a girl from among the people of the plains went, as usual, to fetch water. There she saw the chief buffalo and his followers (the herd ?) on the cliff. To induce him to come down she said to him, that she would marry him if he went down along with his herd. He accepted and told her to abide by her promise. So, he came down as promised, and carried her away with him. Not seeing her return home for a considerably long time, her father was worried and tried to search her. He saw a magpie bird and asked it to help him. He requested the bird to report to him immediately, if it located her. The bird flew here and there, and saw the girl among the buffaloes, and with their chief. He reported to the father and both went to the place where she was. Now, the magpie met the girl, as it saw the chief baffalo having a nap, and told her that her father was waiting for her, and that she should go back to him. She, however, told the bird that she had promised to marry the buffalo and that she could not break the promise. Meanwhile, the buffalo-chief woke up and asked her to fetch some milk in a horn which he gave to her for the purpose.[11] As the girl went out, her father met her and asked her to follow him home. But, she said it was dangerous; because, in that case, the whole herd of buffaloes would follow them and destroy them. So, she went back to the chief and the father remained out, waiting and thinking what to do! The buffalo said to her that he smelt the blood of a Red Indian. Though she denied, thinking to save her father that way, the chief bellowed to the other buffaloes who readily assembled. They all started their 'buffalo-dance', enveloped the father by their rounds of dance and trampled him to death. The pieces of his body got scattered all over the place. When the chief buffalo saw the bereaved girl, he said to her that, if she could bring her father back to life, he would allow her to go back with him. She asked the magpie for help, and he was ready. She asked it to fetch any piece of the body of her father; it saw a bone and brought it. She, then, placed a blanket over the bone of her father and muttered a song as a charm. As soon as the song ended, her father stood up alive. The buffaloes were amazed and requested her to do the same trick in the case of those of the buffaloes that had died (in the dance ?), her reward being that they would teach her their special buffalo-dance.She did it and learnt the buffalo dance (Ed. Betty S. Flowers, *op.cit.*, p.76ff). Campbell opines (as recorded by Flowers) that the idea central to this myth is the belief in the efficacy of the ritual-dance in rejuvenating the slaughtered buffaloes. True, But, then, it could be said that the idea is also the killing of a stranger (here the father of the girl) as a charm, or actually, with the dance. There is no denying the fact that, for the tribals, their dance is an important part of their ritual. But, the myth does not appear to be exhausted only on this message. The points to be noted are: (i) The buffalo chief is not an actual buffalo. He regularly takes the girl away with him (cf. the myth of Lion-man, discussed in the main book, where the Lion-man carries the princess and begets children on her). He smells the blood of an Indian (Red Indian), which indicates that tribe to be antagonistic/exogamous to the buffalo tribe, of which he is the chief. The probability is that the myth hints at the first exogamous marriage between the Buffalo tribe and one of the Red Indian tribes, involving the killing of the father, in strife. A human sacrifice, in ritual, got fused with the memory of the father being killed. The ritual-dance, sacrifice and the exogamous marriage gave rise to the myth, which came to be used, and told, as a charm at the hunting, or for the prospective fall from the cliff, of actual buffaloes for food in the winter season. An important part is of the sexual relationship between the buffalo shaman, both in the myth and the probable ritual. The hint to that effect is in the beginning itself. It was for the procurement of the buffalo-flesh in the winter season that the girl proposes to marry him. She goes with him, and remains as promised, with a view that her tribe of the Algonquin Indians should get food (buffalo-flesh) even in the difficult winter season.

It has been said that the Horse-sacrifice in ancient times and the Durgā-pūjā festival involving the killing of the buffalo (the mythical Mahiṣa demon) has to be taken as the relic of the bloody expeditions (for the opinion see Ch. on the "Goddess and the Buffalo Demon"). But, in that case, the associated myth and ritual involving sex and sexual abuse do not get explained. It cannot be explained by saying that sex indicates victory-revelling. But, then, why sex-abuse ? We have to take both, the bloody sacrifice and the element of sex, together. If that is done, the hypothesis of bloody expeditions recedes; it gives place to sacrifice and ritual-sex for fertility alone. The employment of a pseudo husband (or, lover of the goddess) acts as a spell for the goddess, which represents the earth. The sacrificial blood is the essential 'seed' for the fructification of the earth. The same is the case with the Horse-sacrifice, though in the Vedic ritual blood is avoided. Here in the symbolic act the 'seed' of the horse is believed to be directly transferred. If we compare the myth and ritual of the buffalo-dance with the ritual of the Horse-sacrifice and the myth of the Devī and the buffalo demon, Mahiṣa, the same two traits appear to be common: (i) Sacrificial killing for the gain of continued food (which is hard to get); and (ii) Charm by a young woman. However, in the case of the buffalo-dance the person to be killed is the father of the girl; yet there is an indication of the killing of the buffaloes (the line between the members of the tribe and the animals being very thin in the myth), probably having a totemistic value. That sacrifice and sex are significant traits in rituals and myths indicating fertility of the field (or, newly converted land) is clear from many other instances. We may compare another North American Algonquin myth about the origin of maize. According to it, a boy has a vision in which he sees a young man having green plume on his head. He invites the boy for a wrestling match. The bout is repeated, and repeated. At the end the youth with the plume asks the boy to kill him, bury him and to guard the place. The boy does as he is asked to do. After some time the boy sees maize shoots at the place where the youth was buried. Campbell, who has narrated this myth, interprets as follows: The boy's vision was due to his anxiety of finding a way of livelihood when his old father would not be able to go out hunting (Flowers, *op.cit.*, p.102ff). Whether this explanation could be accepted in toto is a different thing; but, it is clear that wrestling and death are associated here with the gain of maize. It is not improbable that the (vision and the) myth reflects a ritual at the planting of maize. It is also not improbable, that at a later stage this myth served as an oral charm and was customarily told and heard at the time of the first sowing of the season's maize (cf. the Hindu myth to be told at the time of the polā festival included in the pages to follow).

There is another myth from Polynesia, told by Campbell, which could be compared with the myth of the vision of the boy noted above. According to it, a girl often takes bath in a particular pool, in which there is also a big eel swimming around. Whenever the girl bathes, the eel scratches her thigh. One day, he assumes the form of a young man and says to her that he loves her. She accepts his love. He, then, changes his form and becomes the eel. They go on making love for quite some time. One day he askes her to cut his head and bury it. She does so. From the spot where the head is buried a coconut tree sprouts after due time has lapsed (Flowers, *op.cit.*, p.104). Apart from the fact, that the shorn coconut resembles the head of a man with three hole-spots appearing like two eyes and nose, the myth suggests the point of sex and bloody sacrifice (or killing) as a stimulus to vegetation. A ritual, as it enacts a myth at the planting of trees from New Guinea emphasizes the same. It is also an occasion for the initiation of young boys into manhood and they are to have the very first experience of sexual intercourse. A shed is erected on upright props. A young woman adorned with ornaments like a female deity arrives in the shed. Six or seven young boys, that are to be initiated, have sex with her one after the other. When the last boy is in close embrace with her, the supporting logs which serve as props to the shed are suddenly withdrawn and the whole structure crumbles down on the couple in embrace, killing both of them. This is followed by an orgy in which men and women freely take part. Then the dead couple is dragged out of the rubble and roasted. It is eaten that very evening. This is believed to result in bounteous crop for the year (Flowers, *op.cit.*, pp. 106-8). Though this appears to be very grotesque, the content of the ritual is clear. The orgy and sex here compare with the sexy language used at the festival of the Goddess Mahiṣāsuramardinī, wherein Śabarotsava is prescribed. The same is the case in the festival of the Devī Dayāmāva, along with Durgāmāva. We may compare the rites and jubilation at the Vedic Mahāvrata.[12] In the present case the killing of the young woman appears to be to maintain her status of a deity, which she would certainly lose if kept alive. But, more probably, she and the last partner are seen as a divine couple, sacrificed for good harvest in the coming year. We might place all these myths and rituals side by side, with similar myths and rituals we have mentioned:-

Sexual Element	**Killing and gain**
I Black-foot	
Buffalo enticed by a girl; takes her away; marries her.	i. Girl's father killed; is rejuvenated; dead buffaloes rejuvenated. ii (Gain of buffalo-meat)
II Algonquin	
Boy has a vision of a plumed youth; no sex; wrestling and close contact.	i. Boy kills youth; buries him ii Produce of maize.
III Polynesia	
Eel scratches the girl's thigh; takes the form of a young man; loves her.	i. Eel's head cut by the girl; buried. ii. Emergence of a coconut-tree indicating means of subsistence.
IV New Guinea	
Sexual freedom in orgy; woman ornamented as deity; initiates young boys in sex.	i. The last couple killed ii. Roasted and ritually eaten; indication of continued food and prosperity.
V Hindu	
(a) ***Post-Vedic***	
(Myth) : Buffalo demon (Mahiṣa) expresses his love and desire to the goddess to marry her.	(Myth): i. Fight between the demon and the goddess; and the demon is killed;
(Ritual): Śabarotsava; also sexy songs and abuses to the goddess.	(Ritual): i. Buffalo sacrificed to the goddess;

	ii. Sprouting season; fresh corn in the fields (north India); preparing the fields; running, saying *'poḷi poḷi'* (south India), meaning 'crop', 'food', 'prosperity'.
(b) Vedic:	
****Horse-sacrifice*:** The solar-horse is the 'seeder' of the Queen; has symbolic sex with her.	i. Horse sacrificed ii. Prosperity to the king-sacrificer.
**Vṛṣākapi*—(myth and lost ritual) Vṛṣākapi abuses(!) Indrāṇī in sexy terms; suggested sex (ṚV X.86.16-17)	i. The ape Vṛṣākapi killed. ii. Prosperity to Indra.

How myths and rituals from such far-flung sources have ideas quite similar to each other is out of question at the moment. The point to be noted is that sex and killing are seen here to go together for the specific motif of vegetational creation. Two points bear out from the discussion uptil now: (i) Myths cannot be studied in isolation if the meaning of a myth-type is to be understood. Myths from the same region have to be taken note of; also, where possible, those from other regions and peoples should be collected and compared; and (ii) Though myths may differ and take various turns, particular types of myths have some details common. The myths mentioned above could broadly be said to concern vegetation and the involvement of gods and goddesses therein is to be taken as secondary. This is not the place to try to isolate the various types in myths, or even the Hindu myths for that matter; the work would require another study. Even similar looking myths may differ in the meaning depending upon the conditions in which they were floated. However, a single myth might be sufficient to understand its meaning provided the symbolic details in it are known and are familiar.

Reference has been made above to the probable types of Hindu myths. A broad classification at this juncture would help support the right view that all myths are not göttersage, or tales of heroes. It is also granted, that even a single myth is not entirely a whole and independent unit. Some types are common to myths seen among various peoples. An example is that of the myths regarding creation. The Hindu myths at the Vedic period show a diversity of facets. Some may be noted below:

Primeval Waters

There was water everywhere. In that primeval water, however, the gods were already present. They danced in it, and a particle of dust (*reṇu*) was created. (This was the earth). This pseudo myth (ṚV X.72) could be taken as the prototype of all other myths that speak of the creation of the earth from the primeval waters. Though the Vedic literature does not indicate any identification between *reṇu* and any earth-goddess, the point is how a goddess (though the word occurs as the name of the wife of Jamadagni) named Reṇukā is popular in the Puranic period. It should be noted, that most of the Vedic literature (apart from ṚV and AV and the Upaniṣads) is about rituals and there is a probability of the word *reṇu* slipping away from the earth mythos. Reṇukā, in the Puranic period, occurs as an earth-goddess and is also seen in the form of an ant-hill, and the ant-hill is not only popular in the Vedic ritual context, but is said to be the ear of the earth. Thus, the circle gets to be complete. In another myth, popular throughout the Hindu mythical tradition, the earth is brought out from the waters by the boar named Emuṣa, with the embroidery that it was stolen by a demon and had been hidden in the waters. The concealment of the earth by the demon follows the pattern that all important things were in the control of some evil power or a demon. Later, Emuṣa is said to be an aspect of Viṣṇu. In fact, both Viṣṇu and the so-called demon are additions to the main mythical concept of the earth being in water. This is a piece of observation common to the myths in various tribes and people, and a Viṣṇu here may be called by some other name elsewhere. The Hindu myth noted above gets further additions when it is said that the earth, fished out of water, was spread on a lotus-leaf. As it was spread, it was called *pṛthivī* (fr. the root *prath*, 'to spread'), where etymology steps in to support the name and the original myth takes a subtle turn. On the other hand, the lotus-leaf gets the status of a symbol; it stands for the birthplace of the fire-god (actually the fire kindled by the process of churning) in the Vedic ritual-context. Out of the ritual context, it is seen as the seat of gods and of the goddess Lakṣmī, giving rise to various myths. In icons and pictures it is employed to serve the same purpose. One of the most popular myths in this context is that of Viṣṇu, reclining on the serpent, in the primeval waters seen with the lotus sprouting from his navel-pit and shooting up, with the god Brahmadeva seated on it. A variant of the myth of creation from the waters is that of the tortoise as the basis of further creation, whose position is usurped by the Vedic god Prajāpati and later by Viṣṇu, who relegates the primeval creature to a lower status making him his *avatāra*. In ritual-symbolism, however, the tortoise has its place retained. Thus, it is placed alive in the first layer at the Agnicayana ritual where four more layers are to be built upon it.[13] It retained its place also in the myth of the churning of the ocean by the gods and the demons. Further, it is placed at the entrance of the main shrines in the Hindu temples and at the base of the whole temple, called Meru, in the Balinese Hindu tradition. A further development of the myth of the primeval tortoise is that of the cosmic egg, both being suggested from the sun.

About waters on the terrestrial and ritual plane

One of the important myths is that of the god staying in the confluence of the rivers, or rivers. In the Vedic context, this god, named Apām-napāt, is an Indo-Iranian god known also to the Zend Avesta. While in the Avesta he remained confined to the rivers, in the Veda he is also associated with the fire-god. His identification with the fire-god is complete in ṚV, though he retained his association with waters. This is clear from the fact that when water for use in the sacrifice was required it was fetched from a river, tank or a lake, and he was offered oblation in the water prior to water being collected from the river, or such other places of water. In ṚV there is no full-fledged myth about this god like his Assyrio-Babylonian counterpart like Enki and like Atargatis.[14] He has only some pseudo myths about him informing us that he has the form of a horse, three women to feed him and a cow specially his (ṚV II.35). The Puranic counterpart, or his own new aspect located in the sea, is of the *vaḍavānala* (mare-fire) and has some definite mythical accounts about him. His identification with the fire in the waters is developed in the Puranic myths where the rivers are said to be the wives of Agni. But, the name Apām-napāt did not cross the precincts of the Vedic fold.

According to the Vedic ritual tradition he was offered at the confluence of the rivers Sarasvatī and Dṛṣadvatī,[15] indicating that he was the spirit of the confluence, or chiefly of the Sarasvatī. This identifies him with Sarasvant, the male aspect of the Sarasvatī (ṚV VII.96.4-5). The Mahābhārata gives a faint indication of this god in Apāntarātmā, who is said to be the son of the Sarasvatī from Nārāyaṇa, or from the semen of Dadhīci (Śanti 349: 38-39). Probably, the name is a confusion as Apām-antarātmā. He is also called Sārasvata, and born to the river from Dadhīci (*ibid.*, Śalya, 51.7-11). Apām-napāt has the sense of 'son-of-water' or 'source-of-waters' (*napāt*;cf. *nābhi* and Latin *nepos*). Apām-antarātman would indicate the 'inner soul of waters.' The concept of the fire-in-water that is seen about the Vedic Apām-napāt, with his having three female deities caring for him and who were seen both as his mothers and wives, got further developed into the idea that all rivers are the wives of the fire-god, Agni. This gave rise to some very interesting myths. In one such myth it is stated that Aṅgiras was married to Ātreyī. The father of Aṅgiras was the Agni. (The relationship of Agni and the sage Aṅgiras is already well established in Vedic myths).[16] It is stated that Aṅgiras was always very harsh with Ātreyī and addressed her in caustic words. She brought this fact to the notice of her father-in-law, Agni. She was advised by him to take the form of water and envelop her husband, as he was an aspect of fire. So, she got herself turned into a river and took Aṅgiras inside her current. By this act of hers, she came to be called Paruṣṇī, which is the famous river of that name.[17] It is obvious that the myth explains the name of the river. A number of such myths occur, which could fit in the category of 'charter'. In such names the influence of Vedic ritual details is very clear. An important couple in the Vedic ritual tradition is the jar of waters and the fire in the altar. The waters in the jar are called Praṇītā-s (Praṇītāh), as they are collected and carried to various places in the altar before finally being placed to the north of the fire-altar. The sacrificial chamber always faces the east (hence it is called Prācīnavaṁśa,' whose roof-bamboos face the east'). Naturally the fire and the jar of waters are supposed to face the east. In that position, the jar (and the waters) would be on the left side of the fire. The reason given is that this is the way, on the left of the husband, does the wife lie.[18] The relationship of the waters and the fire in the Vedic rituals is clear. The example of the river Paruṣṇī would indicate that the myth is suggested from this unique relationship. According to one myth, the god Brahmā poured out water from his beaked jar (*kamaṇḍalu*). As the waters turned into a current and flowed on, they became the river called Praṇītā. Such myths indicate also the progress of the Vedic sacrificial culture and its direction.[19] Some myths tell us that rivers arose from the milk of cows that streamed out and flowed, where we are reminded of the identification of the river Sarasvatī with a cow and her udder (ṚV VII.96.6). In some myths rivers are said to have taken their form from the rays of the sun, and we are reminded of the Vedic belief that the orb of the sun is full of waters (ṚV I.23.17). In the case of myths where the rivers are closely associated with fire, the Vedic belief and the concept of *payasvān agni* (ṚV I.23.23), apart from that of Apāmnapāt, play part.[20]

Water, especially the cosmic water, is said to have been produced from the body of a divinity in some myths. Perspiration heads this list, though other fluids do figure. They are blood, urine and even semen. The last is a common motif in Vedic myths. Thus, the Ait.Br. (III.33) tells us that the semen of Prajāpati that fell on the earth changed into a big lake. ṚV has numerous instances of this type (cf. *apām retāṁsi,* ṚV VIII.44.16; and X.64.14, *puru retāṁsi*, 'much water'). In the Puranic myth of the creation of the river Narmadā, it is said that when the penis of Śiva was dropped off from his body due to the curse of the sages the semen that flowed from it gave rise to the river. Some portion of the semen that solidified got turned into the mountain Amarakaṇṭaka (SK.P.VI. 259.3-5). The basic belief at the back of such myths is that the waters are organic fluids; hence they are fertile. Another type of myths is a step forward in the same direction. Such myths say that body-fluids generate vegetation. Thus, barley is said to have been produced from the liquid dropped from the swollen eye of Prajāpati. The Purāṇas tell us in a myth that the sesame seeds were produced from the perspiration of Viṣṇu and the sacred grass (*darbha*) from the hair of his body. It is said that when the battle between the gods and the *asura*-s raged, drops of blood that fell from the body of the *asura*, Bali, gave rise to garlic, salt and such other things, also that sugar-cane was produced from the drops of the juice of Soma that fell on the ground as Indra drank it.[21] These may appear to be stray beliefs as mentioned here; but, they are woven into myths, and have to be understood as myths. In many cases gods and goddesses occur as adjuncts, as in the cases of the creation from the fluids of the body. Creation from the body of a god or an *asura* is a constantly occurring phenomenon. The principle at the back of it is that both are superhuman. In other words, any astounding event or myth gets tucked on to any popular god or demon. In the Vedic context it is often said that almost all important things were in the control of demons (*asura*-s) first, and gods won them over from them. This need not be understood as a lesson in history. It boils down to be a pattern of expression that has to be taken as part of a myth. The meaning is that the gods (and even the humans) have had to attain things by efforts, or trickery, and that when things are not in their possession, they are with the 'demons'. As Prajāpati creates things from his own body (being believed to be androgynous), so does 'Vrtra' conceal things in his body; and Vrtra is just a name for the 'withholder demon'. The powers, demoniac or divine, that are believed to reside in the trees, waters and such other things (on the principle of animism) come to be created from fire, when it is deified, or is supposed to be some supernatural visible power. Oblations cast into it would create things. The myth of the creation of Vṛtra from the oblation of Soma cast into it by Tvaṣṭṛ[22] explains this shift. The same is the case when in another myth Manu is said to have cast the oblation of milk in water, there being no fire, with the result that his daughter Iḍā was born from it.[23] In both these examples along with the belief in the creativity of fire and water, the influence of the idea of efficacy of the sacrificial offering is a subtle shift. In later times, creativity from the part of a living body brings in even the hair cast into the fire. Thus, it is said that Tvaṣṭṛ plucked a hair from his locks and offered into the fire. The result was that Vṛtra came out from it. Some more details are added. He had a flaming body and, in appearance, he was like a huge lump of soot (Mark. P. V.1ff.;Sk.P.V.23.5.5ff). Production from the body of gods and demons sometimes takes the interesting turns. They create anthropomorphosed powers each, which fight between themselves. In a typical myth Bala, the demon, creates three evil women. Actually, as he yawns they come out. They are named Kāminī, Svairiṇī and Puṁścalī all indicative of sexual freedom. They are said to be in the habit of seizing men, giving them a drink called *hāṭaka* which intoxicates them and also makes them strong. Then the women indulge in prolonged sexual intercourse with them (Bhāg.P.V.24.16). This is the description of the region called Atala, indicating how in the kingdom of the demon women behaved and how men were strong; but, the mythical detail of the birth from a single person (demon) reflects the problem of birth, autochthonic or through union of two persons of the opposite sex. It is true that there did not exist such a problem at the time of the Bhāg. P., and it ceased to be so long back. Yet, this myth presents a fossil of that problem. The following is the myth about another Bala. According to it, Bala performed a sacrifice and invited even gods to participate in it. As is usual with a sacrificer, Bala requested the gods, in all good faith, to ask for any gift they wanted. Again, as is usual in many a god-demon myth, the gods asked from the demon the gift of his beastly nature. Keeping to the norms of sacrifice, Bala parted with his beastly nature. But, as soon as he was devoid of that nature of his, the gods killed him at the same sacrifice. From his body many gems were created.[24] The trick of deceit and gain on the part of the gods, on the one hand, and the control of power but stupid simplicity on the part of the demons, on the other, is clear in this myth. A number of such myths obtain.

A notable aspect about the myths involving demons (=*Asura-s*) is that, in certain cases, they indicate seismic change or the formation of a geographical region. The myth of Dhundhu (included here) is an example of the former; the myth of the demon Karṇāṭa is of the latter. Like many myths, the myth about Karṇāṭa is a complex one. According to it, this demon was in the habit of troubling *brāhmaṇa*-s who lived in Dharmāraṇya. He would attend the marriages in the guise of a *brāhmaṇa* and would spoil it by throwing the couple in the sky. So, the *brāhmaṇa*-s approached the Mother-goddess Śrīmatā (also called Śrīdevī). On hearing about the mischief of the demon the goddess produced from the lustre of her own body another goddess, called Mātaṅgī. Śrīdevī's abode is said to have been under the Nyagrodha tree (called also Vaṭa) and she held a thorned branch of the jujube tree (*kaṇṭakādhyā badarī*), indicating that she was a deified tree. Mātaṅgī, created by her, is said to have eighteen hands. Śrīdevī commanded Mātaṅgī to punish the demon if he indulged in the same mischief again. Once, at the festive period of the marriage of Gaurī with Śiva, in the month of Caitra (March-April), the demon arrived and tried to carry away the couple, viz. Gaurī and Śiva. Immediately Mātaṅgī stopped him and, in the fight that ensued she swallowed him. But, the demon escaped through her nostrils. The goddess, however, was too smart for him to allow him to escape. She caught him, put him in her mouth and tried to chew him with her teeth and jaws. But, the demon escaped through her ear (*karṇa*). He assumed a fair body and asked Mātaṅgī to marry him. But, Mātaṅgī laid down a condition that he should first defeat her sister, Śyāmalā. The demon accompanied Mātaṅgī to Śyāmalā, and the former told her the purpose of her visit. Śyāmalā immediately engaged the demon in fight, which went on for three months and, on the third day in the month of Māgha (about February) Śyāmalā almost killed the demon at noon. As he lay bleeding he said to the people residing in Dharmāraṇya that, if they desired to be healthy and free from calamities, they should observe a vow (which we leave here). Then he assumed a huge form, faced the southern quarter and walked till he reached the southern sea. The region travelled by him came to be called by his name[25] (i.e. Karṇāṭaka, though it is not specifically stated). The account is important for various reasons: (i) It shows that the region called Karṇāṭaka in south India is named after the demon, as Dhundhu is the demon of the west Indian arid region. (Actually there is a town called Dhandhūkā, a junction of the Western Railway, to the south-west of Ahmedabad. The region is in the vicinity of Kaccha, a known arid region). (ii) It shows a periodic fight, initiated in the month of Caitra. The third day of Caitra bright-half, even this day, is marked with the festival of Gaurī indicating the last day of the home-coming of Gaurī, after marriage. Another such month is Bhādrapada (August-September), when the third bright is auspicious to Gaurī. In both cases the festival and the vow for Gaurī go on for three days. On the first day of the respective month (Bhādrapada or Caitra) Gaurī is installed. In Bhādrapada she is mostly in the form of the fresh and home-sprouted shoots of corn (wheat in north India, paddy in some parts of Maharashtra). The third day is for her departure. The myth mentioned above would indicate that the day, 3rd of Caitra, was not for home-coming, but the marriage. Such variations do occur, but they are not much important for the meaning of the myth. Now, as the myth specifically mentions the Third of the two months and Gaurī, it is clear that the mention of disturbing the marriages of *brāhmaṇa*-s has to be restricted to the mytho-ritual marriage of Śiva and Gaurī. But, this and the mention of other goddeses do not make it a myth about gods or demons. Gaurī, at both these periods, is the earth—sprouted (Bhādrapada, not mentioned in the myth) or to be made ready for the next harvest after tilling (Māgha, which is also the month for collecting dried produce from the worked field). Essentially, Gaurī (fair, white) contrasts with Śyāmalā (dark), being also an aspect of the former. This is like Gaurī and Kālī, in their aspect of the field—the former fair due to the dried up stalks of corn in the field (in Caitra) and the latter, due to the fields being tilled and ploughed (Māgha), looking dark. The bloody subdual of Karṇāṭa at the hands of Śyāmalā would remind one of the killing of Mahiṣa, with the difference, that with Karṇāṭa there is no sacrifice as an added ritual like that of the buffalo (Mahiṣa) and with Mahiṣa there is no association of any region in the myth as such. Though such names as Mahiṣapura (Mysore?), Māhiṣmatī etc. may be associated with his name, he is not localised to a particular place. The detail that Karṇāṭa faced the south and went to the sea, his name given to the region, would indicate that this myth is about the development of the region of that name after clearing the forest visualized as a demon. (iii) Mātaṅgī is not known in the Vedic period. She is not mentioned in Mb. as a goddess, though she is said to be the daughter of Krodhavaśā and Kaśyapa, credited with giving birth to elephants (Ādi 66.67;66). However, she was a famous goddess by the sixth century (A.D.) and was associated with the Pallava kings as their protectress in battles.[26] This would show that she was of south Indian origin, though she got to be popular all over India. With her association with Śrīmatā (Śrīdevī), Gaurī and Śyāmalā the myth indicates a fusion of different goddesses. Gaurī is known to Mb. as the daughter of the mountain Himālaya, while Śrīdevī and Śyāmalā are her new aspects (or, new goddesses of the *brāhmaṇa*-s settled in south India). All these were fused with Mātaṅgī, the special goddess of the Pallavas, who, however, made a strong effort to fuse the Vedic Hindu religion with the Hindu religion in south India.[27] Śrīmatā is said to have produced Mātaṅgī from her own lustre. This clearly answers the mythical way of showing assimilation of two independent goddesses. The case is like Reṇukā and Yellammā, with the difference that Mātaṅgī, unlike Yellammā, could be taken as indicated in Mb, though not as a prominent goddess, in her being the daughter of Kaśyapa. In the case of Yellammā such supposition is wanting. Dharmāraṇya cannot be easily located,[28] and it is not improbable that it is fictitious or was some place in south India.

Another case faintly similar to that of Karṇāṭa is that of Huṇḍa. But, as is common with myths, here we have further 'Hydra-heads' to the central myth. Huṇḍa, the demon, is said to be the son of Vipracitti. He loved Aśokasundarī, daughter of Śiva and Pārvatī (which does not fit in the Śiva-Pārvatī mythical structure, as no daughter of this couple is mentioned anywhere). This daughter is said to have been given to Pārvatī by a *kalpavṛkṣa* ('desire-fulfilling tree'). Aśokasundarī was to marry Nahuṣa, the yet-un-born son of Āyu and Indumatī. This would mean that Aśokasundarī, who was quite young as Huṇḍa loved her, would be far too older than her husband when he would be born and would attain youth! The point was made clear by Huṇḍa to Aśokasundarī. However, she rejected him. So, as soon as Nahuṣa was born, Huṇḍa entered the delivery-apartment in the guise of a maid servant who had gone out. He carried the babe, without giving rise to any suspicion, and brought it home to his wife. He wanted to eat it; so, he asked his wife to kill it and prepare soup from its flesh. The wife, in turn, gave it to her female cook and she to her husband to kill it. But, the cook took pity on the child. He took it out of the city, placed it in the hermitage of the sage Vasiṣṭha,[29] killed some beast and his wife prepared its flesh and soup for the demon. Vasiṣṭha found the child, took care of it and brought it up. When the child grew into youth, he killed Huṇḍa (Padma P. Bhūmikhaṇḍa Chs 103-117). The myth is not found elsewhere and Mb. does not mention it; but, it refers to Huṇḍa as the name of a country (Mb. Bhīṣma 50.52-53). The myth employs various motifs :(i) Killing of the infant as soon as it is born, with the fear that it would be a rival and a danger; (ii) A demon proposing love and marriage to a human or a divine girl; (iii) The saving of the infant by some benevolent person or power; and the gain by the infant of its legitimate right, when it grows up; and lastly (iv) Demon and territorial identification, here, Huṇḍa and the country called Huṇḍa, taking a clue from Mb. The last motif is seen also in the case of the demon named Loha and the place called Lohāṇa or Lohāṭigrāma, where he was killed and his body produced *loha* (iron).[30] As indicated above, such myths have meaning in the belief of a forest being infested with demons, and the clearance of the forest being understood, and believed, as the killing of the 'demon'. In such cases it is hardly correct to say, that they are myths about demons, as such. Yet another interesting motif involving a 'demon' or a 'god' is where the 'demon' gains from the guileless 'god' the gift of no-death by any cause exterior to himself. Also, he gets the boon that the person on whose head he will place his hand would be reduced to ashes. The demon, then, runs to try his new magic on the 'god' who gave the boon, and gets himself reduced to ashes through the trick of Viṣṇu who deceives him taking the form of a woman (the Mohinī-motif).[31] The source of the myth appears to be in the custom of keeping the head covered, or, at least, not allowing any stranger to touch the head. Another motif that commonly obtains in myths, both Hindu and others, is of the Question-answer type. The sphinx in the Greek myth of Oedipus kills those who do not answer her question exactly; but when Oedipus answers it she gets killed on her own. The Hindu myth of the 'Questions of the Yakṣa' is similar to it in meaning. In the Hindu myth the five Pāṇḍava brothers figure. They reach a lake and want to drink water therefrom. There is the Yakṣa on a tree on its bank, who stops each one who approaches the water, and forbids him to touch the water before answering his question. If he answers correctly, he could take water; if not, he would die. So die four brothers. The eldest approaches last. His name is Dharmarāja. He answers all the questions, is allowed to take and drink water and gets his dead brothers rejuvenated (Mb. Vana;Ch.s 312-313). In an inversion of this myth we have Kāmakaṭaṅkaṭā who had a precondition of marriage, that she would marry a person whose question she would not be able to answer. Ghaṭotkaca, the son of Bhīma, came to know about this precondition and travelled to Prāgjyotiṣa (modern Assam), where she stayed. He confronted her and asked a question, after spinning a long story. The situation was, that a man proposes to marry his own daughter (cf. Prajāpati= Brahmā and his daughter; also similar myth from Europe). For this, he tells her a lie that she was not his own daughter, but of the neighbour who is no more alive, and that he brought her up in his absence. So, he says, there is no harm why she should not marry him. The girl marries him, and they have girl born to them. The question of Ghaṭotkaca is, "Is the new-born the man's daughter or his granddaughter?" Kāmakataṅkaṭā cannot answer this question and has to marry him, but not before she challenges him to a fight and is defeated by him. The son born to them is Barbarīka (Sk.P.I.2.59.37-61; 60.37ff.). This myth does not occur in Mb. and other texts. It cannot be said to be a demon-myth, or a god-myth simply because the goddess Kāmākhyā had prophesied that Kāmakaṭaṅkaṭā would marry Ghaṭotkaca, and that she was the daughter of the demon Mura. The central idea in such myth is that the correct answer acts as a charm.

Yet another type that could be isolated (though not unmixed with traits from other types; because, myths could hardly be simple and un-complex!) is that could be named 'Vegetation and Fertility myths'. A couple of examples may be cited. Once there was a demon named Kūṣmāṇḍa. When this demon was killed by Viṣṇu, on the ninth of the bright half of Kārttika, from his hair(s) were produced creepers that bore large cucumbers (Sk.P.II.4.31.2). This myth occurs in connection with a vow to be observed on the ninth of the bright half of Kārttika in which cucumbers are prescribed to be gifted to a priest. At another place (Sk.P.VI.206.76-77) it is said that when the gods Viśvedevas, as a group, wept because Indra did not invoke them at a *śrāddha* (funeral feast, or feast in memory of the manes), from their tears[32] innumerable eggs (*aṇḍāni*) were produced. From them came out fierce creatures with black teeth and having conic ears, hair on their bodies standing erect. Certain trees have myths regarding them, independent of gods or demons. About the Āmalakī tree it is said, that when the whole earth was submerged in deluge Brahmā, astonished at the deluge, released saliva from his mouth. From it this tree was produced (Padma P. Uttarkhaṇḍa 47.7-11). At another place it is said that when Brahmā was engrossed in penance, his eyes dropped tears of joy, from which this tree was produced (Sk.P.II.4.12.13f). These accounts can be understood as pseudo myths, as indicated before. But, in some cases there are fuller accounts which qualify for being named myths. Thus, according to one account, king Nṛga observed the vow of fast on the bright eleventh called 'the Ekādaśī of Āmalakī'. In the night he slept under the Āmalakī tree as part of this vow. His enemies saw him in this condition and went to attack him. But, from his body emerged the Ekādaśī in human form. She killed his enemies and again merged into his body (Sk.P.V.2.28.45-55; also Varāha P. 47.15ff.). Āmalakī produces fruits that are called *āmalaka*, which are round in shape and of the size of round pebbles with which children play. In taste they are sour and astringent, and are of great medicinal value.

Now, we may note a myth which is of a different type from the ones seen above. According to it, in a place called Ajāgrahā there lived a king by name Ajāpāla. Both names have association with she-goats (or goats), the previous meaning being 'seizer of she-goats' and the latter 'protector of she-goats'. Once a *brāhmaṇa* came to that place in the night. As he was fatigued due to travel on foot, he went to the temple of the goddess Ajāgrahā, the deity of that place, to take rest. But, tired thoroughly as he was, he fell asleep. When he got up next morning, he found himself suffering from leprosy. As he was bewailing his fate, the king came on the scene as a commoner. He asked the *brāhmaṇa* why he was worried. The *brāhmaṇa* told him what had happened. The king called aloud goats, each, one after the other. As the goats gathered there, he asked the *brāhmaṇa* to take a dip in the water of the holy place there. This the *brāhmaṇa* did. Then the king explained to him that the goats were, indeed, various diseases that had infested his body, and that they had gone out (Sk.P.VI.130.1ff.). Further it is said, that the holy water-place was called Candrakūpikā ('moon-well'), and that a dip in it would cure a person of his diseases including tuberculosis and leprosy (*ibid.* 133.55-65). The name of the goddess is said to be also Ajāpāleśvarī, and that it was established by king Ajāpāla (*ibid.*95.1ff.). It is not clear if the goddess had the face of a she-goat; but, there is a probability that she was a deified she-goat.[33] It may be noted in this connection that in the Āyurveda system of medicine a person suffering from tuberculosis is advised to stay for a specified period in the same enclosure wherein goats and she-goats are kept. He is also advised to take specified dozes of the juice of the root of the herb called 'the eye of Śvetakokilā' (*śvetakokilākṣimūlam*) in the milk of a she-goat (Agni P. 189.11-12). Fever is described as a man having three feet and three goat-heads. According to a myth, a type of fever was produced from the fore-head of Śiva and the other from that of Kṛṣṇa (Viṣṇu). They were called Śaiva-jvara and Vaiṣṇava-jvara respectively. Both had three goat-heads and three feet each (Sk.P. V.1.49.33; cf. Brahma P.206.14-15; earlier, at Brahma P. 40.112 he is said to have been produced from the perspiration of the god). These could not be taken as myths about gods. In many such cases the names of gods occur just as caps, due to the practice of associating such things with a superhuman power. In the myth about the 'demon' Karṇāṭa, we have referred to above, it is said further (Sk.P. III.2.18.166ff.) that, after the demon was banished by Mātaṅgī and Śyāmalā, he was born as the disease *yakṣman* (a general name for diseases with fever; *rāja-yakṣman*, king of *yakṣman*-s, or 'Chief *yakṣman*'—is the name given to Tuberculosis). Yet another myth about the appearance of *yakṣman* is that, when Brahmā completed his sacrifice at the place called Hāṭakeśvara, there arrived Disease (*yakṣman*) who was beyond cure even for Dhanvantari, the physician of the gods. He wore a black garment, held a staff for support in his hand and was emaciated. He kept on coughing without stop and moved slowly with faltering steps (Sk.P.VI.190.62-76).

We might, now, close this brief survey regarding the types of Hindu myths (and defer the publication of a fuller survey to a later date) with a couple of myths regarding the creation of gods. The Vedic period is not supportive to the idea of idol-worship, except certain unclear references to it (cf.IV.24.10 where Indra is indicated to be sold for ten cows and such other very few). However, up to the beginning of the Christian era the practice appears to have come into vogue. This change was marked by the mention of images of deities in wood and also in stone.[34] The practice of making stone-idols is reflected in a myth, which also provides a reason for it. It starts with the old myth and pattern of the sexual union with Śiva and Pārvatī and says that gods sent Agni to deliver the message about the urgency of creating a leader for the gods to destroy the demons. Though Agni entered in the form of a bird, Pārvatī was disturbed on seeing him. Knowing that the gods were responsible for this, she cursed them that, as they cut her chance of conceiving, they would not have children from their own wives through them. When they pleaded for pardon, she said that they would go to the world of the mortals, where they would be changed into images and idols. She said, that they would also be born as children of humans, who got married according to proper sites (Sk.P.VI.246.22; 251.11-12). The import of the myth is clear. The myth tries to account for the practice of worshipping stone-blocks as gods; also, the practice of preparing idols from stone; further, it tries to support belief in incarnation, as Rāma and Kṛṣṇa were the incarnations of Viṣṇu and such descriptions as that the gods decided to be born as humans to punish the demons who had already arrived on the earth as kings such as Śiśupala, Kaṁsa and so on.[35] According to another myth the goddess Sarasvatī (actually the river) was carrying the fire, called Vaḍavānala, in her hand. She was taking it to the sea. As she was going along her course, a mountain came and stood across her path. He asked her to marry him. However, Sarasvatī was shrewd. She asked him to hold the fire in his hand, for a while, as she was tired. The mountain agreed, and took the fire from the hand of Sarasvatī. The result was that the fire heated the mountain and the stones on it became soft. They remained soft even when years rolled on. Later, they were used by artists to make idols from (Sk.P.VII.1.33.54-90). This latter myth suits more the practice of carving out idols in the caves.

The vast Hindu literature comprising the Veda and the Epics and the Purāṇa texts, not to speak of the Kathā literature (cf. Kathāsaritsāgara) is full of myths and other stories. In the pages to follow explanation of the term 'myth' has been attempted, taking note of important earlier opinions. Though opinions about the exact nature of a myth may differ, there could be one opinion on the point, that a myth is a phenomenon—what is imagined as opposed to what actually is. From this angle it would appear that a myth is, essentially an imagined situation; or, we could say that it is an expression of an understanding that is imagined as true, and which has got rooted in the tradition. Its use as charter is a later stage. So, if some myths appear as tales of gods and demons, it is because they are imagined as such. As we have seen, in most cases, gods and divinities are attached to such tales as attestations. The same is the case with most hero's tales, especially when they are set in patterns. In Part I various theories regarding the meaning of myths are reviewed and discussed with examples gathered from various sources, with additional examples also from Hindu sources. In Part II some Hindu myths are analysed and studied, the selection being made on the basis of the variety they show, and also on the basis of the variety of beliefs central to their formation. In some of the chapters included in Part II the central figures appear to be humans, and the accounts woven round them are mythical. The same is the case where known human heroes, like Alexander for example, are at the centre and mythical accounts are woven round them. In such mythical accounts it is not difficult to discern familiar patterns. In such cases, it is customary to call these accounts 'legends'. The same may be said about the accounts to extol names of holy places. The effort in all such cases is to show the persons and places, in a supra-human supernatural halo. The way this is done is the way of a myth. And, if this is true, the basic idea behind a legend is more of a myth and less of history, or the actual. When a person, or a place, becomes the centre of a legend he, or it, is sought to be removed from the actual and the normal and gets lodged in the mythical sphere. The only difference between a myth and a legend is, that the former is free from any actual and personal event in history, unlike the latter. But, this does not mean that, "Legends are on a different plane from myths, which are imaginative tradition about the nature and destiny of the world, the gods and the human race" (Cavendish, R., 1994, p.11), or that myths are set on the divine levels. Such statements are too restrictive for the nature of myths.The same has to be said about the observation that

"A myth is a mask of god", though we could accept that, a myth is "a metaphor for what lies behind the visible world" (Flowers, Betty Sue, 1988, p.xvii). A legend is, in the same way, a metaphor and a myth on what is actual. This would vouchsafe the inclusion, in this book, of some legends under the general title 'Myths' (Part II)

References

1. Macdonell, A.A. and Keith, A.B., *Vedic Index*, Vol.II, under Śambara.
2. Ludwig, in Held, G.J., *The Mahābhārata*, London, Amsterdam, 1935, "Introduction".
3. *Ibid.*
4 Max Müller, *Chips from a German Workshop*, London, Bombay, 1907, Intr., p.xiii, where he admits that he was called so by others. Peter Munz,' *When the Golden Bough Breaks*, London, Boston, 1971, p.81, about him–"appears nowadays as a slightly comic figure". D. Mackenzie regarding him and his method: "scholarly stupidity", in *Myths of Crete and Pre-Hellenic Europe*, p.80. Mackenzie's remark, in very early twentieth century, and a similar remark by Lang about the same time, is representative of the opinion about Max Müller in the other schools at that period. This opinion, however, is a bit extreme.
5. Cf. the opinion of Bruce Lincoln on the sacrifice of Puruṣa, mentioned by O 'Flaherty in *Sexual Metaphors and Animal Symbols in Indian Mythology*, Delhi, 1981, p.243, *puru+vṛṣa*, suggesting that the Vedic sacrifice was, in fact, "the sacrifice of a man who was a bull".
6. The Chinese 'Blue Boy' resides in the well on the earth. He is one foot in height; rises from the well on the back of a carp, goes high up in the skies; in the clouds; gets transformed into a dragon; thunder and rain follow. After calm has been set, he comes down from the clouds on the back of the same carp and enters the well; Mackenzie, D., *Myths of China and Japan*, London, p.80f.
7. Whatever is left out in the sacrificial rites belongs to Rudra; cf. Ait.Br.III.34, according to which the *vāstuha* (Sāyaṇa, *vāstau*

hīnam) belongs to Rudra. However, the concept was unclear; cf. Taitt. Sam. III.4.10.2 *rudraḥ khalu vai vāstoṣpatiḥ*, which makes Rudra himself Vāṣtospati. Śulagava; the special rite for this god was performed outside the locality. See Kane, P.V., *History of Dharmaśāstra*, Vol.V, pt.ii, Poona, (Second Ed.), 1974, p.83.

8. Dange, *Encyclopaedia of Puranic Beliefs and Practices* (*Encl;P.B.P*; hereafter), Vol I, Delhi, 1986, p.194.

9. Hamilton, Edith, *Mythology*, Boston, p.45.

10. This is the position, in which the woman is up and the man below; see Anaṅgaraṅga, by Kalyāṇamalla, Bombay, Vikrama Saṁvat 1981, p.45, v 42.

11. The horn does not figure here because the buffalo is in the picture. Drinking from the horns obtains as a practice. For example, drinking from the horn of a rhinoceros was a practice in China; Mackenzie, *Myths of China and Japan*, p. 248. In the Hindu context, ṚV mentions *śiprā* in the dual, which were used for drinking from. On this, Dange, *Pastoral Symbolism from the Ṛgveda*, Poona Un., Poona, 1970, pp. 107-14 where other opinions are examined. At the coronation of the Monkey-king Sugrīva, he was sprinkled over with consecrated water from the horns of bulls, Rām., Kiṣkindhā, 26.33.

12. Keith, *The Religion and Philosophy of the Veda and Upanishads*, Part II, Delhi, 1989 (1925), p.351; Kane, *op.cit.* Vol.II, Part 2 (Second Ed.) Pune, 1974, p. 1243f.

13. Kane, *op.cit.*, p.1251.

14. One of the epithets of Enki was 'Lugal Ida' (=king of the rivers). Atargatis was a female deity in the form of a fish and controlled floods. It was also located in a sacred pool; but, in the first version, in the Euphrates, in which she is said to have jumped along with her son; both were turned into fishes; see Mackenzie, *Myths of Babylonia and Assyria*, p. 28, where he compares the case with the Hindu myth of Manu and the fish.

15. Keith, *The Religion and Philosophy of the Veda and Upanishads*, Part II, p.352.

16. Cf. Ait.Br. III.34.

17. Dange, *Encl.P.B.P.*, Vol.IV,p.1183. The river Paruṣṇī is men-

tioned in the Ṛgveda at various places. The association of fire and the river is seen also in the river Payoṣṇī ('She having hot water'), mentioned in Mb.Vana, 61.22;85.40 and so on. For myths of rivers mentioned here, see Dange, *Encl.P.B.P*, Vol.IV, "Rivers".

18. Śat.Br.I.1.1.18-20. For a detailed examination of sexual imagery in Vedic rituals and myth, see Dange, *Sexual Symbolism from the Vedic Ritual*, Delhi, 1979, and for the point in question, p.52.

19. Cf. the mythical account of Māthava Viḍegha, Śat.Br. I.4.1.10-18. According to it, king Māthava of Videgha carried the fire, Vaiśvānara, in his mouth. It would not come out. However, the priest, Gotama Rāhūgaṇa chanted a verse having the word 'butter' (*ghṛta*), and the fire came out and proceeded east up to the river Sadānīrā, from the Sarasvatī, where Māthava was; cf. Eggeling's Tr., SBE, Vol.12, p.104f, and n. on p.104.

20. Dange, *Encl.P.B.P.*, Vol.IV,p.1183.

21. *Ibid.*, Vol.I,p.162.

22. Śat.Br. I.6.3.9-17; Eggeling, *op.cit.*, pp.166-67.

23. *Ibid.*, I.8.1.7-11; Eggeling, p.218f.

24. Dange, Encl.P.B.P., Vol.II, p.393f.

25. *Ibid.*, p.407f.

26. Kersenboom-Story, S., *Nityasumangalī—Devadāsī Tradition in South India*, Delhi, 1987, p. 22.

27. *Ibid.*, p.17.

28. The timings mentioned in the myth are suggestive. It is said that,before the demon was defeated in the month of Māgha, the fight lasted for three months. This means, that it started late in the month of Āśvina or early Kārttika, which period is closer to the traditional killing of Mahiṣa (a buffalo sacrificed), in the fight between the Devī (Durgā) and the demon, on the Dasarā day (the tenth day of the bright half of Āśvina; *daśa-ahan(r)*, called Daśerā in north India). This is about the middle of the year starting from Caitra. This would show that Caitra, Āśvina-Kārttika and Māgha are characterized by the exploits of the Devīs, which are three aspects of the earth.

29. This is a very common motif. Cf. Kaṁsa and Kṛṣṇa; Perseus and his mother; Oedipus; Romulus and Remus; these are some

famous instances.For the present myth, Dange, *Encl.P.B.P.*, Vol.II, p.402; for more details, Vettam Mani, *Puranic Encyclopaedia*, Delhi, 1975, p.515f.

30. Dange, *Encl.P.B.P.*, Vol.II,p.409; cf.also p.401.

31. *Ibid.*, p.405; also p.421, myth of Vṛka, a king; not a demon.

32. For the motif of tears and vegetation, *ibid.*, Vol., p.171.

33. Cf. the myth of Barkarīśa, *ibid.*, Vol. IV,p.1353; for the idol of a she-goat being worshipped, Vol.III, p.781, "Barkarī-kuṇḍa".

34. Cf. Mṛcchakaṭika, Act II, *kāṣṭhamayī* and *śailamayī pratimā.*

    The Mṛcchakaṭika is dated variously from 2nd century B.C. to 6th century A.D.

35. Bhāg.P. X.1.21-25; earlier, Rām. Bālakāṇḍa, 17, the whole chapter; 18.11-14, where Rāma is said to have been born from the half of Viṣṇu; from one-fourth was born Bharata; from the remaining fourth part were born Lakṣmaṇa and Śatrughna. Śiśupāla, the king of the Cedi-s, was the demon Hiraṇyakaśipu in his former birth, Mb. Ādi.67.5, while Kaṁsa was the demon Kālanemi, v 67;cf. Harivaṁśa I. 54. 64-65 for Kaṁsa as Kālanemi.

Part I

General

One

Myth—Problem of Formation and Complexity

There is no one opinion regarding the 'meaning of myth', nor is there agreement about what a myth is. It has been said that myth narrates a sacred story; that it narrates an event that took place in primordial times. It is also said that a myth is always an account of creation, and that the actors are superhuman beings. Myth is said to take man from his own time — the historical time — and project him into the Great Time, to the Suprahuman plane.[1] It is also proposed that every genuine myth is a myth of observation - the observation of men of a state of primitive culture, of a fact which had struck home to their mind;[2] also that myths were not evolved in times of clear civilized thought.[3] As myth is generally relegated to a primordial time, it has to be assumed that myth cannot be a product of modern times. Also, it will be a paradox to say that myths can be created, or made, in the future also. Hence it is not surprising when Grote says, "mythology is a past which was never present". We are reminded, in this connection, of the 'Mythical Theory' of D.S. Strauss (1808-1874) in respect of the scriptures of the Christians, according to which Gospels are mainly a collection of myths, developed during the first two centuries after the death of Jesus Christ, from the imagination of the followers of the Jesus.[4] This statement, like the others, which say that myth is 'göttersage' (story about gods) is obviously influenced by the popular practice of mixing 'myth' and 'mythology'. The popular connotation of the term 'mythology' includes stories of gods, heroes-turned divine and all sorts of fictitious narrations. On careful observation, however, the term 'mythology' should connote a systematic study of myths, and not a mere collection of myths. In the earliest connotation of 'myth', however, there is hardly any case for a 'myth' being only a story about a god, or a superhuman person, though the characters in a 'myth' appear to be supranormal.[5] Zenophon (565-470 B.C.) differentiated *'mythos'* or *'muthos'* from *'logos'*, suggesting 'mythos' to be an utterance prone to imagination rather than truth, which is the meaning conveyed by the term 'logos'. It is not right, however, to presume that in imagination there is positive untruth; for what one takes to be imagination, may be a real experience or a faithful understanding for the person who experiences it, or tries to faithfully comprehend a situation. Even when the word 'muthoi' connoted to the Greeks 'stories' or 'narrations', and not a reasoned discourse, one wonders if these stories were accepted as untrue; for, a known untruth can very rarely have the halo with which myths were not only tolerated but also respected even by the Greeks, whose language gave the word 'muthos' which is the basis of the English word 'myth'. To say that 'myths' are fictional, or fictitious,[6] is to look at them from our angle of assessment. For the early Greeks *muthoi* were traditional tales of gods, or heroes seen as having divine power. Even then, it is clear that they did not take them to be false. In the present day study of such narratives we separate pure myths from fictitious accounts of historical persons. The latter are called legends. The legends draw on myths; they are, hence, mythical accounts of real persons. In this stratum patterns or details of myths pad up heroic tales. It must also be remembered, that imagination need not necessarily be fictitious, or fictional. Imagination and fiction are two different approaches to a situation. Rightly putting it, imagination is, in essence, simply the process of forming an image from an experience or a situation, while fiction entails a *deliberate* effort, or we may say *'art'*, to create a situation. In the popular usage, however, both are (con)fused; and the one is often mistaken for the other. A myth, though a traditional tale like other types of stories, has to be differentiated from them on the point of its being (i) Non-artful; (ii) Fostered by faith in a tradition; and (iii) Indicating inquisitiveness. The other types are—Legend, which we have noted above, Allegory, Parable, Fable and so on. Though all these are generally taken to comprise Mythology, along with myth, the latter has to be differentiated from them on the points mentioned above, taken together. Though myth is differentiated from History, like the former, the latter word has also undergone a change in later times. History came to connote a record of facts, as against myth. In the early period, etymologically, history denoted just 'knowing', from the Greek word *'histor'*. The popular connotation of the word history is of a systematic account, against myth, which is rarely systematic and coherent. Like the folktale, a tale which is commonly called myth is characterised by elements which, apparently, are mostly irrational. The irrationality about the myth is due to the mysterious, or wonderful experience that lies at the basis of its formation, or due to a non-regular (not to say 'irregular') problem, or situation, faced by an inquisitive mind, which takes the form of a riddle. This is true not only in the case of a natural phenomenon, but also in that of social behaviour or mode of life. However, hardly any myth solves the riddle. It simply expresses it in the form of a tale, which is mostly short. A 'long myth' can rarely be there. And, if it appears long, as that of Gilgamesh, in certain cases, it is due to additions to the earlier version, or due to mixing of manifold threads of experiences, and problematic situations.

It should be remembered that, in its origin, the term 'myth' might not have had the meaning of a traditional tale which it gained later; also that even prior to the Greeks, who used this term, tales of a special nature as indicated above had been in use among various tribes and peoples; for, such problems and situations are common to all peoples; so is the desire to express them. Thus, the Hindus have the term *kathā*, which has the meaning of 'story' usually attached to it. However, the etymological meaning of the word is -- 'In what way?', 'how?' (*ku thā; ku* being from *kim*, 'what?'). The word *kathā,* in its earliest stratum had the sense of inquiry.[7] Another term, that is closely associated with *kathā,* in the Hindu tradition is *itihāsa,* which means 'History' in its popular sense. However, etymologically the meaning is 'this way *(iti)* - indeed *(ha)* - it was' *(āsa)*. The term *itihāsa* was often used along with the term *purāṇa* from the early Vedic period. The term *kathā* was not used in the sense of 'story' or a 'tale' in the early Vedic literature. The Ṛgveda used the word *kathā* (RV I.41.7; IV.3.5 etc.); but the meaning of the word was just - 'In what way?', as noted above. *Kathā* is mentioned in the later Vedic period (*Chāndogya Up*.I.8.1) in the sense of discussion; and the sense is that of inquiry. When, the word *kathā* became popular in the sense of 'story' or 'tale', this original sense was not noticed, even though it lay at its back. By the period of the *Rāmāyaṇa* or the *Mahābhārata*, however, the word *kathā* came to mean 'tale' (the root being *kath*, to 'tell'); and *kathā* denoted all sorts of tale. Yet, in the Vedic tradition, it is interesting to note, often the word *itihāsa* remained as denoting such tales as the following -

> Once, there was a girl named Apālā. She suffered from some sort of a disease; hence, her husband discarded her, thinking that she would bring misfortune. Having returned to her father's house, she performed penance to please Indra, with the hope that he would cure her. Once, thinking that the juice of Soma was dear to Indra, she went to the river to fetch it desiring to press it and offer it to Indra. Having taken bath in the river, she obtained Soma and returned. On the way she chewed the Soma-shoots with her own teeth, which generated sound. Hearing it Indra came along and asked her what she desired. Having known her desire Indra dragged her through the hole of a chariot-wheel, then through that of a cart; and lastly through that of a yoke. At every dragging some sort of dirty substance got scrapped off from her body; and she got cured of the disease. She also got sun-like lustre. From the scrappings were created such creatures as a lizard, an alligator and so on.

The commentator (on ṚV VIII.91), who refers to a later Vedic text, the Śāṭyāyana Brāhmaṇa for this tale, calls this narration *itihāsa,* which word indicates a 'tradition'. In fact, it is a tale *(kathā)* of a later period than the Ṛgveda. This would indicate that tales of this type were termed *itihāsa*. Whether the narration mentioned above is a myth or a folk-tale, in the present terminology, is beside the point at this place. The point is that without a tradition a tale cannot gain the status of 'myth'. The term *Purāṇa*, likewise, indicates an old (*purā*) tradition, though, in the absence of a suitable term in the English language, it was denoted by the term Mythology with a loose sense, as we have already noted. However, even in the Hindu tradition the term Purāṇa does not indicate a single tale, but a collection of traditional tales, faithfully preserved. Well! Though it is difficult to define the term myth, we may try a definition (which might well be tentative) — A traditional tale involving non-artful expression of a wonderful experience, or of a problematic situation, faithfully accepted by a society or a tribe. Now a curious problem presents itself viz. of myths that are similar among people widely separated. Thus the myth of the separation of the sky and the earth obtains among various peoples.[8] The ancient Egyptian who conceived the idea of the primeval god, Atum, masturbating in the watery abyss, called Nun, and producing two children—Shu and Thefnut - as the first ever couple and further of Shu separating Geb (male earth god) and Nut (sky-female)[9] may be giving out his true conviction; for, it is very difficult to say, positively, that he was just trying to explain the process of creation knowing also that it was false. Unlike other myths of this nature, where the 'son' is the separator of the Sky-Earth parents, here Shu is the father who separates them. Yet, the narration compares with the Ṛgvedic narration of creation, where it is said that prior to creation there was only water engulfed in total darkness;[10] or with a later version that formerly there was only water everywhere, and Brahmā put his hand in it and there was an egg created.[11] In the case of such accounts of creation which may be said to be based on speculation or imagination, the demarcating line between truth and untruth, and untruth and false-

Indra separates Sky and Earth (parents)

hood is very flimsy. It is clear that these are not expressions of actual observation. Abyss or mass of water is one aspect, while the separation of Sky-Earth is another. In the Egyptian myth both are fused together. Now a narration from among the Maori. According to their belief, Sky and Earth, the primeval parents, were in close embrace. The gods got born from them; but, as there was not enough space for them to move about, they sat in a council and decided to separate the parents. Tane, the forest-god, fixed is head in the chest of the mother, the earth, and stretched his feet upwards lifting the father, Sky. He is still there, as the forest-god, in the shape of the tree and continues to stay in the vertical position. It is further said, that the sky-father occasionally sheds tears due to grief (tears = dew or rain).[12] This myth seems to have some basis of observation. The dark night does not show the sky and the earth as separated, especially in the dense forest. Separation is marked as the rays of the sun usher in the light in the morning. In the Vedic myth, Indra and other important gods are credited with the exploit of separating the sky and the earth.[13] A myth from the Vidarbha region states that formerly the sky and the earth were very close to each other. The primeval old woman found it difficult to move out of her hut. So, once she struck the sky with her broom-stick. It suddenly went up, and is still in the same position. A further step in the same line of narration, suggested in the Ṛgveda, is that these separated 'parents' are to be again brought together for sexual embrace resulting in the advent of rain, which is symbolically described at various places as 'semen' of the sky-father. Later ritual texts exploit this motif to suggest a regular marriage of Sky and Earth *(devavivāha)*[14] which shows a clear influence of a well established institution of marriage. These texts add to it the marriage of the Lauds (Sāman). But, earlier in the ṚV, even without the mention of marriage, we have Indra bringing the Heaven-Earth 'parents' together for (sexual union) for the release of profuse *retas* (semen = rain, ṚV I. 155.3). Now, as in the Maori myth the tears are seen as rain or dew, here rain is imagined as the semen of the sky. The general principle in such identification is that the fluids or waters from the sky, the clouds or those on the earth are animated, and that they are body-fluids of a supernatural person—may be divine or demoniac. There are a number of examples of this type in the beliefs of various people in the world. And, such narrations cannot be set aside as false or untrue or fictitious in the orbit of the beliefs in those particular people or tribes, in the period when they got formulated and continued with faith. They are termed 'false' or 'untrue' or fictitious at a later stage, when more knowledge is available. In the case of such narrations, where apparently fictitious elements are discussed at a more advanced stage, these become 'myths' or mythical accounts in the modern sense of the term. To revert to the opinion of Strauss (D.S.) mentioned above, purposeful narrations introducing miracles in the events of the life of Jesus cannot be called 'myth' in the real sense of the term. It is to be particularly noted that, in a pure myth, there is hardly any effort to metaphorise an experience. A pure myth has two main phases - (i) Experience of a wonder or a riddle-like (puzzling) phenomenon in a natural or social context; and (ii) Its expression in the form of a pure and simple faithful narration, without an effort to gloss over it. It is a different matter, if this narration *appears* irrational to us today. Outwardly a myth,—especially a nature-myth—might look like a metaphor. But, while a metaphor indicates a conscious effort at superimposition of a thing on another, a myth is totally devoid of this effort. As against the observation of Strauss, we may cite the example of the visions of Ezekiel. From the narration of the vision of Ezekiel by some one else, it may appear that the vision is attributed to the saint at a later period. But, if the saint had himself experienced (as he specifically says), that, by the side of the river Chebar, he saw a storm coming from the north,[15] and so on, the position is different. He saw—Lightning was flashing from the cloud. At the centre of the storm he saw four living creatures in human form, but each having four faces and four wings. Their legs were straight and they had hooves like those of a bull. Their hands were human, one under each wing. Two wings of each creature were spread out, so that the creatures formed a square with their wing-tips touching. When they moved, they moved as a group without turning their bodies. Further, each living creature had four different faces—a human face in the front, a lion's face at the right, a bull's face at the left and an eagle's face at the back.[16] The vision records many other details, ultimately pointing to the seat of God and his august presence. This god was of the complexion of fire and shining bronze. Ezekiel lived in the 6th century B.C. and witnessed the fall of Jerusalem (in 586 B.C.). Now, it is very difficult to say whether the saint actually saw the vision, or whether he was simply posing that he saw it. But, there can be no doubt that his vision uses various creatures he might have actually seen; and the vision is a unique combination of all such creatures and objects. Another point is that he speaks of the god, as he saw in his vision, as being of the fiery complexion or looking like shining bronze. At another place, we have his another vision. Here also he sees a fiery human form. His body from the waist below looked like fire, and from the waist up he was shining like polished bronze.[17] The narration goes on to say that the fiery human form caught the saint by the hair and took him to Jerusalem. Once at the temple in Jerusalem, the saint again speaks of the dazzling light of the gods rising up from the winged creatures (*Ib*.9.3), which is, obviously, out of the vision; for, he specifically says that at the temple he saw what he had seen in the vision by the side of the river Chebar (*Ib*.10.15). The historical fact of the existence of St. Ezekiel being granted, his vision shows a mixture of his own imagination of a throne moving everywhere, the main creatures, probably, coming from popular experience. The figure of a lion was already used by King Soloman in his ivory throne, which showed a total of twelve lions on its six steps, each step having one lion-head at each end. At the back of the throne was the figure of a bull's head and beside each of the two arms was a figure of a lion.[18] Soloman and his line of kings flourished in or before the ninth century B.C. The fame of his wealth and the unique throne continued. It is not, hence, improbable that the vision of Ezekiel was influenced by it, with the additions of some new details of the other faces, wheels and all. The point of truth regarding the vision apart, one can safely believe that the vision got formed on the basis of some factual experience. A myth gets similarly formed. We may note one from the Orphic Cosmogony. According to this myth (which develops further into the account of a gigantic egg being the source of the Cosmos), at the beginning of the development of the Cosmos there were only two elements - water and primitive slime, which developed into a solid mass and formed the earth. (This part is common to many Cosmogonic myths). From the mass of water and slime which formed the earth there arose a dragon with the face of a god (human-face?). He was winged and on one side of the face of the god he had the head of a bull, while on the other the head of a lion.[19] If we compare these details with those from the vision of Ezekiel, we could see how the vision could be influenced. Unless we have definite proof to the contrary, there is no reason to believe that the vision is untrue as far, at least, as the person who experiences it is concerned. The same can be said about an experience expressed in a myth by the person who experienced it and the people who believe in it. However, the difference between a myth and a vision could be marked. While in a vision the visual is not necessarily related to the actual phenomenon, being the creation entirely of the person's own mental eye, inspired or padded up by his previous factual experiences, a myth is an understanding of the actual phenomenon, or situation, on the part of a person who confronts it and gives an expression to it. Both, the vision and the expressed riddle-like experience which is a myth, could be further compared to a dream, which is - (i) a rearrangement of previous experiences; and (ii) true for the dreamer, as long as he does not wake up to know that his dream is contrary to reality. A vision enters the realm of the mysterious as the person who visualises it desires never to come out of such experiences. A myth, though apparently riddle-like, does not become mysterious; because, it gets distributed as their own among people through generations of tradition, for a particular society and for others who adopt and adapt it for various purposes.

A considerable number of myths deal with the problem of creation — the riddle of the first couple, life after death, initiation and so on, which are basic; they gain traditional sanctity. In a good number of myths of this nature, spread wide apart, some common traits appear. Thus, according to a myth in ancient Egypt, when Rā (the sun-god) became old, he would not control his limbs. Once saliva dripped from his mouth. His daughter, Isis, mixed it with dust; and from it she created a venomous serpent.[20] Here dust, or moist earth, creates a creature but not the humans. According to a Mesopotamian myth the primeval god Bel severed his head from his body. Other gods mixed the blood with dust, and from the red clay that formed thereby, they created the humans and other creatures.[21] According to the Old Testament, god created the universe, earth and then light. He created all creatures, and lastly man. For that, he took some clay from the ground; from it he created man.[22] He breathed into his nostrils. It should be noted, in this connection, that the word for man and clay (or ground) is about the same in the Hebrew language: man — 'adam'; and ground - 'adamah' (which is feminine). Though not specifically mentioned, another word - 'adom' - indicates 'red' in that language.[23] After creating man god breathed in his nostrils, to give him life. Then, when man was asleep, god took out one of the ribs of man; from it he created a woman.[24] Before we go further, we may note that in these myths from the Middle East (Egypt included, as being adjacent), along with clay, contact from a living organism plays an important part. It is marked in three different forms - (i) saliva; (ii) blood; and (iii) breath. This would mean that, in the imagination of the person who first expressed his imagination about creation of human (or living) beings, a life-principle was necessary. The narration from the Old Testament is more polished, and discards blood in favour of the nicer principle of breath. But, in discarding blood, it does not entirely do so; for, the red colour of the earth (*adamah*), suggests it, if we look to the word *'adom'* (= ed). Far removed from the Middle East, the Pelew islanders believed that a primeval pair of Brother and sister created the humans out of clay, which was kneaded with the blood of various animals,[25] indicating that the clay contemplated was red. According to the Korku of Madhya Pradesh (India), Rāvaṇa complained to Śiva that there were no people on the earth. So, Śiva took a handful of red clay; and from it he created the first couple, the man being called Mūlā and the woman Mūlāī.[26] Though the Korku version mentions a popular Hindu god and the demon-king, the red clay subtly indicates blood-colour. When the birth of the Hindu god Gaṇeśa is said to be from the dirt on the body of his mother, Pārvatī, we have also to take into consideration that the dirt is termed *rajas*, which has a double connotation - (i) dust (clay); and (ii) menstrual blood.[27] It may also be remembered, that *rajas* connects with *rāga* (red colour) and *rakta* (red colour; and blood). The myth about the birth of Gaṇeśa, though sophisticated, works on the same lines as we have noted, i.e., clay mixed with blood (= fluid from a living body). In place of blood it uses a symbolic word *rajas* with the double connotation. One need not doubt the possibility that these myths indicate a sincere belief regarding the creation of beings, though in a polished version of the same myth some sort of artfulness may not be denied.

We need not dwell upon the question how similar looking myths were produced among people far removed from one another. Prof. Daniel Brinton,[28] while studying the bird and serpent myths, suggested the spontaneous generation of myths on the basis of the uniformity of religious ideas. In this he followed Dr. Edward Seler.[29] Both Edward Seler and Daniel Brinton, actually revived the old theory of Prof. William Robertson, the eighteenth century Historian, the author of *History of America* (1777), who was the pioneer of the stratification theory, which taught the principle of spontaneous origin of ideas. Hugh Miller (*Scenes and Legends*, London, 1835) applied this theory to folk-stories and myth. Danial Wilson followed him (*Pre-historic Annals of Scotland*, London, 1863). Hugh Miller's view was that man in a savage state is the same animal everywhere. Following him Danial Wilson observed, that a singular unity of character pervades the primitive acts of man, however widely separated alike by space and Time. Placed under similar circumstances, the first efforts of his mechanical instinct everywhere exhibit similar results (*op.cit.*, p.337). Donald Mackenzie, taking note of these earlier views, rightly, points out that they may account for "striking resemblances though not equally striking differences".[30] He points out, however, that similar symbols and signs may not always have the same significance everywhere; also that the human mind is not like a mould which produces, automatically, the same shapes for the same purpose, or the same idea to account for the same problems. About similarity in such cases he suggests the possibility of contact through travels.[31] What appears to be generally acceptable, in such a debate about the similarity among myths from lands and people far separated, is that certain basic ideas of creation from a supernatural being are common. We have noted how the creation of humans from clay has been one such example. Water is another entity to be believed as the source of creation; for even experience shows how water produces vegetation. Clay could be only another step on the same lines, as far as the human and other creatures are concerned. Yet another common concept to be marked is of the creation of heaven and earth from one single whole, or from a single unit splitting into two. Myths of this type are strewn among various peoples. The hymn to Puruṣa from the Ṛgveda (X.90) states how the primeval Man was sacrificed, and from his various limbs creation came to be. Devoid of the adjunct of sacrifice, the plain fact is that of the universe being created from the dismemberment of a primordial Man. The Chinese myth of P'an-ku's sons cutting him into three parts, and each part being a division of China works on the same pattern. It is said that from his blood water of the rivers and sea was created; his bones got formed into rocks; his hair became trees and plants.[32] According to the Babylonian myth Merodach (Marduk) killed the female dragon, Tiamat; and he formed the heaven with one half of hers, and the earth from another half. In the Tiamat myth, there is a combination of water as the source of creation along with that of creation from a primeval (here female) giant. According to another myth of creation from the Babylonian context, Marduk laid a reed upon the face of the water. He poured some dust upon it and also beside it. Thus he also created mankind.[33] In the Hindu mythology the myth of Viṣṇu creating the earth from the fat of the demons Madhu and Kaiṭabha has a similar motif. It is said, that these two demons got the boon from the god Brahmā that they would not die either in water, or out of it. As they harassed the gods, it was necessary to kill them; but, it was difficult due to the boon they had obtained. So Viṣṇu sat in water; and, taking them on his lap, killed them. The fat *(medas)* that flowed out from their body got solidified as earth. As it was created from *medas,* it came to be called *medinī*.[34] Though it is clear that the Hindu myth works on etymology and cannot be said to be an original myth, it cannot be denied that it is formed on the already existing belief that water was the primeval element for creation, a motif seen in many such myths. In addition, the added imagination is that creation is closely related to body-fluid. It is clear hence that some common belief, based on common experience, does account for similarities in myths from various quarters. However, cultural contacts also may contribute to such similarities.

Another phase of the myths of creation is that of the problem of relationship between the primeval person and his first created counterparts. This is also common in motifs found among people far removed from one another. We have noted earlier that according to the Old Testament, God created the woman - Eve - from the rib of Adam. This will mean that Adam and Eve were brother and sister, (or father-daughter?). It should be noted, however, that here the brother-sister relationship is not the responsibility of Adam himself. The responsibility lies with god. Likewise is the case of the Korku myth, where it is Śiva who is responsible for creating the first couple as brother-sister. In a myth from the Aztecs, the god Xolotle places some bones in a jar and blood of gods is sprinkled over them. The result is, that a boy and a girl come out of the jar. They are the first couple.[35] The case of Izanagi and Izanami from the Japanese myth, is similar,[36] though they are not said to have been created as above. Here also they are not responsible for being mutually brother-sister. But let us take the extension of the Maori myth, we have referred to earlier. Here it is for a new point - Creation from clay. Tane creates a female figure from clay. With her as partner he creates many things but not the humans yet.[37] (We shall come to it later). Here the relationship changes to that of the creator (= father) and his daughter.

However, the Father-Daughter motif presents some complex images, and this motif does not remain restricted to the riddle of the first couple. On the Indian side the famous myth of Prajāpati and his daughter forming a copulative pair does not answer creation in the earliest (Ṛgvedic) occurrences,[38] though creation of various types gets tucked on to it in later versions, when Prajāpati as Puruṣa, and his female half (Daughter?) are said to have assumed forms of various animals - man-woman, horse-mare, bull-cow, goat-sheep and so on.[39] Also, there is no indication whatsoever, in the early text (Ṛgveda) that Prajāpati created the Daughter from his own body. The Father and the Daughter are already there. In the versions (in the Puraṇas) the father (Brahmā) is said to have created the daughter from himself.[40] In such accounts, as they occur in the earliest layer, there is no mention of the sin of incest.[41] In the Vedic data, it is the post-Ṛgvedic account from the Aitareya-Brāhmaṇa (13.9-10) that first mentions that the act was out of the normal (cf 9, *akṛtam vai prajāpatiḥ karoti*). In all such accounts, what is reflected is just the riddle of the first couple, which is sought to be solved, but which has no real solution. As contrasted to myths dealing with a natural phenomenon, in the myth about the first couple there is hardly any actual experience. The only experience is that of the beasts, where such relations as father-daughter, son-mother, brother-sister and the like are not expected. It is not improbable that on the basis of the experience of the behaviour among the beasts, such myths were floated. But even here, the relationship between the *primeval parties* was accepted as natural without any idea of sin or incest. In most myths of this type there does not appear a real solution of the problem of the first couple. What, even ultimately, comes to the fore is just the problem. In many cases the couples are seen to represent the aspect of nature, which are deified; and the myths revert to the general pattern of "tales about gods" (göttersage). In the Aitareya Br., a post-Ṛgvedic text, there is a hint that the first male human (*mānuṣa*) was born of divine energy, and that he could be taken as the first active creator of the human race.[42] From other accounts, it becomes clear that this *mānuṣa* was Manu. But, this does not solve the problem. How did Manu generate the human race? Leaving apart the many myths that try to speculate on this point, we may refer to one (from the Brahmavaivarta P.I.8-9; 13-21; 23-24). According to it, from the mouth of Brahmā (the Purāṇic aspect of Prajāpati) came out a boy shining like gold, *along with his wife,* named Śatarūpā. Manu and Śatarūpā are, thus, brother-sister and also husband-wife. According to another version of the same myth, Prajapāti (= Brahmā) divided himself in two parts — the male part was called Virāj or Manu Svāyaṁbhuva, and the female part was called Śatarūpā (Śiva P.VII.1.17ff; also II.16.10ff; also Brahmā P.I.52). In the Greek myth of Kronos and his sister Rhea, and in that of their children, Zeus and Demeter, there is no mention of the human race being born from them. Even here what may be taken as incest in human relationship, cannot be validly seen. As a matter of fact, hardly any Greek myth directly deals with the creation of the humans or other creatures on the earth, the personalities in many of them remaining shadowy, or, at the best, personifications of natural elements, or older gods being vanquished and superseded by newer gods, seen as father and son respectively. Though the myths of Ouranos, Kronos and Zeus are not associated with the riddle of the first couple, as is the case with other myths mentioned above, it will be interesting to mention them here for a different reason.

What we gather from Hesiod's Theogony is that Ouranos and Gaia were the couple (we refrain from using the terms 'husband' and 'wife'). They were in constant union, or, rather, Ouranos would very rarely leave Gaia, lusty as he was. He produced many illustrious children (all gods) but hid them all away, as soon as they were born, in an 'inward' place of Gaia, not giving them any chance to see light. This evil act of his, in which he rejoiced, gave Gaia much affliction, though she was huge and expansive; and she groaned within with the crowding burden of her children. So, she fashioned a big sickle from out of grey adament and suggested to her children, who lay inside that spot of hers, that they should avenge their father's cruel treatment. All the children were afraid; but Kronos agreed to go by the advice of his mother. So, she gave that adament-sickle to him and instructed him how to accomplish the deed. She also hid him in ambush, in her 'inner place.' After a while Ouranos came along, *bringing night with him.* He stretched himself, spreading all over Gaia, desiring union with her. Kronos came along from his place of hiding, sickle in hand. He swiftly sliced off the genitals of his father, Ouranos, and flung them behind. The drops of blood that dripped were received by Gaia herself, from which she gave birth to Furies and Giants, spears in hand, and also Ash-tree Nymphs over the boundless earth. The genitals reached from land to the seas; and white foam rose from their flesh, from which a girl was born. Her name was Aphrodite, the word meaning being 'one who came out from foam.'[43] Aphrodite was the goddess of love. Though this myth is more complex than that of the Maoris we have already noted, there is no possibility of any borrowal, due to the fact that the two regions are extremely apart from each other. Though in the myth of Ouranos it is not said clearly that Ouranos and Gaia formed a whole and were forcibly separated later (as we have seen in other myths above), there is an indication to that effect in Gaia being the earth. Also, Ouranos is suggested to be the sky and having control over the night; for he is described as starry. This would mean that Ouranos was seen more in the noctrnal sky, rather than the sky in the day time. The dark Night would combine the sky and earth into one unseparated whole, and sunrise would be seen as causing separation of these two elements. We need not get stuck up into the other details. At the moment we stick to the first step in creation, as described by Hesiod -

> Earth, the beautiful, rose up,
> Broad-bosomed, she that is the steadfast base
> Of all things. And fair Earth first bore.
> The starry Heaven, equal to herself,
> To cover her on all sides and to be
> A home forever for the blessed gods.[44]

It is clear, hence, that Gaia and Ouranos were natural elements. The myth does not clearly speak of either of them being created from the other. It would be seen, however, that the first element created was the earth, which was followed by the sky; or, mythically speaking following the words of Hesiod, Earth created sky *from herself,* (cf. the word 'bore', if the translation is correct). In plain words, could we believe that Hesiod got the myth from the tradition as saying that Earth and her son, Sky, formed the first couple? However, in the myths of this nature, Sky and Earth are rarely said to be born of each other. The cutting off of the genitals of the father (Ouranos here) by his son is a detail that was, perhaps, added later; and it was, probably, to suggest how the later progeny was created. But, even here, it came from the earth (Gaia) itself, from the planting of the body-fluid (blood) from the 'penis' of the sky. In this latter part of creation, the creative fluid is seen in two forms - (i) blood; and (ii) foam, which is only symbolic of semen. It should be marked that blood rarely symbolizes rain, though it is the source of water, or gets transformed into water in many myths. Hence, the separation with blood cannot be understood as a flat parallel of separation and rain.[45] Here, though human behaviour is superimposed upon elemental forces, it is not exactly human. Hence, human behavioural norms are out of question. That is why these acts - 'divine' acts—are not to be imitated by the humans, nor do they represent human behaviour in the remotest past. The maxim in the Hindu tradition is clear in this context, "One should not act the behaviour of the gods" (*na deva-caritam ācaret*).

Apart from the point in the above myth of Ouranos which hints at the primeval couple—Sky and Earth—and that it is a nature-myth, or a myth of creation, the detail of the cutting of the penis of the father by his son poses a problem. It has a parallel in a Hurrian story. Here we have the god Kumarbi and his father Anu. Anu is the sky-god; and he is deposed by his son, Kumarbi, who bites off his father's phallus, and himself swallows it.[46] He, thus, becomes pregnant and delivers the storm-god. These details from the human physical structure are superimposed on the elemental parents. But, in these details it is futile to see any natural phenomenon. These reflect the problem of mutual superiority between the male and female partners in the early stage, on the one hand, and, on the other, between the senior male (father) and the younger (son). The first is seen in the case of Gaia and Ouranos (and Kronos) and the second between Anu and Kumarbi. To these we may add the story of

Kronos and his son Zeus, from his sister Rhea. It is said that Ouranos and Gaia had told their son Kronos that he (Kronos) would be subdued by his own son. So, as soon as each child was born it was swallowed by Kronos. By this act of Kronos, Rhea was much disturbed. So, when Zeus was to be delivered she resorted to her parents, Gaia and Ouranos for a plan to save the child, who could take revange on his father (Kronos). Ouranos and Gaia sent her to Lyktos in Crete, when she was to deliver the child. Gaia took on herself the responsibility to nurture the child. When Rhea reached the place, under cover of the night, and delivered the child, she deposited it in a cave. Coming back she presented to Kronos a big stone, wrapping it in swaddling clothes. Kronos took the stone in his hand and, without doubting that it was only a stone, swallowed it. As years rolled on Zeus grew up to be a youth and defeated Kronos. He brought out all the children devoured by the latter, the stone leading the trail, by making Kronos vomit them out. He also set free all the brothers and sisters of Kronos (his own uncles and aunts, if we speak in terms of human relationships) from the places where Ouranos had hidden them in his constant infatuation for Gaia. Commenting on the structure and the implication of these myths,[47] Kirk rightly suggests that the myths emphasize relationships and neatness of patterns. He points out that the myths show the unnatural retention of children within a parent. Thus, in the myth of Ouranos Gaia is forced to retain the children in her womb, while in the Hurrian myth Kumarbi bears the foetus of the Storm-god, himself being pregnant with the swallowed penis of his father. But, the difference has to be noted. In the Ouranos myth, though it is natural for the woman (Gaia) to bear children, the unnatural thing is not to be able to bring them out due to the dominating cruelty of her male partner. In the Anu-Kumarbi myth, it is unnatural for the male Kumarbi to bear children.[48] In the Zeus-Kronos conflict, the latter swallowed not any generative organ (as that of his father) but his own children, the effect being that he becomes the 'mother'. Though Kirk says, that there is a common point of castration in both the myths (in the acts of Kronos and Kumarbi), a difference has to be made. In the Ouranos myth, according to Kirk, castration is the result of sexual excesses and in the Kumarbi myth castration leads to sexual abnormality in the male becoming pregnant. He admits that some kind of sexual norms and functions lurk beneath the surface; but he is not able to indicate what. Comparing the swallowing of his children on the part of Kronos with the details in the Hurrian myth, he poses a question - "But then is Kronos swallowing his children a symbol—not of penis—but of uterus—envy?" Though he does not make it clear, he, probably compares the case as follows: Kronos swallows his children, imitating a woman 'swallowing' the penis and the semen with her vagina. Thus he imitates a woman in sex, who later delivers the semen in the form of children. In the Hurrian myth, Kumarbi swallows the penis (and the semen), and gets pregnant; his mouth acts as the vagina. The point of uterus-envy would indicate the power of the male to imitate the woman. In other words, his power to be able to generate, or create, even without the female partner. In that case this detail is only a variation of a male primeval god procreating from his own body. However, another angle is to be marked in these myths. They show a kind of competition between the members of the opposite sex. Ouranos and Gaia, from the point of flat human relationship, are a normal couple. The domination of the male member is torturous for the female, as is clearly reflected in Ouranos hiding all children in her womb, never letting them out. Here the myth reflects the general pattern of the creation myth where Sky and Earth are in close embrace (cf. Maori and the Vedic myths noted above); but to it is added the resentment of the woman who would like to show her superiority. Gaia's instigation to Kronos reflects her desire. The sickle prepared from adament is suggestive. Though it is wielded by her son, Kronos, actually it is she herself who fashions it and holds Kronos in her vagina (inner place). This would give the vagina a different status and power to cut. Here we have the concept of '*vagina dentata*' (vagina having tooth). Thus, in essence, it is the 'sickled vagina' with the jagged-toothed sickle. The cutting of the penis of Ouranos by his son Kronos is, in essence, its cutting by the Vagina itself. In the myth of Kumarbi, his teeth stand for the sickle; and, as noted above, his mouth symbolizes the Vagina; for, through it he gets pregnant (a motif that widely obtains). In one case the woman punishes the man through her vagina; in the other the man imitates the woman, trying to usurp her power of procreation. If we compare the swallowing of his children by Kronos, it would look apparently, that Kronos acts as the mother. But, a difference has to be made. The swallowing of the penis of Anu by Kumarbi and the swallowing of his children by Kronos mark a subtle difference. While in the case of Kumarbi it is castration, like in the case of Kronos who cuts off the generative organs of his father, the swallowing of the children in the case of Kronos is not castration. It is jealousy and fear of being superseded by his son, as the myth clearly states. It would appear that castration involves the usurpation (Kirk, 1974, p.118) of power from the elder god; but, it has to be noted that it is not unmixed with the motif of '*Vagina dentata*', especially when teeth or tooth-like objects are in the picture.

As the Kumarbi myth is older than the Greek, there is a probability of borrowal by the Greeks, showing the eastern influence; or that both are borrowed from a common west-Asiatic model as Kirk suggests (*op.cit.*, p.117). The motif of conflict between the parent and the son is available in the Babylonian epic between Tiamat (mother) and Marduk (son), and also between Apsu-Tiamat and Ea.

It may be worthwhile to adduce parallels from Hindu myths. In the Vedic context, Tvaṣṭṛ (the father) is challenged and even deceived by Indra (Son), who destroys also the sons of Tvaṣṭṛ, Triśīrṣa ('Three-headed one') and his younger brother Vṛtra ('Enveloper') caused to be born after him. In the Vedic sacrificial context, Tvaṣṭṛ is said to have kept Indra away from the drink of Soma, the sacred beverage after learning that Indra had killed his son, Triśīrṣan. Getting angry, Indra steals Soma - he actually pours in his belly the whole of the liquid, kept secure by Tvaṣṭṛ. Whatever drops of Soma are left, Tvaṣṭṛ, then, offers them into the sacrificial fire, with a desire to get a son who would kill Indra. Vṛtra emerges from the fire; and challenges Indra, who smites him, and splits him into two. The myth then turns into a creation myth; and it is said, that from the fiery portion in Vṛtra's body (as the drops of Soma were cast in the fire) the sun (celestial fire) was born; from the Soma-portion the moon was produced.[49] In other references, Indra is said to have killed the 'Father' catching him by the foot (ṚV IV.18.12; X.27.4), though the name Tvaṣṭṛ does not appear there. We do not have here the castration motif, nor any mention of the generative organ. This will mean that the motif of castration does not always go with that of deposition, or that of usurpation of power. It is more related to the aspect of creation, or with the creative power of the creator god; and in the earliest stratum it is closely connected with the female power of generation being transferred to the male, especially when coupled with 'swallowing'. This would show how various threads get mixed in the formation of a myth; and it is first necessary to sort them out to comprehend their implication, before being able to arrive at the meaning of a myth. According to one of the Hindu myths, Śukra was the preceptor of the *asura*-s who were constantly at war with gods. Śukra had with him the lore called 'Sañjīvanī' ('Restorer of life'), with which he would bring back to life the *asura*-s that fell dead in the war. Hence the gods were unable to liquidate them. The gods, then, approached Śiva who decided to help them. He sent his vehicle, Nandī (Bull), to fetch Śukra. As Nandī produced Śukra before Śiva, the latter simply swallowed Śukra for the duration of the war. After the war was over with the victory of the gods, Śiva reproduced Śukra from his penis (Śiva P.II.47ff). Though Śukra means also 'semen' in the Sanskrit language, the myth cannot be said to rest only on this point. More pertinent is the detail of swallowing and reproduction, which shows the pattern in the Kumarbi myth. Śiva swallows the preceptor of demons, and acts as his 'mother'. He, then, 'gives birth' to him; but the generative organ is of the male. According to another myth, Śiva fights with the demon Jalandhara and kills him. But, as Śukra tries to rejuvenate him, Śiva creates Kṛtyā (a terrible personified female power) and asks her to hold Śukra in her vagina till the war ends. She at once catches the preceptor and places him as directed by Śiva (Padma P., Uttarakhaṇḍa 18.26-86).[50] The power of the female gets emphasised in the myth, which is an inversion of the above noted myth of Śiva, who, sort of, 'mothers' Śukra. In the myth of Ouranos, from the drops of blood Furies and Giants are created; and from the foam Aphrodite is born. This poses an interesting point, which is that the *membrum virile* can produce even if it is severed from the male's body. Blood-drops producing animate beings like demons is a familiar theme; and, as we have noted earlier, it forms part of the general motif that body fluids, even when separated from the body can produce. In the case of the penis, the belief seems to be that it is procreative, even independent of the body. In the myth of Ouranos, the foam indicates the semen.[51] For the *Vagina Dentata* motif parallels from the Hindu myths are available. One of them may be mentioned here. Āḍi, the son of the demon Andhaka, performed severe penance and pleased the god Brahmā, who asked him to choose a boon. Āḍi desired the boon that he should never be killed. Brahmā did not agree; but he granted that Āḍi would not be killed as long as he did not change his form permanently. Having got the boon, once Āḍi decides to kill Śiva. He assumes the form of Uma=Pārvatī the wife of Śiva, learning that she is away getting angry with Śiva. He then approaches Śiva. On seeing Āḍi in the form of Pārvatī Śiva thinks that she has returned; and he embraces her. Umā (= Āḍi) now invites Śiva for sexual union, and creates teeth, like the thunderbolt, in her vagina (cf. Gaia). However, Śiva comes to know the trick and places in his penis the thunderbolt, whereby the false Umā (Āḍi) suffers destruction of 'her' vaginal teeth and ultimately dies.[52] The motif of the *membrum virile* being independent of the body, and causing creation is seen in the myth of Ouranos, as we have noted earlier. A myth about Śiva, in its repeated versions, describes how Śiva's penis got cut due to the curse of the sages whose wives were enamoured of him. From the semen that flowed out the river Narmadā was formed, and also the mountain Amarakaṇṭaka (*Skanda* P.VI.259.3-5).

From what has been noted above, we could now say that, the motif of the separation of the Sky and Earth is very faintly suggested in the myths of Ouranos; and what comes to the fore is the problem of mutual superiority between the sexual partners. This is more prominent in the Kumarbi myth, where the separation motif is not present. As such the myths cease to be pure cosmic creation myths, and indicate the curiosity regarding actual generation of the human race, adding more details such as conflict regarding usurpation of status. Such details, being close to the very life of the tribe, or early society, often get reflected in the well set traditional narrations, or stories of the tribe. Like the creation of the universe, or the birth of creatures, the sprouting of the corn gives rise to many myths in a semi-settled tribe. The seed that is cast in the earth sprouts up giving corn. Though the experience is routine in later years, the very first experience of the phenomenon is enough to arouse one to imagine with a firm faith that the earth is a female that gives out the sprout. The actual experience in the context of the humans and beasts serves as an impetus and the earth is seen as the mother, the father being the rain-god or the sky; and later the apparatus of seed-sowing in the semi-settled agricultural phase works as the male organ. The next stage is to ritualise the concept. In both the phases the vision is sexual. The god of fertility and that of agriculture get to have a prominent sexual overtone in myths of this nature. We may note a myth from the Rathwa tribe in the province of Gujarat (India). Ābh Kaṇbī and his wife were living happily. As years passed on, the husband became old, and he could not perform his duties to her. However, the wife was still young. So, with mutual consent, the husband appointed Nandyo to perform his manly function towards his wife. This Nandyo had a horn. In it he placed all types of seeds and had union with the wife of Ābh Kaṇbī. Thus was produced corn of various types.[53] The myth is self-expressive. Ābh is the word for sky (It has its Sanskrit origin in *abhra*; and in Marathi it is ābhāl). The wife of Ābh is none else than the earth, or, better, the seedable corn-field. Kaṇbi is the name of a caste of tillers (Kuṇbi in Maharashtra). Nandyo is the bull (Nandī in Sanskrit). The detail that Nandyo placed seeds in the horn is not apparently clear; but it reflects the method of tilling and seeding, prior to the use of the regular plough. In that period, a horn may be used in that particular tribe, or may be a hoe. The digging and seeding of land is seen as a sexual act. This practice like the observation of rain and the Sky-Earth parents, would generate similar myths in regions wide apart, which proves the point that similar experience might give rise to similar myths. We may turn to a Maori myth. The Maoris were originally hunters and even practised cannibalism. In 1769 Captain Cook came in contact with these people, when they had begun to produce sweet potatoes. According to the myth, the cultural hero Rongo contemplated how the tribe could grow more potatoes. So, he went to heaven to the god Whanui, who knew the secret and requested him to give him some seeds of the potatoes. But, the god refused. Rongo was dejected and started back; but, before returning to the earth, he went to the backyard of the house of Whanui without being seen by the god. There he saw many 'seeds' of sweet potatoes. Stealthily he collected some of the seeds and hid them in his penis. Then he returned to the earth and had sexual union with his wife, Pani. And, she 'delivered' many sweet potatoes.[54] Like the Rathwa myth, here also the sex-act between Pani and her husband is nothing but the digging of the earth and laying the seeds of sweet potatoes in 'her'. Rongo, being the cultural hero, is presented as the husband. The generative organ of Rongo, filled with the seeds, stands for the digging apparatus, or the horn with an aperture at the end through which seeds could be dropped; or, in conformity with the harvest of sweet potatoes, it is suggestive of the long sweet potato itself. Such and other tales linger on in the tradition of a society and get the status of myth. In certain cases this motif of the seeding of the earth is seen in the ritual set-up though no specific myth or a narration is available. An example in this context is that of a festival in honour of the Greek Earth-goddess, Demeter. In this festival, named Haloa, it was customary to fix in the earth male generative organs made of clay and water them. It was for the fructification of the land. The festival and the custom in it were marked by the presence of women and especially prostitutes.[55] In this connection it will be interesting to note that the word for plough in the Sanskrit language is *lāṅgala,* which has also the connotation of the male organ; and the ploughshare is denoted as the male organ (*kapṛt,* ṚV X.101.12; also ṚV khila, - Apocryphen-V.22.11). The various examples noted above, show that sexual imagery even verging on 'incest', plays an important part in the myths of creation and fertilization of land, with super-imposition of human behaviour on the actors in the myths. Yet, they are not humans. They are supra-human. In this sense only these myths could be termed 'stories of gods'. But, all myths are not stories of gods.

References

1. Mircia Eliade, *Myth and Reality,* Eng. Tr., New York, 1951, p.1ff; also by the same author, *Images and Symbols,* New York, Sheed & Ward Galimard, 1952, excerpted in "Observing Sacred Time", *Parabola,* (Spring 1990). Vol.XV No.1, February, 1990, (pp.21-29), p.22. While focusing attention on hermeneutic ontology in the limited context of religion, Ricoeur's view is that myth is the existential and expressive unfolding of man's understanding of himself before the sacred. Further, according to him, myth provides an antidote to man's distress and reflects his desired unity with the sacred; P. Ricoeur, *The Symbolism of the evil,* Harper and Row, New York, 1967, pp.161-74.

2. G.L. Gomme, *Folklore as an Historical Science,* London, 1908, p. 9.

3. Andrew Lang, *Myth, Ritual and Religion,* London, 1913(1887), p.6.

4. *Chambers Twentieth Century Dictionary,* Indian, Bombay, 9th Reprint 1983 (1972), under 'Myth'.

5. On this, see G.S. Kirk, *The Nature of Greek Myths,* Penguin, Harmondsworth, and other places, 1976 (1973); Ch. "Problem of Definition".

6. *Ibid.,* p.22. According to the Hindu grammatical tradition the meaning of the negative particle ('*non*' in English) has six senses, out of which similarity (*sādṛs'ya*) is one. In that case *a*+ *satya* (truth) would mean 'something similar to truth'. In this context, the remark by Thomas Keneally, the author of *Schindler's List,* is interesting: "a thing about myth is not whether it is true or not, nor whether it should be true, but that it is somewhat truer than truth itself"; cf. *op.cit.,* Rockfeller Centre, Avenue of the Americas, New York, 1993, p.232 (Earlier ptn.1982).

7. To distinguish what is known as 'myth' from other tales, the present author has used the word *purākathā* in his book (in Marathi), *Purākathañcā Artha—Vād āṇi Vivecan,* Continental, Pune, 1994.

8. See A. Seidenberg, "The Separation of the Sky and the Earth at Creation", Folklore, Vol. 70, London, 1959. According to a Zuni Indian myth the children lifted the Sky father from the embrace of Earth mother, with the bow (rain = bow). D. Mackenzie, *Myths of Pre-Columbian America,* London, p.176.

9. R.T. Rundle Clark, *Myth and Symbol in Ancient Egypt*, London, 1959, p.48f.

10. Ṛgveda X.129.3. For the similar Greek belief, see Edith Hamilton, *Mythology*, Boston, 1942, p.77, "formless confusion of Chaos brooded over by unbroken darkness". This compares favourably with the Ancient Egyptian belief and the Ṛgvedic one; cf. the *Old Testament*, Genesis, I.1-2, which is obviously influenced by the older Egyptian account.

11. Sadashiv A. Dange, *Encyclopaedia of Puranic Beliefs and Practices (Encl.P.B.P.)*, Vol.I, New Delhi, 1986, p.363.

12. Andrew Lang, *Custom and Myth*, Vol.I, London, 1884, p.46; A.L. Kroebar and T.T. Waterman, *Source-book in Anthropology*, New York, 1931, pp.444ff. The names of the parents are Rangi (Sky) and Papa (Earth).

13. Ṛgveda, Indra II. 12.2; Viṣṇu p.31 I.154.1 etc.

14. Dange, *Sexual Symbolism from the Vedic Ritual*, Delhi, 1979, p.71ff. Bodewitz, H.W. in his paper "The 'Marriage' of Heaven and Earth" (WZKS, Vol.xxxi, pp.23-36) has taken objection to my stand ("Marriage of Heaven and Earth", *Proceedings of the All India Oriental Conference*, Dharwar, Nov.1976, published Poona 1978, pp.213-18, later incorporated in *Sexual Symbolism* noted above), suggesting that it was not a marriage between Heaven and Earth as such and that it was marriage of the lauds (*sāman*-s), in which Heaven and Earth, at the ritual, got things exchanged. He strictly follows the texts, and, naturally, his interpretation is too textual. The difficulty is about the conceptual marriage and the ritual-marriage. Now, the lauds are both masculine (*sāman* is always seen as a male; the *ṛc*-verse is the female in the Vedic tradition); so 'marriage' between two *sāman*-s will be awkward. On the other hand, Earth is always a female; the Sky (Dyo/Dyaus) is sometimes seen as a woman, but in the sexual coupling it is always the male. So, their marriage is the basic theme. At the most, the ritual marriage of the lauds has to be taken as a charm to that effect. The marriage is mentioned as 'marriage of gods' (*deva-vivāha*). The Sky and Earth are the deities; the lauds are not - they are not so termed. The myth of this 'marriage', where it occurs, always begins with the note that the Sky (Heaven) and Earth were close in embrace, but separated. Here they are brought together; this act is to be connected with the exploit of Indra in bringing them together

for profuse *retas* (= rain). In the present phase of the myth, a social norm of marriage is inserted. It has to be understood that this phase of the myth is not independent; it has to be understood as part of the whole 'behaviour' of Heaven and Earth. Actually the old myth is used here as a 'charter' to extol the part of the lauds in ritual. The meaning of 'charter' will be made clear at a later stage in the book.

15. At various places in the Old Testament there is reference to such calamities and attacks as coming from the north, see *Good News Bible,* Delhi, 1988 (1970), p.737 (People); 799 (Storm) etc.
16. *Ibid.,* p.799; Ezekiel (I.1.4-27).
17. *Ibid.,* p.805, Eekiel, *loc.cit.,* 8.3.
18. *Ibid.,* p.347, Kings, I.14.18-20.
19. Hajime Nakamura, *A Comparative History of Ideas,* Delhi, 1992 (First Indian ed. earlier, 1975), p.58, where he refers to Edward Zeller, *A History of Greek Philosophy from the earliest period to the time of Socrates* (Eng. Tr. of the original German by S.F. Alleyne, 2 Vols., London, Longman, Green and Co. 1881, pp.100-01).
20. Donald Mackenzie, *Egyptian Myth and Legend,* p.3.
21. J.G. Frazer, *Folklore in the Old Testament,* London, Vol.I (Vols.I-III), 1918, p.6.
22. *Ibid.,* p.3; *Old Testament,* Genesis, II.7, there is a slight variation as regards the sequence of other creatures and man created in I.20ff and II.7.
23. Frazer, *op.cit.,* p.19.
24. *Old Testament,* Genesis II.7.21.
25. Frazer, *op.cit.,* p.19.
26. *Ibid.,* p.18 (where he refers to R.V. Russel, *Tribes and Castes of Central Provinces of India,* London, 1916, p.551 ff.)
27. For the myth, see Dange, *Encl. P.B.P.,* Vol.II, p.580.
28. Danial G. Brinton, *Myths of The New World,* Philadelphia, 1905, pp.37; 120f.
29. Edward Seler, *Mexican and Central American Antiquities,* Bureau of American Ethnology, Washington, 1904, p.275.
30. Donald Mackenzie, *Myths of Pre-Columbian America,* London,

pp.39-42; *Myths of Crete and Pre-Hellenic Europe,* P.xxiif. We shall touch this point in the next chapter.

31. *Ibid.,* p.xxiii; also same author, *Myths of China and Japan,* p.4.

32. *Myths of China and Japan,* p.259ff; cf.H. Nakamura, *op.cit.* p.68 continuation of n.13.

33. Donald Mackenzie, *Myths of Babylonia and Assyria,* p.xxxiii.

34. Devī-bhāgavata, Skandha 1; at the Mahābhārata (Mb.) Sabhāparvan, 38 after V29, according to the Southern version, these two were created from the ear-wax of Viṣṇu. Obviously the later account from the Devī-bhāgavata shows addition, and is based on etymology.

35. Donald Mackenzie, *Myths of Pre-Columbian America,* p.186.

36. Donald Mackenzie, *Myths of China and Japan,* p.349.

37. F. Allan Hanson, "Dynamic Forms in the Maori Concept of Reality", *Ultimate Reality and Meaning,* Vol.6, No.3, Toronto, Sept., 1983, p.182.

38. Dange, *Sexual Symbolism from the Vedic Ritual,* Delhi, 1979, pp.141-60.

    But, the first stage is of Puruṣa splitting into two. And they are said to be husband & wife and create human beings. Then the female feels ashamed and changes her forms, because she thinks herself to be his daughter.

39. Bṛhadāraṇyaka Up. I.4.1-4.

40. Dange, *Encycl. P.B.P.,* Vol.I, p.201ff.

41. Wendy Doniger O'Flaherty, *Hindu Myths,* Penguin, 1982 (1975), p.25, calls it incest even in the Ṛgveda. This is applying later norms.

42. Ait.Br. 13.9-10; the details are in Ch.II.

43. G.S.Kirk, *The Nature of Greek Myths,* Penguin, 1976 (1974), p.113ff.

44. Edith Hamilton, *Mythology,* Boston, 1942, p.78.

45. Kirk, *op.cit.,* p.46, about the myth of Ouranos and Gaia, "symbolic representation of the interplay between rain and soil that makes plants to come to life and grow." But, this does not explain the sickle, cutting of the genitals of Ouranos, and the blood-drops creating (not plants) but Furies and Titans (p.114).

As here the blood-drops create Titans, so in the Hindu myths, they create demons, in the myth of the demon Rakta-bija; see Dange, *Encl. P.B.P.*, Vol.II, under 'Demons' 'Raktabīja'. For blood turning into water we may note such accounts as that of Samantapañcaka, *ibid.*, Vol.I, p.147f. According to a popular myth from South India, Paraśurāma washed the blood of the Kṣatriyas, whom he had killed, and which smeared his axe (*paraśu/parśu*); as the blood flowed away, it gave rise to the river named Aihole. The word means, "oh (*ai*) the stream (*hoḷe*)."

46. Kirk, *The Nature of Greek Myths*, p.117.

47. *Ibid.*

48. In a Hindu myth (Mb.Vana, 126.10-31) Indra suckles an infant delivered from the side of king Yuvanāśva who is said to have drunk a foetus-causing potion, through mistake. The child born is named Māndhātā, as Indra said "He will suck my milk" (*mām dhātā=dhāsyati*).

49. Śatapatha Br.I.6.3.1-24; Dange, *Legends in the Mahābhārata*, Delhi, 1969, p.172. A similar myth obtains from the Wintu tribe of America, according to which in a competition of pine tree-bending a crafty Father-in-law, named Sas, gets killed by falling to the earth; from his split body the larger part becomes the sun, while the smaller one becomes the moon. In the language of the tribe, the sun is called Sas (the same as the father-in-law) while the moon is called Canas (= Chanas). Does the myth, indirectly, hint that the moon was produced from the sun? In any case, the competition between the Father-in-law and the Son-in-law reflects the marital conflict in that society. For the myth, W.T. Olcott, *Sun-lore of All Ages*, New York, 1914, p.14ff. This conflict has to be differentiated from the conflict between the Father=god and the Son-god. The latter is reflective of importance of the gods in tribal belief.

50. Dange, *Encl.P.B.P.*, Vol.IV, New Delhi, 1989, p.1326.

51. G.S.Kirk, *op.cit.*, pp.114; 116. However, it is reasonable to take foam as symbolising the womb. According to a Zuni myth foam is associated with the mother-goddess. Foam provided by her gives birth to deities, when the sun eyes it. It produces two children - male and a female, Donald Mackenzie, *Myths of Pre-Columbian America*, p.175.

52. Skanda P.I.2.29.1-7; Padma P. Sṛṣṭikhaṇḍa, 41.45-72; see *Encl.P.B.P.*, Vol.III, p.391.
53. Jyotindra Jain, "Painted Myths of Creation", *The India Magazine,* Vol.V-II, (Jan.1985), p.24ff.
54. F. Allan Hanson, *op.cit.*, *loc.cit.* (see note 37 above).
55. G.S.Kirk, *Myth - Its Meaning...*, 1973, p.230.-

Two

Form and Meaning

We have noted, how there is similarity in some of the myths relating to the problem of the first couple, or relating to the creation of the sky and the earth from the dark watery chaos. In such cases, it is very difficult to assume, and prove, if the myths have not been formed independently due to similar experience. But, it is more pertinent to note that in many other myths in similarity of narration there is not always the same meaning. In other words, outwardly similar looking myths do not necessarily convey the same meaning. In this connection we take three myths from three different regions. The Vedic myth of the Father and the Daughter, we have passingly referred to earlier. Now, more details. According to the earliest version, as can be gathered from pieces in the Ṛgveda (I.71.5; X.61.5-7), the father ran after his daughter. As he united with her he spilt his seed (X.61.7). From the usual symbolic expressions used later in the hymn (X.61) it becomes clear that the seed is rain. The expressions are (i) the milk of the cow that oozes *sabar* (nectar); (ii) the hidden treasure of the demon Śuṣṇa; and (iii) 'milking' of non-falling i.e., non-releasing-cows, (clouds). This will show that the myth of the Father uniting with 'his own' daughter is used as a charm for rain. This myth, as it occurs in the Ṛgveda, nowhere mentions creation of beings from the couple of Father and

Daughter.[1] Yet, it shows memory of a myth involving union of one Male who sexually united with a female created *from* him, as the words *svā duhitṛ* shows.

Another place in the Ṛgveda (III.31.1) reflects the same memory in the expression "when the Father sprinkled his semen in the daughter" (though here the commentator explains away the word *pitā*, as 'protector' (from the root *pā*, which could also give the word *pati* 'husband'). However, from the symbolic expressions used in the hymn later, it is clear that there is the desire of the gain of rain (v.11 shattering of Vṛtra and release of 'cows' etc.).[2] Here also the Father-Daughter relationship does not result in the creation of beings. The myth, hence, is not in a complete form, nor is there any possibility of a clear meaning. As in the references noted above, the fragments of an earlier myth are set here in a sacrificial context for the gain of rain, or general weal. A full version of the same myth appears in the Aitareya Br.(13.9-10) with the added gloss that the daughter was the sky, according to some, or the dawn according to others. Further it is stated as the opinion of this text, that the Daughter took the form of a doe and the Father (Prajāpati) that of a stag. This is, obviously in view of the awkwardness and the idea of sin (of incest), of this relationship among humans. The bringing in of the stag and the doe serves to eliminate the awkwardness. However, from the semen that fell on the ground, a lake is said to have been created (in line with the Ṛgvedic imagery of *retas* = (i) seed; (ii) water; also rain). We also have a hint that a man was born from it. The birth is explained as follows — The gods said, "let not that seed be spoilt (*mā duṣat*); hence the word *mānuṣa* (man)." This would mean (even with the etymological explanation) that man came into being from the primeval god, here Prajāpati, himself, and not out of the womb of a female.

However, this seems to be a sort of palimpsest over the original myth of Father creating man from his daughter - a riddle which persists. It would appear that man was born prior to the gods, as it is further said that various gods got created from the seed, when it was surrounded and heated by Agni (the fire-god). They were Āditya, Bhṛgu and a group of Ādityas (the first Āditya being the sun); then the sages Aṅgirases; and then Bṛahaspati. Thereafter, suddenly come various types of cattle - the charred coals producing black cattle, the reddened earth producing tawny cattle, and from the ashes came the buffalo, the ox, the antelope and so on. Later, the Bṛhadāraṇyaka Up.(I.4.1ff) states that the first couple was Ātman, in the form of a man and his half (woman - daughter?); they sexually united and created men, and other animals. But in this account, and in those in the later texts (Purāṇas), Prajāpati, or now Brahmā, is not said to have a further union with a girl born to him and his female half or daughter. As has been pointed out earlier, the earliest reference to the Father-Daughter relationship, on the Hindu mythical stage, is in the context of rain or water, though later on the details of creation of humans or other animals come in. We are not certain if they were already known in the Ṛgvedic period, though the myth about the Father-Daughter union was known even then. In the absence of a specific indication, we can say that the meaning of this relationship in the Vedic period has to be seen in the advent of rain, which is the 'seed' of the Sky-father, or the god of Rain;[3] and that the Daughter is the earth, specifically seen in the word *Kṣmā* (ṚV X.61.7).

We have a similar tale from the European context, obtaining in England, Scotland, Russia, etc. It is called a 'nursery tale'. According to it, a certain king's wife dies. He has a young daughter. After his wife's death he has a desire *to marry this daughter* of his. The daughter does not know how to get rid of this situation. After some deliberation, she asks her royal father to prepare three dresses - one of the sky, the other of the sun and the third of the moon. The king readily furnishes these dresses. The daughter is again in a fix. She knows that her father has an ass who is his favourite. This ass produces gold every day. So, as a precondition to marriage, the daughter asks her father for the skin of this ass, feeling certain that he would not do so; for that would mean killing the ass. But, the father kills the ass and gives her the skin. When she gets it, she covers herself with it. She also smears her face with soot and runs away. Gomme, who records this tale, comments that it reflects the behaviour of persons in a kinless society when the concept of family was not known.[4] Whether this nursery tale can be taken as a myth is not the point here. It appears that it is not restricted to a particular society, unlike the Vedic myth mentioned above. It has currency. But, even then, this currency cannot be taken as a tradition; for the term tradition is used in the context of a particular society or a regional unit. Similarity in myths and tales of various, mutually far separated, regions is seen; and even though there is a probability of borrowal, myths are regarded as special tales; or, in other words, sacred tales, in the particular social context as against tales for pure enjoyment or recreation. Even so, we take this tale for the purpose of comparison as it involves the point of relationship which is similar to the tale from the Vedic tradition, and with the tales that are to follow. However, on the very face of it, the difference between this tale and the myth noted above is, that in this tale there is no mention of ejection of the sexual fluid, the symbolism of rain being totally absent. Moreover, the Vedic tale does not speak of marriage. The suggestion of Gomme, that this European tale has its source in a kinless society cannot be accepted. Even if we accept it tentatively, it will have to be understood that - (i) when the tale was traditionally kept alive by such a society, even in its advanced stage, or (ii) when it was adopted by such societies as had an established institution of marriage, it served the purpose of pointing out the awkwardness of such a situation. It could also be, that it reflects a stage when kinship was beginning to be a familiar concept - especially the role of the male as the procreator is clear from the terms 'father' and 'daughter' used. Prior to that, as actual birth was seen as being only from the female, the male was not thought as connected with it in any way. At a later stage the male came to be called 'father'. In any case, it has to be understood as a tale from a society which knew the kinship terms used in the tale. Without these terms, how such relationships were expressed remains dark. On the other hand one can explain the term *pitā* and *duhitā* from the earlier Vedic myth, on the basis of etymology. But, to propose that even the Ṛgvedic myth is from a kinless stage is superfluous; for, the *pitā* is simply 'protector', (from *pā*), who rains down his seed in the 'milker' (*duhitṛ*, from the root *duh*) who is said to be the earth (*kṣmā*). This will absolve the Ṛgvedic myth of the element of incest, and the myth will be a purely nature myth. The same cannot be said of such myths where the riddle of the first couple, creating the beings, faces the investigating curiosity. To brand all such myths as being the vestiges of a kinless society will be disastrous, leading to a no-win situation. The fact is, that it is unsafe to see any social behaviour in all such tales, or myths.

With this, we take a myth from the Sumerian-Babylonian context. Enki impregnates Nintu, who is an aspect of the goddess Ninhursag. The name Ninhursag indicates, that she is the goddess of the earth or of the primeval 'stone-heap' (Nin = "goddess"; hur - sag = the earth, or mountain'). Nintu gives birth to a daughter after nine days. Her name is Nin-mu. Enki decrees that no one should wander in the marshy land. But, once this daughter does walk in. When Enki sees her, while himself crossing the river in a boat, he reaches her and impregnates her. She gives birth to a daughter named Nin-Kurra. The name Nin-Kurra signifies (goddess of) 'plant'. This girl also wanders in the marshes and catches the sight of Enki, who impregnates her. She gives birth to a daughter, called Uttu. This name indicates 'fruit', 'grain'. Fearing that even this girl might come in sight of Enki, Nintu (the wife of Enki) tells her that, if Enki sees her and tries to impregnate her, she should ask him to fetch for her cucumbers, grapes, and some fruit out of the desert. This happens; and Enki fulfils Uttu's desire by irrigating the desert, before the girl agrees to impregnation. But, now, Nintu-Ninhursag removes Enki's seed from within the womb of Uttu and plants it in her own womb. From it eight different plants come out, which Enki eats up turn by turn. Seeing this, Ninhursag gets furious; and, cursing him, she withdraws from him 'the eye of life'. The result is that he gets diseased in eight parts of his body and Ninhursag also disappears. The result is that there is a drought. There is despair everywhere. But a fox brings Ninhursag back. She now places the sick Enki in her Vagina. As Enki is diseased in eight parts (corresponding to the eating of eight different plants), Ninhursag causes eight different deities to be born. They heal Enki in each of the eight parts of his body.[5]

The myth has been understood by Kirk as indicating irrigation; and he sees in the continued motif of 'incest' only a dramatic elaboration of the same motif rather than new stages of irrigation.[6] He also suggests that over-irrigation causes failure of Enki's efforts leading to the condition of drought, and that thoughtless and irregular sexual activity carried too far leads to his disease. Now, before examining other details in the myth, the analysis of Kirk's suggestions is necessary. It would be somewhat as follows -

(i) There is only one and the same stage of irrigation, which is overdone;
(ii) Due to this act of one irrigational activity, overdone, Enki gets sick;
(iii) The result is drought.

In that case, how is one to agree with his suggestion that irregular sex wastes Enki. In the case of one irrigation, understood symbolically as an act of sex, the act could be between Enki and Ninhursag, the first couple. What, then, is irregular in it? Irregularity comes with the idea of incest; and it is to be seen in this act between Enki and his daughter; and, further, between himself and his daughter's daughter. The conflict seems to be symbolically presented as between regular 'sex' and irregular 'sex'; and, if irrigation is the point in the myth, which rightly is as said by Kirk himself, one has to understand three phases of the land. In the first, there is regularity. In the next there is irregularity, as the second phase of the land must be seen as the 'daughter'. This is the land that can produce, as contrasted to the unproductive land (the mountainous or rocky land indicated by the name Ninhursag, as Kirk explains and further says that she is herself Nintu). This second phase is the result of the act of Enki, who is the god of sweet water; and, in the kinship terminology, he is the father. That he crosses the river in his boat[7] shows his lordship over sweet water courses. This is further supported from the detail that obtains earlier in the myth. According to it, Enki's wife called Ninsikilla[8] (=The pure goddess' or 'goddess of purity'), an earlier phase of earth indicating a non-differantiative appellation, asks him to supply water to the earth. He calls the sun and the moon for help and becomes successful in bringing water on the earth, which appears to be rain and, through it, floods.[9] The control of Enki over rain is only one aspect. He was, primarily, the god of all sorts of water (Kirk, 1970, p.91). As a river-god, with inundation he generates a different phase of land, now the fertile land, which is his 'daughter'. A further phase is through a second inundation, or irrigation through a canal-system, which generates the 'daughter's daughter'. While there is no substantial change in the form of water, the form of the earth changes. These changed forms are seen as 'daughter' and 'granddaughter'. The pure land and marshy land, and further the desert are all 'impregnated' by the same Enki with his waters-'seed', with the result that there are different types of crops. What Enki does here is done by Enlil in a separate myth; but the themes of these two myths appear to be mutually different.

Other points in the myth of Enki are to be seen in the context of the *main theme of the fertilization of land.* There is mention of the drought, the reasons for which are -

(i) Ninhursag curses Enki as he devours the eight plants each by turn; she withdraws from him the 'eye of life'. He sickens;

(ii) These plants had sprouted from the seed of Enki, which had been planted in the womb of Uttu, but which had been taken out by Ninhursag and placed in her own womb;

(iii) Ninhursag disappears.

Examined carefully, this part marks a difference from the part of the myth which indicates repeated 'incest'. But, to understand this as presenting a polarization between regular sex and irregular sex and, further, as suggesting that irregular sex wastes Enki's fertility (Kirk, 1970, p.96) is difficult to accept. The point is, what is the main suggestion in the myth - a conflict between irregular sex and regular sex or the modes of irrigation-based produce from land? There are clear indications in the narration of various types of produce in the last stage; and the girls that are born one after the other are all phases of the earth which originally appears in a double aspect - Nintu and Nin-hursag. Enki has another 'lady' as wife; she is the pure lady, which might indicate the land scorched by the sun, the word 'pure' indicating also lack of moisture. The point gets strengthened from an important detail in the earlier part of the myth, where it is stated that Enki is asked by Ninsikilla to supply water to the earth. The action of the myth takes place in Dilman, which is, itself, said to be 'clean' and 'bright', but always short of water (Kirk, 1970, p.91). This could be in spite of rain which, if at all it arrives, is very scanty. All this points to the main theme of the myth, which is the watering of the land for produce through irrigation depending upon occasional inundation and through canals. Kirk notes the point of irrigation through a well-knit canal-system and states that irrigation is "associated with sexual activity". The latter, in that case, has to be seen only as symbolic. It is, hence, necessary to take the sexual imagery as only secondary to the main theme. Hence, it is not correct to see here the conflict between regular sex and irregular sex, or to say that irregular sex wasted Enki's fertility. That would shift the theme to actual human relationship, which is only metaphoric. Actually, the myth revolves in the frame of productional activity. So the detail of the removal of the seed from the great granddaughter, Uttu, to her own womb by Ninhursag is nothing but the transplantational activity. The sickness of Enki is the condition of the diminished flow of water in the irrigational canals and its getting stagnated at various points. There is a minute similarity between Ninhursag, and Enki, in spite of difference. Ninhursag appears in various forms in the 'daughter' while Enki appears here in the same form (of canals), though he is the god of all waters, including rain. This is the difference. The similarity is that both have a generic status and are also seen in the species. The placement of Enki in her vagina by Ninhursag is the complete absorption of water or complete lack of the inundation water. A comparison with the phenomena associated with the river Nile helps make the point clear. Entirely dependent on the inundation of the Nile, the ancient Egyptians used to store water for domestic use in large jars during the inundation period and prior to the change of colour of the water-course. This latter phase was marked by the water turning green, indicating disease. During this period the water was unwholesome. The river was at the lowest during April through June. From the middle of June it began it rise, the water having a reddish hue due to mud it carried. Then for a short period till July end it turned green. By the beginning of August the Nile ran high. At this period the canals were opened up for irrigation up sto September. By the end of September the flood receded, giving scope for sowing that started in November.[10] In the Enki myth the mention of devouring the eight types of plants and his getting diseased in eight places, eight deities being created and also being cured by Ninhursag may not be explained with certainty; but it could, probably, indicate small shrines at places where the water in the canals or inundation got stagnated, and later disappeared. So is the case with the detail that Nintu gives birth to a girl after nine days. The number may stand for the period for the sprouts to show up, reflecting the period of nine months, the usual period for delivery; more probably, it might have reference to the duration of some ritual, since lost.[11] The detail that Ninhursag withdraws from Enki 'the eye of life' is closely associated with his getting diseased. If Enki is the god of water, the 'eye' that is causatively intimate to him is to be taken as also the controller of inundation, or flood. There is no doubt, hence, that this 'eye' is some star whose rise showed the surge in water, and whose setting corresponded to the ebb of streams. Here, again, we have parallels from the adjacent (ancient) Egypt. The annual inundation of the Nile was called 'the flood of the Eye of Atum'.[12] This corresponded to the 17th of June, because it was called the "Night of the drop" (Leylet - en - Nuktah). This drop was believed to be from the star Sirius (as it is known to the Greeks). Accòrding to the ancient Egyptians this 'eye' was of Rā; and it was called Hathor. They also believed that tears from the eye of Isis caused floods. In the Summerian myth (of Enki), as it obtains, there is no reference to any ritual; but the appearance of the 'eye' in ancient Egypt was marked by a curious rite. When the Nile began to rise, a young virgin was decked in gay apparel and was thrown into the river, as a sacrifice to obtain plentiful inundation.[13]

We are now at a stage to mark the points of difference in the myths from different lands. The myth from the Hindu tradition, at the period of the Aitareya Br. onwards, tries to solve the riddle of creation - how the human and other creatures were created—though in the Ṛgveda it appeared as a rain-myth. The folk-tale from Western Europe centres round the theme (or a problem?) of marriage with a daughter in the absence of the wife (who is no more). There is nothing of the sort of a riddle of creation in this myth, as marriage does not take place at all. Even according to the narration, the father does not make any advances towards the daughter; and the tale revolves on the point of marriage. The point is the awkwardness of such a proposal. The mention of the ass producing gold may lead one to take the tale as a nature-myth, the colour of the ass taken as the nocturnal darkness fading in the advanced dawn, which produces the 'gold' of the sun. The mention of the dress of the moon and the sun might be taken to add to the conjecture of the nature-myth. But, all these details are superfluous and do not even touch the main theme of awkward marriage. They only form metaphoric side-light. However, there is a psychological cord that this tale strikes. The continued proposal of marriage to the daughter, with restrained or totally absent sexual emotions, is apt to divulge other feelings in the father. These could be his intense love for his deceased wife and the pangs of having to be without her. The daughter could be very much like her mother. And the father, somehow, wants her not to leave him. This creates a riddling situation, which the tale presents. In the early Vedic myth of the Father and the Daughter there is no problem of the first couple, which is seen in its later phase. At the Ṛgvedic period the point is only of rain fructifying the earth. In the Enki myth the same is seen; but the Father is not rain; he is the inundation and the canal that helps irrigation, which hints at settled agriculture. Both, the Enki myth and the Ṛgvedic Father-Daughter myth have the basis of observation. There is no riddle, or problem. The later Father-Daughter versions of the Hindu myths, involving Brahmā and his daughter, reflect a riddle - of creation. Here we could, possibly, make a difference as myths of observation and myths of speculation, though observational myths do turn into speculative myths in many cases. Thus, both myths - the Ṛgvedic myth noted above and the myth of Enki—show speculation about the relationship between rain and the irrigational canal on the one hand and the earth or its phases of the fertile field on the other. One more point to remember is, that in the rain-earth relationship (Vedic) there is no further relationship between the Father and the granddaughter, and again the latter's daughter who becomes the Father's great grand-daughter. But this is a marked trait of the myths of irrigation. However, in certain cases a myth of creation shows the Father-granddaughter speculation. As an example we again take a Maori myth.

The Maori god Tane performs the act of separating the parents - Sky and Earth - called Rangi and Papa, as we have noted. This is the myth from observation. As a further exploit, in the speculative myth of the first couple, he is stated to have created various species of creatures after mating with a series of female beings such as insects and birds. He also creates trees and plants in the same way. But, he could not create the humans. Frustrated, he forms a girl from clay.[14] He breathes into her nostrils to instil animation in her. He then copulates with her. From this act a girl is born. Tane leaves his first mate and now copulates with this daughter. From this union mankind is created.[15] This shows the myth in the same form (i.e., Father-granddaughter relationship) as the Enki myth; but the meaning differs, here the point being of creation; not production from land. In the Hindu mythical context, the Prajāpati-Brahmā - Father syndrome, in relation to the Daughter, is further seen in the myth of Manu and his daughter, Iḍā. Here the daughter is the offering (*iḍā*) itself. It is said that when a fish saved Manu from the great deluge, he saw himself alone and he desired to create (cf. the case of the Egyptian Atum, the Vedic Prajāpati and later Brahmā). He desired to create a girl, by a regular sacrifice. He did not have the usual apparatus (*araṇi*) for kindling the fire out. So he cast clarified butter, curds, etc. in the water itself. From that offering a fully grown young girl came out within a year's time. Manu asked her who she was. She replied that she was his daughter and that he should use her at sacrifices. Manu used her in the sacrifice to be performed with cooked grain. She is said to be the same as Iḍā.[16] He used her variously. He also created progeny with her help. That came to be the progeny of Manu (Śatapatha Br.I.8.1.7ff). Here, though the first couple is contemplated as Father-Daughter, there is no mention of copulation between the parties. "With her help" or "through her" (*tayā*) does not mean 'from her'.[17] As such, this narration cannot be taken as a pure myth, though it uses the popular theme of such myths. Here the stress is on sacrifice as the source of creation; and, at best, it could be taken as a Charter-myth (to use Malinowski's term). In this myth though Manu is said to have created progeny *with the help* of Iḍā, the point of copulation is not clear; because the old myth of Father-daughter is used here for a different purpose, which is to extol the portion of the sacrificial cake (*puroḍāśa*). This portion is called Iḍā. It is used in the sacrifices that do not use the juice of the creeper called Soma. These sacrifices are called Pāka-yajña (cf. The New-moon and Full-moon sacrifice). Independent of this sacrificial context, Manu and Iḍā are not mentioned. Manu and his daughter Iḍā, as the first copulative pair are hardly, or never recorded. It would be, hence, unsound to say that Manu took Iḍā as his female partner in the creation of the human and other animate species. What can be gathered from this version is only that Iḍā (sacrificial offering) is presented in place of Manu's daughter, who was, probably, known in popular belief even in the Vedic period as his female partner in procreation. However this is not recorded at that period. Iḍā (Iḷā as per the Ṛgvedic method of pronunciation) is mentioned as a goddess.[18] So is also Manu as the ancestor of the humans; but these two do not form the creative couple in the Ṛgveda. So, the position is that even in the Vedic period the riddle of the first couple being Father and Daughter was already known. On the basis of this myth Iḍā, the personified offering, was presented as the daughter, aetiologically, to extol sacrifice. The strain of this new myth is that the human race was born from sacrifice, through Manu. This will show how the original Father-Daughter myth of creation, rather shadowy in the early Vedic period, was used in two different contexts with different meanings - (i) Rain as noted earlier; and (ii) offering. This would also show two stages in the history of a myth - one, the stage of formation; and two, the stage of its varied usage.

We have referred to the myth of Kronos swallowing his children and vomitting them out, later, when Zeus cheats him. The swallowing motif is seen also in the myth of Kumarbi who swallows the penis of his father Anu, though he does not vomit it but gives birth to the storm god. Though the form of swallowing is the same in both, in one case the children come out as they were swallowed without getting changed. In the other case what is swallowed is the penis, but what comes out as the result of the act, is the wind god. This has the setting of the strife between the high-god and the new divinity, his son. In the case of Śukra and Śiva, in the Hindu myth, a new point is seen in the mythical narration, which is that of rejuvenation. The strife, though subtly present, is relegated to the background. Śukra, the priest of the Asuras (demons) is said to possess the lore of bringing the dead to life (*saṁjīvanī vidyā*), with which he could revive the dead demons. The gods were devoid of this lore. Hence Śiva gets Śukra to be brought to him and swallows him when he arrives. Ultimately Śukra comes out with the lore called Śāṁbhava.[19] The same motif is seen in the myth of Kaca and Śukra The latter has the lore of rejuvenation, while the gods do not possess it. The gods send Kaca to get the lore from Śukra. Kaca stays with Śukra as a disciple. The demons see to it that Kaca is killed. But, Śukra brings him back to life. Ultimately the demons kill him, burn him and put the ashes in the drink of Śukra. As the ashes reach his stomach Śukra feels uneasy. Due to the intervention of his daughter, Devāyanī, Śukra teaches the lore to Kaca (who is in the form of ashes in the stomach) so that when he comes out he could rejuvenate Śukra who would die as Kaca would tear open his belly in the act of coming out. Kaca comes out alive and also rejuvenates his preceptor, Śukra[20]. Here the form of the narration is almost the same as in the myths of Kumarbi, and of Kronos. But, while in these myths the swallowing and destruction indicate the strife between the old god and the new god with the Father-son relationship and the usurpation of power, subtly mixed with fertility, in the Kaca-Śukra-Śiva myth there is no strife between the new and the old individual nor the Father-son relationship. The strife shifts to the gods and the demons as groups. The suggestion of fertility is seen in the Ouranos-Kronos myth, but there is no swallowing of either. The Kumarbi myth may come nearer the Śukra-Śiva myth in terms of fertility as the birth occurs from (or due to) the generative organ. However, the latter is totally different as far as the meaning is concerned. As noted earlier we might see in such myths the speculation of the capacity of the male to produce without the female (as for example Zeus 'giving birth' to Athena from his head in the Greek myth). In this context, we may note a Sherenté myth, from South America. According to this myth, men practised homosexuality before women existed. One of them became pregnant; but he was unable to deliver; and, died![21] In this myth, there is no 'swallowing' in the strict sense of the word; and the problem remains unsolved - or, rather solved for good; because the male dies, suggesting that a male cannot take upon himself maternity, which is a speciality of a woman. The myth, at the best, can be taken as reflecting the superiority of the female in this sphere. It is also to be noted that the myth has human relationship as the central point, and not gods or superhumans, in whose case such births are no problem, nor do they form part of this meaning. The Śukra-Śiva and the Kaca-Śukra myths use swallowing and rebirth from the swallower to suggest initiation for a new lore and the ultimate identity between the preceptor and the pupil. A further step is where the motif of 'swallowing' in the myth is enacted in ritual. The preceptor closes his eyes and places his right hand (palm) on the head of the pupil (= initiate) and takes him inside his own body, symbolically. This is done by inhaling the breath. The process is called *saṁhāra* ('in-carrying', 'contraction'). Then follows the 'keeping in' *(kuṁbhaka;* or *kuṁbha*) wherein the mouth and the nostrils are closed lest the breath should go out. This is the process by which the initiate is kept in his body by the preceptor as a foetus. Then follows the 'release' (*recaka*), wherein the breath is released through the nostrils. Then the preceptor opens his eyes and looks at the initiate and takes his palm off the head of the pupil, thus bringing him out, fully equipped for imparting the *mantra.*[22] The strife and displacement of gods that mark such myths may indicate even social strife and tension between the older people and the younger generation, through the stories of gods; but a combination with the motif of swallowing gives a new angle, the motif giving signals of different meanings as the situations change. Sometimes an aetiological addition gives notice of this change as is seen from the Vedic myth of Śuṣṇa. This myth also has association of the

God-demons fight. Śuṣṇa is said to be a demon (*dānava*). He always kept nectar in his mouth. Those of the demons who died in the battle with the gods, Suṣṇa brought back to life. If the gods died, they did not revive. Now, Indra learnt that Suṣṇa had nectar in his mouth. So, he took the shape of a lump of honey and lay in the path of Śuṣṇa. Śuṣṇa swallowed that lump; and, now Indra got inside the stomach of Śuṣṇa. Indra caught hold of the lump of nectar that was in the mouth of Śuṣṇa, changed himself into an eagle-hawk and flew out. Hence is the eagle-hawk strongest of all birds, as he is a form of Indra. The myth has an aetiological note - "Nectar does he hold who knows thus. Whosoever one desires to live without disease, him should one breathe out (*abhivyanyāt*) after having taken inside (*vyādāya*). With immortality does he breathe him out. He (the one taken in and brought out) attains full life. Not before his (full attainment of) life does he die".[23] The myth ends with Indra getting inside the belly of Śuṣṇa and coming out with nectar (*amṛta*). It does not require much thought to see that 'nectar' here corresponds to the *saṁjīvanī* lore that we have in the later myth of Śukra-Kaca (from the Mahābhārata) and that of Śiva-Śukra later from the Purāṇas. The tailpiece of aetiology cannot be taken as forming part of the original myth of the eagle-serpent fight, that is set in the strife between gods and the demons; and Śuṣṇa, modelled on the serpent, like Vṛtra, is here the prototype of Śukra (for Kaca), and Śiva (for Śukra). However, it is not the myth, but the aetiological appendage, that has the root of the symbolic rite of initiation, as it speaks of 'breathing out after taking in' while the myth proper does not mention it. The 'swallowing' and bringing out appears in the later myths of Śukra-Kaca and Śiva-Śukra. The homologues in these versions can be seen as follows-

I *Vedic*	II *Mahābhārata*	III *Puranic*
1. Śuṣṇa, the Asura-demon, has the rejuvenating liquid in his possession, in his mouth.	1. Śukra, the priest of the Asuras, has the rejuvenating lore.	1. Śiva—gets the priest of the Asuras, Śukra, called to him,as the latter has the rejuvenating lore.
2. Indra approaches Śuṣṇa (and lays in his path as honey).	2. Kaca, on behalf of the gods, approaches Śukra.	2. Śukra approaches Śiva, being taken forcibly.
3. 'Snaking' along his path, Śuṣṇa swallows the honey-Indra.	3. Śukra is made to swallow Kaca with the drink.	3. Śiva swallows Śukra (no drink or honey).
4. Indra takes the rejuvenating liquid from inside the stomach (mouth) of the swallower and comes out with renewed strength, with the rejuvenating fluid (taking the form of an eagle-hawk).	4. Kaca learns the lore while inside the stomach of the swallower and comes out of the stomach with renewed status and the lore.	4. Śiva releases Śukra through his generative organ; and Śukra comes out with the lore called Śāmbhava (indicating that Śambhu-Śiva taught him).
5. Aetiological detail.	5. —	5. —

Myth III is an inversion of the two earlier myths; because it shows the 'swallower' (*Śukra*) being swallowed and his original lore getting the name Śāṁbhava. But, apart from this change, due to the prominence of the Śaivite faith, there is no difference in this version. Version I has the liquid of immortality and not the 'lore'. The post-Vedic versions of the myth have the meaning of initiation - lore (*mantra,* for rejuvenation) which gives the status of a 'twice-born' to the initiate, after symbolically 'killing' him in the tonsure of his head and other details, at the rite.[24] The Śuṣṇa myth, using the word *amṛta* has a different meaning, though the appendage has initiation or consecration in view. For that the main myth has to be compared with such other myths where the words 'honey' (*madhu)* and *amṛta* have been used symbolically; also where the strife between the god(s) and the Asura(s), or more particularly between Indra and this demon is seen. Indra is said to have smashed the citadels of Śuṣṇa and released rain-waters (ṚV I.51.11) and at other places; also he is said to have broken the testicles of Śuṣṇa to release the divine waters (ṚV VIII.40.10.11). The Indra-bird-honey-lump equation in the myth is suggested from the Ṛgvedic detail where he is said to have brought 'honey' taking the form of an eagle-hawk (ṚV IV.18.13); and honey often symbolizes rain-water in the Ṛgveda; the same is with *amṛta* (in water is *amṛta*, ṚV I.23.19). From *amṛta* (liquid of immortality, 'honey' rain-water), the myth takes the meaning to the lore of immortality, as the period and the situation changes. It is probable that the original myth of the fight between the controller of rain, conceived as a serpent (demon), and the Eagle (Indra) as the releaser of rain[25] was used in the later Vedic period of the Kāṭhaka Saṁhitā, to exemplify the principle of new birth in initiation. In that case, it will mean that the symbolic swallowing of the initiate on the part of the preceptor to give him a new ritual birth was already getting enacted by breathing him in and breathing him out (cf. Kāṭhaka Sam., *loc.cit.*, *vyādāya abhi-vyanyāt, vyanyāt* has the root *an*, which signifies breathing and life-breath). And the myth was suitably fashioned to make Śuṣṇa the swallower. Even then, the expression 'one should breathe him in and then breathe him out' ill-suits Śuṣṇa [26] (who is said to be a serpent with horns = dragon) and does not obtain in the other two myths about Śukra and Śiva. The reason is that those myths do not require elaboration of the symbols that get embedded in them, while the corresponding ritual being an act has to express the same symbols in acts. Such acts are also to be taken as having symbolic meaning. In the present case, 'breathing' - both breathing in and breathing out - is symbolic for 'swallowing and letting out', and this is further symbolic for taking in the womb (conception) and giving a new birth (delivery) for renewed vigour, or a new status after initiation. This will be enough to show how even other popular myths get used in a variety of situations resulting in a change of the original meaning, as the situations solicit. In such cases, with the change of meaning is noted a slight change in the form of the original myth. This change could best be taken as of 'pattern' rather than of the form. Thus, in the case of the myths mentioned above, the form is 'Taking in - taking out'; but the patterns would be (i) Taking in - taking out; (ii) Entering - coming out; (iii) Breathing in - breathing out; (iv) Swallowing - letting out. The meaning would depend on the words used. Thus—

1. Penis: castration/loss of status/birth;
2. Honey: rain/liquid of immortality.
3. Whole person: conception and new birth/initiation/consecration.

The same applies to other myths appearing similar, but differing in meaning.

References

1. For a detailed examination of this myth see Dange, *Vedic Concept of 'Field' and the Divine Fructification,* pp.123-53; *Sexual Symbolism from the Vedic Ritual,* pp.141-59; Wendy Doniger O'Flaherty, *Hindu Myths*, Penguin, pp.26ff.
2. In the Ṛgveda Vṛtra is the serpent that holds all waters, including rain. At this stage, the concept of Vṛtra presents a mixture of a water-holding serpent and a demon often superimposed on the rain-cloud, while that of Śuṣṇa is of a demon-dragon of drought; see A.A. Macdonell, *Vedic Mythology,* under sections 68-69.
3. For a probable borrowal of the Father-Daughter motif by the Ṛgveda from the middle eastern sources, see *Sexual Symbolism,* pp.152ff.
4. *Folklore as an Historical Science,* p.50. I have examined this tale earlier (*Sexual Symbolism*). Here it is studied in a slightly different light, and improved opinion.
5. G.S. Kirk, *Myth,* p.91ff; also J.B.Prichard, Ed. ANET (*Ancient Near Eastern Texts Relating to the Old Testament),* Princeton, 1955, p.38ff.
6. Kirk, *op.cit.*, p.95f.
7. Like Enlil, who is also said to wander in a boat.
8. Nin is common for some names indicating 'lady', 'goddess'; so Nin-sikilla; Nin-tu; Nin-mu; Nin-Kurra.
9. J. Hastings, *Encyclopaedia of Religion and Ethics,* vol.II, p.295.
10. D. Mackenzie, *Egyptian Myth and Legend,* London, p.24.
11. Nine like seven appears to be a favourite symbolic number among various people. The Hindus have the Navarātra (nine nights) at the Autumn festival of the goddess, and also at the start of the Spring (Rāma-navarātra; on the ninth, Rāma is said to have been born, in popular belief). In ancient Greece, the festival of Demeter came once in five years but lasted for nine days in September, Edith Hamilton, *Mythology,* p.54; according to the myth she wandered for nine days in search of her daughter Persephone (Proserpine in Latin), when the latter was carried away by the dark god of Hades to the underworld (p.57);

the Lycian king entertained Bellerophone for nine days. King Menos had declared that every nine years the people of Athens should pay him tribute of seven maidens and seven youths (p.212). The female demon Hydra had nine heads (p.231).

12. R.T. Rundle Clark, *Myth and Symbol in Ancient Egypt*, p.84, where he refers to the Coffin Text IV.140.

13. D. Mackenzie, *Egyptian Myth and Legend*, p.25, who refers to E.W. Lane, *Customs of Modern Egyptians.*

14. cf. Genesis II.7, first account of creation. In the second account in the same chapter, Adam (= man) is said to have been created before other animals.

15. F. Allan Hanson, *op.cit.*, p.183.

16. From another little portion of the *puroḍāśa*, is made what is called *prāśitra*. This is said to represent the portion of flesh that got stuck to the tip of an arrow shot by Rudra at Prajāpati, who had run away in the form of an antelope; for *prāśitra* see P.V. Kane, *History of Dharmasastra*, Vol.II-ii, Poona, 1974, p.1064f. The birth of Iḍā, however, is from the offerings of heated and cooled milk, and its other products (Sat. Br., *loc.cit.*).

17. The words of Iḍā are "employ (*avakalpaya*) me in the sacrifice" and, "If you employ me (*mām avakalpayasi*) you will prosper in progeny and cattle" (Ib.9); further "with her he performed worship and austerities, desiring off-spring", which would indicate that she was a divine ritual-aid for progeny, rather than being an active copulative partner. The words are abstruse; hence they might indicate a copulative association. This dubiosity is due to using an older myth (of the riddle of the first couple) as a charter in the sacrificial context. Wendy D. O'Flaherty in her *Hindu Myths*, p.25, n.1, says that the primeval incestuous act is attributed to Manu in later mythology. However, she gives no reference. She obviously has Śatarūpā in mind, (see Index to her book, under Śatarūpā and the page 50 as indexed; but even here it is not made clear if Śatarūpā is Manu's daughter, and also wife). Even so, the Manu-daughter myth has to be taken as a meta-myth; for it is Prajāpati himself, who is Brahmā (and even Viṣṇu), who is substituted by Manu in a later myth, see Harivaṁśa I.52; II.1.

18. For Idā (Iḷā), ṚV III.4.8 = VII.2.8; X.70.8 etc.

19. Dange, *Legends in the Mahābhārata,* Delhi, 1969, p.212ff.
20. *Ib.*, pp.157-162.
21. Kirk, *Myth* (1970), p.216, who takes it from Claude Lévi-Strauss.
22. Dange, *Encl.P.B.P.*, Vol.III, p.915.
23. Kāṭhaka Sam. 37.14
24. Dange, *Legends in the Mahābhārata,* pp.194ff, 201ff.
25. *Ib.* Ch.1, esp. pp.67ff; Mb.Ādi I.16; 33.6.
26. Śuṣṇa is said to have not only horns, but even has his eggs, and is born of an egg, ṚV I.33.12, VIII.40.10-11; see A.A. Macdonell, *Vedic Mythology,* under 69.

Three

Nature, Ritual and 'Charter'

As the twentieth century advanced, some theories about the meaning of myth got settled. However, the earliest effort towards unravelling the meaning in a myth was made, in the Vedic context, by Yāska (Nirukta, about the seventh century B.C.), who classified tales as - (i) Aitihāsika (narrative involving a person); (ii) Nairukta (based on etymology; *nirukta* = 'etymology'); and (iii) *Mantra-Brāhmaṇa-vāda*(eulogy relating to a prayer or ritual). The first type has already been referred to (Ch.I) while explaining the connotation of *itihāsa*. The second type is seen in explaining a myth on the basis of the etymology of the names in it. Thuṣ Vṛtra, the demon, is the 'enveloper' (fr. the root *vṛ*, 'to cover'., 'envelop'); or, Śuṣṇa is the demon of drought (fr. the root *śuṣ* - 'to dry'). In such cases Vṛtra and Śuṣṇa would be seen as the 'holders' of water, whom Indra is said to smash to release the rain and other terrestrial waters. Yāska, who follows this method, gives all sorts of etymologies without minding the grammatical irregularities, which he sets at naught by proposing that the letters and suffixes should be ignored to give a plausible meaning. In this, Yāska follows the Brāhmaṇa texts (that specify various rituals) which are replete with such etymologies to explain a particular ritual or a name in the ritual context. The third comprises narrations to support the ritual or a prayer-formula. An example of this type is the tale of Manu and Iḍā, his daughter, noted earlier. This tale is specifically told (or made up) to extol the *iḍā* offering at the ritual in the context of the New-moon-day and the Full-moon-day sacrifices.

It may be mentioned, that etymology was resorted to even by modern scholars, while trying to unfold the 'message' or meaning in a myth. Thus, in the myth of Ouranos-Kronos (referred to in Ch.I), Aphrodite is said to have been produced from the foam of the sea, where drops of Ouranos' semen fell. The name suggests, etymologically, 'one who was born from the foam'. 'Aphros' means 'foam' in Greek. Claud Lévy-Strauss explains the myth of Oedipus on the basis of the etymology of the names therein, saying that the message therein lies in the conflict between the beliefs regarding beings born out of earth and out of the union between man and woman. He explains the names as follows - Labdocos (father of Laios) = Lame; Laios (Oedipus' father) Left-sided; Oedipus = swollen foot.[1] But far before Lévi-Strauss, etymology was made a strong basis of the interpretation of myths by Max Müller and early writers on this subject. Max Müller, who was nicknamed the 'Sun' or 'Solarist' by scholars in the field of Anthropology, said, "I fully admit that animism is the true key to many secrets of mythology, but the true key to animism is language".[2] This was a reference to the animistic method of interpretation and to such scholars as Tylor and others. Max Müller (1907, p.xvii) mentions three methods or schools in this context - (1) Etymological or Geneological; (2) Analogical or Comparative; and (3) Psychological, or Anthropological or Ethnological. He stressed that the original constituent elements in a myth were words and phrases about the most striking phenomena of nature such as day and night, dawn and evening, sun and moon, sky, earth and sea, in their various relationships to each other and to man (*Ib*.vi). Hence his method was to seek the meaning of the various names in a myth in their etymology and thus to arrive at the meaning of the myth. But etymology and the slant towards seeing nature in almost all myths sullied the efforts of Max Müller. He believed that, in order to become mythological, it was necessary that the radical meaning of certain names should have been obscured and forgotten in the language to which they belonged. According to him mythology is only a dialect, an ancient form of communication, that it was a type of language; but Lévi-Strauss laid stress on structures and bundles of relationships to go to the inner meaning of myths. It is not untrue that myths of a particular class are representations of natural phenomena. The Greek myth of Apollo, that of Ouranos and Gaia, of Hades and Proserpine, or that of Aphrodite's birth from the foam cannot be unconnected with the natural phenomena. On the Hindu side the myth of Vivasvant and Saraṇyū, and its later version of the Sun and his two wives - Sañjñā and Chāyā have their source in the observation of nature. But, to say that all myths are convertible to the working of natural phenomena is not true. The excesses of the Nature-myth theory could be seen from the example of the tale of the frog-girl. The Mahābhārata (III.192) records a tale according to which (in short), Parikṣit, the king of the Ikṣvāku family, once went ahunting in the forest. When he was deep in the forest, he heard a sweet melody. He followed it and saw a beautiful young girl singing near a lake. Being attracted by her beauty, the king proposed marriage to her. She also accepted, but on the condition - viz. she should never touch water. This was simple, thought the king. He took her to his city. (He married her). He decreed that a palace be built for her and that water should never be brought in it, or in its vicinity. He enjoyed his days and nights with her and became rare for his other queens. The queens were no less surprised than they were angry at the whole situation and taking the chief minister into confidence asked him to help them. The chief minister got a mini forest grown around the new palace. He also got dug a stepped well in one of its quarters and got it hidden amidst creepers. Having done all this he informed the king. Once, the king took his new wife for sport in this newly made forest. They strolled about for a long time and wandering away, got thirsty. The king noticed the spot, dark green with thickets and went there. To his surprise he saw the stepped well and invited his beloved queen for a sip of water. She approached, saw the well and, as soon as she dipped her cupped palms in the water, she got turned into a female frog, which was her former form.[3] On the very face of it, the tale cannot be taken as a Nature-myth. But, Max Müller who relates it as the story of Bhekī (female-frog) takes the disappearance of the girl at the touch of water as suggesting the setting of the sun in the sea.[4] The blow to the Nature-myth theory was given by Andrew Lang, who also criticised Max Müller's etymological method, which sought to explain away the repulsive points in a myth or a legend to yield a pure and harmless sense. Calling such efforts apologistic, he branded the scholars and commentators who resorted to such explanation[5] as 'Apologists'. Lang, who believed that myths are formed in the savage stage of human beings, criticised the 'physical philosophers' (of the Nature-myth school) who thought that the early people, in whose brain and speech myth had their origin, must have been philosophers, like themselves, intelligent educated persons,[6] who could never have meant to tell stories about gods so full of nonsense, irrational and blasphemous. So, according to him, they believed that such irrational and inconvenient elements in myths must, originally, have had harmless meanings. Hence they commented with the help of etymology and other interpretations.[7] Andrew Lang does not reject that Nature-myths do obtain, and he has recorded some such myths (Lang, 1913, p.124f). However, he ridicules the theory that all myths are Nature-myths. His own contribution to the study of Nature-myths could be said to be that the savages supplied the material to science through their myths and now mythicised names. We should never think, says he, when a new planet comes into our ken, of calling it Kangaroo or Rabbit; but the names of stars we inherit from Greek mythology, such as the Bear, Castor and Pollux and so forth are such as no people in our mental condition would originally think of bestowing. According to him these older Greek names of stars are derived from a time when the ancestors of the Greeks were in the mental and imaginative condition of the Bushmen, Murri and New Zealanders. These and such names provided Greece with the raw material for their astronomical myths and the savages handed these names to science. Quoting Bacon, he says that we listen to the harsh ideas of earlier people "blown softly through the flutes of the Grecians".[8] He does not accept any kind of etymological explanation for the Sanskrit word *ṛkṣa* for constellation as Max Müller does. Max Müller (fr. the root *ṛc* - *ṛkṣ* - *arch* etc.), says, that the original meaning of *ṛkṣa* as 'bright' was forgotten, and the popular meaning of 'bear' came to stick.[9] Lang would call this 'apologistic'. Lang suggests the following steps for the formation of such myths: (i) the savage man wonders; (ii) he marks the movement and the position of the stars; (iii) he connects it with the beasts or men of his own experience; and (iv) he expresses in the form of a story.[10] From what Lang has said about the savage mind loaning the names of constellations to science, he appeared to Kirk as suggesting that myths constituted "a kind of proto-science".[11] While commenting on the aetiological theory of myths, Kirk criticises Lang for taking myths to be explanatory,[12] or trying to explain myths. True, Lang uses such expressions as "explain" (*Custom and Myth*, p.52, 57 etc.) or "we explained the survival of the bull-roarer" (*Ib.*,p.63). But, he hardly says that he tries to explain a whole myth, or even a part of it, or that a myth explains something. On the contrary he says, "we do not even pretend to explain everything" (*Ib.*). In the case of the Hindu myth of Urvaśī and Purūravas he suggests that the myth points to the importance of a custom in respect of wives and gives examples from various tribes.[13] In contrast, Max Müller tries to explain the myth on the basis of words as — Urvaśī is from 'wide' (*uru*) and 'shining' (*aś*, 'to shine'); so Urvaśī is the morning Dawn for him, or evening twilight; and Purūravas is the sun (fr. *rava*='sound') having 'crying colour'. Here also Lang does not take the whole myth.[14] However, Kirk's proposition that aetiology cannot be taken seriously as a help in understanding the original meaning of a myth (always) is acceptable. We have taken the example of the myth of Śuṣṇa, earlier, and the aetiological tail-end. There are a good number of such narrations in the Hindu mythical literature and elsewhere which are marked by what may be termed aetiology. However, it is diffiult to say in all such cases if they formed an integral part of the myth, or were appended at a later period. In the latter case, we could postulate two stages in the history of a myth— the first is the formation stage; and the latter is to be taken as the stage of its usage, depending on the details in it thought to be suitable for aetiation. Aetiology could be seen in such mythical accounts as explain the name of a city, or a tank or a holy water-place.[15] Whichever mythical narration seeks to give a causative explanation may be of this nature. However, in most such cases the accounts could be made to order, and need not be given the status of myth. In any case, aetiology, like etymology, cannot be taken to be a safe criterion for all sorts of myth, as it is very difficult to sift later made-to-order accounts from the pure ones where aetiology is just reflected through the genuine expression of a wonderful experience.

The next theory to be noted is what may be called the ritual-myth theory. The best known adherent of this theory appeared in J.G. Frazer whose volumes of the *Golden Bough* sought to show a close relationship between ritual and myth. His volumes of information regarding the priest-king being killed after a certain period and being replaced by another—the very killer in many cases—lends support to this theory, which gets a firmer ground in the myth and ritual of Adonis, or the myth and ritual of Attis, or the myth and ritual of Osiris, or the myth of Balder and its dramatization in ritual and the sanctuary for him in the Norwegian mountains, called Balder's Grove. Frazer's observations regarding the interrelation between myth and ritual had very wide influence. Myth and ritual came to be seen as two sides of the same thing. Accordingly, a myth was said to be the '*legemenon*' (the thing said), while ritual the '*dromenon*' (the thing acted). To some extent the close association between a myth and ritual, or, in other words, that a ritual may give rise to a myth, or a myth may be enacted in ritual could not be denied. But, the point cannot be stressed to hammer that all myths have a parallel ritual-context, or that the myths that obtain in later societies could always have their prototypes in primitive rituals.[16] Examples of correlation between myth and ritual obtain. The Delphic myth of Charila may be taken as an example. According to Plutarch the king distributed barley to people in times of famine, but he refused it to a doll called Charila and struck her with his shoes. The doll was taken to the ravine and buried with a rope round its neck near the traditional grave of a person called Charila. This was the ritual. According to the myth Charila was a poor girl who was refused grain at the famine. She, hence, hanged herself. As a result the famine became acute due to the plague that followed. The Oracle enjoined that the girl be propitiated with a ritual. Kirk, who cites this tale in this context suggests that in origin, Charila was, actually, a demoness of famine, or a spirit of fertility that had to be renewed and that she was a scapegoat.[17] The point needs examination. Whether there was an intimate connection between this tale (= myth?) and the ritual—in other words, whether this myth was a counterpart of the ritual—is not easy to understand. Kirk says, that the instance "exemplifies a different aetiological technique whereby a special but somewhat pointless and improbable tale is manufactured to match the manifest details of the rite" (Kirk, 1973, p.236). If one scrutinizes the manifest details of the rite, one could see that the girl could hardly be a spirit of fertility; for in that case, hanging and 'shoeing' her would go against that suggestion. In the ritual, hanging and shoeing are done by the king who represents people. In the tale the girl is said to hang herself, in desperation(?); and plague follows. The Oracle decrees that the girl be propitiated with ritual. There is an apparent contradiction in the two. The ritual shows Charila to be an evil spirit. The tale indicates that she was a wronged good spirit. Hence this cannot be, apparently, taken as a case of myth and ritual being parts of the same situation. However, there is no doubt that these two parts are closely related. But, then, which one was the source? The tale which says that the girl should be propitiated cannot be taken as the source; because, the ritual cannot be taken as 'propitiating' her as is clear from the shoeing detail, though the noose round her neck could be explained as an imitation of her of hanging herself. This would show that the ritual does not conform to the tale. There is also no doubt that the tale did not form part of the ritual. There is one more point. The ritual was well set in tradition; for, there is mention of the 'traditional' grave of Charila, which was out of the locality—in the ravine—near which the doll was buried. The tradition of ritual dies hard and is more sticky than a tale, which is more prone to variations. It is not improbable that the ritual in the present case was an imitative preservation of an actual sacrifice of a girl to ward off a long spell of famine in the past. This girl was destitute or, might be, she was sold away by her parents for grains in the famine. In both cases, she would be termed 'poor'. In the present case the ritual indicates that the doll stood for evil which— (i) brought the famine; or/and (ii) which she could destroy if she was hanged and taken out of the locality. On the other hand, the tale gets sanctity as it is associated with the Oracle at Delphi, where it is current. The tale and the ritual correspond to each other in the following points:

Ritual *Doll—*	**Tale** *Girl—*
(i) was refused grains;	(i) was refused grains
(ii) was shoed;	(ii) —
(iii) taken to the ravine;	(iii) —
(iv) was fitted with a rope round her neck;	(iv) hanged herself;
(v) was buried near a grave.	(v) (buried in a grave?).

The narration seems to lose certain details (ii and iii); but, it almost tallies with the ritual. The oral tradition being prone to variation, some details are not seen in it. Though one cannot be said to be the source of the other, it seems probable that both are records of the same event which was set in tradition. The enactment in ritual is one phase of it, while the tale is the other. Both have the sanctity of tradition. The ritual is sacred; and the tale is as sacred as the ritual; because, both enshrine the memory of an event that was connected with the very life of the society. The tale is, hence, a myth. However, it has to be remembered that, though the tale is sacred, it is not about a god or goddess. As we have noted above, here the doll is a representation of the girl who (in all probability) was sacrificed to avert famine. A later step is that the event could become an (yearly) ritual to ward off famine; or it could be performed whenever a famine-like situation presents itself. In Charila we have a case where the same person (or object) is a representation of evil and a scapegoat to help ward off the evil. In the latter case, the object is not an evil in itself. It is burdened with evil. In other words, it is benevolent and carries away evil. This twofold value is a marked characteritic of a ritual-victim in certain cases. In the case of Charila[18] a ritual and myth both obtain. Such, however, is not always the case. A ritual might become obsolete and die out in course of time; and only a myth that faintly corressponds to it may survive—either in the oral or a written tradition. In such a case a ritual corresponding to the myth current in the same tradition could give a clue to the meaning of the hazy myth. An example is the Hindu Vedic myth of Vṛṣākapi (Ṛgveda X.86). The hymn which comprises this myth and appears in the form of a dialogue, has been much misunderstood by earlier scholars, who felt that the hymn is obscure.[19] From the fragments in the hymn we gather the following account. A huge virile ape (Vṛṣākapi) was obtained by Indra. The monkey had his mate and also young ones from her; but they were not brought along with him to stay with Indra. Indra loved the monkey who stayed in his abode. Gradually the monkey got familiar with Indrāṇī, the wife of Indra. The familiarity got ripened into intimacy and the ape[20] would praise Indrāṇī in erotic terms, extolling her fleshy hips. And once he said to her, "lady, may my organ join that of yours; may my thigh-bones join those of yours". Indrāṇī complained to her husband; but, he connived at it. (There is description of a coitus position between the ape and?-Indrāṇi?—a ritual-woman! vv 16-17). The ape is desired to get the dagger, the pot for boiling flesh and is desired to proceed out on the 'cart of fire' (which indicates his being sacrificed and offered in the fire). Indra, now, was sorry and expressed his grief at the absence of his dear friend—the ape, whose liquid offering went to the gods in heaven. Indra called the ape (who has vanished = sacrificed) to arrive again saying that he was 'bundle of sins' (*pulu-agaḥ* - having many sins)[21] and the 'sparer of people' (*jana-yopanaḥ*)[22] from sins (v 22).

The main details from the narration here exactly tally with details from the hymn about the Horse-sacrifice (ṚV. I.162) and from the ritual at the Horse-sacrifice from other Vedic texts.

The following chart would be useful for comparison:

Vṛṣākapi-hymn Vṛṣākapi and Indrāṇī	***Horse-sacrifice*** Horse—the eldest queen
1. *Sexual overtone*: "Whose generative organ dangles between his thighs"; "whose hairy one'' waxes as he takes the position (vv 16-17).	1. *Sexual overtone:* "Let us spread out our four feet (two of the queen and two hind legs of the horse)". "O Horse, sprinkle semen on the genitals (of the queen)" (*Vājasaneyi- Samhitā*) xxiii.20-21).[23]
2. *Indication of ritual*: "May the ape carry with him the dagger, the plate for keeping flesh and a new jar of cooked rice (*asim sūnām navam carum).*	2. *Ritual*: May these go to the gods with the horse : the wooden rod to test the flesh being boiled *(nīkṣaṇam māms -pacanyā ukhāyāḥ)*; the pots in which the boiled juice of flesh is poured, the lids for the jars (*pātrāṇi yūṣṇa āsecanāni... apidhānāḥ carūṇām sūnāḥ)* (ṚV I.162.13)
3. May he (carry or) get the killed in his honour (*hatam vidat)*— (i.e., prior to his own sacrificial killing) (*Ib*.18).	3. The goat led before the horse as an offering for the god Pūṣan (it was killed with a stroke on the head) (I.162.3).
4. May he get to the well arranged fire-cart (*Ib*) (The fire was believed to lead the offering to the gods, when cast in).	4. "May not the smoke-smelling fire cause you to utter a cry, O horse" (*Ib*.15).
5. "Whose liquid offering goes to the gods (v.12).	5. "you are not going to die nor injured. You will go to the gods."

These are the homologues. The point which is not common is that Vṛṣākapi is said to be 'bundle of sins' and 'people-sparer' while the sacrificial horse is not so described. The homologues would show that the Vṛṣākapi-myth, reflected in the hymn, could be a record of a ritual of the Horse-sacrifice type. Let us, now, take the (myth of the so-called) fight of Mudgala with the robbers(!). The 'fight' with robbers is not supported by the earliest record (Ṛgveda).[24] The later tradition concocts it; and modern scholars follow this later tradition which, sort of, labyrinths them.

In the myth of Mudgala and his wife Mudgalānī, the terminology of fight is the outer cover for a ritual of the fertility of the field, the details being—Mudgalānī, called also Indrasenā, the wife of Mudgala rides a 'mock-chariot' (*Mithū-kṛtam ratham*) for the gain or cattle and grain, which is said to be *bhara* (= of 'total gain'); the word means also 'battle'. Here the battle is against evil forces that would thwart the produce. The 'mock-chariot' is the plough-turned chariot. Mudgala has a bull, whom his attendants approach and lead it into the midst of the field (not 'battlefield', which image makes the myth obscure). They give him water to drink and cause it to urinate on the corn-field— the symbolic act between the bull and the field (cf. the Nandyo-Ābh kaṇbi—earth myth noted earlier. The urination of the bull ill-suits an actual battle). The bull is yoked to the 'chariot', (a bull can hardly be yoked to an actual battle-chariot!). As the bull runs, it releases dung (fertility symbol for the earth). Later a block of wood (*drughaṇa*) is harnessed to the yoke along with the bull (mistaken as a hammer thrown against the enemies, by scholars). The block of wood is led and placed in the middle of the other boundary with the words, "away sins". This hardly suits an actual fight, or battle. With this *bhara* Mudgala, through his wife (Indrasenā-Mudgalānī) earned prosperity (ṚV X.102). Bereft of the symbolic expressions, the narration (or myth?) will be obscure. The narration in the hymn, as it has been generally supposed to be, is as follows. (Brackets are for connecting the narration, not present in the hymn proper)-Some robbers wanted to rob Mudgala of his property. But, his wife Mudgalānī, was resourceful. She got prepared a mock-chariot and rode it. As she rode along, her garment was blown up by the wind (X.102.2 *ut-sma vāto vahati vāso asyāḥ*). (Mudgala or his wife invoked). "O Indra, break away the thunder-weapon of the enemy ('robbers') who wants to kill us, hating us". (With this) the bull drank (water) from the reservoir; and, he having prominent testicles, ran ahead. They (attendants) approached the bull and caused him to urinate in the field of battle(?). With this Mudgala gained thousand-fold cattle in the 'battle' (*pradhane*). Mudgala then threw the *drughaṇa* (hammer?) at the enemies and drove them away. (The myth of an actual battle, as told by modern Sanskrit scholars leaves away some important symbolic expressions). But, the hymn clearly says that: (i) the *drughaṇa* (wooden mace) was placed in the next boundary (*kāṣṭhā*) which cannot be of the battlefield, which has no fixed boundary; (ii) they did not offer him (the wooden block) water, grass to eat (v 10), though the wooden block was co-yoked with the bullock. Thus deposited, the block is said to drive away sins (*Ib. āre aghā*). This also ill-suits an actual battle. Seen closely, the block compares with *vṛṣākapi,* who is "bundle of sins" and the "people-sparer". Details that tally are—

Vṛṣākapi-hymn	*Mudgala-hymn*
1. Pairing Indrāṇī Vṛṣākapi;	1. (a) Bull-field; (b) Mudgalānī (=Indrasenā)-Bull (single one yoked to plough?);
2. Coitus-pose (X.86.16-17);	2. Bull urinates in the field (X.102.5)

Contd...

3. Vṛṣākapi (a) Bundle of sins (also 'people-sparer' (*pulvagha janayopana*); (b) Goes away through sacrifice, after being killed; (c) Is invoked to come again back (*punar ehi*);	3. Mace of wood (shadow-bull; yoked along with the bull); (a) symbol of sin (āre aghā); (b) Discarded beyond boundary; (c) —
4. Indra gains vigour through Indrāṇī (+Vṛṣākapi).	4. Mudgala gains cattle and prosperity through Mudgalānī (+ plough and Bull).

The tradition identifies Indrāṇī with the earth, as she is said to have hips spread over thirty *yojanas* (1 *yojana* = 6 or 8 miles)[25]; again *senā* is said to be the earth.[26] In that case—
As—Mudgalānī = Indrasenā;
and (Indra)senā = Earth
(∴) so: Mudgalānī = Earth (field)-symbol.

The obscurity and riddles in these narrations, which could be called myths, get clear with ritual-reconstruction which gives the meaning of both as the gain of produce and cattle. So these myths have fertility as the meaning. In both the cases there is no record of their occurrence in the post-Vedic literature either in the form of a myth or a complete ritual. However, Vṛṣākapi is identified with the sun (as the horse in the Horse-sacrifice)[27] and the word is explained, with the help of etymology as — "as he sprinkles his semen "*(reto varṣati;* hence *Vṛsā*, from the root *vṛṣ*, "to rain", "sprinkle") while vibrating (fr. the root *kamp→Kapi*) he is called so indicating Vṛṣākapi as the "raining sun".[28] Though the whole myth, as such, in a prose-story form is not found associated with a ritual, the hymn, or at least the portion which indicates the coitus-position (vv 16 and 17), is enjoined as a fecundity-charm at a ritual in the case of an issueless woman.[29] In both these myths (as they are reflected in the hymns) there is the point of discarding the evil. The ape Vṛṣākapi is a fertility aid and also the 'bundle of sin' to be discarded in one, while in the Mudgala-myth the bull is the fertility aid and the wooden device is to be discarded. Actually, the wooden device serves as the alter-ego of the bull, being with the bull in the field and separated and discarded out of the field as 'sin'.[30] It may be said that the hymns have in themselves details of ritual which surface by comparison with other known rituals, and that, as they are not retained in the tradition in the form of tales, they cannot be regarded as myths. However, by the 7th century B.C. the Mudgala hymn appears to have strode into the realm of myth. Yāska (the author of the Nirukta), of about that period, believed that Mudgala gained victory over some enemies in a battle which he fought with the help of a bullock and a wooden mace (Nirukta IX.23f); and the Sarvānukramaṇī, a text of a later period[31] states that Mudgala fought a battle with some robbers of his cattle whom he defeated with a wooden mace, pursuing them on a chariot drawn by a single old bullock. The same is the version of the Bṛhaddevatā (VIII.10ff).[32] However, these texts which are ancillaries to the Ṛgveda appear to explain away the details in the hymn; and they are not traditional texts in the real sense of the word. Yet the mythical accounts in the hymns mentioned above do seem to have an intimate relation to ritual as noted above.

Another instance of a myth which shows a close relationship with ritual is that of Vāmadeva cooking the entrails of a dog in an effort to bring rain as seen in a hymn (Ṛgveda IV.18). The hymn appears in the form of a dialogue,[33] and, according to a unique style common in ṚV, the seer identified himself with Indra. From the narration we learn that the usual gods were helpless in destroying the spell of the famine (*avarti*). So the seer (Vāmadeva - Indra on the basis of identification) is questioned: "Who desired to smite you, as you lay motionless and then moved on?" The seer Vāmadeva answers— "In distress I cooked the entrails of the dog; and lo! the eagle hawk fetched honey for me" (vv. 12 and 13). The Bṛhaddevatā explains (IV.126;131) that, in the famine, when Vāmadeva cooked the entrails of a dog, Indra approached him in the form of a hawk and gave him, 'honey' which stands for rain and sustenance. In the case of this myth we have further records, with Vāmadeva giving place to Viśvāmitra. Thus, according to an account from the Mahābhārata (Śāntiparva 141.43-49) in the remote past at the junction of the Tretā and the Dvāpara ages there was a spell of drought which lasted for twelve years. All people began leaving their usual habitats and started wandering in search of water and food. The sage Viśvāmitra also left his place with his family and wandered. As he once strayed away from his family and went alone in search of something to eat, he fell unconscious. Gaining consciousness he saw nearby the dwelling of a *cāṇḍāla* (a lowly man). He crept along slowly and peeped into the dwelling and saw the ham *(kutantri?)* of a dog.[34] He also noticed that the owner of the dwelling was lying with his eyes closed. He crept ahead and was about to steal the ham when the owner, *cāṇḍāla*, opened his eyes. He said, "Hallo! I am not asleep. You would be killed now". But he learnt about the condition of the sage; advised him that it was not good on his part to eat the flesh of the dog and that he would give any other thing in place of of the ham (jāghanī, v 92). But, the sage insisted on the ham; so, the kind *cāṇḍāla* gave it to the sage. The sage took the ham to his wife and children. He decided to sacrifice to the gods and kindled the fire. As the offering was about to be cast into the fire, Indra sent rain, and the spell of drought ended.

Later the account occurs in the Brahma P. (93.5-27). According to it, in one of the worst famines, the sage Viśvāmitra bade his disciples, to bring anything to eat. The disciples roamed about and fetched a dead dog. Viśvāmitra asked them to clean it and cook it on the fire, which they did. Viśvāmitra, then, got ready to offer the flesh of the dog into the fire. But, the fire-god appeared before him and forbade saying, that the flesh of a dog was never to be offered to the gods. Now, Indra arrived on the scene in the form of a hawk and stole jar of flesh. As the sage fumed with wrath, Indra brought the jar back substituting the flesh by honey, which he offered to the sage, who, in turn, declined when other people were tortured by hunger. Finally, Indra summoned the clouds with the result that there was rain. The place where this happened came to be called Madhu-tīrtha ('Ṭhe holy place of honey'). According to yet another account (Skanda P. VI.90; also VII.3.30.8-16), in a drought Viśvāmitra was reduced to a skeleton. Once, as he was wandering in a forest he saw a dead dog. He took it, washed it and cut it into parts. Then he offered the flesh for the manes into the sacrificial fire. But, now the fire-god was angry at this act and disappeared. He was angry with Indra himself, as the latter was responsible for the drought by not sending timely rain. (Here this main myth gets fattened up by the myths regarding the disappearance of the sacrificial fire and its reappearance. It is left out here).[35] Ultimately the god Brahmā finds out the fire-god and entreats him to come along and accept the usual sacrificial offerings. The myth indicates that the offering of dog's flesh brought rain, but also indicates that it was an unusual offering. From all these accounts it is clear that the unusual ritual of the offering of dog's flesh was an actual event; but its non-occurrence in the later ritual tradition got it turned into a myth. In such cases one has to accept the correlationship between a myth and ritual. But it is impossible to contribute to the general theory that a myth is a counterpart of ritual, and that myth implies ritual and ritual implies myth; or that myth is a statement in words and that ritual is a statement in action.[36] A point to be noted in the case of the last mentioned myth and its versions is that the earliest version gets explanatory support from later versions as regards the expression: "The hawk brought the honey". For readers (or the hearers in the event of only the oral tradition), who are conversant with the symbolism of the Ṛgveda, it is not difficult to know that 'honey' stands for rain.[37] But, even to those who are not so conversant, from the later versions which speak of rain and honey in the same breath, it becomes easy to understand that 'honey' stands for rain. A comparison involving these versions would show the additions and identifications:

Vāmadeva (ṚV) *(Famine)*	**Viśvāmitra (Mb)** *(Famine)*	**Viśvāmitra (Purāṇa)** *(Famine)*
1. Who desired to smite you as you lay motionless, and then moved on;	1. He fell un-conscious; gained conscious-ness; crept along; the *cāṇḍāla* said, "you would be killed".	1. Viśvāmitra and his disciples wandered;
2. (Dog sacrificed).	2. (Desired ham).	2. Found a dead dog.
3. Dog's entrails.	3. He gives the flesh.	3. Dog's parts.
4. Cooked the entrails of the (sacrificial) dog.	4. Cooked the ham and wanted to offer.	4. Dog's parts (flesh) about to be offered into the fire. The fire-god got angry.
5. Hawk (Indra) brought 'honey'	5. Indra showered rain	5. Indra replaced the flesh in the jar, with honey; clouds arrive, rain follows.

(How the entrails in the original account changed to the ham is not relevant. This is probably due to the reference to killing by holding the leg in an earlier verse in the hymn at the ṚV., v 12 *pāda-gṛhya*)[38]

The versions, though similar generally, have certain differences. The Puranic account does not mention any altercation between the sage and the owner of the dog's flesh, as is seen in the Mb. account. The altercation at the Mb. has its origin in the ṚV account where we see question and answer. Another point is, that in ṚV, and Mb the sage is seen as lying and creeping ahead, which is not seen in the later accounts. However the point of offering the flesh is common to all the accounts. The lying and creeping, probably, formed part of the ritual in its origin (ṚV). It began getting faded prior to the period of Mb., and it is here that the ritual got getting the form of a myth, bereft completely of the ritual. It would be right to think that after Vāmadeva, a priest of the Viśvāmitra family performed the same ritual in the post-Vedic period, but far earlier than the Mb. period. Or, the original ritual of Vāmadeva was never again performed; but came to be tucked on to Viśvāmitra, who has been known to be, sort of, a reformist and to have introduced many new trends. Vāmadeva who recorded the ritual in the oral tradition by incorporating it into a hymn also used in the narration, the then popular symbol of honey for rain, and also the popular myth of an eagle-hawk bringing the liquid of immortality from heaven. In this, another symbolic identification was used by the seer, viz. the eagle-hawk = Indra. These examples, together with those cited earlier from the Vedic and later Hindu sources (Apālā, Kaca-Śukra and Śukra-Śiva etc.) would show that, myths could take rise from lost ritual traditions. On this point it will be proper to examine the opinion of Kirk who refers to the statement of Gaster about Semetic myths. According to Gaster (as quoted by Kirk, 1970, p.13), Semetic myths are embodied in poems designed originally to be chanted or recited at ritual exercises; that their object was to provide an interpretation of ritual in terms of connected stories. In course of time, many of the underlying rituals fell into disuse, so that the myths survived as purely literary compositions to be modified or elaborated at will. Kirk objects to this observation of Gaster "at least in so far as Semetic myths are concerned". As will be seen, this observation of Gaster could be profitably viewed in the case of Hindu myths seen above,[39] though, as Kirk says (*Ib.*), all myths cannot be taken to have source in rituals since forgotten or being out of use.

An offshoot of the ritual-myth theory was what is known as the functional theory, or the theory of functionalism. According to this theory all myths, like rituals, have a specific function to indicate in a tribe: social institutions such as marriage, economic institutions, kinship and mores—i.e., customs, manners etc. Actually functionalism tried to give a blow to the domination of the ritual-myth theory under the leadership of Bronislow Malinowski. According to it, only the functional analysis of a series of myths in a particular tribe or society, could give the real meaning of a myth or series of myths. It was also proposed that myths did not contain any truth regarding man and the cosmos. However, when Malinowski studied the myths of the Trobriand islanders (lying to the north-east of Australia), he did not so much contemplate the functional nature of myth as a charter, a term he applied to it on close study, (*Myth in Primitive Psychology*, London, 1926). The latter term envisages that in a traditional society every custom or institution has to be supported by a myth, which need not try to explain the custom or institution.

In other words, the sanction for the custom is sought in its origin in the past; and this past may be historical or even imaginary. In a way, this is like giving merely a causative support for the present act or custom, or ritual, continued in tradition. But, this resembles aetiology, though Malinowski would not prefer the term. He mentions that the Trobrianders differentiated between two types of tales, one being just for entertainment and the other being sacred. The latter may be termed myth. Even then, all such sacred tales do not have relationship with ritual, though they are 'charters', as they support tribal behaviour or custom. His pupils, including E.R. Leach, however, regarded myth and ritual as counterparts of each other, and both as symbolic statements about the social order.[40] In line with this observation falls also the opinion that myth and ritual have a common psychological basis, that ritual is symbolical dramatization of the needs of a society, while myth is the rationalization of the same.[41] What is clear from these views is that the functional approach is one step ahead of the ritual-myth theory with the other step on it. The difference is that, according to the ritual-myth theory, myths are, in many cases, derived from ritual, or are counterparts of rituals, which position is not exactly the same as the functional appraoch. Another point to be noted is that, while the ritual-myth theory takes its sap from the religious context, functionalism focuses attention on social needs. Yet another point is that, while the ritual-myth theory takes the narration in a myth as the final unit of meaning, the functionalist approach takes narration as secondary to the under-current augmented by the narration. In this case, myths are not a counterpart of rituals and on equal footing with the latter. On the contrary, rituals are the integral aspect of a tribe or a society; myths function only as supports and seek to offer causative background. As will be seen, it is difficult to draw a clear-cut line between the charter-theory and the functional theory, though it is possible to say that in both, religion and gods have no front seat. In the Hindu context, the function of myths as a support to rituals is best exemplified in the relation of chants (*mantra*-s) with rituals. The Vedic view is that *mantras* are 'form-enhancers' of the rituals.[42] Actually they are an oral aid to the ritual, which is physical. A myth likewise, in such a case, acts as an oral charm. The next phase is that of a myth, apparently, completely independent of ritual, due to loss of the ritual. The myth of Vṛṣākapi (noted above) has to be taken as one such example. As a typical charter myth may be pointed out the tale of how the metre Gāyatrī or the other metres (the one called Jagatī and the other named Triṣṭubh) were regarded as important. According to it, Soma, the liquid of immortality, was in heaven; and the gods who desired to sacrifice were here (on earth). So, they requested the metres to fetch Soma. The Jagatī metre (conceived as a female bird) flew first; she had fourteen syllables in each of her four feet. Without Soma she returned; but she lost (in effect, she bartered)[43] her two syllables (i.e., she remained with twelve letters) with which she brought here to the gods, sacrificial beasts and the method of consecration for the sacrifice. Hence Jagatī, of all metres, is the most endowed with beasts. Then flew up the metre Triṣṭubh having thirteen syllables. Even she returned without Soma; but she brought back penance (*tapas*) and sacrificial gifts (*dakṣiṇā*), losing two of her syllables thus retaining only eleven. Hence, in the sphere of the Triṣṭubh, i.e. at midday, sacrificial gifts are given. Then flew up the Gāyatrī with her four syllables. She not only fetched Soma but also the two syllables each of the Jagatī and the Triṣṭubh (totalling four); she, thus, became eight-syllabled in each of her three feet. The 'knowers of sacrifice' (*brahmavādin*-s) say, "wherefore did Gāyatrī, though the youngest of the metres, circumambulate the head (of the sacrifice)?" (The answer is—) she did bring here Soma; hence did she go round the head of the sacrifice. Hence is she the most brilliant of all...etc.[44]

The myth accounts for the following— (1) why these three metres are very important at the Soma-sacrifice, and why are they traditionally employed at the three pressings—morning, noon (i.e. midday) and evening— of the shoots of Soma at the Soma-sacrifice; (2) Why the metres have now, respectively, twelve syllables (Jagatī), eleven syllables (Triṣṭubh) and eight syllables (Gayatrī) in each foot; (3) Why is the *dakṣiṇū* kept ready at mid-day.[45] There are a number of such myths in the Vedic ritual context; and in later literature, especially in the context of vows. A point to be noted, in the case of the myth just mentioned, is that it uses an already popular myth— viz. the fetching of Soma from heaven, which is only a version of the gain of the liquid of immortaity from heaven. In the present context, the tale cannot hence be taken as a pure myth. It is a meta-myth; as it is derived or structured on an earlier myth. It should not be confused as a variant of the earlier myth; for, the change is purposeful— to account for some details of ritual. Can we call it, following Malinowski, a 'charter'? No, not exactly. Malinowski's idea of charter is not of a meta-myth. For him a charter-myth appears to be original myth, accounting for a ritual, a custom or a tribal practice. In any case, such a myth has to be differentiated from the nature-myth or a myth of creation. The latter has nothing like a custom to account for. And there are a good number of myths that are not 'charters'; nor they have any 'function' as such to point out. Here we see the limitations of the 'Charter' theory, or, for that matter, of the 'Functional' theory. Myths comtemplated by the charter-functional theories would appear to be more artificial than natural, though traditional sanction is common in both. The same could be said about a meta-myth, with the difference that a meta-myth is a secondary myth, but not necessarily a 'charter' in all cases.

A good number of myths are related to rituals in another way, in addition to the type of myths that indicate a lost or discontinued ritual as noted above. In this case the myths are to be narrated, either orally or from texts if they are thus recorded, to emphasize the glory of a particular deity, or as oral charm for a particular occasion. Regular prayers with narrations, extolling a god and his exploits, are of this type. The myth of Marduk's rise to power and the establishment of order in the universe at the new year festival in Babylon is of this type. The recital, in ancient Egypt, of the myth of the defeat of the serpent Aphosis each day for the safe return of the sun is another example. In the Hindu context, the story of Śunaḥśepa could be cited. Traditionally, it was to be told and heard by a king at the sacrifice called Rājasūya. The story can be said to be a legend, as there is some indication of the historicity of Śunaḥśepa and his family. The Vedic tradition mentions him as the seer of some hymns (Ṛgveda I.24 to 30; IX.3). Actually, it appears to be a story tailored on purpose, in which case it has the nature of a 'Charter'. The name of Śunaḥśepa and those of his two brothers indicate the 'tail' of a dog (*śvan→śun*-dog'). His name means 'dog's tail' (*śunaḥ*-'of the dog' + *śepa,* 'tail'). His brothers' names are Śuno-*lāṅgūla* ('tail') and Śunaḥ-*puccha* ('tail'). It is said that king Hariścandra of the Ikṣvāku dynasty was issueless, though he had a hundred (= symbolic for 'many') wives. The sages Nārada and Parvata advised him to solicit the favour of the god Varuṇa; for, it was necessary for a man to 'see' a living son's face. He did solicit Varuṇa's favour. Varuṇa granted him a son, as the king assured the god that he would sacrifice the son to him (= Varuṇa). The king, obviously, took the words of the sages literally, that he should 'see' the son's face, as that alone was enough to reach heaven after his own death! When the son was born, Varuṇa approached him and asked for the son. But, now, the king got emotionally involved with the son and began postponing the sacrifice by some excuse or the other—"let him have teeth", "let his teeth fall", "let his fresh teeth rise" and like that, till the child grew into a youth able to put on an armour. When Varuṇa approached him now, the king called his son, who was named Rohita, and told him, "Well! This god gave you to me; and now I have to offer you to him in sacrifice!" The boy, saying "no", ran away. So. Varuṇa seized the king with dropsy (as Varuṇa controlled all waters, including the bodily fluids). The boy, Rohita, came to know of it in his wanderings in the forest; and he started for the capital. But Indra met him and dissuaded him. This happened for seven years. Ultimtely Rohita approached a needy brāhmaṇa, named Ajīgarta (the word means, 'Not having eaten anything'), who had three sons, to purchase a boy to offer in his own place. Ajīgarta and his wife did not want to part either with the eldest or the youngest. So the middle son Śunaḥśepa was purchased for a hundred cows. He was brought to the capital and was fixed to be offered in the sacrifice. Varuṇa also was satisfied that a *brāhmaṇa* boy (Śunaḥśepa) was better as a victim than a *kṣatriya* (Rohita). As Śunaḥśepa got tied to the sacrificial post, none was ready to kill him. So, his own father — Ajīgarta— came forward to kill him with a dagger for a hundred more cows. Now, Śunaḥśepa praised various gods; but they could not help him; so ultimately he praised the goddess (of) Dawn (Uṣas). She favoured him and he was set free. The king also got free from dropsy. The verses of praise by Śunaḥśepa formed part of the Ṛgveda and Śunaḥśepa became a seer. He was adopted as son by Viśvāmitra and was named Devarāta ('god-given'), as the latter took resort to the lap of Viśvāmitra. This, in short, is the story, which came to be narrated to the king at the Rājasūya (royal consecration) sacrifice.[46] Hence, it fits in the type of myths called 'charter'. But, the story, (as it occurs at the Ait. Br.) has an aetiological note, that a person who desires a son should recite, or hear, this story. We shall return to it later.

As is rightly pointed out by Kirk (1976, p.60) charters are validations and are aetiological in one sense. The only requirement is that such stories must be striking and entertaining. The plausibility and historicity in realistic terms are not important. If this be accepted—and there is no difficulty in accepting it—such tales as try to explain, or account for the place-names, or tales that seek to account for a particular ritual, or even a non-ritual practice could come under this heading. Thus, the Vedic tale of Iḍā (sacrificial offering, personified) going to the gods and *Asura-s* and observing their method or carrying the freshly kindled fire to the three altars, and advising that the real method was to see that the fire is carried always eastward and finally established in the eastern (Āhavanīya) altar, is of this type.[47] Thus, the method of establishing the fire first in the Gārhapatya altar (at the west), thence part of it to be carried to the Dakṣiṇa fire-place (altar) that required moving to the south-east and thence to the eastern quarter of the Āhavanīya was supported by this tale. And, as the tale was rooted in the tradition it could be called a myth of the Charter-type. Likewise tales told to account for the name of a place could be a myth of the charter type. Thus, the places called Lohāṇa, Lohāṭigrāma, and Lohayaṣṭi are all said to have been so named as the demon Loha was killed at two places; at one place (Lohāṇa) by a goddess;

at another by Kṛṣṇa (Lohaṭigrāma) and at the third place because the gods Viṣṇu and Śiva and Brahmā came to compromise with the same demon, that they all would stay at that place along with the demon (Loha).[48] But, it will be seen that in most such cases there is hardly any tale as such and the aetiation tends to be just a phase of etymology and assimilation of sounds. Lohāṭi and Lohayaṣṭi may appear different; but, they could be originally the same (*Loha+yaṣṭi→Loha+yaṭṭhi→Loha+(ya) ṭhi→lohāṭi*). The account of staying together does not explain the part *yaṣṭi*, which means 'stick'. If we believe that the killing of the demon gave the name, we could very well understand *Lohāṭi as Loha-hati* ('killing of the demon Loha); and *hati* changed to *haṭi*, though irregularly. In the same way Lohāṇa could be explained as *Loha+hana* (killing'); then *haṇa→hāṇa*. There would be no proper justification for all such cases to be termed myths. Such cases would better be grouped under folk-tales rather than myths. Hence, tales that are told to explain place-names or names of persons, which are included by Kirk under speculative myths (1970, p.257) could hardly be called myths, much less charters though they account for some name. The same is the case with tales accounting for names of other holy places. In many cases such tales take the form of meta-myths, as older myths are adapted and retold to suit these new requirements. However, tales accounting for a custom, or tales told on important occassions, rituals or even without a ritual, as such, could be termed myths; and myths of the charter type. Thus, the following tale is usually told on the occasion of the Sunday-fast in the month of Pauṣa (roughly December-January) in the Maharashtra (especially Vidarbha) region of India. Mostly restricted to women, the vow rquires taking food only once on all the Sundays, at midday. On this day twelve tiny circles, one enclosing the other, are drawn on a plank with red (sandal) paste. These circles represent the twelve digits of the sun, who is believed to stay in the figure for that day till sunset. In the form of these circles, the sun-god is worshipped in the morning and offered whole green beans and jujube fruits. Finally, a lighted wick is moved around it. When the sun is at meridian, a regular meal is taken, preferably after the tale is told; and thereafter nothing is to be eaten till the next day. According to the tale, once there was an old destitute woman who lived on alms. She was very poor, but she observed this vow. Once, it so happened that, as she was just about to take her frugal meal, a boy presented himself. He was not from the village, and naturally she had not seen him before. He said, he was very hungry; and the old woman was very glad to give him some food. As he took his seat and began to eat what was served, the woman looked at him with compassion coupled with gratification. On and on, the boy went on eating and the old woman began to worry that nothing would be left for her. And nothing was left when he finished his meal and prepared to go. He took leave of the woman and darted out of sight. The woman starved for the day, as there was nothing to cook. But, she was satisfied with the thought that she could feed the boy sumptuously. Came the next Sunday; the woman completed her sun-worship, prepared food for herself and for the boy, expecting that he might arrive. And he arrived. The same was the experience. The boy ate the whole amount of food; and she had to remain without food for the whole of that Sunday. Sunday followed. She prepared enough food; the boy came; ate; and no food remained for her. She thus fasted on the three Sundays of that month. But, on the last Sunday something unusual happened. As the boy started to go, after taking leave of the old woman, he suddenly dropped bits of excreta, as he traversed the small courtyard and vanished. The woman was amazed and also was a bit annoyed. But, the boy was out of sight within a moment. The woman, her lips curved in anger, took steps to clear her court-yard of the matter; and, lo! the bits of excreta turned into solid gold!! The woman looked up to the sky with submission and overpowered with devotion—where the sun appeared to be mischievously smiling at her. She became rich. Such was the outcome of her sustained devotion and worship of the sun-god on the Sundays in the month of Pauṣa. The meaning of this myth (or charter) is not much out of the narration; though it is just beyond it. It is in the suggestion of periodic Sun-worship; and the period is Pauṣa, when the sun gets turning towards the earth and getting nearer to 'her' and is about to change its course from the south to north. The month is also marked by the saṁkrānti (crossing) of the sun to the northern hemisphere according to the Hindu calendar. The myth enshrines also the symbol of the sun in the gold,[49] which the excreta gets changed into; and the boy represents the sun-god. The charter-status of the tale is in its being told on this special occasion (like that of Śunaḥśepa). Though it is associated with a vow, it does not get causatively related to any ritual. In other words, the tale is not developed from a ritual, nor does the worship of the sun-god here, in the form of the circles, has any direct relationship with the narration in the tale. There is no replica or an idol of a boy indicative of the boy in the tale, to support the conceptual need of the ritual-myth theory. In plain words, there is no indication also of the tale being specially made for this particular ritual. The fact seems to be that a tale was in vogue; and, then, it came to be traditionally used on the occasion of the vow. As such, the tale could be taken to be a myth; but, it was used as a charter. It cannot be taken as a meta-myth; because in that case the essence of the narration remains practically the same; only the parties (actors) change, as is the case with the myth of the metres who are substituted for the original bird that brings the liquid of immortality, the liquid (or tablets in the Babylonian myth) giving place to, or adding, the various requirements in the sacrifice. In the case of the story of Śunaḥśepa also the meaning is not in the narration alone, but slightly beyond it. It is in the suggestion of human sacrifice, coupled with the deposing of Varuṇa as a prominent god in post Ṛgvedic period, though the actual event of a human-sacrifice is not attested by the Vedic rituals. In such cases, the story itself serves as an oral charm in place of human sacrifice. As the story forms an integral part of the rites at the Rājasūya-sacrifice it has the halo of the sacred, which reminds us of the division between sacred types of stories and those only for amusement. Though all myths are not embedded in religion, or they are not all 'stories of gods', the stories believed to be sacred have to be taken as myth. As such, the story of Śunaḥśepa gets the status of a myth. One cannot argue that the story is a *göttersage because* gods are mentioned in it. On the contrary, it is not a story of gods at all. They only add spice to the main story which, in essence is: King Hariścandra had no male issue. For gaining a male issue he performed a sacrifice, as was the belief and practice in those days. It was necessary that according to the belief, a person, has at least to see (*paśyet cet* are the exact words) the face of a male child, lest he should fail to reach heaven after death! As the king was always worried, the sages advised him to perform the sacrifice saying that he could sacrifice the son as a victim.[50]

In the Mahābhārata, which refers to the account in only two verses, Śunaḥśepa is said to be the son of Ṛcīka (not Ajīgarta); that he was a victim and that he got himself released due to his prowess at the great *sattra* (not Rājasūya). Viśvāmitra adopted him as his son and named him Devarāta (Anuśāsana, 3.6-8. Devarāta means 'god-given'; the name appears also in the account at the Ait. Br. noted above). According to the Rāmāyaṇa (Rām.I. i.e. Bālakāṇḍa 61.16 ff.), the king sacrificer is not Hariścandra (as is the case with the Ait.Br.). He is Ambarīṣa, who is also said to be a king of the Ikṣvāku dynasty. The account here says, that Ambarīṣa decided to perform a sacrifice (not the Rājasūya as the Ait. Br. says). As he started the sacrifice, Indra (the king of gods) stole the beast which was the victim fixed for being sacrificed.[51] So, the family priest of the king said, "O king! Here is a case for an urgent expiation. Now, you have to obtain a human victim". Hearing the speech of the priest, the king began searching for a human victim even in exchange for a thousand cows, at a variety of places including the hermitages. After a long search, he found a sage called Ṛcīka who had three sons. When the king told him about his difficulty, the sage sold his middle son Śunaḥśepa for a hundred thousand cows together with crores of gold-pieces and gems (Rām.I, end of Ch.61). Now, the king seated Śunaḥśepa in his chariot and drove along. On the way he rested at Puṣkara at midday (Puṣkara is in the present state of Rājasthan, in the region logistically to the west of Ayodhyā, the capital of the Ikṣvākus). As the king was taking rest, Śunaḥśepa wandered away; and, by a stroke of happy surprise, saw the sage Viśvāmitra who was practising penance there along with certain other sages. The account says, that Viśvāmitra was the maternal uncle of Śunaḥśepa (62.2 and 3). Śunaḥśepa threw himself on the lap of Viśvāmitra, saying, "I have no father, no mother, no relations, no friends. Kindly protect me. Devise a way that I be spared and also the king should have his sacrifice accomplished" (to cut the account). Viśvāmitra advised Śunaḥśepa to sing two *gāthās* (popular verses that could be sung, as against the verses from the Ṛgveda that would require accentual recitation), which he readily taught him, when he would be tied to the sacrificial stake. When Ambarīṣa got Śunaḥśepa tied to the stake (*yūpa*), the latter sang the two verses in praise of Indra and his younger brother (*anuja* i.e., Viṣṇu). And, Śunaḥśepa was released; also the king got his sacrifice accomplished. (We do not know what happened to the victim earlier stolen by Indra!). Another account occurs in the Devībhāgavata Purāṇa Skanda 7); but, it, more or less, tallies with that at the Ait. Br. The name of the sacrifice occurs in this account as Rājasūya; but it is said that this sacrifice was performed after Śunaḥśepa was set free, after the son of Hariścandra returned from the forest. It is not the son, here called Rohitāśva, who purchases the middle son of Ajīgarta; but it is the minister of the king who does the job. These later accounts are devoid of any aetiation. But even the aetiation that is marked in the very first coherent account (Ait. Br.) does not conform to the actual tradition. The Vedic tradition uses the account as a necessary part of the Rājasūya sacrfice, while the aetiation at the account at the Ait. Br. is a sort of prescription of this tale for a person who desires a son, and also for a king who has been victorious, though he may not be involved in the performance of the Rājasūya sacrifice. Whatever might have been the original status of the account, one thing is clear, which is that the account came to be closely associated with (the Rājasūya or) some sacrifice in the Vedic tradition. This itself should be sufficient for it to be treated as a charter. Whether it could be taken as a legend (which has often a mixture of mythical details) or a myth is beside the point, as noted above. However, it is necessary to extend the scope of the term charter to cover all such cases where a myth, or a mythical account, serves as an oral charm, or is reminiscent of a ritual. If we take the term charter to mean only validation, or confirmation, such accounts as of Śunaḥśepa would require an actual, continued, custom of human sacrifice at the sacrifice like Rājasūya; or it will have to be seen accompanying a human sacrifice, to support which this mythical account is to be associated. This is not supported by the Vedic tradition. Hence, the account has to be taken as filling the gap of a human sacrifice which got extinct; and, impliedly, it is a reminiscentary myth. When it is traditionally recited at a particular occasion (here, Rājasūya) it assumes the status of charter, in a wider sense. We may close this discussion with a couple of more recent popular examples. In the Vidarbha region of Maharashtra (India), on the occasion of a festival regarding cattle the following tale is customarily told and heard. The festival is named Poḷā (*poḷ*, means 'bull' or 'bullock' in the Marathi language); and it is celebrated on the dark fifteenth of the month of Śrāvaṇa (roughly August). Cattle, especially bulls and bullocks are worshipped and given sweets to eat. In the evening they are taken in a procession round the village. In the night members of the household gather together and hear the tale told. The tale is as follows: In the long gone past, a certain farmer and his wife's brother went out of the village to fetch a bundle of green grass for the cattle. While they were out, may be certain altercation cropped up between them; the farmer, while cutting grass, gave a stroke of his sickle at the neck of the brother-in-law and killed him. He then bundled him with the mass of grass and carried him to his house. He placed the bundle of grass containing the body in the cowshed. When his wife asked him repeatedly where her brother had gone, he remained silent. The bereaved woman then broke a cucumber (called *kākḍī*) on a wooden plank and threw its seeds which flew in the direction of the bundle of grass. Some of the seeds fell on the bundle. And, suddenly her brother came out from the bundle and stood before her. The farmer, who was already sorry for his rash act, was emotionaly moved and owned his guilt. They were all happy. This is the tale. As it is regularly told on this occasion, it gets the status of a charter myth. The myth further says that in the bundle other was a leafy vegetable, called *karḍu* (*celosia cristata*) in the said region. The blood of the brother had been splashed on it. Hence, it is (aetiologically) said that, because of the bloodstains the leaves of *karḍu* turned red; hence, this vegetable becomes unsuitable for being eaten. So, after this day of Poḷā, it is not eaten. Now, there is also a ritual-act associated with this tale. Before, or after the 'myth' is related, a woman, or a girl, who has her brother in the house at that time, touches a *kākḍi* to his back, and breaks it. Then it is sliced and eaten by all, sometimes along with specially prepared spiced flour. If the brother is not near, the fruit (*kākḍi*) is broken on a wooden plank and the seeds are thrown in the direction of the village (or town) where the brother is living at that particular time. Why the 'brother' of the woman is killed out of the locality, when her husband, the farmer takes him for grass-gathering is a dark point. Again, was he a human brother, or zoomorphic 'brother' (bull), in reality, also is a dark point. In the present context we need not go into these details. Suffice it to note that the 'myth' is not only customary but also traditional and hints at a close relationship between the bullock and the family of farmer in the economy of village life. The cucumber of the type mentioned in this myth is actually among the first of the fruits in this season from the sprawling creepers that mingle with the growing mass of grass. It is possible to say that the breaking of the *kākaḍi* fruit comes on par with the killing of the 'brother'. It is not improbable that it is symbolic of a ritual-sacrifice of a bullock (bull) in the remote past.[52] The festival of Poḷā marks the sprouting up of the seeds sown earlier at the beginning of the rainy season. Another example is of a tale told in the context of the 'festival of lights' (Dīpāvalī). This festival lasts for five days, starting from the twelfth dark of the month of Āśvina (roughly November). The first day (i.e., the twelfth) is called 'The Twelfth of the calves' (*go-vatsa-bārasa*).[53] On this day the cows and calves are worshipped. In the afternoon the following tale is told (in a group of famiy members). In short the tale is as follows: In the remote past there was an old woman. She told her daughter-in-law to cook and keep ready '*gavhāḷī-mungāḷī*' as a speciality for that day, while she would be out visiting some people. Saying this, she went out. When she came back, she asked her daughter-in-law if she cooked what she was asked to. The daughter-in-law answered in the affirmative and showed her what she had done. Actually, she had killed two calves, one named *gavhāḷa* and the other *mugāḷa*. The mother-in-law was not less angry than she was amazed at her daughter-in-law's folly. What she had intended was that the younger woman should cook *gahū* ('wheat', Sanskrit, *go-dhūma*) and *mūg* (green gram, Sanskrit *mudga*). The charter status of the 'myth' is clear. It also reverts to the same implication— a probable and lost ritual of offering calves of two different types for prosperity and cattle-wealth (*vasu*, in Sanskrit means, 'wealth'; also there is ground for a probable pun; *vasu—vatsa*, 'calf'. In the Marathi language, the word for calf is *vāsaru*).

The point is—Are such tales to be given the same

status as the myths seen earlier, such as that of the Father-Daughter, Indra-Tvaṣṭṛ, Anu-Kumarbi, Atum-Shu/ Thefnut and so on? In comparison with the earlier category, these other 'myths' appear to be made to purpose or used on purpose. In the case of Nature-myths or Cosmogonic myths, the myth is an expression of an extraordinary phenomenon—a sort of an honest belief expressed, without any effort to artificiality. Such is hardly the case with a 'myth' that balances a ritual, or a discontinued ritual that develops into a myth, which could be best called Reminiscentary. In the case of aetiation, later attached to an already known myth, it could best be seen as a meta-myth. The same is the case where a known myth is retold (or set) in a different garb to serve a new purpose, in which case it cannot be taken as simply a Version of the original. A myth seen as a charter, hence, cannot be taken as a pure un-artificial myth. In the case of the functional approach, it could be legitimately believed that the myth reflects a function, though the purpose of the myth may not be to show or indicate a function. In any case, as the myths are a complex phenomenon it is not quite possible to be sure of the purpose of their formation. Nevertheless, it is possible to mark the formation stage and the later stage of multiple usage on the one hand and, on the other, the original stage and the stage of variations or versions. However, there is no guarantee that the message or meaning will be exactly the same in these two stages.

References

1. *Cultural Anthropology*, Eng.T., Penguin, 1969 (1963), p.213f.
2. *Chips from a German Workshop*, Vol.IV, London, 1907, p.xii.
3. The story occurs also at Skanda P. V.2.84, 2-38; see Dange, *Encl.P.B.P.*, Vol.III, p.1028.

4. Dange, *Legends in the Mahābhaṛata*, pp.339-42; Max Müller, *Chips from a German Workshop*, Vol.II, London, p.251; for a similar tale from another source see A. Lang, *Custom and Myth*, Cambridge University Press, p.79. Max Müller uses the word *bheki* (female frog). He says that the king first saw her at a well. I think he narrates the tale from his memory. The Mb., or even the *Skanda P.* does not have the version exactly as he narrates. He says, that the condition of the frog-maiden was, that the king "should never show her a drop of water. One day, being tired she asked for water.... The king brought water and *Bheki* disappeared". He further thinks that the name Bheki was given by some fishermen.
5. *Myth, Ritual and Religion*, Vol.I, London, 1913 (1887), p.15f.
6. It may be noted that according to Lévi-Strauss myth-makers of early period had no less intelligence than modern men, *Myth and Meaning*, London, 1980 (1978), p.16ff.
7. *Myth, Ritual and Religion*, p.16ff.
8. *Custom and Myth*, London, 1884, p.135ff.
9. *Ibid.*, p.140, where he refers to Max Müller (*Lectures on Language*, pp.359, 362).
10. We may compare the concept of bricolage.
11. Kirk, *The Nature of Greek Myths*, Penguin, 1976 (1974), p.53.
12. *Ibid.*
13. *Custom and Myth*, p.71.
14. *Ibid.*, p.68.
15. For such examples, see, Dange, *Encl.P.B.P.*, Vol.III, under "Holy Places", pp.771-867.
16. For elaboration,-see Kirk, *The Nature of Greek Myths*, p.66f.
17. *Ibid.*, p.235ff., also *Myth*, p.16, where he refers to J. Fontenrose (*Python*, and L. Farnell, *Greek Hero Cults*).
18 The name is Charila. Was it a symbolic name? cf. Greek, Charis - grace; English 'Charity'. The girl was gracious as she averted the calamity of famine by her own sacrifice.
19. A.B. Keith, *The Religion and Philosophy of the Veda and Upanishads*, Vol.I, Delhi, 1989 (1925), p.133. However, see Dange, *Vedic Concept of 'Field' and the Divine Fructification*, University of Bombay, Bombay 1971, pp.49-67.
20. There is no doubt that Vṛṣākapi was an ape; he is referred to

even, simply, as *kapi* in the hymn (X.86), v 5.

21. *pulu* is *puru* - 'many'; K.F. Geldner, "unheil stifende".

22. *yopana,* causal fr. *yu* 'to separate' and also 'to unite'; also *yup* 'to efface'; but Geldner "Leutestorer" (trouble-maker for the people), which I very much doubt.

23. cf. Tait. Sam. VII. 4.19.1-4; Mait. Sam. III.20.20

24. For fuller study, Dange, *Vedic Concept of 'Field' and the Divine Fructiction*, pp.108-22, where parallel details from vedic domestic texts are cited. The fight-theory is based on the word *pradhana,* which occurs twice in ṚV, and at two places it occurs with the meaning of 'gain of wealth' (*pradhanasya) sātau I.* 169.2; battle for gain I. 116.2 *pradhane ājau.* This would show that *pradhana* is different from battle, āji.

25. See A.A. Macdonell and A.B. Keith, *Vedic Index of Names and Subjects,* London, 1912, under *yojana;* for the Puranic meaning, Dange, *Encl. P.B.P.*, Vol.III, p.1008. *Vedic Index,* under Mudgala, admits that the tradition and modern scholars like Pischel, Geldner and Fon Broadkey are not of one opinion about the meaning of this hymn.

26. cf. *senā ha nāma pṛthivī dhanañjayā,* Mait. Sam. IV.12.1a; Kāṭhaka Sam. VIII.17[a]; Taitt. Br. II.4.2.7[a].

27. Gopatha Br. Uttara, VI.12.

28. *Ibid.*, The sun stores waters in its orb (evaporating it), and releases it as rain; cf. ṚV I.23.17; Vāj.Sam. IX.3; Taitt. Ā.I.8.1.

29. Ṛgvidhāna III.119-127. This is a treatise on the application of the *mantras* from the Ṛgveda to domestic rituals; see also the Paddhati (text) on the Kauśika-sūtra (of AV) 76.18.

30. This part of the ritual appears to have developed in the later Ṛgvedic period; cf. the driving away of Alakṣmī, who is asked to seize a wooden block and go away. She is described as ungenerous, deformed in the eye and cruel, RV X. 155.1. Varuṇa, as evil power, is driven away with the sin of the sacrificer, if any, at the final bath at the Soma-sacrifice. He is called Jumbaka, Keith, *The Religion and Philosophy,* Vol.I, p.304; also Śat.Br. XIII.3.6.5.; Tait.Br. III.9.15. In the Nagpur region of Maharashtra (India) such a female evil is called Mārbat and is asked to take away with her all troubles—even mosquitoes and flies— from the locality.

31. Ed. A.A.Macdonell, p.158.

32. Ed. and Tr., A.A. Macdonell, HOS, Vol.Vi.

33. For a fuller discussion Dange, *Sexual Symbolism from the Vedic Ritual*, pp.161-74.

34. The word *Kutantri* does not occur in Monier William's Dictionary, nor that of S.S. Apte. Later in the narration *śvajāghanī* (dog's ham) is mentioned. In older Sanskrit *jāghanī* denoted the tail of a beast (cf. Śat.Br. III.8.5.6); later, however, it was taken to indicate the ham.

35. The account is a mixture of — (i) The legend of Devāpi; (ii) The usual myth of the disappearance of the sacrificial fire; and the newly incorporated element of (iii) the offering of dog's entrails; and (later) flesh.

36. See Kirk, *The Nature of Greek Myths*, p.66, where he refers to Jane Harrison and Leach; also *Myth*, p.23.

37. cf. ṚV II.24.4; X.30.3 and other places where such expression as 'honeyed wave', or 'honeyed waters', occurs.

38. See *Sexual Symbolism*, p.169ff.

39. The present writer had come to a similar conclusion independent of Gaster's observations (1971; 1979).

40. *Political Systems of Highland Burma*, London, Cambridge, 1954, p.13f.

41. Clyde Cluckhohn, *Harward Theological Review,* XXV, 1942, p.78.

42. cf. Yāska, Nirukta, I.16; Ait.Br. 3.5, uses the expression *rūpa-samṛddha* in this context; also that the *mantras* are (should be) *abhirūpa*, i.e., suitable to the sacrificial ritual.

43. Such exchange, or barter, is often marked in the Vedic ritual context; cf. Śat.Br.III.3.1.13-16—Cow for Soma-shoots; another example is that of the marriage of gods (*deva-vivāha;* here that of Heaven and Earth), where sacrificial smoke and saline earth or rain is exchanged between them; see Ch.I, n.14

44. Dange, *Legends in the Mahābhārata,* p.71.

45. Gāyatrī is the metre associated with Agni, and the verses in this metre are to be employed in the morning pressing of Soma. The Jagatī is for the evening pressing.

    I have not given a literal translation of the passage here as being not necessary. For the translation, see A.B. Keith, *The Veda of the Black Yajus School,* entitled *Taittiriya Sanhitā*, 2nd (Indian) Issue, Delhi, 1967 (*HOS*., 1914), pp.492f. The myth had become popular in the Vedic ritual literature; cf. Mait. Sam. III.7.3ff; Śat.Br.III.2.4.1ff; 3.1.13-16; Jaim. Br. I.287f. For a detailed study of this myth, Dange, *Legends in the Mahābhārata*, pp.1-153.

46. Ait.Br. 33.1-6. The Tait. Sam.V.2.1.3f has no story, but just a reference. The story of Śuṇaḥśepa is prescribed to be recited by the Śānkhāyana Ś.S. (XVI.11.1) at the human sacrifice (puruṣamedha), and not at the Rājasūya. However there it seems to be just a portion of the story at the Ait. Br. from where we have taken it. For a discussion regarding the point of actual human sacrifice and nature of the story, see A.B. Keith, *Rigveda Brāhmaṇas*, Delhi, 1981 (London, 1920), pp.61-67.

    I have mentioned it here to illustrate its type as 'Charter'. The story is mentioned also in the post-Vedic times, as we shall see below.

47. Tait. Br. I.1.4.3-7.

48. Skanda P. I.2.65.91f; 115f; III.3.29.5ff; see Dange, *Encl.P.B.P.*, Vol.II, p.409.

49. Gold as symbolizing the sun can be attested from a number of examples. In the horse sacrifice, a golden disk symbolized the sun as also the heavenly world. In the Soma-sacrifice the waters used in the shoots-pressing ritual were collected on the previous day while the sun was still shining. But, if the sun did set, they were collected touching a piece of gold. Among other peoples the Aztecs showed a pominent belief in this symbolism, Berdan, Frances F. *The Aztecs*, New York, 1989. For the story see Dange, Sindhu S., *The Bhāgavata Purāna*—Mythosocial study. Ajanta, 1984, p. 287f. who recorded it for the first time.

50. Though the practice of sacrificing the first male child is noticed (cf. the story of Ciliyā, being offered to Śiva, who rejuvenates him later), this story can hardly be taken in that light. For a similar suggestion by Hillebrandt and his criticism by Keith may be seen A.B. Keith, *Rigveda Brāhmaṇas*, p.62 and note 3.

51. The word for the sacrificial victim (generally, a goat, a bull, a horse etc.) is *paśu*; and it is properly used in this account (from the root *paś*, 'to bind'; and the victim is bound, or tied, to the stake). Vettam Mani, in his *Puranic Encyclopaedia*, (English), Delhi, 1975, p.29 (under Ambarīṣa) translates the word *paśu* as

'sacrificial cow', which is not correct. He is obviously influenced by Malayalam which is his mother-tongue. In Malayalam and also in Tamil *pasū* (*paśu*) means 'cow'. This is not the case with the Sanskrit language. Though Malayalam and Tamil have borrowed this word from Sanskrit, the meaning has been contracted in those languages.

52. We may compare the Vedic domestic ritual of Śūlagava, in which a bull was sacrificed to Rudra; here, too, the sacrifice took place out of the locality. Rudra, like his later aspect, Śiva, was the lord of cattle; *paśupati* is a famous epithet of Śiva. For Śūlagava see P.V.Kane, *History of Dharmaśāstra*, Poona, Vol. II, Part-II, 1974, pp.831-32. This rite was performed either in the autumn or in spring; the Poḷā festival falls in the latter part of the rainy season (Varṣā), just prior to the autumn.

53. It has also a variant name, Vasu-bāras (Twelfth of Wealth; Vasu = 'Wealth').

Four

Structural Approach and Meaning

The structural method, or, better, the method of structural analysis, rejected the earlier methods and tried to provide a critical approach to go to the 'subconscious' level of a myth which alone, according to it, held the meaning inherent in it. What is seen, however, is that it relied more on the material from tribals, or the pre-writing records, extending the generalizations to the more advanced contexts.

Structure indicates a non-individualistic characteristic of a society and points to a possible system of concepts and beliefs. For structuralists it was necessary to examine the tales, rituals and life styles not only as reflected in recorded literature, but also from actual contact with tribes. This would help arrive at a system of concepts *behind words*. This system of concepts would also divulge (what is called) the 'problematic' behind the mass of words that fashion tales and behind traditional beliefs. This is the process of trying to discover the undiscovered. This in the phase of the absence of writing in a particular tribe or society, would point to the mode of communication of tribal knowledge. In line with this, the structuralists believed that myths (or a class of myths) had the prime function of solving problems that faced a particular society or a tribe, in that particular stage of the formation of myths, which might include the creation of the world, relationships between the opposite sexes and so on. In this context it is advisable to examine afresh the views of Claude Lévi-Strauss. According to him natural phenomena are the medium for explaining social facts and they are not restricted to nature in themselves.[1] In his view mythical thought works like a bricole (1966, p. 22) and results in the building of structures, grouping various events that percolate in a tribe's march in time. The exact implication of this reasoning would be, that there is no conscious effort in the formation of myths. Bricole is an ancient type of engine used for throwing stones. The word is also used for the rebounding action of a tennis-ball thrown against a wall. As a mere one throw does not give any idea about the working intention behind the throw and, as a group of throws would be required to understand the implication of the action of throwing, so is the case with a myth. A number of (similar) myths or versions of a myth have to be examined to get at the meaning. Like magic and totemism myths, studied this way, would require the analysis of concepts and bundling them together. According to Lévi-Strauss, myths looked from this angle, cannot be taken to be as opposite of science. On the other hand, they are an alternative to science. In other words, they present a science in their own way. Myths and science (in the popular sense of the term) have to be taken as parallel ways of presenting knowledge. Deploring, as early as 1963, Tylor, Frazer and Durkheim who, according to him, "were psychologically oriented although not oriented to keep up with the progress of psychological research and theory",[2] Lévi-Strauss had already voiced against "pretending" that a meaning has been found. In his view the functional approach to the myths of pre-writing stage was utilitarian, while that of Lévy Bruhl (Levy Bruhl, L., *La Mentalité Primitive*, Paris, 1922) was that the primitive thought was entirely determined by emotion and mystic representations. Lévi-Strauss believes it to be disinterested (as against the utilitarian) and intellectual (as against the emotional and mystic). For him the primitive man is as intelligent as the modern. Hence myths do reflect logic (1980, p. 16), according to him. He posed a question — If there is no logic or no continuity in myths, apparently, and that if they are arbitrary, why should there be the astounding similarity between myths collected in widely different regions?. He compared myths to language and said, that the similarity between language and myths is that both have the purpose of communication. In language it is not the sounds themselves that give meaning but it is a particular combination of sounds that gives the meaning. However, the same combination of sounds (we may add, in the same order) may not give the same meaning in another group of people. Impliedly, we are to suppose that the same or similar myth may not have the same meaning (or substance?) in different groups of people, the order notwithstanding. But, he also marks a difference between language and myth. According to him, a myth always refers to events alleged to have taken place long ago. But, what gives myth an operational value is, that the specific pattern described is timeless; it explains the present, the past, as well as the future. Referring to Saussure's distinction between *langue* and *parole*, the former indicating the structural and expression side and the latter calling for explanation (or interpretation, to be clearer), in the case of language, he assumes a third level for a myth which makes it an absolute entity, whereby, though linguistic by nature, it is, nevertheless, distinct from the usual two characteristics of language though it combines the properties of the two. In this, according to him, "myth has to be placed at the end opposite of poetry. Poetry is a kind of speech that cannot be translated except at the cost of serious distortions, whereas the mythical value of myth is preserved even through the worst translation." Myth transcends the garb of language it is expressed in, and is felt as myth anywhere; even if it is presented in a different language. "Its substance does not lie in its style, its original music or its syntax, but in the story it tells" (1969, p. 209). From what is said above, it can be gathered that, for Lévi Strauss, myth is a language; it is a means of communication through ages. However it needs to be pointed out that communication is only one way in the case of myth, reciprocation back to the past being absent; for there is no way, and nothing to convey to the period, or to the stage of society, which was witness to the formation and fattening of myth. We may say, with Lévi-Strauss that "to be known, myth has to be told; (and that) it is a part of human speech" (*Ib.*); but, we must admit that it could only be told now or forward; never told back; or to be clearer, it could be read forward to the present and future, never read back to the past. This is true also of written records of language. But we have to mark an important difference between language and myth. Conversation is an important aspect of human speech; but in the case of a myth this is hardly possible. Conversation is the basis of reciprocation in terms of human speech. Myth cannot be a medium through which we can converse, though we may converse about a myth. This will show that the similarity between language and myth is not total. When Lévi-Strauss says that the substance of a myth does not lie in its style, its original music or its syntax, but in the *story* it tells, he diffentiates the manner and the outer frame of the narration from the message it has to communicate (myth being language); and this message is the substance that lies in the 'story'. It is not clear at this point what Lévi-Strauss means by 'story'; but from the examples he has given, and the method of analysis he has suggested in his writings, it becomes clear that 'story' for him was a very complex concept—or, rather, he is not clear about this term. He obviously makes a difference between a myth and "the story it tells". We, thus, have three different levels in a myth according to him - (1) Myth; (2) The story it tells; and (3) Its substance. Thus, before we arrive at the 'substance' (or the message) we have the myth which is in the form of a narration. This narration, which we may call mythical narration here for convenience, may have more versions; these could be taken as versions of the myth itself. It may be in the form of a poem or a song (cf. music, as he says) or may be a simple prose narration recited or told in a ritual (though Lévi-Strauss does not seem to bother about that, nor about the functional use of a myth). The nucleus of a mythical narration, or of all available versions of that narration, is the 'story' which holds the substance. The 'story' could be arrived at by analysing the narration (the myth, or mythical narration) for the structures it (or the many versions) might show. Therein lies the substance (meaning) of the myth (narration).

Following the linguistician concept of language (cf. his reference to Saussure noted above) Lévi-Strauss names the gross constituent elements of a myth 'methemes' (cf. the linguistic terms 'phoneme', 'morpheme', etc.) and says that these gross elements can be arranged into a number of 'bundles of relation'. It is only as 'bundles' that these relations can be put to use and combined so as to produce a meaning. He says, "Relations pertaining to the same bundle may appear diachronically at remote intervals; but, when we have succeeded in grouping them together we have organised our myth according to a time reference of a new nature, corresponding to the prerequisite of the initial hypothesis, namely a two dimensional time referent which is simultaneously diachronic and synchronic, and which accordingly integrates the characteristic of *langue* on the one hand and those of *parole* on the other.... It is as though a phoneme were always made up of its variants." The natural sense of this reasoning, in short, will be that, as a single phoneme has more than one allophones, a 'metheme' will be a whole myth having a variety of 'allomyths' i.e., the variations, or versions, of a particular myth, which might obtain diachronically, or synchronically (and, we may add, even diaterrenely). But this is not what Lévi-Strauss means by a 'metheme'. For him, a 'metheme' is a gross element, which is just a facet of a whole myth; and in a myth there may be more than one such 'methemes', though they are bundles—not of myths, properly speaking, but of "relations", as if a myth or its version deals only with 'relations', or 'relationships' which can best be understood in terms of the relations in a society or of a human family. There is hardly any doubt that, here, the social anthropologist gets on top of the mythologist in Lévi-Strauss; because, myths are not restricted to family or blood relationships, or social relationships. The example he gives in this context discloses the restricted scope that he allots to a myth. It is the example of Oedipus. His method (or 'technique' as he calls it) is to break the 'story' (and not 'myth'? What he means is the myth—i.e., narration) into shortest possible sentences, and write, each sentence on an index card, bearing a number corresponding to the unfolding of the story. In this, each card will show a certain function, which is linked to a given subject at a given time. In this way "gross constituent units" (he means 'bundles') will be available, which will consist of a relation. The relations pertaining to the same bundle may appear diachronically at remote intervals, the scrutiny of which will lead us to the meaning (or substance?) of the "story" (= myth). The analysis of the Oedipus myth given by Lévi-Strauss, in columns according to his method, is as follows (1969, pp. 213, 214). The myth is too well known to warrant a full record here. However its narration, for recollection, and analysis would be helpful.

King Laius (also spelt Laios) of Thebes is said to be the third in descent from Cadmus (also Cadmos). He married his distant cousin, Jocasta.[3] Apollo's Oracle at Delphi, whom the king consulted, warned Laius that he would die at the hand of his son. But the king decided to disprove it. So, when the child was born, he bound his feet together and got it exposed on a lonely mountain expecting it to die soon. But a shepherd rescued him and brought him to Corinth. Many years rolled along. Once the king was away from home and many years had passed. And it was reported in the capital that the king was killed by robbers on the way to Delphi along with all his attendants, except one. The one that escaped brought the news of the destruction to the capital. There were no efforts made to investigate the matter, as Thebes was controlled at that span of time by a terrible monster, the sphinx, who was shaped like a lion having wings but having the face and breasts of a woman. This creature stood by the way and would not allow a passerby without putting him a question, which the person had to answer. The failure to answer correctly would result in the person's being devoured by the sphinx. Hence the famous city remained closed and was stricken with famine. Now, it so happened that a man, a stranger, passed by about the same time. His name was Oedipus. Actually he had come from Corinth, where he was held to be the son of the king there, by name Polybus. On knowing from another Oracle of Apollo, that he would be the cause of his father's death, he had wandered away from Corinth, resolving never to see Polybus again. In his wanderings, he had come to the sphinx in the vicinity of Thebes. The sphinx, now, asked him— "What creature goes on four feet in the morning, on two at noon and on three in the evening?" Oedipus answered, "Man! In childhood he creeps on his fours - two hands and two feet; in his youth he walks erect on two feet; and in old-age he supports himself with a staff, in addition to his two feet''. On hearing it, the sphinx said that it was the right answer. And, she (sphinx) killed herself. When the Thebans heard this, they took him to the capital and made him king. (According to the custom) Oedipus got everything that belonged to the earlier king, Laius, including his wife, Jocasta, whom he married. They lived happily and had two sons born of them.

Time passed along and the sons grew into full men. But, now a terrible plague came upon Thebes. Having concern for his subjects, Oedipus sent Creon, the brother of Jocasta, to consult the Oracle of Delphi; and he came back with a comforting news. The Oracle had said that the plague will vanish if the murderer of King Laius would be punished. Oedipus was very glad and proclaimed it to the subjects. He also sent for the blind prophet, Teirestias, to ask him if he could know the murderer through his special powers. The prophet readily arrived but refused to say anything. The king, Oedipus, implored upon him to speak out and, fretting with wrath at the prophet's continued silence, accused him to have had taken part in the murder. Now the prophet said, seething with anger, "You are yourself the murderer!" Oedipus thought the man was out of his senses. And, even Jocasta added how the Oracle of Delphi had prophesied the death of Laius (her former husband) at the hands of his son, but how he was actually killed by robbers on the road to Delphi. Oedipus was more shocked than surprised on hearing this and asked her when it had happened. She answered, "About the same time— just before you had come here!" On being asked how many were with the king, she replied, "There were five; all were killed along with the king, except one. But why do you ask me? You are disturbed!!" Then did Oedipus tell her, ''Oh! I did come upon a man with five attendants; on the narrow path; he would not give me path and struck me away with his staff, which angered me. And I killed him and his four attendants." But Jocasta insisted, on the testimony of the escaped attendant, that Laius was killed by robbers. Just at this time a messenger came from Corinth and announced that Polybus was dead. Oedipus exclaimed joyfully that he was relieved that he was not the cause of his father's death. But the messenger clarified that, Oedipus need not have any fear at all, as he was not the real son of Polybus and that a wandering shepherd had given him as a child to Polybus, and that the shepherd was the servant of Laius. At that moment the shepherd himself arrived and the whole truth came out. Jocasta ran out and reached her apartment where she killed herself, being shocked and feeling ashamed. Oedipus put out his eyes, though he lived on.

This story of Oedipus is one in a chain of two others. One preceding, the other following, all relating to the royal house of Thebes. According to the preceding story, when Europa was carried away, her father, the king of Sidon,[4] sent his sons in search of her. One of them, Cadmus, went straight to Delphi. The Oracle told him that he would see a heifer and he should follow her and build a city. He obeyed and followed the hiefer. He founded Thebes on the spot where the heifer stopped. But, first he had to fight and kill a terrible dragon which guarded a spring and killed all his companions when they went to get water. Then he killed the dragon. Now, the goddess Athena appeared before him and asked him to sow the earth with the dragon's teeth. But, when he furrowed the land and sowed the teeth, to his horror, armed men sprang up from the furrows. (They were named Spartoi- 'sown men'). However, they did not harm him. On the contrary, they fought amongst themselves and all were killed, except for five. They helped Cadmus to found the city of Thebes. The rest of the incidents in the life of Cadmus need not be told here; and we leave them.

The one that follows the account of Oedipus is as follows. Oedipus' two sons from Jocasta were Polyneices and Eteocles; and he had also two daughters, Antigone and Ismene. Oedipus relinquished the throne. His elder son also was not interested in being king. So he also kept himself aside. The people of Thebes accepted Creon, Jocasta's brother, as regent. After some years, Creon and both the sons of Oedipus sent Oedipus away from the city, for reasons not specific. One of his daughters, Ismene, stayed back in the city to look after his interest, while Antigone went with him to take care of him. When Oedipus was gone, his two sons fought for the throne;

but Eteocles succeeded. He drove away his elder brother Polyneices, who took refuge with Adrastus, the king of Argos with an intention to invade Thebes. He, along with Adrastus and others, marched on Thebes. In the meanwhile Oedipus died and both his daughters were near him at Athens, where he was earlier received by King Theseus. The two sisters returned to Thebes only to learn about the strife between their brothers. When the battle was joined, the seven gates of Thebes were guarded and also attacked. At one gate Eteocles faced his brother, Polyneices. The sisters waited anxiously inside. But, on the prophesy of Teirestias that Creon's younger son, Menoeceus, alone would save Thebes by his death in the battle, Menoeceus jumped in the battle, unmindful of his father's entreaties not to do so. As the battle raged on and yet did not come to a decisive end, it was agreed that there should be a combat between the contending brothers. This was done and the brothers joined in the combat. But, both were killed. Thereupon the battle resumed. Ultimately the Thebans defeated the invaders. Creon (the brother of Jocasta, and the material uncle of the contesting brothers and father of Menoeceus) decreed that Polyneices should not be given a burial as he was instrumental in the disaster of Thebes by invading it. One who buried him would be punished by death. But Antigone, under cover of a dust-storm, buried her brother and was ultimately put to death.[5]

There have been various interpretations of this unit of tales; and various dramas came to be based on it. Lévi-Strauss who did not give the accounts, being well known, analysed them structurally and arranged in columns in main points ('bundles') as follows (1969, p. 214):-

(1)	(2)	(3)	(4)
I. Cadmus seeks his sister Europa, ravished by Zeus	—	Cadmus kills the dragon	(Meaning of names)
—	The spartoi kill each other	—	Labdocos (Liaus' father)='lame'
II Oedipus marries his mother, Jocosta	Oedipus kills his father	Oedipus kills the sphinx	Laius = 'left sided'
—	Eteocles kills his brother Polyneices	—	Oedipus= 'swollen foot'
III. Antigone buries her brother Polyneices despite prohibition	—	—	

Having presented this analysis, Lévi-Strauss comments as follows (p.215)—

1. All the events grouped in the first column (i.e., column1) on the left have something to do with blood-relations which are over emphasized, that is they are more intimate than they should be. Let us say that this column has its common feature as *overrating blood relations.*
2. The second column expresses the same thing, but inverted. This is *underrating bloodrelations.*

3. The third column refers to monsters being slain.
4. Regarding this column he has a few words for clarification, which is that all the "surnames" in Oedipus' father's line have a common feature: "All the hypothetical meanings (which may remain hypothetical)'' (the brackets are his) refer to difficulties in walking straight and standing upright.

He draws our attention to the third and the fourth columns and argues that the dragon is an autochthonian being which has to be killed "in order that mankind be born from the Earth." He suggests that the sphinx is a monster unwilling to permit man to live, and that (hence?) "the last unit produces the first one which has to do with the autochthonous origin of man." He adds that, "since monsters are overcome by man, we may, thus say that the common feature of the third column is the denial of the autochthonous origin of man." This immediately helps us understand, according to him, "the meaning of the myth" (meaning is equal to 'substance' for him here). He adds that in mythology it is a universal characteristic of men born from Earth, that at the moment they emerge from the depth, they cannot walk, or they walk clumsily. He gives some examples for this from the mythology of the Pueblo. Happily, he says that this is a "provisional formulation of the structure of mythical thought." In his opinion this myth tries to explain the contradiction between the belief that mankind is born from the earth and the belief that it is actually born from the union of man and woman - a conflict between nature and culture.

It will be seen that Lévi-Strauss leaves of many details as unnecessary for arriving at the substance of the myth, and says that Jocasta killing herself and Oedipus blinding himself do not alter the substance of the myth. He also says that this method does away with the problem of the quest of the true version or the earlier one. But, can we take whatever Lévi-Strauss has suggested to be the meaning of the whole myth? Apart from structuralism as such, the method of Lévi-Strauss, came under heavy criticism, though he became popular as a structuralist and has his own place in the review of interpretation of myth. Miriam Glucksmann opines[6] that "Lévi-Strauss tries to make a reading of his work as difficult for the reader as the deciphering of a myth was to himself." She adds, "The reader is expected to 'work' at reading his books, since the jigsaw nature of the writing is in fact a carefully thought out strategy for particular intellectual purpose" (1974, p. 47f). Later she says, "To analyse myths as Lévi-Strauss does must require a good deal of individual flair and genius... but he is so individualistic that practically no one else would be able to learn the method" (p.92). How far this criticism can be accepted, and how far one should follow the method of Lévi Strauss is up to the individual interested in unavelling the meaning behind a myth. However, at the outset, a question arises as to why only certain details have to be retained for examination and others have to be rejected. Moreover, why should the belief among the Pueblo regarding the origin of men from the earth and lameness be taken as universal? It may be noted, that Lévi-Strauss takes the help of etymology for the meaning of the names (the English translation has "Surnames", which is doubtful) of Oedipus' father's line. It is true that the word Oedipus (Greek Oidipous) indicates 'swollen foot', and Labdocos and Laius may be taken to indicate defect in walking (of which even Lévi-Strauss is not quite certain). But, why should he leave off the meaning of the name Cadmus, who is said to have introduced the Greek alphabet. Actually even here there appears to be some association with the earth.[7] The myth reflects the association of Cadmus with earth very clearly in the sowing of the teeth and reaping of the corn - though, the corn is not the usual one! One fails to understand how a brother (Cadmus) seeking his sister could be taken as an overrated blood-relation. The ravishing of Europa by Zeus is out of question as regards blood-relationship, far less its being overemphasized. The killing of the spartoi (if they could be taken to be brothers of each other, all being born from the furrow, though this point is not made clear by Lévi-Strauss) may be seen as a parallel to Eteocles killing his brother, Polyneices, and Oedipus killing his father. But, then, should we leave away the difference between parties that form this 'metheme' (or 'bundle'), viz. the spartoi's awareness of their mutual relationship being doubtful and Oedipus completely oblivious of Laius being his own father, and Eteocles and Polyneices knowing full well that they are real brothers? If the killing of the near blood-kin be taken as underrated blood-relationship, how is it to be reconciled with the substance of the myth which is the riddle of birth - 'Birth from one (= earth) or born from two (Male-Female)'? How do columns one and two together are to be read with columns three and four? If they are to be kept mutually apart, why are they to be shown at all? But, then, how is one to understand that "the last unit produces the first one" (p.216). If it means (at all) that conflict between birth from earth and that from a pair (sex), what about point III? Further, if the decision of ultimate victory is reached by the combat between real brothers, one killing the other, what happens to the prophecy which led Menoeceus to die for his country? The final point is—is the whole of the Theban cycle a pure myth or is it mythicised history? In other words, are the human characters in the whole cycle, or in each individual account, purely mythical, or they are historically important and came to be coated (or embroidered) with symbolic elements which usually form an important ingredient of myth and folklore? To be plain, it appears that these are accounts of heroes whose achievements turned them into legends. It will not be wrong to state that here history and myth are fused together. And, it is futile to overrate the hypothesis that here the substance of the myth (which part of the accounts?) is "inability for a culture, which holds the belief that mankin is autochthonous, to find a satisfactory transition between the theory and the knowledge that human beings are actually born from the union of man and woman". And this, on the basis of etymology, which is uncertain and of doubtful use in the present context.

More probe in the cycle is required. Apart from the cryptic mention of the cycle by Lévi-Strauss there are other details that obtain in this case; and, though it may not be necessary to seek out the true myth as Lévi-Strauss suggests, it is of help to examine certain details and see if they suggest something. Cadmus is seen to have come to Greece from the near east,[8] from Phoenicia. He was sent by the Oracle to go and settle in the wheat-bearing plains. In his march westward he was guided by a heifer and was to build a city where she would stop, or go underground. Where the heifer lay down he stopped and wanted to purify himself with some water from a spring. As he and his companions went to the spring, he saw it being guarded by a huge dragon-serpent, who killed all his companions. But ultimately he killed it, took out his teeth as he was counselled by Athena, and sowed them. From these sprang up the spartoi, who spread everywhere; but fought among themselves.[9] The detail of the killing of the guardian dragon and sowing its teeth occurs also in the account of Jason. Even there the sown teeth give the crop of armed men (Kirk, 1976, p. 160). The dragon in the Jason account is said to guard the golden fleece. There are a number of stories from folklore which testify to the belief of serpents or dragons being guardians of water or treasure.[10] But, the sowing of the teeth of a dragon is unique here, along with the production of heroes from them. When the spartoi fight among themselves, only five survive; and they help Cadmus to found the city of Thebes. They are considered as the ancestors of the Thebans. No such thing is said about the teeth-men in the Jason account. Python-killing occurs also in the Apollo-myth. Kirk sees in the Cadmus-spartoi their autochthonous nature; but, he does not say, and rightly so, that this is the substance of the Cadmus myth. It is very probable that this detail in the popular Cadmus myth influenced the later Jason myth. The case of the sphinx in the Oedipus myth is different. The sphinx is not a serpent dragon; but a lion-bodied winged woman. However, like the serpent, the creature is associated with the earth, though as her guard, and has its origin in Egypt. According to the Egyptian mythology, the sphinx is an aspect of Aker, the human-headed lion that is said to guard the two limits of the earth.[11] The questioning sphinx in the Oedipus myth has the same function. In a way the serpent and the sphinx here are aspects of the earth and the killing of these creatures indicates full control - or, the gain— of territory. The two events place Cadmus and Oedipus on equal level. They also join together two heroes probably of mutually separate clans (Kirk, 1976, p. 104). It will be interesting to note that, when Cadmus and his wife Harmonia ultimately fled from Thebes and reached distant Illyria, they were both changed by the gods into serpents. The mythical element of the serpent, its teeth[12] and the ultimate transformation of Cadmus into a serpent, together with the serpent symbolising earth and the word Cadmus itself having a bearing of the meaning of earth (as we have noted earlier) indicate the employment of a symbol. The same appears to be true of the spartoi, who, most probably, have to be taken as 'children of the serpent-teeth', together with 'those of the earth'. According to Kirk (1976, p. 158) the myth suggests the autochthonic nature of the spartoi. But the point has to be explained on the basis of a double symbolism—of the serpent and the earth; and, with due credit to the structuralist interpretation, we can say that the serpent and other symbols for earth indicate a set of emotional structures in the human mind. The spartoi are autochthonous in a double sense— (i) born from themselves; hence, divine; and (ii) sons of the soil; hence indigenous, which means that they were the first human settlers in Thebes. This myth was a necessity to make Cadmus, and his clan-men sons of the soil and bestow superhuman status on them. The in-fight among the spartoi has to be seen as internal rivalry with the prospect of prosperity. One feels, there is hardly any point for 'bundling' the dragon with the sphinx; for, though both may be related to the earth, the sphinx is not associated with creation anywhere — not even here. The etymological meaning of lameness or of 'swollen foot' does not suit the question-answer motif nor does it go well with the sphinx. It is tempting to add that the teeth of the dragon/serpent might well be taken as the shares of the plough as associated with the sowing of grain (wheat?). In that case, Cadmus may be taken as the leader of the first agriculture-settlers on the land, the cow (heifer) symbolising ploughable earth, though there is no other Greek-myth to substantiate it. Interestingly, Zeus abducts Cadmus' sister taking the form of a bull; and Cadmus is led by a heifer—an unfructified cow, the expedition resulting in sowing and reaping! By another interesting contrast we see the Zeus-bull abducting Europa, while his wife, Hera, is often seen as having the face of a cow; and the Cow (and also a peacock) was sacred to her, though the myth of Cadmus does not specifically strike the identity between Hera and the heifer that guides Cadmus. The thought-reflection in the mythical part of the story of Cadmus could be outlined as follows:

I.	Zeus (Bull)	Europa (co-wife with Hera)	(continent)	Earth
II.	Cadmus	heifer (quasi-Hera who is *cow-face*)	(merges in)	Earth = Thebes

we would not be wrong in supposing that a historical figure, Cadmus, has been associated with the symbolic value of Cow and serpent, both having identification and association with earth. It is often seen that historical persons are made legendary with the tucking on of popular mythical symbols and symbolic narrations— that of the defeat of the dragon in an actual fight, in the case of Cadmus and that of the sphinx in a wordy duel in the case of Oedipus. The questions and riddles that the hero has to answer cannot be dispensed with by saying that it is simply a folklore element. It is a set pattern[13] and has the same importance as that of a word charm which conceals the effective will. In the Oedipus myth it takes the verbal form for an actual fight, resulting in the sphinx's death. Even granting the widespread prevalence of, and historical support for, the belief that the primordial creatures of the early marshy earth were reptiles, and conceding to the belief that these creatures got established in myths as the controllers of earthly treasures and nourishment which were to be obtained by vanquishing them, it is difficult to see in the myths of Cadmus and Oedipus the *problem* of the creation of the human race—whether from one or from a sexual union of two. That does not require the incest, which remains unexplained. The plain substance seems to be—(i) Cultivation of virgin and marshy land (heifer) and the control of fresh water-sources (defeat of the dragon/serpent by Cadmus by vanquishing them); and (ii) (which is the extension of the same thought but in a different way). The defeat of the earth-guard (dragon or sphinx). This here (in the Oedipus myth) mixes with the belief that the earth has a husband, who is also her son viz. that the seed (fructifier) is also the sprout (the son), and *vice versa.* That the story of Oedipus is more mythical than legendary (i.e., less history and more myth) is clear from the fact that, though the name Oedipus does not have variations, Jocasta has (cf. Iocaste and Epicaste). Even if Jocasta and Iocasta(te) be taken as variations of the same name, Epicaste appears to be different. Exposing of a child to the ferocity of nature, or contriving its death, because of its being a future danger is not restricted to Oedipus nor to the Greek mythology. We may take another example from the Greek mythology. King Acricium was told by the Oracle of Delphi that his daughter would have a son who would kill him. However, he shuts her up in a house built of bronze and sunk underground. She gives birth to a child from Zeus; he was Perseus. He was put in a great chest, along with the mother, and the chest was cast into the sea.[14] A very similar account about the birth of Gilgamesh obtains. According to one such, reported by Aelian, a Roman writer of the second century A.D., the Babylonian king was told that his daughter's son would seize the kingdom from him. So he shut the girl in the citadel and had her closely guarded. However, she became pregnant by an obscure man and gave birth to a son. The guards were taken aback and got afraid of the wrath of the king, as they would not be able to explain the situation. So they threw the baby over the walls of the citadel to kill it. But, as the babe was falling down on the earth, an eagle saw it and gently caught it on its back, flew to a nearby orchard and placed it there, whereafter it flew away. When the keeper of the orchard arrived and saw the babe, he took it up and nurtured it. The babe grew up to be Gilgamesh.[15]

The same pattern is seen in the Hindu context. Kaṁsa was the maternal uncle of Kṛṣṇa and was informed by the divine speech that the latter would kill him, being the eighth male issue of his (Kaṁsa's) sister, Devakī. So Kaṁsa imprisoned Devakī and even her husband Vasudeva. In spite of this precaution, and the killing of all earlier issues of Devakī, Kṛṣṇa was rescued and carried out of Kaṁsa's capital Mathurā and kept in Gokula, across the river, where he attained boyhood. Later he went to Mathurā, along with his brother Balarāma, and killed Kaṁsa.[16] The divine speech in the story of Kaṁsa compares with the speech of the Oracle in the Greek (and even the Egyptian) myths and obtains as a common motif. In the case of the narration about Oedipus, apart from mythical elements being added, and apart from strict congruency not being expected, there are a few points that indicate weakness of narration. The king is said to have been murdered just before Oedipus came to the city. If the sphinx controlled the city, and lay in wait for any wayfarers, the attendant of the king who brought the news home must have been specially favoured by the sphinx to let him in! There is no mention of any band of followers for Oedipus in his wanderings. He seems to have come alone; and he was brought with admiration to accept the throne and the dead king's wife. Had the escaped guard been in the palace, as is expected, being the chosen one of the king, he would have at once recognised that the saviour was the same 'murderer'. If Oedipus wandered alone what about the band of robbers? Oedipus specifically says he came upon a man (king) with four attendants (not five), all of whom he killed. It is possible that the fifth who escaped never saw him, as they all filed behind the king due to the path being narrow. This would explain why the only witness of the murder could not recognise the murderer. Surprisingly, he is not on the scene when Oedipus, after many years, tries to investigate the cause of the plague. This is when his children from Jocasta have grown up to full youth. And why should the plague seize the city for the sin of Oedipus after so many years? This version of Sophocles (496-406 B.C.) appears to be a dramatized product of the fact of a stranger being grafted on the family line of Cadmus-Laius, being given the status of 'son' for legitimacy. This was done on the mythical patterns of—(i) The likely-to-be-dangerous son cast away; and (ii) The 'sprout' (son) is also the 'seeder' (husband) of the earth, together with the custom of the vanquisher taking also the wife of the vanquished.

As has been indicated earlier, the Cow in the Cadmus myth appears as the symbol of the earth. She stops at (or merges in) the earth at a place where Thebes comes up and also Cadmus 'sows' the 'teeth' reaping the 'corn' of men. It should be noted that the region around Thebes was called Boeotia, "heifer's land"[17] (though the term 'boeotian' came to signify dulness in English). Coupled with the belief that Cadmus introduced alphabetic script, the myth reflects that he was also the one who introduced systematic agriculture in the land. In this sense, the mythical detail (not the myth as Kirk says) tends to assume the characteristic of a charter. In the Greek mythological literature, it may be rightly said, we do not have Cow as symbolizing earth or ploughable land. In any case, the myth that got attached to Cadmus has to be taken as a clear case of this symbolization, though an exception. The Greek goddess of earth and of corn-field, Demeter, was not a cow; she was depicted as a mare. Actually the name Demeter is formed from two words - (i) *de*, from *deai*, which is a Cretan word for barley; and (ii) *meter*, meaning 'mother'. The whole word would give the sense of 'mother-barley' (or 'mother of barley' or even 'corn-mother', as a secondary meaning). Her figure, as the Black-Demeter, had a mare's head and was made of wood. According to Pusanias (VIII.12), she had above it figures of snakes and other monsters (the symbols) associated with the earth as their mother, in addition to a dolphin, in one hand and a dove in the other.[18] Did the Cadmus myth indicate introduction of a cow-faced corn-goddess, which, however, did not stay?

On the Indian side, the Hindu mythology has a similar myth where king Pṛthu figures, the earth being symbolically suggested as the Cow. Pṛthu is mentioned right from the Vedic times.[19] He was the son of Vena, born from the latter's right arm when it was churned.[20] When he was installed as king he is said to have 'milked' the earth, suggesting the earth to be a cow. Later texts give a myth according to which Pṛthu was angry with the earth that had run away taking the form of a cow. So, he threw a burning arrow at her and she agreed to get milked. According to a variation of the same account, Pṛthu darted many arrows at the earth-cow which entered deep into her body. On her request that he should take them out, Pṛthu took them away with the tip of his bow; the result was, the mountains got formed from the lump that came out along with the arrows.[21] The 'milking' of the earth-cow after the shooting of an arrow is a symbolic (or metaphoric) way of seeding the earth after furrowing with a shaft-like plough or a hoe. According to the Avesta the earth is Spenta Armaiti, and each time Yima (the first king) presses her with the golden ring and bores her with the poniard called *aṣṭrā* (which is, in fact, the goad to manage cattle), she spreads; and from 'her' flocks of cattle, herds of sheep and even men come out.[22] This Middle-Eastern myth of Yima, which dates at least about the eleventh century B.C. has probably influenced, through Phoenicia, the Cadmus myth of 'sowing' (by) the 'teeth' and reaping the harvest of men from the earth.

The part of the Oedipus myth that makes the son the husband of the mother has a parallel in the Egyptian myth of Anpu and Bata. But there are many other points; and it is not sufficient to see the meaning of the whole myth in a part, as Lévi-Strauss has done in the case of the Oedipus myth-cycle. Anpu and Bata are two brothers, who loved each other until the wanton wife of Anpu sowed the seeds of jealousy in her husband's mind. Bata, the younger, was strong and Anpu's wife desired him. Bata told her that she was like her mother, and the elder Anpu was like his father. One afternoon as Bata came back home earlier than his elder brother from the field, she expressed her desire to him; but Bata went out, and away to the fields. In the evening when both returned Anpu went into the house, and Bata went to the byre to keep the oxen. In the house, Anpu's wife did not light the lamp and lay quiet, her garment away from the body. When Anpu asked, she told him that Bata had made advances towards her. On hearing this, Anpu got furious and waited for his brother, who, however, escaped and ran away. Anpu followed him, dagger in hand. On the request of Bata, Ra created a river filled with crocodiles in between them. Now, Bata told Anpu from across the river what had happened. He also told him that he would not return, that he was going to the 'region of flowering acacia' and that he would leave his soul in the highest blossom of acacia. If, and when, the tree is cut down, Anpu will see his soul fallen on the ground. Anpu would find it out even after seven years. When the soul is placed in a bowl filled with water, Bata would come back to life. The indication of a disaster to the life of Bata would be the bubbling of the beer kept with Anpu. Bata left. He stayed away for many years. In the meanwhile Anpu's wife died; but even knowing of it Bata did not return—he never wanted to. Ra asked the 'nine gods' to fashion a wife for Bata. And the seven Hathors prophesied that she would meet a speedy death. (To cut the narration short). Bata and his wife lived happily for a long time. One day Bata told his wife the secret of his soul. Once it so happened that the sea-god carried a lock of her hair to the shores of Egypt, and into the victinity of the royal palace. It fell in the hands of the washerwomen of the palace, who gifted it to the king. The king sent messengers to the land of the flowering acacia to bring the woman, on knowing from the royal scribe that the lock belonged to the daughter of Ra. But, Bata killed them all. Ultimately the king sent a shrewd woman along with presents to Bata's wife, who, allured by them, went to Egypt to become the queen. Now, she wanted to get rid of Bata and divulged the secret of Bata's soul to the king, who sent messengers and quietly got severed the blossom from the acacia. The soul of Bata in the blossom of the acacia was disturbed and fell to the ground leaving Bata in the grasp of death. Back home Anpu saw the beer bubbling and sighing with foul smell. He got the indication, rushed to the land of the acacia, searched for the seeds of the acacia, found one and immediately placed it in a bowl filled with water. As night approached, the body of Bata quivered. Anpu gave him the water from the bowl to drink. And Bata came back to life. He told his elder brother that he would take the form of a bull, that Anpu should ride him and he would take him to the king of Egypt, as a gift and that Anpu should present him (the bull = Bata) to the king; but then he should return. Next morning Anpu set for Egypt on the bull and stood in the audience of the king, who accepted the bull as a gift and gave Anpu much gold and silver.

The queen (= the faithless wife of Bata) liked the bull very much for his strength and beauty. Once, however, the bull told her who he really was. Afraid, the queen told her husband to get the bull killed as she wanted to eat its liver and also that the bull was inauspicious to him. Though sorry, the king commanded the bull to be sacrificed. As the bull was killed, two drops of blood fell on either side of the palace gate; and, from the spots they fell on, two trees sprang up. Later, when the king and the queen were passing through the gate in a chariot, the trees whispered to her, "O false woman, I am alive". Later the trees were cut down at the queen's command far making two fine seats from them. As the trees were being cut, the queen went to see, and a chip from one of the trees entered her mouth; she swallowed it, became pregnant and gave birth to a son. The king appointed him as the ruler when he came to age. After some years, he appointed him heir to the throne of Egypt. When he died this son became king of Egypt and took the queen (his mother) as wife, according to the custom. This myth is known from the time of Ramses II, 1300 B.C.[23]

The new king summoned all people to tell them what actually the history was. The queen (mother = wife) was brought before him and all people; and he revealed himself before her. The king asked the judges to pass the judgement. And she met a speedy death! The new king (Bata, in the new form of his son from his wife) summoned Anpu and made him the royal heir.[24]

In the Egyptian mould the son-husband motif is subdued. Bata is an alter ego of Osiris, dying and coming to life serially, and the bull is the Apis bull. The narration is fine and sophisticated in the later part showing certain differences from the Oedipus account. Yet the similarity cannot be overlooked. One of the marked differences in the relationship is, that the Bata story shows his wife to be faithless to him, and presents a sort of a triangular relationship, the king of Egypt coming in between the main parties. But, for a Lévi-Straussian analysis this should not pose any problem; for, Lévi-Strauss allows myths, even from contexts that are not culturally related, to postulate bundles of relations, leaving away minor (or even major) differences. According to him Oedipus has a double personality - he is thought to be dead, yet he is alive. But such double personalities are seen in many other cases. Bata, for example, is both dead and non-dead; dead as Bata, but non-dead as the soul in the acacia flower and so on. With the Greek Oedipus myth he compares a myth from the Iroquois tribes of North America which has a girl visited at the night by a person who, she believes, is her brother. So, this person has a double personality—a brother and a non-brother. In both the myths, even with intervention of precautionary details, the sexual union of the type of 'incest' takes place. For Lévi-Strauss these relations of son-mother and brother-sister form a bundle, and the brother-sister relationship is an inversion of the son-mother relationship. In the same way the question-answer forms a bundle that is related to the riddle, the parties changing in various myths. To these he relates the death of the Buddha as being the result of the disciple failing to ask the required question. So, in certain cases, there is a question which has no right anwer; in others, there is an answer which has no question. The latter is the inversion of the former. This, according to him, gives the types that obtain from analysing myths structurally— by arranging sentences horizontally in the case of each myth, the perpendicular columns revealing the 'bundles'—homologues, inversions etc. So the analysis indicates types. But what about the meaning for the whole myth? Such situations as question-answer, sexual relationships tending to what culture (of which society, in any way?) calls incest, the varied tests—by the father of the son, of the would be son-in-law by the father of the girls, a sexual act by an instrument other than the generative, parts of the body producing various creatures, fire producing creatures and so on are commonly met in stories, specially fostered by tradition (and hence gaining the status of a myth); and these could be bundled as 'methemes' (or whatever name we give them, including 'type'). However the point is whether these, as parts (bundles) of a whole, could be taken as forming an essential part of the whole myth? In other words, can such structural analysis lead to the inherent substance of a myth in which they form 'bundles' (even indicating relationship in themselves)? Thus, has the question-answer syndrome, together with the reflection of incest in the Oedipus myth, to be taken as necessary to reach the level of meaning in the Oedipus myth? How can 'killing' by different parties on the one hand and that of the dragon by the main character in the myth, on the other, be connected with the idea of incest; and how can incest (not only a sexual act) be connected and contrasted with the autochthonic nature of the birth of man? If all things together do not form a coherent whole, from which part or 'bundle' is the substance, that lies in the unconscious, to be gathered? This would mean that from each different bundle a different substantial message would be flashed. And, if we are to see a binary relationship based on a unit of doubles that stand in mutually opposite positions, are we to take the message of a conflict between nature and culture in all such relationships? In other words, are all such bundles of contrast, reflected (or seen by the analyser) in a myth, to be taken as motivated as the myth got formed and, later, developed due to additions and embroideries? If yes, each addition, or original part (which?) will have an independent motivation. But, this would go against the very basis of Lévi-Strauss' concept of structuralism, which proposes that the proof of the analysis is the snythesis and that structural unity is effected by the constituent structures. According to him, content is closely associated with, and gets its reality from structure. It is not necessary to examine the influence of the Linguistic method on structuralism or the philosophy of structuralism, and take a survey of the criticism of Lévi-Strauss on these points.[25] He has been criticized for developing a general theory on the basis of myths of South American Indians. He has also been criticized as having deliberately chosen examples from cultural areas where, in myth, structure predominates.[26] Kirk admits that Lévi-Strauss' idea about myths being especially concerned with mediating contradictions is a productive one in the case of the Bororo Indians, but may not be exactly applicable to myths recorded by the literary tradition. He also concedes the non-applicability of the concept of polarity and mediation to such other myths due to their being disturbed in the literary tradition and their structural emphasis being concealed. How far this could be true is a matter of separate investigation and would require thorough scrutiny, which appears to be a far cry. But, as he says, there is no denying that Lévi-Strauss' concept of structural analysis, as applied to the study of myths in general, is absurd in its stringency (Kirk, 1976, p. 84). This seems to be the case also with the Bororo Indian myths, in spite of Kirk's partial recommendatory concession (*Ib.*; but see,

p. 284). We shall see presently. However, bereft of the stringency, the method of locating the structures, in itself, without the halo of philosophisation that is attributed to it, is useful. The deficiency in the method is that the structures do not all relate to the meaning. Even the basic stand that "myths think themselves in men without their knowledge"[27] is acceptable inasmuch as it suggests myths to be *formed* and not artificially *made*. It suggests that myths have a hold on the human mind. But, beyond that, any rigid position is difficult to be accepted. Let us have a fresh look at the Bororo Indian myths. This is, as hinted above, in view of the concession that Lévi-Strauss' method has been given in the case of these myths.[28] The first of these myths[29] is as follows -

I. The myth of Geriguiaguiatogo

Long long ago, a man named G. (for short) followed his mother into the forest, where she went to collect some special leaves for the initiation of young boys at puberty. G. raped the woman (his mother) His father came to know of it and, as a punishment, sent him on a *mission* to fetch various kinds of ceremonial rattle from the lake of the soul. The mission was dangerous. But, G.'s grandmother advised him to take the help of a humming bird; and G. was successful. The father, then, asked him to go on other *missions,* the last being the one of catching parrots. In this, the father *stranded him on a cliff;* and G. hung on the *magic stick* given to him by his grandmother. Now, while on the mission G. catches lizards and tucks them onto his belt. These creatures get rotten; and vultures are attracted to them. They eat the lizards and also G.'s buttocks, with the result that the food eaten by G. goes straight out. The vultures, however, become friendly to him and give him fruits; and G. cannot retain them in his interior. G. suddenly remembers a tale the grandmother had told him; and, taking clue from it, makes potato-mash and forms his buttocks out of it. The remedy works and he can digest. He gains strength and comes back to his village in the form of a lizard, assumes his own human form and meets his grandmother. Now, there is a storm and all the fires in the village get extinguished except that of his grandmother. All women including the new wife of G.'s father ask for the fire and the father pretends to forget the past. But G. assumes the form of a stag and throws his father into the lake of souls with his antlers (thus killing him). The latter is devoured by large fishes. His lungs come up to the surface in the form of a special kind of floating leaf.

II. Now we take another Bororo myth

A boy follows his mother into the forest, where she is to gather fruit. He beholds that she is raped by a member of their own moiety (which is like a phratry of the same tribe). The act is considered an incest in that tribe, which is exogamous. He tells his father, who kills the offender and also the mother of the boy (his wife). He then buries the woman under her hammock, with four different kinds of armadillo (which are a kind of teethless mammals, and are ant-eaters). The boy searches his mother, but the father misleads him. The boy continues the search, now taking the form of a bird, which drops excrement on the shoulder of his father. The excrement turns into a tree which gets shorter every time the father stops; ultimately it diminishes completely and vanishes, giving rise to a tank. There is happiness all round. The father, who is the chief, makes ornaments and decoration.

III. There is yet another myth. (Brackets mine)

A young man refuses to leave his mother's hut, though he is expected to do so and mix with other men at the period of puberty. The grandmother does not like it. So, she goes to the man when he is asleep, clasps him tightly and smothers him with her belly-gas. The man gets up and kills her by thrusting his arrow into her anus. He buries her secretly with the help of four kinds of armadillo. An expedition to the river to catch fish, by suffocating them, follows. This is the usual method followed by the American Indians. The next day, the women go to the river to collect the dead fish. The young man's sister desires to keep her child with the grandmother (the one mentioned earlier, of course). When she does not find her (as she is no more), she keeps the child in a tree. There the child turns into an ant-eater (armadillo). The sister eats so much of dead fish that she suffers and releases vapours that give rise to diseases. Her brother kills her and throws the parts of her body into two specific lakes.

Lévi-Strauss has seen the conflict of nature and culture here; Kirk has also commented on them. But a fresh analysis is required. It is not necessary to give the details of homologues in horizontal and verticle columns; they could be jotted down, with differences —

I

★ Son goes to the forest with mother;

★ Mother has to gather special leaves;

★ The leaves are to be used in initiation of young boys at puberty;

★ Son rapes his mother;

* * *

★ Father *punishes* him - sends on dangerous missions—

(a) sends him to fetch ceremonial rattles;

(b) from the lake of the souls;
Another punishment by father, but,

(c) Grandmother helps the boy. On her advice,

(d) Boy takes help of the humming bird; becomes successful.

(e) Parrot-catching;

(f) Boy stranded on a cliff.

(g) Grandmother helps him; gives him a magic stick;

★ The boy gets lizards; ties them to his belt (cannot eat them enough); the rotten lizards turn to be disadvantageous; because the vultures eat them and also his buttocks;

★ The lizards are tormentors, yet turn friends;

★ The boy is helped by the grandmother - indirectly. The boy gets buttocks healed—turns healthy.

★ He takes the form of a lizard and returns - and assumes his own form.

* * *

★ Storm causes all fires to go out; but the boy's grandmother has it. (So the boy has control over it; the father stays away from her with his new wife).

★ Father proposes reconciliation; but is killed by the son, who becomes a stag;

★ Father thrown into the lake of souls; his lungs become special kind of floating leaves.

The dominant theme in the story, which could be divided as we have done, appears to be— (1) Initiation; (2) Sexual union, appearing to be incest (son X mother); (3) Testing of the boy on the part of the father; (4) Grandmother always helping the boy; (5) The control of fire; (6) The boy killing his father; and (7) Lake of the souls - with the ceremonial rattle, in which also the father's body is thrown.

The story begins with initiation and ends with the dead father thrown in the lake of souls.

II

Now, let us analyse the second story, noting the homologues and differences:-

★ Son goes to the forest;

★ Gathering of fruit.

★ Mother raped by a member of the same moiety — amounting to incest.

★ Father misleads the son; and the son tries to punish him in his own way, turning into a bird (which might compare with the helping bird in the first story, with an obvious difference). The strife between father and son.

★ Reconciliation of father and son.

★ Excreta→tree→lake; and ornaments; by stages.

The points of difference are— (i) the killing of the woman, though apparently she is helpless (she is raped); this is in contrast to her being kept alive, but separately, in story I; (ii) killing of the offender here, but not the boy (son) at I. This could be as the secret was not exposed outside, at I. However, the son was expected to die in the expeditions, at I; (iii) No indication of initiation; (iv) No grandmother; (v) The armadillo is an addition, as a help for burying.

III

The third story-

★ Even after nearing puberty a young man does not leave her mother;

★ Grandmother unhelpful; clasps the young man; emits gases; suffocates him;

- ★ The young man thrusts his arrow in her anus (indication? sexual act, but unnatural);
- ★ The armadillos help bury her;
- ★ The child turns into an ant-eater (= armadillo);
- ★ Child on the tree (like a bird?), the bird, ant-eater?
- ★ Sister stuffs herself with fish - gives out evil vapours - diseases; is killed;
- ★ The pieces of the sister's body thrown into two specific lakes.

Lévi-Strauss shows that the myth (with its variations) is about the origin of cooking, though this motif does not appear in the text. The storm in the first myth he takes as indicative of noise, which becomes manifest whenever the expected order (social order) was disturbed (incest?); that the domestic fire which unites the earth and heaven demands respect and silence, the indication, in this particular case, being that the fire went away. But, then, how could the fire be yet and only with the boy's grandmother who helps the boy who was a party to the (incest, though against the wish of his mother; as she was raped, resulting in the) disturbance of the order? And the man (father) who tried to guard the order and left the sullied woman (his first wife) has also lost the fire, along with others in the village! One feels the detail of fire has to be kept away from the earlier part of the myth. Even if we understand that the structure shows mediation between heaven and earth - the boy suspended on the cliff (I), boy turning into the bird (II) and the child in the tree being like bird (III) - what does it all indicate? To say that the mediation reflects a compromise between the extremes - Nature and culture, or hunting and agriculture, grass-eating animals and carrion eating (in the case of animals) does not totally suit in the case of all these myths.

It is not necessary to go into detailed criticism of Lévi-Strauss.[30] Suffice it to say that it is not always true that the meaningful content of a myth is entirely abstract. It may be acceptable that the various distinctions and items exploited by myths consist not so much in the items themselves but in common properties. However, it has been difficult to contribute to his view that they could be expressed in geometrical terms, and transformed into each other by means of operations that are *already* a kind of Algebra.[31] It also cannot be accepted that the purpose of a myth is to provide a logical model capable of overcoming a contradiction or a polaric situation. The point is, that, if myths have any purpose as such, how is structuralism of Lévi-Strauss different from functionalism except for the addition of an elaborate and complex concept of structures, he presents, including the presumption that such structures already exist in the human mind (compare Kant and Hegel). There is no doubt that Lévi-Strauss has been all the while confusing logic with flexible associability of concepts in myths to arrive at meaning. It will be better to say that myths divulge flexible mental or behavioural patterns, rather than rigid structures; the former would go well beyond the mere social structure. As is clear from Lévi-Strauss' own interpretation, he not only descends to etymology but also relies on content to tailor the structures.

In the case of the Bororo myths, the safer and easier way to the meaning is to group together the following concepts that show patterns, without discarding the details that may serve to open the mind of these myths.

(I) *Sexual behaviour*—

a. Son X mother (first account);

b. Mother X moiety-member, the son watching (second account);

c. Grandmother's clasp and the young man's arrow in her anus (third account).

'C' seems to be only a shady variation of 'a'; the 'arrow' standing for the young man's organ. The young man is in fact, the grown up boy at 'a' and his behaviour is on par with the boy in 'a'. One boy (at 'a') follows his mother in the forest, the other (c) does not leave his mother, even when he is expected to, as a grown up boy (man). The common concept in the behaviour is that of puberty. In one case initiation and puberty are clearly mentioned; in the other puberty is mentioned and initiation is implied; because in most tribes initiation is a necessary rite at puberty. In 'c' the fact that the 'man' has to mix with other men, *and leave his mother* (i.e., cease to be a child) indicates that the puberty-rite (initiation) is already gone through. In societies that have advanced ahead of the tribal stage, the initiation is marked by the last meal with children and it is administered by the mother. Among the Hindus, the *upanayana,* which marks the end of the stage of childhood, was performed prior to the boy's being sent to the preceptor, where he mixed with other boys and learnt various lores, *away from* the motherly care. He returned well after attaining puberty, if one calculates the stay out at least for twelve years. The *upanayana* (lit. 'taking near to the preceptor')[32] got fused, later, with marriage; and, it could even be (but must be) done just prior to marriage. If performed at the normal age, the *upanayana* is immediately followed by a mock proposal by the maternal uncle to give the boy his daughter in marriage. In the present case, the grandmother (c) is the shadow of the mother. But, it has to be clearly understood, that they are not from the real life of the boy. They are true only as far as the myth is concerned and serve to indicate the age of puberty. There might have been a necessity of the myth being narrated at the ritual at initiation, in which case it could have had the status of a charter; and if the myth, as it is recorded, did never have any association with the ritual, the backdrop of the ritual of initiation could hardly be denied. If we compare 'b' with 'a', it will be seen that the boy who watches his mother being raped by the member of the same moiety is a shadow of the raping boy in 'a', the point being the *indications of puberty* in the boy, though initiation is not specifically mentioned, as in 'a'. So, in all the three accounts, which may be taken as variations of the same concept, the reference to the acts is only symbolic, rather than a narration of actual human relationships. This is the main theme in this cycle of narrations. It is relevant to note that both in 'a' and 'b', the strife is between the boy and his father and the various tests are for the boy. He is the centre of the narration; and the same is the case with the 'young man' in 'c'. In 'a' and 'b', after the strife there is reconciliation, though in 'a' the boy, as a stag, kills the father, indicating the gain of authority by the son, which is an added point. Like the bird, or the vultures turning friendly, helping the boy in 'a' and like the bird being another form of the boy in 'b', the boy-stag in 'a' killing the father is not relevant to the main meaning of the myths. The excreta tree etc. are additions, subservient to the main theme.[33] It is difficult to say anything about the magic stick given by the grandmother. Wands and magical staffs appear in folk-tales. But, even in such cases, they are not restricted to a particular tribe. They appear to be suggestive of actual practices of gifts indicating attainment of manhood, and could be associated with initiatory or such other rituals,[34] though the association has got dimmed. The Greek Hermes has his magic wand and winged sandals. Heracles has his club (though associated later).[35] In one of the myths from the Asdiwal cycle the hero has his magical weapons in addition to magical shoes given by his father; and in another case in the same set the young boy named Waux, has a magical lance.[36] The lizards do not have a separate importance, in the opinion of Kirk, except for serving as food as the boy was to move on (1976, p. 283 and p. 287). May be. However, the lizard appears to be a totem symbol inasmuch as the boy himself becames a lizard. It seems futile to go in search for a subconscious level when initiation and puberty are clear enough in the myth 'a' and they could explain the main points in other myths. There is also no necessity for 'mediation' (birds, flying in the sky and coming on the earth, or the stick pointing skyward and earthward). One relevant point in all the accounts is the mention of the lake; and, in 'a' and 'c' it is directly associated with the dead. In 'a' the father's lungs float on the surface of the water in the form of a special leaf; in 'c' the sister's body-parts are thrown into the lake. There does not appear any hidden meaning here; these details appear to be from the general practice of the people, and indicate a probable belief that the souls of the dead stay in water.[37] Following Lévi-Strauss' analysis of the Oedipus myth, or the Theban cycle, it is possible here to group sexual details and contrast them with those of killing as—

I.	Son rapes mother	Son kills father	-
II.	A moiety-member rapes woman; son looks on	(a) Father kills a moiety-member (b) Husband kills wife	-
III.	Grandson's 'arrow' in grandmother's	(a) Grandson kills grandmother	-

anus, as she clasps him	(b) Brother kills sister
	(a) Grandmother suffocates grandson with her gas; (b) Sister gets stuff with (fish and) gas; (c) Fishes killed by suffocation.

But these hardly have relevance, except indicating that suffocating is a means of killing and that diseases get originated from body disorder, which is in the very narration. If these myths, collectively or individually, were narrated at initiation, a probability hinted above, all these details—suffocating of fish at the catch, burying with the armadillo, throwing the dead in the lakes and the souls seen as leaves—would appear to be part of general instructions to be given as a lore to the initiatives along with sexual awareness and its dangers, in secrecy, Hence these narrations were sacred, though now collected and recorded by scholars; and made public. One feels that, in a myth, or a cycle of myths, it is not always necessary to believe the substance to be entirely subdued by narration. It is necessary to take clue from symbolic concepts, which are part of the narration and are indicated therein, rather than seeing, in all cases, mediation between opposites expecting a contrast between, or transition from, nature to culture, or even expecting a solution of a contrast, say, in this particular case, between accepted sexual relationship and incest. This is not to deny, however, that such problems do not get reflected in myths; but the groups of myths noted above can hardly be taken to reflect them, essentially. It is always safer and profitable to take the clues from clear contexts rather than to go below to hunt the elusive subconscious, which may help in the case of an individual's dream. The same could be said in the case of myths, or, rather, the four versions of the myth of Asdiwal, collected by Franz Boas, current among the Tsimshian Indians of North America (British Columbia near the southern border of Alaska). Lévi-Strauss' method, even here, is out of focus. It will be proper to examine it. The myth of Asdiwal is more elaborate, and deals with the movement of these people from the river Nass, to the river Skeena, former being to the north of the other. In spring, they move from their usual winter habitat in the usual villages. The first myth is about two women - a mother and her daughter. Both move along the bank of the Skeena, but in opposite directions. The myth is as follows—[38]

The woman and her daugher are both widowed and famine-stricken. They leave their respective husband's villages, move from opposite directions and, when they meet each other they meet also a young stranger from upstream. He is also a bird. The women are poor and have scant to subsist on, having only a rotten berry in common. So, the bird-man offers food to them and takes the younger woman (daughter) as wife. The child born to this couple is named Asdiwal. Then, after some time, the miraculous stranger, bird-man, vanishes, giving the boy (Asdiwal) some magic weapons, snow-shoes and a cloak. In the meanwhile his grandmother dies and his mother moves along with him downstream to the grandmother's birthplace. Asdiwal grows into a youth. Once while hunting a white bear he goes into the sky, following her. There she turns into a beautiful young girl. Actually, she is the daughter of the sun, called 'Evening star'. Asdiwal marries her, after being put to various difficult trials and tests by the sun, his would be father-in-law. He comes down to earth with this wife; but, once on the earth, he deceives her and takes an earthly woman. The divine wife kills him (and not the new woman); but, his father-in-law (the sun) revives him and they both go to the heavenly world. He descends to the earth again, and his divine wife leaves him finally. So he takes up another mortal woman. As the spring starts (and the waters get warmer bringing the fish to move freely) he, his wife and her four brothers move up towards the Nass river. There is an argument about hunting on land (which Asdiwal prefers) and hunting on sea (which the group of four and the sister prefer). Asdiwal is successful with the help of his magical weapons, while the group does not get a good catch of fish. So, the four brothers and their sister leave him. He meets another similar group, and has again a dispute with this group also, when, after a successful fishing season, they return south for late summer and winter. The dispute is about hunting seals. This group of four brothers of his new wife strand him on the slippery reef, which he manages to climb with the help of his magic shoes. He manages to keep up with various tricks, going down at last to the home of the seals under water. There he heals the wounded seals and asks for a boat to go up-ashore. This is granted, and he comes back to the shore, where his sons and wife are waiting. The wife, with him, kills her brothers; and they live together for some time. But, Asdiwal, who loves to wander, abandons his wife and returns to the place of his childhood up the Skeena river. His son also goes with him. In the winter he goes up a mountain forgetting to take his magical implements. Hence, he is stranded and turns into a stone. Even this day he can be seen, it is said, there in the form of a stone along with his dog who also had been turned into a stone.

As pointed out by Kirk, Lévi-Strauss sees here a close parallel between (1) movements up and down the course of the river, on the one hand, and down in the water and coming up, sea-hunting and land-hunting, going up the mountain and getting stranded etc., on the other, indicating mediation between extremes; (ii) The paradoxes are that the mountain hunter gets stranded on the reef, which is a sea-mountain, and that the hunter of seals becomes their healer and gets help from them. (iii) Social relationships - of husband with wife; son with mother and grandmother etc. According to him, along with what is said above, the myth is trying to mediate a contradiction at the root of Tsimshian social life and presents a question, unresolved, about the tension regarding different systems of marriage.

In another version of the same myth, the adventures of Waux, the son of Asdiwal from his first human wife, are related. The main points are that he hunts on his father's hunting land, though forced to separate from him by his matermal uncles. From his marriage with a cross-cousin he has twins; but they get killed on the mountain. Like his father, Asdiwal, he forgets to take his magic lance and gets trapped half-way in the mountain. So, he shouts to his wife below to offer fat to the gods. But, due to some mishearing she eats the fat herself—and excessively, with the result that she bursts and gets turned into a flint. The flint, according to the narration, is still found on the valley. Waux, helpless, himself becomes a stone. Now, Lévi-Strauss' observations are interesting. According to him, the twins are weaker mediators and that even Waux is a weaker mediator; because, according to him, even cross-cousins are twins, and Waux is a twin of his wife as he is her cross-cousin. Thus, impliedly, the twins born to this marriage die on the mountain and Waux also meets the same fate. But, then, what about Asdiwal, who has a similar kind of death - getting stranded and turning into a stone? And there is hardly any indication of his being a 'twin' on any account. It may be noted, however, that Lévi-Strauss has the same observations regarding twins and the concept of twin-relationship even in his later study[39] (published after the examination of these views of him by Kirk, *Myth*, 1970, to which we have been referring above), as we shall note further.

According to yet another version, two sisters (not mother and daughter) travel downstream and upstream. One is married and has a daughter accompanying her; one has a handful of berries, the other a piece of spawn. A stranger meets them and is attracted by the maiden who is young. They unite and have a son born, named Asi-hwil. He marries a woman, having brothers. There ensues a quarrel; but his wife does not abandon him, nor he her. For Lévi-Strauss, this is also a weaker version, that the spawn and berries neutralise each other (how?) and that all values are transferred.

Kirk, who does not agree with the interpretation of Lévi-Strauss, suggests some points that need consideration. According to him the crucial facts are—[40]

1. Asi-hwil marries a stranger and lives happily.
2. Asdiwal marries a stranger girl, but is separated from her and dies because of his mistake, which includes his hunting spree.
3. Waux marries his cross-cousin, and dies because of *her* mistake (she does not hear properly).

He also says that, these conclusions do not require structural analysis. He adds (1970, p. 58) that many of the symmetries derive from the peculiar life-style and environment of the Tsimshians and from the ordinary symmetrical and antithetical tendencies of simple narrative, that do not rest on the general tendencies towards the expression of structures (inherent) in the human mind.

However, he adds, that the various marriages in the episodes may show a persistent structure. This is, by far, a reasonable suggestion, which would mean that—

(i) Structure may be seen, and could be isolated in a narration; but that,

(ii) they need not be inherent to the human mind, in a general way.

Kirk's position is that, in spite of symbolic values for particular objects in a myth - such as birds, excreta etc.— the meaning in a myth is to be found quite explicitly in its content seen in terms of some significant relationships (he has the particular myths of the Bororo in view at the moment) - the young man who clings too long to the women folk and resists initiation into the world of men, the excessive reaction against him by the father, and the role of excrement and decay. However, he does not make it clear whether the behaviour of the father, or the boy's behaviour in the Bororo myths, is a speciality of only these myths. If, as he says, social and inter-sexual tension caused by puberty, initiation and matrilocality leads to the 'disjunction' of the hero, or isloation from his normal locale and family connections, this could be taken as a general tendency (and not restricted to the Bororo myth). And it surely is, though Kirk does not probe the point further by adducing parallels. On the common basis, it serves to evolve a pattern in narration; and this pattern enters or is used in myths, which need not necessarily show or have any consciousness of the psychological tension. In other words, generally speaking, myths present types, which need not be taken as real psychological situations. Hence, what looks as incest in a myth need not always be taken as a real case of incest. These types may be given the name of structure, or even formats; they have a suggestive value and become symbolic. It has been well accepted that a myth, as a whole, may present a combination of many formats, or patterns; and it is difficult to press out one coherent meaning from all these patterns, or 'methemes' as Lévi-Strauss has it, that are found in it. However, some prominent structures do reflect a meaning depending upon the context or persistence of thought; other patterns help the main theme. In the case of the Asdiwal myths, the most prominent theme is hunting and the formation of a family; the migration along the course of the river depending upon the change of season is unimportant. The contrasts appear to be as follows—

1. Marriage with a stranger (exogamous) as against with a cross-cousin (endogamous). The suggestion is that the first is safer. Here, again, the twins do not have anything special to add to the meaning as such, nor is it necessary to stretch the idea of the twin to include cross-cousins.
2. Patrilocality and matrilaterality (as Kirk says); or, better, patrilocality and matrilocality.

In addition to this main problem of marriage and family reflected in these set of myths, the last version reflects the belief that non-offering to the gods results into calamity. The point of mishearing on the part of the wife supports it, as a transgression.[41] The calamity is two-fold (i) death of the hero and his wife; and (ii) transformation into stone. This is common with a similar detail in the main, and elaborate version, where Asdiwal and his dog are said to have got turned into stones, though the reason for this transformation is not given. Whether these details formed part of the original narration is difficult to say. In any case, these indicate an effort to localise the myth, sliding it to be functional, in the sense that it might have come to be narrated (later) in eulogy of particular stones (held sacred?). The practice is common and old popular myths come to be associated with places, at times the same myth getting associated with different places.[42] Yet another point to be noted is that of the exogamous relationship being described in a superhuman light, which obtains as a pattern in many folk-tales. The father of Asdiwal is semi-divine. The mediation in this case is supra-mortal, and becomes symbolic. This stranger is a bird, and imparts special magical implement to his son, who mediates between heaven and earth and ultimately wins the sun's daughter as wife. Here, the myth uses the pattern located also in the Wintu Indian myth,[43] where the father-in-law has the name meaning the sun (Sas). These special powers attributed to the stranger (and his son) place him on an advantageous footing; and he contrasts with the cross-cousin, who is not fortunate, the suggestion being that exogamous relationship is profitable. This pattern (or 'bundle', cf. the stranger in the last variation) enters the main theme and helps it. Other traits from folklore, the magic shoes etc., enhance the same theme, though they are add-ups from a different source and obtain widely.[44]

It will be seen that in a myth, many patterns get added up. Some enter the main theme, as a support, others hang on. Among these hang-ons similarity from other sources is observed. Sometimes, the main pattern resembles a pattern from other myths from a different cultural context. And, it is not always possible to account for it. Hence the alternatives of simultaneous origin or borrowing. For example, the Oedipus-mother forms a pattern as it occurs also in other myths. However, it will be incorrect to see in this an 'Oedipus complex' which was given currency by Freud and now rejected; for, in that case, the examples noted above will have to be interpreted as a subconscious desire in all males to kill the father and possess the mother. A chart of comparison will make the point clear. It will also show how it cannot be taken to be an archetype of the terrible Mother and the hero (Jung); because the patterns get mixed up; and sifting becomes necessary.

Incest (1) Oedipus - mother (Greek)
(2) Bata's son - mother (Ancient Egypt)
(3) Boy - mother (Bororo)
(4) Boy - grandmother (Bororo)

In this connection it may be well to mention a myth from the Hindu context. Dhṛtavrata and Mahī were husband and wife. After a long time a son was born to them. After the death of Dhṛtavrata, her husband, Mahī kept her son, Sanājjāta (lit. 'born after a long time' = *sanāt* "after a long time' and *jāta*='born') in the hermitage of the sage Gālava and went away to lead a free life. The son also was a wandering type and often strayed away from the hermitage. It so happened that, both Sanājjāta and Mahī came together at a place in the region called Janasthāna (This was also the name of the south Indian region where, during their forest wandering, Rāma and Sīta had stayed). Here they met often; and, unaware of their relationship, they got sexually united. The result was that the son suffered from leprosy. When he went and saw Gālava, the latter advised him to take a dip at a holy water place in the river Godāvarī, which flowed through Janasthāna. He did so and got cured. Thenceforth the place came to be known as Dhautapāpa, ('where sin is washed'), also as Pāpapraṇāśana ('Destroyer of sin')[45]. It is very clear that this myth has the charter-value. But, why 'such' a myth (or a secondary myth) got formed is the question. In any case, we can add to the four noted above, this as another example which would be—

(5) Sanājjāta and mother (Hindu; secondary myth).

One more Hindu myth from the Mathurā region in north India. According to this myth, a brahmin from the Pāñcāla country (modern Punjab) had five sons and a daughter. The daughter was married; but soon after her husband died, the young widow took the ashes of her husband and went to Mathurā, where she attracted the attention of a prostitute. The prostitute took her home, as she had no means of subsistence, and taught her to dance and also to sing. As years rolled along, the youngest of her brothers saw her when he had gone to Mathurā on certain business. He happened to meet her and had sexual union with her. He regularly went to the river, called here Kṛṣṇagaṅgā (which, in fact, is the same as Yamunā, whose water is believed to be dark [*kṛṣṇa*] in comparison with that of the Gaṅgā in popular belief). But after that day, as he took bath and came out he saw worms emerging from the pores of his body. This he experienced every day. A sage, Sumanta by name, saw this and asked him one day if he had committed any grave sin, even unknowingly. Later, when they met, the young man (brother) asked the young prostitute that night about her personal history. On hearing and knowing that she was his own sister, he was shocked. The sister committed suicide by burning herself. The brother also wanted to follow the same course, but was warded by the sage to stay on at the holy place, which would clean him of sin that would be discharged in the form of the worms, and that he would be ultimately free from it.[46]

Here in place of the mother, we have the sister; and there is no doubt that even here the story is of the type of charter, and may be called a myth as it is preserved in the tradition, like the one noted above, both being from the Puranic tradition. So, we may list it as—

(6) Brother-sister (Hindu; secondary myth).

But, here is one more. According to it a person named Durvinīta ("of bad behaviour") and his mother moved away from their native village and reached Gokarṇa. Here Durvinīta, once, could not control his passions and raped his mother; but, both repented later, and the sages advised them to go to Dhanuṣkoḍi (near the southern cape of India, known as Kanyākumarī; English mispronunciation, Kamorin). They went and had a bath there at the sea and were freed from their sin.[47] The pattern is—

(7) Son - mother (Hindu; secondary myth).

The last mentioned Hindu myth exactly resembles the first myth of the Bororo, but does not have, even remotely, the context of initiation. As a matter of fact, all these myths from the Hindu tradition occur in the context of holy waters, a bath or stay at which is said to wash away the sin of incest, committed knowingly or without knowledge. In the Bororo myth the context is clearly that of initiation, and the meaning is the attainment of puberty. Two of these myths from the Hindu context show a relationship that resembles one that of Oedipus, but it would, obviously, be straying away from the track to see in all of these the desire to possess the mother as a natural instinct, though killing of the father is absent. In the Hindu myths noted above, the meaning is that of warning about the possible sin,[48] and nothing more, while in the Bata myth, along with the reflection of a probable custom (as in the Oedipus myth) the frailty of a woman's nature is seen. What should be gathered beyond that will require some real exercise. Even granting the possibility, on the psychological level, of adoration of a son for his mother, with the desire to be near her, resulting into an awkward dream, all such myths cannot be taken to be reflecting the same 'subconscious'. The same may be said about the myth wherein the father is seen as running after his daughter. This will also mean that such patterns outstep the set 'subconscious', which is restricted to one aspect of human relationship. This will also show the limitations of the parallel between a dream and a myth, and how it is improper to say flatly that a myth is the dream of a society.

Claude Lévi-Strauss' method neglects the emotional and expressive content of myths even where it is pressing and clear. It tends to be excessively schematic and rigid, actually smothering the clarity which a myth would naturally reflect. This is true also of his later study in which he says, "structuralism, or whatever goes under that name, has been considered as something completely new and at the time revolutionary. This, I think, is double false" (1980, p.9). True. As M. Glucksmann had pointed out earlier (1974, p. 50) the notion of structure goes back to the 1920s and existed in an undeveloped form in the Anneé sociologique school. And the Sanskritist Dumezil's studies of Vedic and Latin religious texts are a point in this direction. But, for Lévi-Strauss, structure has certain fundamental properties that lead to the unconscious meaning, as we have noted earlier. That was his stand in 1955 and remained so later. Even in these lectures (published, 1980), he stresses that the level of intelligence of the primitive man and the modern man is the same. He once more stresses here that, "notwithstanding the cultural differences between several parts of mankind, the human mind everywhere is one and the same and it has the same capacities". (1980, pp. 17-19). But, this could be correct insofar as human emotions or behavioural patterns are concerned. The difficulty with Lévi-Strauss is that the structures and homologues, contrasts etc. he suggests to be in a myth are to be understood as inherent in the human mind everywhere in all circumstances and experiences, and that a myth should 'think' in every human mind as it 'thinks' in his own (Strauss') mind. In this he has logic in mind. This has been pointed out earlier, and will also be seen from fresh examples of myths which he gives in his lectures mentioned above.

The first is about the skate fish, which is said to have controlled the south wind. The skate is said to have released the south wind only when he promised not to blow all the time, but at a specific period. Since that time the south wind blows only at a specific period and men in that region fulfil their work in the rest of the period. Lévi-Strauss says that "the story never happened", but that we have to take it seriously; and, as a clue to the inner meaning, he poses a question, "Why the skate and why the south wind"? (1980, p. 21). That the story never happened and that we have to take it seriously (because the people who took it seriously?) is why we have to take it as a myth, because, it had gained traditional faith (a characteristic of a myth; as we noted earlier). The meaning of the myth, according to Lévi-Strauss, depends upon the balanced relationship (subconscious?) between the skate and the south wind, which is— (1) The skate, like all flat fish, is a slippery fish; but it is not slippery totally. It is slippery underneath, while it is rough at the back; and (2) It is large if seen from above or below, while it is very thin if seen from the side. An adversary may think he can easily shoot it with a lance or an arrow; but misses, because the skate can very easily slip. So, it has both a 'yes' and 'no' capacity to answer. In plain words (following Lévi-Strauss) the fish presents a unit of contrasts, a binary position. He further explains—while it is wrong and impossible to assume from an empirical point of view that a fish is able to fight a wind, from a logical point of view we can understood why images borrowed from experience can be put to use. "This is the originality of mythical thinking to play the part of conceptual thinking." As the fish is a binary operator, and so is the south wind, according to him, it presents a binary problem. Like the 'yes'—'no' status of the skate, the wind has 'yes' - 'no' status—Blowing one day ≐ 'yes'; blowing one (another) day = 'no'. This problem, according to Lévi-Strauss, the myth is trying to solve. According to him, though the myth is not scientifically true, according to the working of computers which work cybernetically, the myth is scientific (p. 22; and we may add, following Lévi-Strauss, the brain of the primitive myth-maker works scientifically).

The point is whether the south wind really blows one day and on the other it does not; or the blowing of the south wind refers to certain specific period, as mentioned earlier by Lévi-Strauss. And, if the latter is the case, does the skate fish (actually the group of fish of that type) appear when the south wind does not blow, and does not appear when the wind blows? So, when the fish is present and the wind is not blowing it is understood that the fish's presence checks the wind. In that case the seasonal advent and departure of the fish and the season of the south wind are important rather than the appearance of the fish, i.e., the shape. The periodic advent and departure could be profitably compared with the candle-fish and the salmon in the earlier myth of Asdiwal, necessitating the journeys - North and South— of the tribals in North America near the southern border of Alaska. The myth of the skate fish belongs to practically the same region, Western Canada. In the case of the myth about the skate what appears to be the meaning is that the fish is the main source of subsistence and the principal item in the economy of these people (as is the case with the sweet-potato for the Maori). This gave the fish supernatural status and, on the experience of its alternating with the advent and departure of the south wind, made him the central figure in the myth. This hardly warrants any binary nature, based on the appearance of the fish. The fish was not regarded simply as an aquatic creature. 'He' was on par with a human hero. This is clear from what Lévi-Strauss mentions in the beginning of the myth, reflecting the usual belief among the tribals— "The story is of a time when animals and human were not really distinct; beings were half-human and half-animals. To save themselves from bad winds many human-animals and animal-humans took part, including the Skate".

In other case in the same book Lévi-Strauss, with his structural approach, tries to show that a number of characters in various myths have to be understood as twins (*Ib.*, p.25 ff, "Hare-lips and Twins"). In this connection he refers to a record of a Spanish missionary in Peru (South America), named Fr. P.J. de Arrigava at the end of the sixteenth century (and published in the missionary's *Extirpation de la Idolatria del Peru,* Lima, 1921). According to it, in times of bitter cold, the priest called all the inhabitants who were known to have born feet-first, or who had a hare-lip (split lip) or who were twins. He accused them for being responsible for the cold; because, it was said that they had eaten salt and pepper. He ordered them to confess their sins. Lévi-Strauss tries to explain with the help of three different myths why the twins, the 'feet-first borns' and the 'hare-lips' are to be considered similar. For this he takes a jump (as he says) from Peru (South America) to North America, also conscious of the criticism levelled against him by people according to whom myths of a given population can only be interpreted and understood in the framework of the culture of that population. He takes a view that myths do not remain isolated and this view need not be questioned. In fact, this was also the opinion of earlier investigators which we have taken note of in an earlier chapter.[49] We shall now examine the meaning *he* sees in this fresh set of myths.

According to the Brazilian-Peruvian myth, among the Tupinamba, once a poor woman was on her way to meet her would-be husband who also was reported to be 'god'. While on journey she meets a man, who says to her that he is her would-be husband reported to be a god. (This must be taken to be on knowing from her the purpose of her journey). In fact, he is a trickster; and he succeeds in his trick. He unites with her and she conceives. Later on, she meets her real person; and gets pregnant even from him. After the usual period, she gives birth to two boys. These boys have mutually antithetical features and natures. One is brave, the other a coward. One is the protector of the native Indian tribe, the other of the white settlers. One brings fortunes to the native people, the other ushers in calamities.

From North America, especially in the north-west of the United States and Canada, Lévi-Strauss records a myth for comparison. He says that the myth is "exactly the same except for two differences—(1) Among the Kootney of the Rockey mountains there is only one fecundation resulting in the birth of twins; and these twins become the sun and the moon. (2) A variation obtains among the Okangans of British Columbia, which is a branch of the Salish language group. The region is practically the same as that of the Asdiwal myths. In this case there are two sisters and they are tricked by two men. Each one gives birth to a boy. Actually they are not twins. But, Lévi-Strauss says that, "since they are born in exactly the same circumstances, at least from a moral and psychological point of view, they are, to that extent, twins." By "same circumstances" he, probably, means trickery on the way. "Moral and Psychological" is difficult to comprehend. Whose morals and whose psychology, after all? From these narrations Lévi-Strauss deduces the homologues which would better be jotted down more clearly, to understand Lévi-Strauss' position:-

	Myth	*Parties*		*Result*	
I	Brazilian —Peruvian	One woman and Two Men	Separate concept-ions	*Twins* having mutually different characte-ristics	
II	North American — Canadian				
	(a) Kootney -	One woman and One man	One concep-tion	*Twins* (1) Sun (2) Moon	
	(b) Salish	(i) One sister and One man	One concep-tion	One son	Twins
		(ii) The other sister and another man	One concep-tion	One son	

Lévi-Strauss glosses that in the first version the boys are "not strictly twins as their fathers are different". To accept what Lévi-Strauss says, we should have to believe that the two boys were born at two different periods; which would also mean, that the real (would-be) husband met the woman after the birth of the son from the trickster; and from him she gave birth to another son. In that case, the boys can hardly be called twins. And if the real would-be husband (i.e., the second man) unites with the woman immediately during her first conception, i.e., just after the first man united with her, (and is believed to cause her to conceive?) the two boys born will have to be taken as real twins. It is not improbable that the myth has its basis in the actual birth of the twins, and works on the belief, in this tribe, that twins are the result of two different men having union with the same woman (though in fact this belief is not scientific) and brings in two men *to account for* the twins. In any case Lévi-Strauss' gloss is not clear. The myth, as mentioned by him, states that the woman had only conception from the trickster and also second conception (only) from the real person ('god'); but that she gave birth to two boys. The probability is that these boys were born together. Hence, they were real twins and the explanation in the tribal belief was, that this was because two persons (men) figured. Lévi-Strauss' position about the boys in the II-b (Salish) version is also that they are in *reality* not twins, but are "believed" as being twins. From his record, however, it is not quite clear if the Indians concerned believed them to be twins, though they are born to two sisters from two mututally different men, or whether the *word* the tribals used in their language is the same for these different categories of boys, and it has the *same accent*. Yet he says, "In any case this basic distinction of being twins or being believed as twins is a characteristic of all (these) myths'' (p.28). There is a further detail from the Salish version of two sisters and two different persons begetting a son, each on each sister. It is as follows:

After the tricksters trick them, the elder sister leaves her younger sister and goes to meet her grand-mother. This grandmother is supposed to be a mountain-goat. When she learns that her granddaughter is coming, she sends a hare to receive her. This creature hides under a log which lies in the middle of the road. When the girl lifts her leg to cross over it, the hare has a glance at her genitals; and he makes a remark which infuriates the girl. She hits him with her cane, with the result that the nose of the hare gets split. The myth closes with the aetiological statement, "This is why the animals of the leporine family now have a split upper lip."

Lévi-Strauss comments, "In other words, the elder sister starts to split the body of the animal" (p.29). He explains that, if this split were carried to the end and did not stop at the nose but continued through the body to the tail, she would turn an individual hare into twins (p.30). To support the split in the myth mentioned above as being indicative of the division of one whole into twins, he refers to a belief among the American Indians that, if a pregnant woman turns violently in her sleep, the fluid in her womb would get divided, resulting in the birth of twins. Further, he notes a myth from the Vancouver island about a little girl with a split lip, who succeeds in coming out of the basket, in which she is carried by an ogress on her back along with other children. The girl splits the basket with a seashell and drops out feet-first. Though he does not say so clearly, Lévi-Strauss intends to suggest that the girl's split-lip (= hare-lip) should be taken to be on par with her escape, feet-first. The observation of Lévi-Strauss on the last myth is as follows— The hare on the log has a crouching position beneath the girl's legs. This means that the hare is born from her with his feet coming out first (p.30). This is hard to accept. The hare was already there; and the girl steps astride it. Actually the hare is crouching, and not even standing. And, if he is to be understood as being in the process of *getting* born feet-first, one wonders if he came out with all his four feet! If Lévi-Strauss has in his mind a comparison with the little girl coming out of the basket, feet-first (the basket symbolizing the womb, though he does not mention it), that also is untenable. The girl's feet actually come out while the hare is already in a sitting position. We have examined his observation about the boys, in the previous myths, being twins or believed to be twins, when they are actually not so. This will show that, inspite of the structural analysis of the myths, the interpretation is laboured; and unwarranted. Hence, his statement, "So we see that there is in all this mythology an actual relationship between twins on the one hand and delivery of feet-first on the other" and that "this obviously clears up the connection in Father Arrigava's Peruvian relations between twins, people born with feet first and people with hare-lip" is questionable. The problem in Father Arrigava's account does not seem to be as Lévi-Strauss proposes. The incident recorded has two parts - (i) The twins, feet-first-borns and the hare-lips are accused of being responsible for the spell of bitter cold; and (ii) *because* they had eaten salt and pepper. To take the first. In the belief of these people such boys could be responsible for bitter cold or bad weather[50] as Lévi-Strauss rightly says; but that hardly means that the twins, the hare-lips and feet-firsts are meant to be related. And, one cannot take the feet-first to symbolize, or even thought to be equal to, the hare or the hare-lips, or the twins. The hurry to come out of the womb in the case of twins (as suggested by Lévi-Strauss, but not supported by any example by him) may be understood; but to equate it *metaphorically* (as he says, p.31) with the feet-first appears to be beyond the meaning of the myths, and also of their 'unconscious', though it might suit its ingenious interpreter, who might see in the out-coming feet haste to run out of the womb. And, then, what about the hare-lip?—Is it the same hurry, for which he gets punishment in the womb, though he is coming in the natural way—head first? It seems, one has to be extremely imaginative and patient to understand all this, and also be prepared to see in the girl with the cane the anthropomorphic representative of an uncompromising womb wielding the cane[51]—almost an aspect of the *vagina dentata!* Now, about the second part. Lévi-Strauss does not state if this second part is related to the first as being necessary for the meaning of the myths, which, according to him, seems to be that the three categories, viz. the hare-lip, the 'feet-first-born' and the twins are to be taken as the same. In other words, the hare-lip and the 'feet-first-born' are only twins, and stealthily eating salt and pepper on the part of these 'twins' (and not by others) was believed to bring bitter cold. The coordination of the myths and the report of the Father would give the following points:

1. Even the non-twins are twins (I and IIb = IIa);
2. The hare has to be taken as a twin, the lip indicating the start of a lengthwise cut of the whole body;
3. The girl's feet coming out of the basket stand for the 'feet-first' birth, which would make her a twin if she is cut across the body starting from the lower part where her feet (actually thighs) separate from each other and the cut reaches her split lips and even further;
4. All these categories are dangerous (to the mother and) to the locality;
5. They bring bad weather, and bitter cold, especially when they steal and/or eat salt and pepper.

Actually, the beliefs regarding salt and pepper, independent of the association with the twins and the other categories noted above, obtain.[52] Lévi-Strauss leaves away the point of salt and pepper, focusing attention only on the twins. But, while doing so, he leaves other important details in these myths, probably, as not important for the meaning of the twins he sees. However, these details appear to have relation with the belief regarding twins in these myths. They are: (1) The trickster and the real would-be husband are both outsiders, as they meet the girls outside the habitat; (2) The detail that the would-be husband is a 'god' indicates that he is from outside the moiety and the girls move out; (3) A further detail regarding the difference between the twins born is eloquent in this respect. One of the twins is said to be the protector of the white settlers, which means that the problematic reflected in this myth is not so much of twins, but of taking a husband from the native tribes or from the new white settlers.[53]

Even if it is accepted that twins are inauspicious, or dangerous, especially to the mother, there is absolutely no indication of it in any of the myths seen above. In the Kootney myth, on the authority of Lévi-Strauss himself, that it is "exactly" the same as the Brazilian, the twins are the sun and the moon, the motif being generally similar to that of the Wintu Indian myth of Sas (noted earlier). However, in the Sas myth the sun and the moon (not said to be twins there) appear to be detrimental to him, as they are produced when Sas is split by Chanas, his son-in-law. But, that can hardly be taken as a delivery myth. All these myths (I, II-a and b) appear to swing between sex and matchmaking. For the twinhood of the hare, and his birth, the myth cited above is weak. We have to look to the myth of the birth of the hare among the Winnebago and the Kwakiutle tribes, where the hare is shown as quarrelling with his (twin) brother in the womb (Kirk, 1970, p. 216, n.21). At last they agree to be born simultanously—one through the regular passage, the other from another part of the mother-hare, killing her. At the best, in the present context, we might place the relevant positions in the myths, mentioned by Lévi-Strauss, side by side as follows—

I		II	
Salish—Okangan (British Columbia)		Kwakiutle (North America)	
(A)	Girl-astride; upper position for *feet*,	Girl—Hare-lip (split lip) upper body.	(D)
(B)	Hare (split-lip) lower position (under the girl's legs);	Her legs, out of the basket, lower body;	(E)
(C)	Hare, born 'feet-first'.	'Feet-first' birth	(F)

∴ Conceptually ABC ≑ DEF

Having reached this stage in our discussion regarding Lévi-Strauss and his concept and method of structuralism, it has to be admitted with him that "it is absolutely impossible to conceive of meaning without order", by which he means structural analysis (*Ib.* p.12) and that a (seeming) absurdity, which reappears, is potent with meaning. But, the intricate analysis to which the myth is subjected often misses the meaning, rendering the structures disjointed. In his analysis he even takes recourse to metaphorization, which has to be seen as the first step for symbolization, and also to etymology. This is the acceptance of the fact that structural analysis is a good tool but remains only *a tool*. Taking a step ahead, it has to be admitted that the meaning does not often lie in the subconscious and that his method hangs too much on subjective interpretation. It is also to be accepted that the meaning or substance very often gets reflected in the symbolic patterns and beliefs that go to form the myth, depending upon the context in which they are arranged, if the myth is a complex one, some, or even one, being at the centre, the others getting subtly connected to the central one. Though symbols may appear similar in tribes that are culturally separated, their meaning may differ depending upon the particular tribe. However, it is not surprising that in certain cases, the symbol and the meaning are similar among such separated tribes too. This might indicate borrowal; or, that certain basic concepts developed similarly in the collective mind of these tribes or a society. From the myths treated by Lévi-Strauss, the meeting of a stranger is a pattern that seems to have developed a symbolic value ("foreign seed"); and the hare in the last myth appears as a variant of the same pattern, as he meets the girl on the road, though the situation has been presented with a different curve—the stranger having sexual union, but the hare looking at her genitals and wafting up an awkward(?) joke. To this is added the mythical explanation about the split-lip of the hare, which hardly warrants his being treated as a twin (or, a prospective twin if he is cut through!!).[54] The justification from the belief that the fluid in the abdomen of a pregnant woman may get divided into two producing twins is not appropriate. We have to make a difference between the split fluid developing as two embryos on the one hand and, on the other, one body being cut lengthwise to suggest twins.

From the Hindu context two examples could be suggestive. The Mahābhārata (Mb.) explains how Kṛpa and Kṛpī were born. Kṛpa was the ācārya (teacher) of Kauravas and Pāṇḍavas in archery. Kṛpī was his sister. It is said that they were born from the semen of the sage Śaradvat, which had fallen on a heap of reeds. The semen got divided as it fell. From one part a boy was born, from the other a girl (Mb Ādi 63.107). They were Kṛpa and Kṛpī. At another place the same text says that the semen of the said sage got ejected on seeing the nymph named Jānapadī (*Ib*.12.9.6-14). The text explains the names Kṛpa and Kṛpī as being due to the sympathy (Kṛpā) of king Śantanu, who later found them in a forest while hunting and brought them to his capital, Hastināpura (Ib.14-20).[55] The point to be noted is of the fluid getting divided - may be inside the womb, or outside the body in the form of semen - not one body split into two, unless there is some indication somewhere in the American myth (not referred to by Lévi-Strauss) of the parts of a body being called twins, to substantiate the case of the hare. The other example that could be cited from the Hindu context is that of the twins - Utatthya and Dīrghatamas. The myth reflects a social problem regarding marriage and whether a young brother could have sexual relationship with his elder brother's wife. It also connects with the practice of *levirate*. According to the myth, Bṛhaspati (the preceptor of the gods) was the younger brother of Utatthya. Utatthya had a wife named Mamatā. Once Bṛhaspati approached Mamatā and desired sexual union with her. At that time Mamatā was pregnant from Utatthya. While Bṛhaspati was in the act, the foetus of Mamatā began to object from inside. Bṛhaspati not only ignored the protestations but also cursed the foetus to be blind from the moment of its birth. Later, Mamatā wanted to get rid of the seed of Bṛhaspati fearing the wrath of her husband (as twins would indicate two fathers, according to the belief then prevalent?); but the gods advised her to bear both the foetuses. The son of Utatthya, born blind, was named Dīrghatamas; and the one from Bṛhaspati was named Bharadvāja.[56] The point at the moment is that of twins; but even here, there is no splitting on one body into two - let alone outside the womb. Now, here is the example of Jarāsandha, an Amerindian (American Indian) version of which (if any) might have served as an example of inversion for

Lévi-Strauss. Jarāsandha is said to have been formed of two halves, born from the two queens of Bṛhadratha, the king of Magadha (modern Bihar in India). The king was without a son, even though he had two wives. So with his wives he resorted to a sage, Caṇḍakauśika by name. The sage was sitting at the time under a mango[57] tree, and as the king was telling him the purpose of his visit, a fruit fell into the lap of the sage. He gave it to the king. The king, after returning to the capital, gave it over to the two queens. They cut it into two parts; each ate one part, and conceived. But when they delivered, half a male child was born to each. And they threw the parts out. An ogress named Jarā, per chance, saw them; but, instead of eating them, she joined them at their inner sides. As soon as the parts were joined a whole male child came alive. The ogress presented the child to the king. As it was the result of two parts joined together by Jarā, he came to be called Jarāsandha ("joined by Jarā"). The account says that the two wives of Bṛhadratha were twin-sisters, and daughters of the king of Kāśī, also that the ogress was, in fact, a benevolent spirit called 'House-goddess', to be worshipped, her figure being drawn on the walls. Here two half parts form one whole; they are not twins, though born of twin sisters. Jarāsandha was a real person, a king having a family-line after him. Later on Bhīma, one of the Pāṇḍava brothers, is said to have rent the parts away, which he threw in opposite directions inside-out; so they never came together.[58] Thus, the king was killed. This will make clear that, though myths many times show similar patterns, involving similar situations and characters, they may have different suggestions depending upon the beliefs from the particular tribe. Hence it is, that twins are both good and bad; they might be "killed in several tribes" as Lévi-Strauss says; but, not necessarily in all tribes. Even if the hypothesis of competitive hurry, in coming out of the womb first, be granted in the case of the twins, resulting in the death of the mother, that cannot be taken as the reason for killing them once they are out. Even when in one of the Asdiwal myths, that of Waux, the twins are said to die, that cannot be taken as suggestive of their *being* killed. In another case, where the twins are said to be the Sun and the Moon, there is hardly anything to suggest that they are evil. The beliefs are diverse. Among the Arunta (of Africa) both the twins are killed as being inauspicious; but among the Dahomians of Africa the twins are welcomed, while deformed children are killed. Among the Ainu of Japan only one of the twins is killed. Among the Witotas of Amazonia the second one that comes out is killed or is left in the bush to die.[59] Even among the Kwakiutle Indians of British Columbia (whose myth of the split-lip girl Lévi-Strauss mentioned) twins are believed to be transformed salmons; hence they are kept away from water lest they should become salmons again. The Tsimshian Indians of British Columbia believe that the twins control weather; hence twins are feared, not killed. The same is the belief among the Baronga, a tribe of the Bantu.[60] The same is the belief regarding the 'feet-first' born in some parts of India. But, this does not mean that they and the twins are conceptually the same and that they should be so treated on the physical level. So, simply arranging the homologues by the structural methods does not help suggest the meaning. Though it may be accepted that "myths think themselves in the mind" of man, the mind cannot be taken to possess rigidly fixed structures at all levels and contexts. It has also the natural faculty of mobility which creates psychic images and metaphoric superimpositions, that are adjustible and appear in myths.

References

1. Claude Lévi-Strauss, *Mythologiques,* Vol. II, Paris, 1966, p. 95.
2. Claude Lévi-Strauss, *Structural Anthropology*, (Tr. in English, from the Original French by Claire Jacobson and Brook Grandfest Schoept), Penguin, London, 1969 (1963), p. 206ff.
3. Also spelt as Jocaste, also as Epicaste; see G.S. Kirk, *The Nature of Greek Myths,* Penguin, p. 164.
4. This is according to Edith Hamilton, *Mythology,* p. 37f; according to another account, he was the son of Agenor, king of Tyre in Phoenicia, *Legends of the World,* (Ed.) Richard Cavendish, Barnas and Noble Books, New York, 1994, p. 158.
5. These accounts are from Edith Hamilton, *op.cit.*, pp. 372-91.
6. Miriam Glucksmann, *Structural Analysis in Contemporary Thought,* Routledge and Kegan Paul, London and Boston, 1974.
7. Greek *Kădmia*, Cadmean ≐ earth; on the basis of this myth, there is the expression 'Cadmean victory' which means a victory that is very costly to both the sides.
8. Edith Hamilton, *op.cit.*, p. 372; G.S. Kirk, *The Nature of Greek Myths,* p. 356f.
9. *Ib.*, p. 357 (from Euripides, *The Phoenician Women,* p. 638ff).
10. Dange, *Legends in the Mahābhārata*, Delhi, 1969, p. 292f, where other sources are mentioned.
11. Rundle Clark, *Myth and Symbol in Ancient Egypt,* p. 154; also Donald Mackenzie, *Myths of Crete and Pre-Hellenic Europe,* London, p. 303. There is a probability that the concept of the woman-headed and lion-bodied sphinx is the influence from the Egyptian source; but the concept is inverted. Unlike the sphinx, the ancient Egyptian goddess, Tefnut, was lion-headed; Donald Mackenzie, *Egyptian Myth and Legend,* Gresham Pub. Company, London, (no year), p.1. In the Gilgamesh legend a serpent is said to have seized the plant of life when Gilgamesh stopped to draw water from a well (or a pool); but in an earlier visual of the Etana myth, where a serpent is expected at the bottom, on the earth as against a bird on the tree, we see a lion, cf. Kirk, 1970, p.127.

12. One wonders if the 'teeth' are not suggestive of barley; for barley is referred to as 'white barley', Kirk, 1976, p. 251.

13. From the Hindu context, cf. the questions of the Yakṣa, who controlled a lake of sweet water and would not allow any one to drink from it unless he answered his five questions, Mb. Vana, Ch.s 311 to 315; another example is that of Bhīma, one of the five Pāṇḍava brothers, who was caught by a python. The python would not allow him to go, unless he answered his questions. Here, as in the case mentioned above, the eldest brother, Dharmarāja (Yudhiṣṭhira) arrives on the scene and answers the questions; see Dange, *Legends in the Mahābhārata,* Delhi, 1979, p. 296f. Bereft of the motif of the superhuman guardian, the question-answer motif occurs as easily as the Ṛgveda, in the dialogue called *brahmodya,* I. 164.34, 35. The question posed by the sphinx to Oedipus may be compared with the riddle-like narration, "the 'one footed' runs ahead of the bipeds; the 'biped' overtakes the 'three-footed' from behind; the 'four-footed' approaches at the indication of the two-footed, waits on him and watches the rows of the five'', RV X. 117.8.

14. Edith Hamilton, *op.cit., p.* 197; similarly, Priam, the king of Troy, sent away his son, Paris, because it was prophesied that the latter would be the cause of the destruction of Troy, *Ib.,* p. 256.

15. *Legends of the World,* (Ed.) Richard Cavendish, p. 91.

16. Mb. Ādi 67.152; Sabhā 22, after verse 36, Southern recension; Bhag. P. X Ch.1 and Ch.s 40-44. The account occurs in other Puranic texts. See Ch. "The Eighth'', *supra.*

17. Edith Hamilton, *op.cit.,* p. 373.

18. Donald Mackenzie, *Myths of Crete and Pre-Hellenic Europe,* London, p. 170. It is interesting to note how Demeter got to be the centre of a very late myth (or rather meta-myth). According to it, at Eleusis in Greece, an ancient statue of the goddess Demeter was worshipped, because 'St. Demetra' always afforded protection to crops, until the statue was removed by British archaeologists in 1801. The locals told the story that St. Demetra's daughter had been abducted by a Turk and the St. searched her for a long time. According to the original Greek myth, Demeter's daughter, Persephone had been carried to Hades (underground) by the king of the dead; *Legends of the World,* p. 288.

19. He is known also as Pṛthi and Pṛthī; ṚV I.112.15; VIII.9.10 etc., he is said to be the first king, Śat. Br. V.3.5.4.

20. Mb. Śānti, 59.98-113; later texts follow the account.

21. Dange, *Encycl. P.B.P.*, Vol. IV, p. 1134.

22. *Avesta, Vendidad* II. 10ff; also in SBE, Vol.4, p. 13f.

23. J.G. Frazer, *The Golden Bough* (Abridged), Vol.II, Macmillan & Company, London, 1957, p. 882.

24. From Donald Mackenzie, *Egyptian Myth and Legend*, London, pp. 45-57.

25. Attempted already by Mirium Glucksmann, *op.cit.;* G.S. Kirk, *Myth; The Nature of Greek Myths;* Peter Munz, *When the Golden Bough Breaks*, Roultedge and Kegan Paul, London, Boston, 1973; and others.

26. M. Glucksmann, *op.cit.*, p. 85.

27. *Mythologiques*, I, Paris, 1964, p. 20.

28. Also M. Glucksmann, *op.cit.*, p. 68.

29. From *Mythologies of the Ancient World*, Ed. S.N. Kramer, Garden City, New York, 1961; G.S. Kirk, *Myth*, p.64ff.

30. For which see M. Glucksmann, *op.cit.;* G.S. Kirk, *Myth*, p. 42ff; Peter Munz, *op.cit.*, p.x, 5-16.

31. *Mythologiques* II, Paris, 1966, p. 407.

32. For a full treatment, see Dange, *Legends in the Mahābhārata*, "The Legend of Kaca", esp. pp. 194-222.

33. How the excreta of the boy, himself changed into a bird, then getting turned into a tree which gets itself shorter, subsequently disappearing, can be taken as indicating a change from nature to culture, is unclear, unless symbolic meaning for excreta, tree and pure water is attached, or seen in that tribe. The change of the boy into a bird and a stag indicates new power gained by initiation—a common belief reflected in such myths; see Dange, *op.cit.* at n. 32; also Atharva Veda-XI.5.6-14.

34. In the Hindu initiation, such staffs of various length are prescribed for initiates of various castes, Manu II. 45.

35. Edith Hamilton, *op.cit.*, p. 34; Kirk, *The Nature of Greek Myths*, p. 184f.

36. Examined below.

37. G.E. Simpson, "Ideas about Ultimate Reality and Meaning in Haitian Vodun", *Ultimate Reality and Meaning*, Vol. 3, no. 3, Toronto, p. 192.

38. Franz Boas, *Tsimshian Mythology*, Washington D.C. 1916, examined by G.S. Kirk, *Myth*, p. 51ff.

39. Claude Lévi-Strauss, *Myth and Meaning*, Routledge and Kegan Paul, London and Hensley, 1980 (1978; Originally his Massey Lectures, 1977).

40. G.S. Kirk, *Myth*, 71; and earlier p. 56ff.

41. The detail of misunderstanding, or mishearing in this myth may be compared with that of the daughter-in-law in the Hindu myth of 'Gavhāḷī-mugāḷī' ('corn' meant, 'calves' understood); see Ch. III, p. 96 *supra*.

42. The Hindu myth of Kaca and Śukrācārya, later, got associated with certain rocks in the river Godāvarī, in South India; see Dange, *Lengends in the Mahābhārata*, p. 215; also the myth of the demon Loha and the place called Lohāṭigrāma, p. 87f. *supra*.

43. W.B. Olcott, *Sun-lore of all Ages*, New York, 1914, p. 14ff.

44. See notes 34 and 35 above.

45. Dange, *Encycl. P.B.P.*, Vol. III, p. 792.

46. *Ib.*, p. 810.

47. Skanda P. II.1.35; Dange, *Encycl. P.B.P.*, Vol. III, p. 792.

48. Manu II. 211-215.

49. See ch. I, p. 14ff.

50. See J.G. Frazer, *The Golden Bough*, (Abridged into Vol. I and II), vol. I, p. 86f.

51. Cf. the Hindu Devī with the sword, and the interpretation of Wendy Doniger O'Flaherty, *Sexual Metaphors and Animal Symbols in Indian Mythology*, Delhi, 1981, p. 83.

52. J.G. Frazer, *op.cit.*, vol. I, pp. 258; 261 for pepper, and for salt; Vol. II, p 670, 780, though the tribes differ: but see p. 182 for the belief and practice in a tribe from Nicaragua for salt; also p. 288f.

53. Cf. "Coming of the White Man", in *Legends of the World*, Ed. Richard Cavendish, p. 327f.

54. This idea of splitting the hare lengthwise is difficult to be substantiated even remotely from the belief in any of the tribes, nor has Lévi-Strauss done so. It is *his* interpretation, which one feels is stretched rather too far. Well, a myth which the present writer heard on more than one occasion in India about the creation of woman may be told. According to it, in the beginning of creation god created two figures from clay. To one he added breasts of clay, and gave it a split with an axe, in between the thighs. This figure became a woman. This is a creation myth; but, if one takes the split further up, to the head, it would mean (following Lévi-Strauss) that every woman is a unit of twins! The 'hare-lip', possibly, has to be taken as a category different from the twin, the only similarity being 'lip like a hare' and nothing further, the protrusion of a couple of teeth with the split lip being thought to be inauspicious. Such boys or girls are believed to be demons in their earlier birth, in some parts in India. The axe appears as a symbol of the goddess elsewhere, though not so much in India. For the double-axe associated with the goddess, see D.M. Mackenzie, *Myths of Crete and Pre-Hellenic Europe*, London, p. 160. In ancient Egypt, Neter (the supernatural female power) had her ideograph, which was an axe with a handle. Axe was worshipped in Crete, *Ib.*, p. 311.

55. Apart from this explanation, etymology appears to have played an important role in the names in this case. The Sanskrit root *kṛp* (alternating with *kḷp*, i.e., *ṛ* - *ḷ*) has the sense of 'cutting', 'dividing'. Twins are not generally believed to be inauspicious in India. The famous examples are Yama-Yamī (Veda), Yima-Yimeh (Avesta) and the gods Aśvins (Veda). In the case of Kuśa and Lava (sons of Rāma), there appears to be a faint belief that twins are born due to two persons figuring as seeders. The name Kuśa indicates grass (cf. Kṛpa-Kṛpī from reeds) and Lava indicates 'cut' in essence, from the root, *lū*, "to cut"; the account occurs at other texts also; see Bhāg P. IX.21.35-36.

56. This is according to the Bhāg.P.IX.20.36-39. According to a variant from the earlier period, Mamatā herself tried to ward off Bṛhaspati as she was pregnant through the seed of Utatthya, Mb. (crit.ed., *BORI.* Poona) Ādi 98.6ff; see Sindhu S. Dange, *The Bhāgavata Purāṇa, Mytho-Social Study*, Ajanta, 1984, p. 78.

In both accounts there is no mention of the belief, that twins are due to two men being involved. Such a hint is, however, reflected in the case of the twins of Sītā, who is (hence) discarded by Rāma. We may note an interesting news. An *in-vitro* fertilization resulted in the case of a Dutch couple; twins were born. But one was white (fair) complexioned; the other was black. The hospital sources came to know and accepted the mistake. The mother's eggs were accidentally inseminated with sperm from another man (from the Caribbean island of Aruba) along with that of her husband, in 1993—News, *The Times of India,* Bombay, 3rd July, 1995, p. 16.

57. According to another myth the mango fruit given by a sage to a man is thrown away by his wife. A cow eats it and, later, gives birth to a boy, who however, has the ears of a cow. He came to be called Gokarṇa ('cow-eared'), Bhāg.P. Mahātmya (='glorification'), 4.41-65.

58. Mb. Sabhā, 17.13-52 and 18.1-8; the killing of Jarāsandha by Bhīma, *Ib.* 23.10-24.7, especially 24.7.

59. J.P. Murdock, *Our Primitive Contemporaries,* New York, 1957 (1934), pp. 34, 178, 578.

60. J.C. Frazer, *op.cit.,* I, p. 87.

Five

History, Typology and Proto-philosophy

We have hinted earlier at the concensus of modern scholars, that the method of structural analysis has its limitations in getting to the meaning of a myth. We have also seen how this method adopted by Claude Lévi-Strauss is too individualistic and squeezing. Hence we have proposed, that symbols and symbolic expressions that appear to have developed in the tribes, or a society, may help a long way in reaching towards meaning. It should be noted, however, that the use of symbols, and the search for them in the myths or legendary accounts which get woven with the texture of mythical elements, has been already hinted at far earlier. The theories which are based on such investigations are known as psychological. Even the Freudian school which takes help from structural analysis and tries to get at the subconscious in the sphere of interpretation of dreams depends upon symbols. In a way, even Claude Lévi-Strauss contributes to the power of the psyche when he speaks of the myths "thinking themselves in the mind" of people, and takes the concept of the subconscious in myths from the Freudian school. On the basis of the supposed similarity between dream and myth (Karl Abraham, *Dreams and Myths*, 1909, Eng.tr. 1913), to call a myth "fragment of the infantile psyche" and to believe in an, 'Oedipus complex' (Freud) may be a thing of the past.[1] However, the fact cannot be denied that, like dreams, myths do reflect certain symbols; and they cannot be neglected. Speaking about dreams of flying, Kirk suggests (1976,p.87) that they may help to unfold the meaning behind the Greek myth of Learus flying towards the sun or Bellerophon on Pegasus. He does not elaborate. Actually, the Bellerophon-Pegasus detail is a variation of the Perseus myth. Perseus has the winged sandals and Pegasus is a horse with wings. The source of both is the bird. The flying here need not be bracketed merely with dream-flying, when the bird is a visual in actual life. The hero-bird in the tribal Asdiwal myth and the sun-bird in Vedic symbolism are more examples in the context.[2] The Freudian explanation of floating-on-water dreams as unconscious reference to the embryo is likewise inadequate. Such dreams indicate disorder in the air in the body according to the Hindu medical treatise.[3] But, it is not only the Freudian, including C.G. Jung, who saw in myths and dreams the collective unconsciousness of a tradition. Joseph Campbell, for instance had said that myths and dreams came from the same place.[4] According to him, myths are the world's dreams, that they deal with great human problems. When he says that dreams and myths come from the same place, he means that they are reflections of the mind, i.e., they have a psychological basis. One (the dream) is the product in an individual; the other in the society, through ages. For Jung, the same is the position—personal dream and archetypal dream; the latter has the mythic dimension. The theory that equates dreams with myths works on the belief that their formation is similar, that both have their source in real experiences, which appear rearranged in dreams or myths, with variations and additions, through layers of time. This is true to some extent. But this similarity cannot be stretched further. Like the element of etymology in myths, Anna Faraday has dreams sometimes working on puns; which is only a type of rearrangement in meaning. She avows that she has come to the various observations regarding the meaning (or messages) of dreams through group discussions and examination of dreams of the members of her groups. Thus, as an example of verbal pun she mentions a person seeing himself in dream as being clad in *gilt* (gold), and interprets it as a sense of *guilt* in the subconscious. In another case a recurrence of 'base-ball' game in the dream would indicate, according to her on the basis of discussion with the group-members, some 'base' (low) act which haunts the mind in the subconscious. A tormentor named Long John may give the image of a man wearing 'long jeans' and so on.[5] May it be as found out by Anna Faraday, and she has many other instances gathered from actual group-discussions. But it is the experience of all that events and personalities in real life are stored into the brain and are recast, during the Rapid Eye Movement period, in fanciful combinations. These are 'real' for the duration of sleep, though not factually real. Apart from the Freudian sex-based complexes, these dream-experiences do turn into symbols, or are presented into symbolic indications. From personal investigation (by the present writer), it has been noticed that similar dream sequences, or dream images, would indicate different emotional tensions in different subjects. It has been noticed that swimming in dream would indicate a probable attack of cold in one case, while in the case of another person, a desire for cool air, and in yet another one, it may be the result of actual raining as he is sleeping near the window. Such dreams are only circumstantial. But there are others—deeper. Fear may in some cases take the form of a terrible beast (the common being a bull, a lion, or tiger); and the overcoming of fear in the dream state itself has been, in some cases, seen as the beast becoming friendly, a cobra being cut into pieces or simply receding in a hole in the wall. The last one need not be indicative of sex (as the present writer has verified from a number of cases). In one case (under investigation) a person's most often repeated dream was of missing a train. The person reported that, in the dream, he goes to the station well in time, waits for the train; but when it arrives he sees that it is not *his* train; or, in a variation, he runs and reaches the platform only to see the train already moving. On investigation, it came to the fore that this dream occurred when he was appearing at an interview, or when there was some appointment to be kept. A further investigation led to the detail that he had once actually travelled unreserved and was ordered out by the Ticket Inspector; and he was always nervous when taking travel. Here train-travel is real; so is the interview or some such situation, which caused nervousness. But the dream takes the missing train from real life and joins it, in the subconscious, with an oncoming situation of uncertainty. Thus, the missing train, in this case, becomes the symbol for nervousness. Here is another case. One of the commonest dreams of this person has been the visit to a temple. This temple shows itself in various sizes, sometime, with worship in progress, sometimes not. However, he can very rarely remember the idol in the temple; he even says that no idol is seen in the *sanctum sanctorium*. Investigating into the circumstances of the occurrence of this type of dream revealed that it occurred mostly when the person was heavily worked up with some problems. And, did he frequent temples in any period of his life? Yes! Way back in boyhood his father used to play on the harmonium when his (father's) *guru* performed *kīrtana* (a particular type of devotional story-telling with solo acting in a temple before the idol of a god). In his later busy life, this sort of dream acts as a pacificatory aid and removes tension. The temple, with its atmosphere, stands as a symbol, even as in real life, for pacification—the god, or his idol does not matter! A further step is the codification of dreams and relating them to expected future events. This starts divination and fixed symbolization.[6] But the process has its root in an individual's dream-experience, which, when made public, sets in motion the process of generalization. Myths act on similar lines. An individual's reaction to a situation, or to an experience, in real life gets expression; it fattens up; gets currency and the details get a symbolic status. Both, a myth and a dream, are rearranged and recast fragments of realities that assume fantastic forms. They are not false; they are quasi-real. In the Hindu tradition the dream is described not as false (*mithyā*), but as *anṛta* (ṇon-real'; may be ḷike-real[7], cf. ṚV VII.86.6 *svapnaś cana-id-anṛtasya prayotā*, "The sleep [dream]; is, indeed, the mixer of the non-real)". The similarity in the formation of a myth and that of a dream is this much; and only this much. But, beyond this it cannot be stretched to say, with Jung, that a dream is a myth of an individual and a myth is the dream of a society. It is possible to delve deep into the subconscious of an individual on the basis of a series of *his* dream. It is not possible, nor it is necessary, to assume a subconscious of a society (or a tribe) which could be reached through a series of myths, even structurally analysed; more so if the versions of myths are separated from each other in time and territory, getting embroidered with additions. It is also not possible to comprehend the 'collective unconscious' in relation to a society.

Peter Munz, taking a brief critical survey of the various theories regarding the meaning of myth noted above, and not agreeing with any of them as constituting "a royal, let alone, absolute" way, complains that Lévi-Strauss neglects the historical nature of seriality because he sees "every member of the series (of a myth) as a mere repetition of a message." He advances what he calls, a theory of typology, or "theory of the significance of substitution".[8] According to him, the substituted version of a myth stands to the version substituted for as a symbol, not a sign. To point out the difference between a symbol and a sign he says—

(i) A sign merely duplicates the thing it signifies. It can be dispensed with without any loss of meaning and be replaced by the thing itself. A symbol is more specific and precise in meaning. A thing is the meaning of a sign; but a symbol is the meaning of its thing.

(ii) A sign and the thing are easily interchangeable. But the thing and symbol are not. The word 'sheep' is a sign for the beast and can be substituted by the actual beast. However, a 'spire' is a symbol for the phallus. The phallus receives a special meaning when it is symbolized by the spire; and the spire is, therefore, the meaning of the phallus, "because its meaning is more specific than the meaning of the phallus taken by itself" (*Ib.*, p.xii).

The difference between a sign and a symbol, mentioned above by Munz, requires to be examined in the context of the myth. He has already stated (as noted above) that the 'substituted' version of a myth stands as a symbol for the earlier (or, the original) version. In this he assumes, that (i) the later version is a deliberate effort; and (ii) it is an effort to make a symbol (or, to leave the option for Munz, we could say that the subsequent version assumes the status of a symbol). Read with his statement, that this symbol (in the form of a later version) "is irreversible because it presents the old theme in a more specialized shape" (p.xi), we have to believe that the real meaning of the earlier version of a myth has to be seen in the later one. But, he goes on to say that "since the symbol does not receive its meaning from the thing symbolized (in this case, the earlier version of a myth), *the symbol itself lacking in meaning, unless there is a further symbol for it,* a series of symbols feed back the meaning to the original thing" (p.xii). Earlier he has stated that "a symbol is a meaning of its thing"; and now he says that even the symbol lacks in meaning, unless there is a further symbol for it. This appears, on the face, confusing and self-contradictory. However, if we put it systematically and more clearly, it would help understand what Munz has to propose - A symbol gives a special meaning to a thing (or to a concept, or a story or a statement, or what not!); but, that symbol and that meaning are only a temporary phase. It should be taken, as the first stage in proper (?) symbolization. In a subsequent period, or context, that meaning may change depending upon the additions to, or substraction from, that temporary symbol. Thus, we have to go on expecting changes in the same symbol. Till the final form of the symbol is known, the meaning of the thing cannot be decided. But, in that case, when do we (or, rather, a posterior person, or society) arrive at the final meaning?— Who knows? In our present efforts to know the 'meaning' we have to take a series *and stop somewhere* at the records at hand. *Historically* speaking (as Munz would want us to be satisfied), we stop at the last *available* (or recorded) version and 'Feed back' to the original the meaning that obtains in the last *available* version. However, the meaning may have to be modified (later - now or in future—) if something as can be called a version of the same historically gathered 'ṣymbols' of the original thing crops up afresh. This will mean that a symbol would never give the exact meaning, as it is always in a flux, like one's reasoning (cf. the famous Upaniṣadic saying, *tarko' pratiṣṭhaḥ*). The difficulty about Munz's argument is, that it confuses a total myth with a symbol. Also that he is hardly clear about the concept behind a symbol. He admits that, as time passes, the substitutes of a myth (which he equates with symbols) do not occur in the same society and in the same place. In that case, there will be a diversity of symbols; and the meaning of the original will yet be a far cry. It should be noted that Ricoeur, P. (1967,pp.15-18) has already hinted at the historical method in his historical-philosophical studies of religious myths, and symbols. According to him, myths are merely elaborated symbols. Munz does not evince acquaintance with this view of Ricoeur, which is, however, restricted to religious myths. But, it will be better to examine the view of Munz, that a whole substituted version of a myth is a symbol, in the light of the view of Ricoeur. Giving the different facets of symbol, Munz (p.60f.) supports its importance, because lingual or literary expressions are many times unable to give an exact idea of a concept or feeling. Using the words of T.S. Eliot ('Hamlet and His Problems", in *The Sacred Wood*, London,1926), he says that a symbol works as an "Objective correlative". He explains that, in certain cases, the same symbol may stand for many diverse feelings (and, we may add, more than one objects), thus incurring the fault of 'poverty effect', while in other cases many artificially conceived images (read symbols) indicate the same feeling showing the defect of 'abundance effect'. Whether the second case can legitimately be taken as symbol is a different question, the point being that symbol has to have a tradition. A symbol may be in the form of a design, an image, or even in that of a lingual expression; but it stands for some thing which is beyond it and to which it is sought to be correlated. As Ricoeur says, a symbol has 'ḍouble intention'. First is of a 'lịteral meaning', while the second is the one to which the first points. This second one has relation to the Ultimate reality of the sacred. In this context of the sacred, Ricoeur says that myths are merely more elaborated symbols. The implication is, that already conceptualized ideas that gained the status of symbol become myths when explained and communicated through the medium of lingual or literal expression. This comes close to Cassirer's view that myth and religion are continuous, and that myth is a 'ṣymbolic form' of expression (*The Philosophy of Symbolic Forms,* Vol. II, New Haven, 1955). Cassirer's position is that a myth cannot be tested on intellectual norms; because it is not allegorical in nature. This compares with the view of Ricoeur that myth resists an allegorical interpretation, which would do away with symbolical understanding (1967, 167f). Writing six years later, Munz says that myth fills the gap between the logic of theology and the belief in incarnation (p.64). It will, thus, be seen that Munz's thoughts regarding the mutual relationship between myth and symbol show a reflection (or influence?) of the views of Cassirer (1955) and Ricoeur (1967); but, while these earlier scholars have the religious context in view, Munz extends it to areas beyond religion, rendering his contention, that a whole substituted version of a myth is a symbol of the earlier 'type' or the initial actual event, unacceptable.

As is very well known, a symbol (Greek *symbolon,* 'A token', fr. *syn*, 'association' and *ballein*, 'to throw') implies continuous association of the thing which it is expected to stand for. The main difference between 'sign' and a 'symbol' is that the former works in a narrow limit of application, while a symbol has no such limit. A sign may even be individualistic, as is the case with the 'signature' or the 'signet' ring. A symbol has to be accepted by a group, tribe or a society as indicating what it implies. A sign, as has been said by Munz, stands for a thing itself; but a symbol indicates something else—in many cases, beyond itself. Thus 'अ' in the Sanskrit language (and the languages derived from it) is a sign for the guttural back short vowel; but, 'ॐ' stands for all the vocal sounds - and, even further; it stands for the ultimate 'syllable - Brahman', the cosmic sound and even sublime peace in almost all faiths that originated in India. It breaks the limit of sign, becomes a symbol. Likewise, the lotus goes beyond its own objective and pictorial limits and stands for various objects and concepts, including the sun, the universal womb, the first ever expression of light and so on, depending upon the context in which it is accepted. A myth is a narration. It is extremely rare that it is wholly a symbol. It uses already current symbols and symbolic concepts on occasions, as it grows, or gives rise to new ones which get currency. In each such case the use might tend to introduce a different shade in the meaning. For example, the motif of the mother-son sex is, formally, similar in the Oedipus myth and that in the first Bororo myth, as we have already seen. But, while in the former it works on the practice of a winning king taking the wife of the defeated and killed king coupled with the apprehension of the winner being, possibly, a long lost son, in the latter it reflects the new manly status of the son.[9] In both, however, the *act* of sexual union might never have taken place. For this the Bata myth is a testimony, though the Oedipus myth mentions the sons of the hero born from this union. However, an important lever in the myth is the status of the Oracle of Apollo at Delphi and the determination of Laius to counter it. Looked from this angle, the myth appears as a charter to heighten the importance of the Oracle, and casts doubt on the reality of Oedipus being a son of Laius, after all. Moreover, in the version at *Thebais* there is no incest.[10] A faint hint to this effect obtains from Kirk's doubt about his name and that of his grandfather with the comment that he does not fit well in the early history of Thebes, though Kirk is hesitant and never touches the point of the status of the Oracle vis-a-vis the determination of Laius. Another detail in the life of Laius is that he had raped Chrisippus, the son of Pelops. For this Pelops cursed his line. The inversed juxtaposition is - somebody's son is wronged by Laius; and his own son, now, wrongs him; both involve sex and curse.[11] In the light of what we have proposed above, the mother-son act appears more symbolic than real, and may be compared to a dream (not unusual, as verified from reports) of a similar nature. This act in a dream might indicate intense attachment to one's mother, or a strong desire to get a wife who will be like one's mother, which is only an inversion of the motif in the European myth of the king who proposed to his daughter to be his wife, as noted earlier (chapter Two).

We have pointed out how Munz's suggestion that a substitute version of a myth is a symbol and the assumption of a whole myth being a symbol is defective. But it is necessary to see the purpose for such an equation on his part. This lies in the basis of his method, which he calls 'Historical' and regrets that earlier scholars, including Lévi-Strauss, missed it. He admits that, in his study of myths, Lévi-Strauss is aware of the historical dimension, inasmuch as the latter takes into consideration the necessity of collecting all available versions of a myth; but he complains that in his study Lévi-Strauss pays scant attention to the history of a myth and its versions. In his approach, according to Munz, history plays a subordinate and accidental role. This is true, as Lévi-Strauss feels it unnecessary to hunt for the authentic version; for, his structural approach has no need for it, as it fixes attention on the subconscious and undermines the narration as such. Munz blames Lévi-Strauss for taking Freud's version of Oedipus as part of the material to be considered and comments, that Lévi-Strauss "does not attribute any importance to the fact that the Freudian version is later than that of Sophocles and that this time-relationship between Sophocles and Freud should make some difference" (Munz, p.23). He stresses that a historical approach makes a significant difference in the meaning of a myth. He feels it "strange that Kirk, one of Lévi-Strauss' most elaborate if sympathetic critics should go even beyond Lévi-Strauss in his rejection of the historical life of every myth." (The present writer is unable to find such rejection in Kirk). Munz does not approve of the belief of Kirk that, as a result of changes a myth gets 'heavily polluted'. On the contrary, he says, the various shifts and displacements are not due to carelessness, but design (Munz, p.25). Munz does not stick to the idea of studying the myths of a particular tribe or of a particular region and proposes the selection "from different cultures and traditions". He proposes the division of a myth into episodic components (which is not unsimilar to the division already suggested by Lévi-Strauss, and far earlier by G.L. Gomme, 1908). One must, he says, sort out all myths in which a hero is wandering through the world etc., or in which he is sacrificed, and such other components. One must search for the earliest tales, add to them the more literate treatments and end up with the most sophisticated ones. This is all very well acceptable; and there is not much difference in this method and the one adopted even by Frazer. However, with Munz, we have to correlate history with the collection and arrangement according to themes. And this not only from one tribe or culture but even from different cultures and traditions. The difficulty about the mutual correlatibility in the method of his has not been considered by Munz. This division and arrangement of the myths would lead to a typological series, according to him, and what would be gathered from this process is—(1) That myths have a history; and (2) that myths are not generated or created as fully-fledged, but are gradually elaborated from simple general tales into more and more specific tales. The earliest stage in this series is not of an uncorrupted version. It is of a type. His method is for the search for a type which, according to him, is the most unspecified version, while the subsequent accounts are progressively specified. The earliest is type, while the subsequent ones are anti-types. As an example he refers, in short, to the various (historical) stages in the myth of Oedipus:

- Oedipus, a warrior killed in battle and buried with traditional funeral rites (*Iliad*);
- Marries his mother (incest), after killing his father and continues to rule even after her death (*Odyssey*);
- Begets children with Euryganeia (hence, no incest) (*Thebais*);
- Incest established; parricide happens on the road from Thebes to Platea, at a place called Patniae, the meaning of which indicates 'place of the Furies' (treatment by Aeschylus);
- No Furies; introduction of the Delphic Oracle (Sophocles) (p.26).

According to Munz's method, the last 'anti-type' is the most specified and holds the meaning, though it is unclear in the earlier anti-types and even in the type (i.e., version 1). He would have us believe that all these 'substitutes' are made on purpose, deliberately. Though this does not help show how these deliberately fashioned substitutes are symbols of the 'type' (and the point of 'symbol', thus, hangs in a corner), we have to believe that, all these earlier sources were striving in complete unison (as if in a common Project). This is hardly the case. The fact is, that deliberateness would tend to bend the original myth (which Munz calls 'type') to one's own purpose, making the effort subjective, which would hardly guarantee the safeness of its original meaning. Actually, the additions, or eliminations, would indicate the influence of later periods; and, though they may not 'pollute' the original myth, there is no doubt that there will be a remarkable modification in the original meaning. On closer consideration it becomes evident, that this method of Typology is not only unsound; it is dangerous; because, it saddles a simple narration with later and unwarranted sophisticated metaphysics. This is not to deny that an ancient myth may be engineered, in later times, into a metaphysical principle; but, with the 'feed-back', the same principle cannot be seen to be the original intention in the original ancient myth. From his example of the Oedipus myth 'A warrior killed in battle and buried with traditional funeral rites' would be the type; and each of the later ones will be an anti-type; the one just prior to the final anti-type will be a semi-final (so to say) anti-type and would indicate that the meaning of the myth depended upon the Furies; and it would be that the Furies control the fate of men. (Will it really be, as a whole?) But, this is again, tentative; because the final 'anti-type' with the Oracle is yet to be reached. When it is reached, the content of the whole myth has to be taken as that 'Oracles played an important part in the life of Oedipus'. And, with the 'feedback' every anti-type to the very 'type' will have to be taken as permeated with this meaning or context. But, is it so? In that case, the myth will become an insipid didactic tale. Or, might it be taken as indicating the status of the Oracle at the period?

Having fixed his attention on historicity, or a typological series in his own way, Munz appears *not* to take into account such types of myths that have their origin in the natural phenomena, or the Bororo myths where history or chronology is hardly in the picture. As a matter of fact, most unrecorded (= unwritten) myths would have to be kept away from this method. His suggestion regarding the formation of a myth, not the typology, however, holds good even for natural phenomena. When he says that "Myths are no more than extreme cases of metaphors" (p.55), this could be taken to apply to natural phenomena. Also is acceptable his suggestion (which, however, is not new) that natural events get turned into myths by deflection or embroidery, and by depriving them of their connection with a location in time. However, when he says that the myth is the first step in a series, "the top (of the series) being a problem to search", he creates a problem for the acceptance of his stand, as far as the meaning of a myth is concerned. He gives an example for his typological system: Jesus Christ is crucified. This is an actual event. The next step is, a story with the addition that he was 'son-of-god'. This is the first deviation for mythicization. A further version is as "The Trinity sacrificed itself in order to redeem the world it created". This can be transformed into further speculation that "the world turns back upon itself in order to continue the incessant creation of itself by 'itself'" (p.46).

But, then, this could only mean that *certain myths* get worked to formulate, or stand as illustrations of metaphysical speculation. But nothing beyond that. How this typological series helps understand the meaning of the very first event is a big problem! This illustrates, as already pointed out earlier, how the simple original event or myth gets burdened (and overburdened) by subjective embroidery, which actually smothers a myth (in this case, the first deviation of an event into a myth), ultimately nailing it on the cross of metaphysics. To see the metaphysical essence of the last 'anti-type' in the first deviation (type) is to put the investigation off the track. Far less is it safe to take every myth as the seed for metaphysical speculation. Munz's another example - this from the Indian context - shows how his (so-called) 'typological approach' is set with awkward presumptions. He gives this example as "perhaps the only case where the whole series from the bottom layer to the top layer could be fully documented" (p.47). Here he takes his start from the Ṛgveda, passes through the Brāhmaṇa texts, and the Upaniṣads and comes to Brahmasūtras, reaching further to Śaṅkarācārya. To quote him, "Ritualism and minimum speculation in Ṛgveda, ... to the Brāhmaṇas, to those hymns in which the science of sacrifice is elaborated, and from there we pass to the Upaniṣads, which bring us through further speculations to the threshold of metaphysical abstraction" and, in the same passage, naturally, going to Śaṅkarācārya. He comments, that the "communal repast" (which is the expression he obviously uses for the sacrifice and the priestly assemblage at it) is the type, while Śaṅkara's metaphysics is the ''anti-type."

It must be made clear at this juncture that this simplistic observation is not only beset with inaccuracies but also, unhelpful in the study of myths. Firstly, he does not give any examples from the texts he mentions to show a steady specification, degree by degree. In this, he keeps his readers in complete dark about the exact material upon which he gives his judgement and expects acceptance from them about his typological method. Those who are familiar with the gamut of the Vedic literature would be bewildered by the comment. Further, this comment leaves the entire range of Ṛgvedic myths, including even such portions where a mixture of ritual and metaphysical speculation helping such 'typology' could be seen as working.[12] And what about the hymn to Vṛṣākapi (*ṚV* X.86), the hymn that refers to the dog's entrails (IV.18), the myth of the eternal combat between Indra and Vṛtra, or the myth of Apālā (*ṚV* VIII.91) and a host of others, including that of the bitch Saramā, where metaphysics is not seen. From the very statement of Munz, it becomes clear that the typological method is of very little use in understanding myths, though, like structures, historical development may provide some aid.[13] Further, there is a trait of overdoing in the method followed by Munz. True, "sexual union of a man and a woman is the type of the return of multiplicity into the undifferentiated one" (p.50, n.1); and there are a number of Vedic instances to indicate the one splitting into the manifold and the principle that all this manifold gets merged into the one. The Vedic texts have already a persistant theme of Heaven and Earth being in close embrace, and later separating (a motif that obtains widely). But, how a stray incident of sexual intercourse can be seen as a type and its meaning could be decided by a metaphysical meaning of, say, *yava-yuma* anti-type (which, however, Munz does not mention) is not very clear. He also mentions the expression *ya evam veda* (erroneously though, as *yo evam veda*) that often occurs in the ritual-texts and the Upaniṣads, but not the *Ṛg-Veda*, and means "He who thus knows" (on the authority of H. Zimmer, *Kunstform und Yoga*, Berlin, 1926, p.22) as explaining typological relationship between such a natural act and a metaphysical doctrine. However, the instance he has in mind (and does not give any reference to), in the immediate context he just touches, has nothing to do with any myth. Actually it forms part of the section on 'offering into five-fires', the last 'fire' being in the form of a woman. The offering is the 'seed' of man and the fire is the female with her generative organ (*Chāndogya Up.* V.8), which produces 'man' (i.e., the child, *Ib.*9). This places the female (= fire) in line with the other four forms of fire—(i) sky, (ii) rain-ful cloud-fire; (iii) Earth and (iv) Man. The sexual intercourse here is not a stray example, *nor is it from any myth*; it forms part of a metaphysical elaboration itself, with the expression *ya evam veda* ("one who knows these five fires... attains the meritorious world - aye! *he who thus knows*", Ib.10). In the present case, we do not have a series of myths, but only five different images from actual observation, avowedly to connect them to a metaphysical principle of 'fire' on various strata for creation of various objects, culminating into the creation of man; and the sexual intercourse is intimately connected with the birth of man (man here symbolizing creatures in this world). The scheme is as follows (*Chānd.Up.* V.5-8).

- ★ Sky=fire; Sun=firestick; rays=smoke; day=flame; moon=embers; stars=sparks; faith=offering; *Soma* produce;
- ★ Rain=fire; wind=firestick; cloud=smoke; lightning=flame; thunder=embers; rumblings= sparks; *Soma*=offering; drops of rain=produce.
- ★ Earth=fire; year=firestick; space=smoke;

night=flame; quarters=embers; sub-quarters= sparks; rain=offering; food=produce;

- ★ Man=fire; speech=firestick; breath=smoke; tongue= flame; eyes=embers; ears=sparks; food=offering; semen=produce.
- ★ Woman=Fire; generative organ=firestick; man's soft words=smoke; vagina=flame; inside thrust=embers; pleasure=sparks; semen=offering; foetus=produce. (cf. also Jai. Br. I. 45)

It will be seen that, in this elaboration, sexual intercourse appears at the last (the lowest) layer, if we have a verticle visual; and in it the human sexual relationship could be taken as 'type' for the upper ones which may be understood as 'anti-types'. But if this be the series Munz contemplates (it is not clear for want of reference, though), there is no evidence of "the return of multiplicity into the undifferentiated one". Moreover, though he has included this "Vedic method" in the chapter, "Myths and Metaphysics", there is no myth here at all, though there is a series of metaphors. Nowhere in Munz we find a series of *myths*, as such. Also he does not make clear *what is a myth*, according to him. And when he does take the example of a known myth (Oedipus for example) he gives its historical deflections and embroideries; but fails to state how the last anti-type (the version of Sophocles) is the most specified one and how it helps unravel the meaning (and what?) in the 'type' in the *Illiad*. The shortcoming in Munz's exposition becomes obvious on his own admission that the final and more specified version is to be used as a 'stencil' on the natural event (read 'myth'); and then, "one and the same myth... *can be made to have a number of different meanings*". This clearly means—(i) That a myth, as such, has its own meaning in its original form; and (ii) That "the multiplicity of its meaning is due to its position in a typological series, depending on the kind of top-myth or doctrine one uses as a stencil" (p.51). But, this is *using an original myth* in various ways for various interpretations. This is the using stage. And it has to be differentiated, 'on the one hand, from the formation stage and, on the other, from the natural (not artificial or purposeful) elaboration of a myth which may or may not develop into a metaphysical principle. In the study of myths metaphysics, like aetiology, has to be taken as a later appendage; and that too is not seen in the case of all myths. In short, though the Historical method is useful, and should be followed wherever possible, its typological phase, as envisaged by Munz, is as lame as the earlier methods he criticizes. However, some creation myths and speculative myths do have metaphysical or proto-philosophical value as is the case with rituals. But that cannot be taken as a rule for all myths. It is also to be understood that historicity and metaphysicality are not mutually interdependent, nor are they, as a rule, mutually compatible - the series of the 'five-fires' is an example in this connection. As has been noted by us above, certain myths may be worked upon, in later periods, to fit in a metaphysical theme, which marks the stage of the use of the myth as apart from its formation.

For Munz's historical approach there is no bar on comparing myths from one region with those from another, the only requirement being that they should have a chronological sequence. There could be no difficulty in accepting this position if, however, the regions are adjacent to each other, or there could be available a clue for borrowal from one region to another. So when he says that the creation story of the Old Testament is an anti-type of the Babylonian creation myth (which has to be taken as the type), there need not be any problem. His contention, throughout, is that any 'type' is of a general nature, while the anti-types go on becoming more and more specific, the final (tentatively? Because, there could be more anti-types from other regions and later in time, anywhere!) being the most specific—and turning into a metaphysical principle. But even for the present, instead of taking the whole (creation?) myth from Babylonia, namely that of Gilgamesh,[14] he takes just a part of it viz. Enkidu's seduction by a harlot. In this he calls Enkidu the Mesopotamian Adam. Actually, Enkidu is the beastly uncultured counterpart of Gilgamesh, who, as the king of Uruk, is abominably free in his sexual life, sleeping with other's wives and maidens in his kingdom.This will mean that there is no problem of creation in this myth. Enkidu is created by the goddess Aruru, not to start creation but, as opposite of civilization (or culture) represented by Gilgamesh. There is, no doubt, a great probability of borrowal and influence of this detail of the Gilgamesh story on the Biblical story of Adam; also that there is the detail of immortality common to both. In the former there is an effort on the part of Gilgamesh to gain the flower (plant?) of immortality to bring Enkidu (his own alterego) to life again, while in the Biblical story, there is the inversion of the motif—the ouster of Adam and Eve from the immortal region in Eden to that of the humans to the eastern quarter. Now, comparing these two accounts, Munz says, "The earlier Mesopotamian version *could mean almost anything*. The later Biblical anti-type, though open to many varying and conflicting interpretations, provides some guidelines as to the meaning, by linking the loss of innocence to a moral decision" (p.124). Comparing the act of the serpent in both these accounts, he says that the serpent's act in the earlier one is "nothing more than an act of greed"... "while in the Biblical version the serpent assumes a phallic role". If that is so, how can we legitimately see the meaning of the later anti-type of the myth, through the serpent symbol, in the former, unless we take the 'greed' to be also indicative of the value of the phallus? The harlot-Enkidu version, though crude and direct, imparts the meaning of seduction; but it does not *depend upon* the more polished Eve-Adam episode. In the earlier one the harlot is specifically appointed for that purpose; she uncovers her breasts and spreads her legs to entice the all-too-natural Enkidu, hairy all over the body and unclothed. But the meaning of 'loss of innocence' (i.e., the knowledge of sex) leading to a chain of difficulties is clear, and does not require to be glossed by a 'feedback' from the anti-type of subtle embroidery that marks the Adam-Eve-serpent-fruit-knowledge of the difference of sex of the Biblical version. So, the point is—myths may get 'embroidered' and continue to be so embroidered; but, in that process, the final product (may it be called by any name - or anti-type) need not have the same meaning as of the original, nor is it strictly necessary for understanding the original. On the contrary, the final may have an entirely different meaning, though it maintains the pattern of the original. It has to be made clear that typology, as it is explained by Munz, does not help understand the historically earlier or earliest myths. Its value should be seen only in comparing typical parts of myths. It has been seen already that a myth often develops into a complex form; and some of its parts appear common to some parts in other myths. For typological analysis, if we follow Munz's suggestion, one has to take versions of the same myth through history, as he has indicated in the case of the myth of Oedipus (p.26). In that case the later myths, grown in size or even slightly changed, could be versions of the *same myth.* But, he also speaks of such versions as substitutes, calling the latter 'symbols', thus mixing the concept of variation with that of substitution, speaking also of the "theory of substitution". In essence his concept of typology appears to be double-faced—(i) versions of the same myth; and (ii) similar myths; in this case similarity of types being the criterion. But for him any earliest myth from either of these two would be 'type' and any later one would be anti-type. This puts undue pressure on the concept of type, which is a fault of 'heaviness' and 'contradiction between two concepts' (according to Indian norms - *gurutva* and *vṛtti-dvaya-virodha*). Legitimately, typology should be a study of types; and it is common experience that myth does use types as it develops. In other words, type is very much akin to pattern. But these patterns, or types, need not have a fixed meaning, which depends upon the context in which they are placed. Thus, we could speak of the Oedipus myth as having versions. The earlier myth of Anpu-Bata would be said to be an earlier type of the Oedipus myth, inasmuch as the son-husband motif is common to both; and the Vedic god Apām napāt being at once the 'son-and the-seeder' of the waters shows the same 'type'. The Akkadian myth showing Etana flying up to the sky and to heaven on the back of an eagle and coming down to the earth is a type, which is seen also in the Chinese Blue boy myth where a red carp is substituted for the bird; but the flight in the sky and return to the earth are identical.[15] The Etana flight is historically subsequent to the eagle-serpent fight in the Akkadian context; but in the Hindu context the serpents are carried by the eagle (Garuḍa) on its back towards the sun and brought down as they get tortured with heat.[16] The Etana myth centres round the plant of Birth to gain an heir, while the Blue boy myth and the Hindu myth of Garuḍa has rain in view as the gain. In the same way, in the Gilgamesh myth, the loss of the plant of immortality on the part of Gilgamesh, who gets it after great effort, is the type that is found in the Hindu myth of Garuḍa (called Suparṇa) in the liquid of immortality being taken back by Indra. However, the Garuḍa myth is more complex inasmuch as in it the liquid of immortality was brought by Garuḍa to free his mother from the bondage of her co-wife, the mother of the serpents; and both the serpents and the eagle were duped by Indra, while in the Gilgamesh myth it is the serpent who robs Gilgamesh of the plant of life. In the earlier Hindu version, it is Suparṇa (eagle); but he brings the plant, *Soma,*[17] the juice of which is supposed to bestow immortality. The following table will show how the same type is worked to give variations in results:

(A) *Etana*	(B) *Gilgamesh*	(C) *Suprana (Garuḍa)*
Plant of Birth for the gain of an heir	Plant of life = immortality	(1) Plant - Soma for immortality; (2) Rain in later versions

A and B could be seen as having the same meaning, as an heir keeps the family line making it, in a sense, immortal. In that case, the comparison between the Etana myth and the Gilgamesh myth would suggest an obsession to gain immortality and a probable consolation that immortality could be gained through the issue, but never by avoiding death.

How the concept of typology, with the 'stencil' of the anti-type, fed back to the 'type', does not necessarily help give the original meaning in the case of myths could be seen from the following example. We take a Hindu myth, from the Vedic period and follow it in the later period. In the first book (*maṇḍala*) of the Rgveda, which is a later phase linguistically, occur the following lines (ṚV I.24.7).

> Varuṇa - the king with pure will—
> Erected in the bottomless void
> A tree trunk with branches shooting (*stūpa*);
> Up (in the sky) their roots rest
> In our hearts are their filaments fixed.

This is clearly a cosmic vision expressed in the form of shortest narration. The sanction of tradition gives it the status of a myth. It is no justice to say that the person (the seer) who first visualised such a branched cosmic column did it on purpose, artificially, as he contemplated the relationship between the earthly creatures and, probably, the sun. The fact seems to be that he knew from his experience the tree, and visualised its roots up in the sun. His knowledge and belief regarding the sun as the source of all light and life gave rise to this 'roots-up-filaments-reaching below' image on the basis of the sunrays. He called it *stūpa* (column/pillar), and visualised it as branched. In this he has a mixed image— that of the tree with that of a column of rays. This is because he is conversant with the concept of the *stūpa* which got forming up in that ancient Vedic period - forming up we say, as the word is not very frequent yet (and the *stūpa* in the Buddhistic concept is yet centuries ahead, though it borrowed it from the Vedic concept and gave it a specified meaning of dome-like structure on the remains of the Buddha). In the early Ṛgveda it is applied to the column of the flames of the sacrificial fire in the altar, though occurring only once (ṚV VII.2.1). It is not improbable that the column of tapering up flames (*stūpa*, in the plural) in the altar suggested the light-column in the cosmos (*jyotirliṅga,* of the later period). With the well set principle of the triple fire (sun, lightning and the terrestrial fire), the source of the cosmic fire—the sun—spreading rays below was transformed into the *stūpa* spreading its ray-filaments down to the earth as source of energy and life for the creatures. Both, the fiery column from the sacrificial altar and the cosmic light-column, are symbols for energy and life, with the difference that the fiery column in the altar is visually opposite of the solar light-column. The *stūpa* is not the tree; but with the root-stump (*budhna* is the word used) and filaments (*ketavaḥ*) the *stūpa*-symbol could easily glide into a tree-symbol. And, this is exactly what happened in the later period. The age of the Ṛgveda (compilation and arrangement into books at least 2000 to 1500 B.C., but the actual *mantras* far earlier) goes back to, probably, about 5000-4000 B.C., if not earlier. The Kaṭha Up. (II.2.1; about 800 B.C.) speaks of the cosmic tree, called Aśvattha, its root being up in heaven and branches going down reaching the hearts of creatures on the earth. It calls it 'white bright Brahman" (*śukram brahma*) in which are settled all worlds including our earth. This is only another version of the lustrous *stūpa*. In it are all the worlds contained. This tree is limitlessly old (*sanātana*). The same symbolic tree is referred to by the Bhagavadgītā (about the third century B.C.), which describes it as spreading its branches far above and far below i.e., far beyond (the sun), though it is called Aśvattha, and far down to the earth, its sprouts getting tied up with the actions of the mortals (Bh.G.XV.1). The Ṛgvedic verse does not specifically speak about the sun being the source of the light-column; but, it is clear enough. The later texts call the 'tree' Aśvattha, which word means 'resting on the horse'. But the horse is a symbol for the sun in the Vedic and later Hindu tradition.[18] This would indicate the Ṛgvedic column (*stūpa*) that has its root up in the heaven, as set in the solar orb. These three accounts are three stages of the same concept. We can say, with Munz, that the image in the Ṛgveda serves as the 'type', while the later ones are antitypes; and, if we start to feed back from the last antitype, the meaning does not change, though the symbols show slight variation. The reason is that all these accounts are metaphysically tinged from the very beginning. They are short myths, no doubt; but they are speculative about the relationship between the mortals and the immortals. So, like such other myths that dwell on the creation of the world and the relationship between the microcosm and macrocosm, they could be termed 'proto-philosophic' in nature. But, now let us refer to a part of a regular and more elaborate myth. It forms part of the saga of the conflict between Garuḍa and the serpents, reaching back to their mothers, who are said to be the wives (and former sisters of each other) of Kaśyapa. When Garuḍa was flying to heaven to fetch nectar (the drink of immortality) he held an elephant and a tortoise, one in each of his claws. On the way, however, he desired to alight on a huge banyan tree (Rauhiṇa or Vaṭa). But, as soon as the bird touched the branch of the tree, the latter broke under the weight of the three creatures. Cognising that the sages - all of the size of a human thumb—were resting on the tree, and afraid that they would perish if the branch crashed with the impact of the earth below, Garuḍa swooped below it and caught it in his beak in mid-air. We are not concerned with the rest of the myth. However, the motif 'thumbkin sages' on the Rauhiṇa (Vaṭa) tree is to be compared with another one in the Garuḍa-saga. According to it, the thumbkin sages were once carrying, all together, a small bundle of twigs meant to be offered into the sacrificial fire. On the way, however, they all got stuck into a small round pit filled with water and could not get out. Seeing them thus helpless Indra (the king of the gods) laughed. Feeling insulted the sages vowed to create another Indra who would challenge this usual Indra. So, they favoured the sage Kaśyapa by granting a boon that one of his wives, Vinatā, would give birth to the 'Indra of the birds'. This was Garuḍa.[19] The thumbkin sages have the epithet *marīci-pāḥ*' ('drinkers of the sunrays' or 'protectors of the solar orb'; *marīci* = sunray, or solar orb; *pāḥ* fr. the root *pā* = [i] to drink; [ii] to protect). The thumb-size is symbolic; and according to the tradition, the soul is of this size.[20] This makes clear that the circular pit, filled with water, in which the sages are said to have got stuck, is symbolic of the sun's orb with the souls in it. That the solar orb is filled with, or is the receptacle of cosmic waters is traditionally well set in the Hindu mythology (going as far back as the Ṛgveda)[21] and elsewhere.[22] On the other hand, both the Aśvattha tree (*aśva*=sun-symbol) and the Rauhiṇa-Vaṭa are closely associated with the sun—the former tree in the Vedic period, the latter in the post-Vedic period, where it figures in the myth of *Sāvitrī* (which word means 'daughter of the sun' or 'energy of the sun'; *savitṛ* is the sun).[23] This will show that 'thumbkins on the branch of the tree' and 'thumbkins in the circular water-pit' are two phases of the same 'type' (type in the sense as Munz understands). Now, to fix our attention on the 'thumbkins on the tree' and go back. The thumbkins are *marīcipāḥ* and also the souls. We compare this image with 'thumbkins in the solar orb' image, and realize that the latter image is of the souls settled in the solar orb, which is the source of the rays. When we compare this image with the very first we see that it is the inversion of the latter. In the earlier one the rays of the sun shoot downwards from their circular source and settle in our hearts, while in the later one our souls (after release from the mortal frame) get settled in the solar orb, through the rays. This metaphysical concept is explained through the employment of various mythical images lustrous column→tree with shoots growing down→solar bird (Garuḍa) with thumbkin (or 'soul-kins', if we may say so) on the solar branch. The whole series is lively with one principle. This is how (and there are numerous examples like this) a myth and its versions serve metaphysics; and, as noted earlier, some myths can be understood as embodying proto-philosophy. But this cannot be true of all myths. Even here, in this example, the historically last myth does not serve to throw back light on the earliest one. The streak of light permeates throughout, starting from the earliest, though getting dim in later mythical cover. The tree image seen here gets further specified later in the 'tree' that holds the two 'birds' - one simply watching and the other that enjoys, the supreme soul and the one that gets caught in the body experiencing this world's sorrows and joys through the senses;[24] and the tree of down-growing shoots, which changes from the Aśvattha to the Rauhiṇa comes to be known as Nyagrodha (*nyak*= 'downwards'+ *rodha*= 'growing', from the root *rudh-ruh*, 'to grow', 'extend'). The Nyagrodha tree has a twofold association in the ritual context. The Ait.Br. (VII.30=35.4) tells us, mytho-etymologically, that it sprang from the Soma juice (drink of immortality), when it dripped down from the (wooden) cups that held it when they were turned upside down. If we place these various versions side by side we have the following structures—

Later Ṛgveda (3000 B.C. to 1500 B.C.)	*Kaṭha Up. (about 1000 B.C.)*	*Bh.G. (300 B.C.)*	*Mb. (300 B.C.)*
Varuṇa erected a *stūpa* in the bottom-less void.	—	—	—
Its root is up in heaven; its branches spread downwards	Aśvattha, the ancient tree; its branches spread down-wards	Aśvattha, the non-destructible (*avyaya*) tree, with branches spreading down and above	The Rauhiṇa (Nyagrodha) tree; its branch held by Garuḍa
The *stūpa* has lustrous branches	It is the bright *brahman;*	—	It holds the 'Soul-sages' thumbkins.
They are settled in our hearts.	In it are settled all the worlds;	Its shoots are related to the action of creatures in the world	—
(Root up in the solar-orb)	(Aśvattha standing in the '*aśva*' horse Sun-symbol)	(Sun-Symbol)	The thumbkins are residents of Sunrays

Prajāpati, Daughter and Rudra

All have the same metaphysical principle.

Now we take another series of myths, as an example, and trace them historically. We have already referred to the Ṛgvedic myth of the father running lustily after his own daughter, in earlier chapters (Second and Third) for a different purpose. Let us trace it further for the historical method and typological study.

(1) Ṛgveda has some details, though the full-fledged myth does not occur at any one place. Accordingly, it is said that, when he (the sacrificer) offered the liquid oblation (*rasam*), to heaven, the knowing one approved of it and ran after the speckled cows (*pṛśanyaḥ*). Noticing this, the archer fitted an arrow onto the bow and shot it aiming at the 'father'. However, the divine father, planted his manly seed into the daughter (ṚV I.71.5). Though the account is not elaborate, there is no doubt that it appears in the form of a short tale and, though not prefixed by such words as, "Once upon a time" etc., it has to be taken as a very ancient occurrence expressed in a rather puzzling way. Who the father is, is not clear. The 'speckled cows' (the word used is *pṛśanyaḥ*,[25] which is pl. of *pṛśanī*) would indicate that the father who runs after them would be some bull. But, among all these 'speckled ones', he selects his own daughter! If the 'father' (*pitā*) is the same as the 'knowing one', who is, again, the same as heaven, we have a triple identification: Heaven (sky) = the knowing one = Father. But the imagery of the Ṛgveda identifies the *pṛśanī* or *pṛśni* with the sky, with the earth (in certain cases) and with the cloud-cow. The words 'to heaven' (*dive*) would take the whole myth to the sky and mid-region sphere, where the cows are the clouds. But, who is the father? If, as a male of the cows, he is the bull, the human terminology of Father and daughter does not suit them well. At another place (ṚV X.61.5ff) we have the same myth with the

details as follows: the sage Cyavāna prepared the altar and arranged the sacrificial material. Then he offered the oblations in the fire for weal on the earth. Then (as if, as a consequential act) the 'father' ran after his own daughter. However, here the daughter is mentioned as 'earth' (*kṣmā*). Combining these two accounts, which appear to be fragments of a well known myth at that period, we get the pair as sky-father and the earth-daughter. And, this without resort to etymology. This would mean that, whoever expressed this myth, had before him the sky (as the male) and the earth as the female. But the point is that he calls the earth, not any woman but, the daughter (*duhitṛ*). This, obviously, would bring in etymology to explain away the word *duhitṛ* (daughter) as 'one who milks' (rain which is) the semen of the sky (= cloud) father, though *kṣmā* (earth) is not born from the *div/dyo* (sky). In any case, at this stage of history, the myth centres round the gain of rain, symbolically spoken as semen (*retas*); and this symbolic use is attested by the Ṛgveda at various places.

(2) In a later period, the myth gets fattened up. But, though the parties are Father and daughter, the identifications differ. As noted earlier the Ait.Br. has more specifications. It states that the father is Prajāpati, but not the sky. On the contrary, the daughter is said to be "either sky or dawn". Yet the semen = water symbolism persists, though with a change. The semen of Prajāpati gets transformed into a lake; and there is an indication of the creation of man from the semen. The gods said, "let not the semen get spoilt (*mā duṣat*)". Hence from it was created man (*mānuṣa*). The myth takes a turn here and it is said that the daughter became a female deer, Prajāpati the male deer and the archer the star called 'hunter' (*vyādha*), later called the 'lord of cattle' (*paśupati*). The same myth, which was a rain-myth at the Ṛgvedic

period, changes here into a constellation-myth, and also a creation myth, explaining the creation of man. In another text (Śat.Br. I.4.4.1ff) the myth occurs practically the same way as at the Ait.Br.; but, there is an addition. It says that, when the gods saw that Prajāpati's (the deer's) flesh got stuck to the tip of the arrow when it was taken out by the archer, now specified as Rudra, they thought that it should not go waste. So they decided that one of the gods should eat it. But, it caused harm to each of the gods and ultimately it was eaten by the god Bṛhaspati. That is why, it is said, in the ritual the priest named Brahmā (who stands for Bṛhaspati) eats the portion called *prāśitra* (the first to be eaten, *pra-aśitra* in relation to *iḍā* which comes next; or 'excellent eatable'). Here the old myth clearly assumes the nature of a charter, and explains why the Brahmā priest came to eat the *prāśitra*. Actually, the portion of flesh remains restricted to the myth. The ritual has nothing of the sort. The ritual has only a portion of the sacrificial cake made from the flour of barley. This portion is called *prāśitra*. On the one hand, this text uses the same old myth to explain the *prāśitra*; and, on the other, just earlier, it uses the then popular myth of the flood, with Manu as the only one to be saved by a fish who guides his canoe getting it tucked to its horn. Alone, and without a fire, Manu offers in the water some milk and butter (which he had carried). Therefrom a young girl gets born, butter sticking to her feet. He generates progeny with her help, the indication being that this progeny is from the father (Manu) and his 'daughter'. This new myth has Iḍā as the daughter's name. Iḍā means 'nourishment' or sacrificial material. But, in essence, it is a portion of the same sacrificial cake (*puroḍāśa*) of which the *prāśitra* is a portion, of the size of a barley-grain. This will show a further embroidery to the original myth, each phase getting more specific. All through, in the Vedic texts, the context appears to be of sacrifice. If we note that Manu and Prajāpati are conceptually on the same level in the Ancient Hindu mythical sphere, Manu being sometimes said to have been produced from Prajāpati himself, the structure of these two myths would be the following in the ritual mentioned above:-

puroḍāśa (sacrificial cake)

Antelope-Prajāpati's own flesh → Prāśitra ↑ ... iḍā ↑ ← 'offering' = daughter of Manu

∴ Prajāpati = Manu

However, the Father-daughter relationship (producer and the produced) does not exactly fit in the human norms. The sky does not 'create' the earth; and though the deer may create the female deer, it does not create man (*māḍuṣa* - *mānuṣa*); and Manu's daughter is not created from his body, though that myth takes the line of the primeval couple (which is a riddle, but a necessity for the first ever phase of creation), but not a copulatory couple, as we have noted earlier.

(3) In the period later than the Vedic, when the god Brahmā replaces the old god Prajāpati, we have interesting variations. As a step ahead of the old tradition we hear Brahmā creating a beautiful young girl from his own body. Being struck by her beauty he tried to embrace her. Seeing this awkward behaviour of Brahmā, other divine damsels and daughters of gods hastily circumambulated him and left the place. This daughter of Brahmā also desired to go round him in circumambulation before leaving him. As she went round him Brahmā turned his face to all the quarters, unable to withdraw his eyes from her. Because of this act he developed four faces. When the daughter finished circumambulating him, she took the form of a female bird

to fly away from him. Brahmā also turned himself into a bird and followed her. Fearing being caught by him, she turned to the mountain named Aruṇācala where there was a shrine dedicated to Śiva. Seeing what the matter was, Śiva came out of the *liṅga* in the form of a hunter, and fixed an arrow onto his bow with an intention to shoot at the male bird. Fearing death, Brahmā at once resumed his form and stood before Śiva to solicit mercy (Skanda P.I.3.5.49-62). Here we have a version of the same myth, the actors being the same but with their new names. Like the Vedic Rudra, Śiva is often seen as a hunter in the later myths.[26] The father and the daughter do not occur in the form of deer here, but the motif of their heavenward flight is seen in the flight of the birds. In yet another version in this period (SK.P.III.1.40.6ff), Brahmā and his daughter assume the forms of a male deer and a female deer respectively (cf. Vedic pattern); but, the daughter is seen also as speech. And, further, the mythical tradition tells us that Brahmā's daughter, Sarasvatī (≐ Speech; called also Bhāratī) was also his wife. Here, then the old myth gets inclined to be metaphysical, suggesting that Brahmā, the god of sacrifice and learning takes his daughter (speech) as wife. This is supported by a myth where Gāyatrī is said to be his wife. Gāyatrī is the metre and is also his daughter. Her other names are Sāvitrī and Śatarūpā. This is, by far, the last variation. So, to follow Munz's typology, the couple of father-daughter (unspecified) would be the type and Father = Brahmadeva and Daughter = Speech would be the topmost anti-type. Could we say, by the feedback method, that this last anti-type holds the meaning of all the previous anti-types and the first type? In that case rain-gain and offering would have to be seen only as aspects of Speech. The fact is, as made clear above, that originally a myth has its own specific meaning; but, when it becomes popular, it gets used in different contexts; and those contexts give a different shade of meaning to it. We could say, that such a change of context slightly changes the status of the original myth. This new status is that of a meta-myth. In the case of the myth that we have been discussing we could say, that the very first context in which the Father-daughter myth is ushered in is that of the gain of rain, though the sky-earth unit does not exactly suit the relationship. For the exact fitting we have to go to the Middle-Eastern myth of Enki-Ninhursag. If we compare the two sets of this myth (Middle-Eastern and the Hindu) we have to accept that the mid-eastern tale is the myth, and the Vedic is a meta-myth. Restricting ourselves to the Hindu context, we could say that the Vedic myth is the basis of the later Hindu myths mentioned above, which could be termed meta-myth. A question may be asked, - what is the meaning of the earliest such myth? The answer is that it depends upon the context. In the context of creation, as in the case of the Maori myth of Tane and his first female creation, or Manu's body producing a fully developed maiden, the meaning has to be seen in the riddle of the first copulative pair of creation. In the case of the Enki-Ninhursag myth, the meaning rests in the particular method of cultivation. And, though it is possible to see reflections of social behaviour at the subconscious stratum, care has to be taken before believing it to be *the only and final* meaning; because, a myth is never straightforward and is often hydra-headed. The Father-daughter myth has to be taken as one of the cardinal myths in the Hindu mythology, as could be seen from the various shoots it developed later. But, before we take leave of it, let us mark one more turn it takes. This is in the context of Śiva's marriage with Pārvatī, who is also called Umā.

(4) At the marriage of Śiva and Pārvatī, who is now the daughter of Dakṣa, himself a Prajāpati, Brahmā looks

at the toe-nails of Pārvatī, gets excited with passion and releases semen. Śiva notices this and gets wild with wrath. He asks Brahmā to touch his feet with his head. As Brahmā does so, Śiva stands on the former's head, and asks him to practise penance at a place, which, hence, comes to be called Rudraśīrṣa. A variation of the myth has Brahmā trying to wipe out the semen with the toes of his foot; and from it were produced the thumbkin sages, Vālakhilyas.[27] According to yet another variation, Brahmā who was sitting near along with others, desired to see the face of Pārvatī, on seeing her feet; but was afraid to do. So, he placed into the holy fire (kindled at the marriage and around which the bride and the bride-groom have to go) a twig, smearing it with clarified butter (such twigs, *samidh*-s, are usually kept near the fire for offering into it by the officiating priest and the bride-groom). Thereby curls of smoke rose up, causing Śiva and others to close their eyes for a while. Seeking this opportunity, studiedly worked out, Brahmā lifted the veil on the face of Pārvatī and eyed her face. Excited, he could not check his semen that gushed out in four drops. But, Śiva, understood his trick and mounted upon Brahmā's head even as the latter bent it in shame capping it with his folded hands. From the four drops four clouds got formed, namely Saṁvartaka, Āvarta, Puṣkara and Droṇa.[28] It will be seen that these accounts regarding Pārvatī take images from the Vedic context and transform them, but not beyond speculative cognets. A picture of these later variations, in comparison with the old mythical details is interesting. It adds a new detail of marriage of the 'daughter' in the older scheme, the archer in the old scheme turning here into her husband. The 'father' in the older scheme remains a passionate seeker of his daughter changing into a pseudo father, on the basis of the equation:

(i) Prajāpati=Dakṣa
Brahmā=Prajāpati
∴ Brahmā=Dakṣa

∴(ii) Dakṣa's daughter, Pārvatī=Brahmā's daughter
(real) (pseudo)

Here Brahmā, the old Prajāpati, assumes the role of a pseudo father, in view of the fact that there is another one Dakṣa, as father. However, according to one account, he yet is linked to Pārvatī in a filial line. It is said that when Brahmā ran after his daughter, here named Sandhyā, the *mahāyogī*, Śiva, condemned him. So Brahmā nursed spite for him. However, Viṣṇu acted as a mediator and got them reconciled to each another. But, Brahmā still nursed ill-will for Śiva. So, he caused his own daughter to be reborn as the daughter of his own son, Dakṣa. She was born to Dakṣa and his wife Asiknī. She was the same as Umā Pārvatī. So, from the earliest Father-daughter to the latest Father-daughter there is a long journey; and it is impossible to see any metaphysical 'stencil' that could give the meaning of the last to the first and to the intervening variations, where some details join up while a good many stray away from the earlier ones. The whole cycle of this myth reflects some symbols. But they do not enter every version. Thus:

★ Semen stands as a symbol for rain, as for water in the tank and even as for clouds into which it gets transformed; and it is on the same level with other organic moistures such as perspiration, blood, spittle and so on, which appears irrational on the face of it;

★ But the semen also develops into organic beings-*mānuṣa* and Vālakhilyas.

However, in certain versions the symbol of semen is not

	I *Father*	II *Daughter*	III *Archer*	IV *Semen (symbol)*	V *Context*
(1)	Sky/Raingod →	Earth (*kṣmā*) (Birth un-specified)	Unspecified	*Rain*	Cosmo- *sacrificial*
(2)	(a) Prajāpati → (b) Male antelope →	a) Sky or Dawn b) Female antelope (Birth unspecified)	Rudra	a) *Lake* b) Man	Constellational; terrestrial; *sacrificial* background
(3)	Manu (one of the Prajāpatis)	Iḍā (= offering) Birth specified as from Father	—	Liquid offering in *water*	First *sacrifice* (terrestrial)
(4)	Brahmā (Neo-Prajāpati) →	Śatarūpā. Birth specified as from Father	Śiva	—	—
(5)	Brahmā	Vāk = Speech; Gāyatrī (metre)	—	—	—
(6)	(a) Dakṣa- (a Prajāpati) (b) Brahmā (Pseudo Father) →	Umā (Pārvatī) Marriage Sees her and ejects semen	Śiva (but no archer) clouds (Rain-*water*)	—	—

employed. In the Manu - Iḍā version semen gives place to an offering of milk and liquid clarified butter; it does not get transformed into water, but is offered into water, which often symbolizes the female in the Hindu tradition.[29] If we give the structure of the variations of the myth it could be as follows. In column I the arrow-sign indicates sexual advance. (see chart on p. 213)

It has been said above that symbols help in understanding the meaning of a myth, partly or wholly. Where a myth shows a composition of manifold details, symbols could help make clear some of them. However, this cannot be taken as a rule. In some versions of the myth noted above, semen is mentioned persistently, and the implication thereof is clear as water in the formation of the lake and clouds. Other places in the Ṛgveda support it. But, in certain other cases, this does not exactly work. Thus, in an account Brahmā is said to have held his semen in a ladle and offered it into the fire, wherefrom were born the thumbkins, Vālakhilyas.[30] Here the semen stands for the liquid offering and comes on par with Manu's offering in the water. This and other instances like this would show that Cassirer's idea of myths using symbolic forms[31] is not altogether unworthy of consideration, if it is not too inhibitive of a religious meaning. We have noted an example where myths go subtly gliding on the path of metaphysics. In the example noted above, the *stūpa*, giving place later to the tree, stands as a symbol and the indication is that the microcosm and the macrocosm are permeated with the same principle. This brings us to a question of the mutual relationship between myths and metaphysics or philosophy. Generally speaking mythology and philosophy are two opposites; and, way back, Prof. Burnet had observed about the founders of European philosophy that "they left off telling tales. They gave up the hopeless task of describing what was when as yet there was nothing, and asked instead what all things really are now."[32] By this he differentiated the ancient and traditional stories about the beginning of the world from those deliberations of the thinkers of Miletus, a prosperous city founded by the Ionian Greeks on the coast of Asia Minor. In other words, he differentiated between the poems of Hesiod and the thoughts regarding the nature and evolution of the world we live in. All the same, he did not deny that the roots of philosophy are discernible in the ancient traditional tales, in howsoever minute forms they may be. Kirk, starting from another book of Burnet (*Greek Philosophy, Thales to Plato,* 1914), traces the views of other scholars on the topic and accepts the attitude of mediation between two extreme views (1976, p.277), which would admit some kind of relationship between mythology and philosophy as far (at least) as Greek mythology and philosophy are concerned. Actually Greek philosophy stands at the top in the history of European philosophy and this period is the sixth century B.C. Kirk argues that, though literacy became established in Greece around 700 B.C., the pre-Homeric period was not a traditional society. He says this to clarify his earlier general statement that myths achieve their greatest prominence in traditional and non-literate societies, implying that philosophy dawns in a non-traditional and a literate society. However this position of dichotomy cannot be taken as rigid. To accept this position as rigid would mean that a literate society would not very much honour tradition or the traditional rituals and myths. Experience does not support this stand. Even in literate societies of this century rituals, traditions and even myths are not totally rejected. The most glaring example of this century (and towards its close), which is about to hold its hand forward to greet the twenty-first century is that of Soviet Russia after the blow to communism. The church and the religious traditions are back again. And fundamentalism, with all its traditions, myths and beliefs is sprouting up in the field of literacy and science! Literacy and traditionalism are not necessarily non-compatible to each other. We can only say that free thinking and traditionalism are mutually less compatible to each other. Philosophy starts not only with free thinking but also with rethinking of the tradition. On the one hand this rethinking takes the form of establishing an order in traditional rituals, concepts and myths; and, on the other, it looks to the absolute reality beyond them. In this process, these earlier records are interpreted or seen as stages to the absolute truth, or they are totally discarded. The first is the stage of proto-philosophy; the latter that of unmoist pure philosophy proper. However, any society, as a whole, hardly accepts the latter—and for good. There is always a cycle of these processes.

The Hindu term for this process to 'see' the ultimate is *darśana*, which implies 'looking through and beyond'. When the Absolute is comprehended, i.e., seen through the mental eye, as the Truth, the stages in the process may be termed what is known later as *dṛṣṭānta* (example). In another pair of terms, very well popular, the final is the *nirguṇa* (non-qualified), while the earlier stages are *saguṇa* (qualified), both being Brahman, and both having their status. It must be noted, however, that myths in this process are of a special nature. Some of them deal with the creation of the cosmos, and the universal order. They are speculative in nature. Such myths having the rudiments of philosophy have a hoary tradition among the Hindus which goes right up to the Ṛgveda. One example - that of the *stūpa*—we have already noted. It is of the nature of an enquiry into the source of all that we see around, and about the relationship between the Ultimate and this created world. In the example noted, the *stūpa* stands as the connecting link between the seen world and its probable source. But, even here this connecting link is said to be the creation of Varuṇa. Hence this myth tends to be religious as it speaks of the god. In the version from the Upaniṣad (Kaṭha), the place of the *stūpa* is taken by the tree that has its roots up and branches down. And, here is a definite step into philosophy when the 'tree' (now cosmic tree) is termed Brahman and *amṛta* (the immortal) in which all worlds rest. This is *darśana*. Here the old and traditional term *brahman*[33] is used; but it is bereft of its earlier meaning of 'prayer and ritual' and gets a new meaning of the 'Supreme' principle. However, it is yet applied to the vision of a cosmic tree which is suggested from common experience; but it is unique. The concept of the supreme *Brahman* is superimposed on it, just to indicate the latter's nature. Thus, *brahman* is explained through its qualification, the *guṇa*. In other words, the image of the unique tree is a visual symbol for the Ultimate, and is the *saguṇa* aspect of the Ultimate. In fine, the *stūpa* and the 'tree' are both on the same level; both fail to impart the exact knowledge of the Ultimate, about which is often said—"nay-not this" (*na-iti, na-iti*). The vision of the *stūpa* or the 'tree' when expressed in the form of a tale is a myth and has the status of proto-philosophy. Such myths, when bereft of references to personal gods, get the status of investigation about the nature of the Ultimate. Both are to be met with in the later Puraṇic tradition, which not only carries old myths but gives rise to new ones. This will prove that it is not necessary to assume that myths get prominence in traditional and non-literate societies. The Hindu society at the period of the Purāṇas was firmly embedded in literacy. Yet it shows a mixture of speculative thinking and free-thinking. And this trait goes back even to the Vedic period.

Such myths in the Vedic tradition which speak of one person, being split, giving rise to diverse cosmic entities, are to be taken as proto-philosophic. The narration of the myth apart, the principle that lies therein is of the ultimate unity of the cosmos. We have already referred to the myth of Indra splitting Vṛtra, the result being that the sun and the moon get freed from its body. This is the latter part of the myth. The earlier is that Vṛtra was created by Tvaṣṭṛ to punish and kill Indra, who had stealthily drunk the Soma juice concealed by him from Indra. This part indicates the strife between the old god and the new one. But, when it is told that from the drops of Soma that were poured into the fire, Vṛtra got created, the indication is that Vṛtra is a unit of the fiery (fire) principle and the moist principle (juice of Soma). These come out separated in the form of the Sun and the Moon, the latter being regularly swallowed by the former and cast out. Here ends the myth; but it is to be read with generalization that there is only the twofold principle - heat and moisture.[34] Here the myth assumes the nature of the proto-philosophic truth, which is already presented in the Ṛgveda (X.129). According to it the first creation in the dark moist nothingness is the ray of light that gradually spreads everywhere. Here, and in such speculation, philosophy is seen stirring behind the veil of a myth.

References

1. For a full criticism of this view see, G.S.Kirk, *The Nature of Greek Myths,* p.73ff.
2. ṚV I. 163.1 addressed to the sacrificial horse at the Horse-sacrifice, describes him as having the wings of a hawk. The next verse in the same hymn has the expression, "The Vasus fashioned the horse from the sun." Elsewhere, and at many

places, the sun is said to be a bird, the imagery developing in the symbol of 'Suparaṇa'.

3. Dange, *Encycl.P.B.P.*, Vol.IV, p.1102f.
4. *The Power of Myth* (Ed. Betty Sue Flowers; questions by Bill Moyers and answers by Joseph Campbell), Doubleday, New York, London, 1988, pp.15; 32.
5. Anna Faraday, *The Dream Game*, Harper and Row, New York, (no year of pub.), p.92ff.
6. As in the case of the mother of Buddha in her pregnancy; for more instances, Dange, *Encl. P.B.P.*, Vol.II, under "Dreams".
7. *svapna*, in the ṚV, has the sense of "sleep" also. The prefix *a* (=*an*) has five other senses in the Sanskrit language, in addition to that of negation; one of them is 'similarity', another is indicative of 'a little'. So, *an-ṛta* would mean 'a little of *ṛta*', i.e., 'a little real'.
8. *When the Golden Bough Breaks* (structuralism or Typology), Routledge and Kegan Paul, London and Boston, 1973, p.ixf; also his chapter "Symbols and Signs", from p.72ff. It is not necessary here to comment on the relationship between the Cosmic mushroom and the Cross, and whether they are 'substitute' or 'anti-type' of the phallus, or if the earlier one is the sign for it later on.
9. G.S. Kirk, *The Nature of Greek Myths*, p.284, says that in this myth (that of Geriguiaguiatogo) incest is "some- how" (but how? He does not explain), gets associated with the gain of fire and sees in it the opposites - raw and cooked, nature and culture, under the influence of Lévi-Strauss. I am unable to comprehend it.
10. In this version Oedipus begets two sons on Euryganeia.
11. *Legends of the World* (Ed.Richard Cavendish), Barnes and Noble Books, New York, 1994, p.158; Kirk mentions the curse incurred by Laius as being due to abducting the boy, *The Nature of Greek Myths*, p.104.
12. For ex. ṚV I. 164; X.26; 27 and so on. How metaphysical speculation, through typology, can help in myths we have already discussed earlier from the Ṛgveda, is yet a further question.

13. Munz's unfamiliarity with the Vedic data is clear when he speaks of 'hymns' in the Brāhmaṇas. Hymns belong to an earlier period of the Saṁhitā-s of the Ṛgveda and the Atharvaveda. Also his mention of "Brāhmasūtras" has to be taken, probably, as a printing error for Brahmasūtras.

14. G.S. Kirk, (*Myth,* p.135f) is reluctant to call it a myth, though he admits that it has many qualities of myth. Actually, the real creation story is that of Marduk from Tiamat.

15. D. Mackenzie, *Myths of China and Japan,* London, p.80f. The blue boy gets transformed into a dragon and is lost in the clouds; rain follows. After calm is restored, he takes his original form and comes to the earth to the well. On its bank he finds a herb, which has the power to restore vitality.

16. See Dange, *Legends in the Mahābhārata,* p.4; also Mb. Ādi, 25 (Gorakhpur ed; crit.ed., Poona,Adi 21).

17. *Ib.*, p.71ff.

18. See n. 2 above. A person offering a miniature horse made of dough was believed to reach the region of the sun after death, Dange, *Encycl. P.B.P.*, Vol.IV, p.1318; image of the horse made of gold was to be gifted in the vow for the son; *Ib.*, Vol.V, p.1545.

19. Dange, *Legends in the Mahābhārata,* p.113ff.

20. Kaṭha Up.II.1.13 and at many other places.

21. ṚV I.23.17; Vāj.Sam.IX.3; Taitt.Ār.I.8.1

22. The Assyrian symbol of the sun was a disc from which flowed streams of water; see D. Mackenzie, *Myths of Babylonia and Assyria,* p.334.

23. For which see Dange, *Glimpses of Puranic Myth and Culture,* Ajanta Publications, Delhi, 1987, pp.59-66.

24. ṚV.I.164-20 = Śvetāśvatara Up.IV.6 = Muṇḍaka Up. III.1.1; further Śvetāśvatara Up.IV.7 = Muṇḍaka Up.III.1.2.

25. Sāyaṇa, the scholiast, renders it here as 'demon', taking it as Nom.Sing.; but at X.73.2 for the sing. *pṛśanī* his rendering is *senā* (army). This will show, he is not reliable here. The word *pṛśanī* occurs only twice in ṚV, as noted here—once in the sing. and once in the pl.

26. Mb., Vana, ch.39-40, where he tests the mettle of Arjuna, posing as a hunter; the same occurs later in the Śiva P.III. 40-41.

27. Probably, here there is a subtle association of the symbolic sense of the toe, which is called *aṅguṣṭha* (the thumb); hence the size of these sages. Vālakhilyas are not associated with semen in the earlier literature, either Mb. or Veda.

28. Dange, *Encl. P.B.P.*, Vol.I, p.203f.

29. The earliest mention occurs at ṚV in the Soma and Water couple, and in Apām napāt (god) and his position in the waters X.30.5 and II.35.4-7 respectively. The ritual perpetuates the imagery further, see Dange, *Sexual Symbolism from the Vedic Ritual,* Delhi, 1979, p.64.

30. Dange, *Encl. P.B.P.*, Vol.I, p.203.

31. E. Cassirer, *The Philosophy of Symbolic Forms,* Vol.II, Eng. Tr., New Haven, 1955.

32. Clement C.J. Webb, *History of Philosophy,* Thornton Butterworth Ltd., London, 1937 (1910), p.10.

33. The term *brahman* is understood by some scholars as meaning 'holy prayer' or something like a 'magical fluid'; see A.B. Keith, *The Religion and Philosophy of the Veda and Upanishads,* Motilal Banarsidass, Delhi, 1989 (originally in HOS, 1925), Vol.I, p.209; Vol.II, p.399. However, the Indian tradition understands by the term also 'ritual'; cf. Sāyaṇa on ṚV I.105.15; 129.4 etc.; and before him Yāska, Nirukta I.3.9 "extended in all quarters", and X.4.36 (on ṚV I.80.16) *brahmāṇi karmāṇi.* The Jaim.Br. I.125 has *brahma akriyata "brahma* was performed".

34. Śat.Br. I.6.3.24 *dvayam vāidam na tṛtīyam asti, ārdram caiva śuṣkam ca.*

Part II

Some Hindu Myths

Six

Wolves that Devoured the Ascetics

There are two mutually connected, mythical and problematic accounts from the Vedic texts. The first is the account of the *yati*-s being devoured by the wolves (*sālāvṛka*-s), and the other one is the account of one Rahasyu Deva-malimulc, who is said to have killed the ascetics (*vaikhānasa*-s) at a place called Muni-maraṇa ('Death of the ascetics').

To take the first. The account of the *yati-s* being devoured by the wolves occurs about eight times in the Vedic texts; but it is not exactly the same at all places. In certain cases the account is associated with Indra, stating that it is Indra who gave the *yati-s* to the wolves; but at other places it is simply said that the *yati-s* were being devoured by the wolves. The passages are as follows:

1. "Indra, indeed, gave the *yati-s* to the wolves; as they were being devoured, Syūmaraśmi, a seer from amongst them, entered a horse (*teṣām adyamānānām syūmaraśmir ṛṣir aśvam prāviśat*); hence, does a horse smell its own excreta.[1]

In this passage, Indra is said to have given the *yati-s* to the wolves. The Taittarīya Sam. mentions Indra in the same context, but adds a ritual detail, when it states that the *yatis* were devoured by the wolves at the south of the raised (*uttara*) altar (*dakṣiṇata uttaravedyā ādan*), by it supporting the throwing of the remainder of the cleansing (*prokṣaṇī*) water to the south of that altar. It is also said that by doing so whatever cruel there be in that quarter gets pacified (*yad eva tatra krūram tat tena śāmyati*)[2]. The raised altar (*uttara-vedi*) is in the eastern part of the great altar, called Mahāvedi. This altar is sprinkled with water. The association of the south to the devouring of the ascetics (*yati*-s) indicates that the quarter is of death; hence cruelty is associated with it. The Aitareya Br. refers to the giving of the *yati*-s to the wolves as one of the bad deeds of Indra[3].

2. As at the Taitt. Sam. (noted above), the raised altar and the southern quarter figure in the Kāṭhaka Sam.:

   The wolves, indeed, devoured the *yati*-s. As they were being so devoured, being clutched, they ran to the (*uttara-vedi*). That is why the wolves could not attack them. But, one of the *yati*-s, now, laughed (as the wolves were, thus, got rid of!); but, as he laughed, the wolves (again) ate them, one by one, dragging them. Hence one should not laugh thoughtlessly (or, fruitlessly, *moghahāsinā*)[4].

In the account noted above, though the point held out appears to be that it is not good to laugh thoughtlessly, the importance of the raised altar is implied. The raised altar is the one that could save from death or danger, as against the southern quarter, which is cruel and has to be pacified. The motif is present at another place in the same text, where it is said that the northern altar is the place of birth, or of those that are born; it is also the place for those that are the "eaters"; the southern altar is the place of those that are to be "eaten"; hence it is that, the northern altar is to be scattered over with sand, and not the southern one. The passage starts with the myth of the *yati*-s being eaten by the wolves. About the two altars, it is also said, in the same context, that the northern altar is to be elevated (by scattering the sand), so that it could be mounted upon (*abhyārohāya*; for protection)[5].

In the passages noted above Indra is not mentioned; and the account of the wolves and the *yati*-s starts straightaway.

3. Yet another mention of the myth is in the context of the *kārīra*-ritual, a rain-charm. It is as follows: "The wolves, indeed, ate the *yati*-s; their (of the *yati*-s) heads fell off; they became the dates (*kharjūrāḥ*); the juice of Soma that was (in the heads) got turned into the *karīra*-fruits, flying aloft; the *karīra*-s bring rain from heaven by being offered."[6]

Here also Indra is not mentioned; and it would not be wrong to surmise that the motif of the wolves eating the *yati*-s is, originally, independent of all the accounts mentioned above. Even so, the myth of the wolves and the *yati*-s must be very old and famous at the time of the formation of these various accounts, and was used to support certain details of the Vedic rituals, as *arthavāda*. The occasions to use the legend are, as noted above, the throwing of the *prokṣaṇī* water to the south of the raised altar; the praise of that altar itself, saying that it is the altar for new birth, as against the southern one or the southern quarter, which indicates death; and the praise of the *karīra*-fruits and the dates. The comparison of the dates with the heads of the *yati*-s also indicates that the *yati*-s had their heads clean shaven, as against those of the *muni*-s, who had long flowing hair.[7] The same is also indicated by the detail that one of the *yati*-s, the seer Syūmaraśmi, enters the horse and is indicated to have come out as its excreta which it smells.[8] That Indra gave the *yati*-s to the wolves has also to be taken as an *arthavāda*, and not a matter of fact; nor can it be taken as an effort of some so-called Vedic Aryan chief punishing the *yati*-s with this cruel fate. It is also to be noted that Indra often comes in rituals only as an indication of divine participation; and many rituals where such divinities as Indrāṇī, Vṛṣākapi and others are said to take part in acts or rituals indicate only this divine participation, the act being accomplished by mortal agents turned divine on the plane of the sacrifice or ritual.[9] What, then is the nucleus of the accounts involving the wolves, and the *yati*-s? The main points can be sorted out as under:

1. The *yati*-s were devoured by the wolves; but they were not offered to them by any enemy.
2. It is probable that they, or some of them, offered themselves to be so devoured, and that they did so in a group; some of them ran away when actually the wolves came, but others, as a rule, did not.
3. The smile of one of the *yati*-s did not stop the wolves from eating them; it appears to be misinterpreted as that of a person who has duped the wolves; it is not improbable that the smile was in spite of the wolves eating them; if so, it indicates complacency.
4. As an offshoot of the previous point, it could be added that the *yati*-s were revered for this act of

theirs; respect for them is clear in the fact that their heads are said to serve, in the form of the *karīra*-fruits, to bring rain in a Vedic ritual; at other places *yati*-s are said to be not particularly enemies of Indra.[10]

5. If what is suggested above is accepted, it appears that the *yati*-s were devoured by the wolves (or offered themselves to them) on the southern quarter of a locality[11] (cf. the motif of the northern and the southern altar).

From what has been said above, it is not improbable that the *yati*-s, who have been known even to the Ṛgvedic seers as wandering ascetics[12], came to a particular place, when completely emaciated, as the last resort and with a determined mind to meet their last fate. The wolves (or dogs; the word is *sālāvṛka*) might be knowing the place by habit. The *sālāvṛkas* are referred to twice in the Ṛgveda, and the references appear to show acquaintance with the custom of offering persons to them, or, at least, the beasts so devouring. In one place Indra is said to have held a thousand *sālāvṛka-s* by the mouth,[13] while at the other Purūravas refers to them comparing with them the hearts of women;[14] it is also said that he may be eaten away by the wolves.[15] The point that strikes one here is, why should Purūravas not refer to any other type of bodily affliction, when being denied the attention by Urvaśī. True, that the customs of the disposal of the dead referred to in the Ṛgveda do not include the giving away to the wolves; but, there can be no doubt that Purūravas is referring to the most grotesque bodily torture in his mention of the wolves devouring him. The words of advice to Purūravas are: "Purūravas! Die not (*mā mṛthāḥ*); fall not: may not the vile wolves (*vṛ́kāso áśivāsaḥ*) devour you. Friendships with women are non-existent; they are the hearts of the *sālāvṛkas*".[16] In the earlier verse, falling to the ground is closely associated with the devouring by the wolves; it precedes the eating by the wolves.[17] The wolves are, here, described as *rabhasāsaḥ*, "speedily attacking"; and, as noted above, they are described as *aśiva*, "inauspicious". These details could not have been without an actual observation. In the passages noted earlier, Indra's agency in the act of the wolves devouring the ascetics is not inherent; and we have given reasons for believing so. Again, in the face of the fact that the *yati*-s praise Indra, as noted above,[18] " there can be no doubt that the eating of the *yati*-s by the wolves, though it appeared to be terrible, was customary for the *yati*-s themselves. In this connection it will be interesting to know that, among a sect of Jains, the dead were given to the jackals; and different superstitions were based on the direction in which the body was carried by the beasts. If the body was dragged without injuring it, the direction in which it was dragged was believed to offer good prospects for alms and sojourn. If the body was injured while being dragged, it was indicative of famine in that direction. The prediction was applicable only to the bodies of the preceptors; in the case of others no such predictions were made.[19] In another case, a future Śākya Muni is reported to have offered his body, being alive, to a hungry tigress.[20] These instances may be from a later period; and similar other instances from the Vedic texts may not be available; but their near absence in that period cannot be granted simply because the texts do not record them. In the case of the Vedic *yati*-s, such a custom cannot be said to be improbable. The probability is of its prevalence, the *yati*-s being living and getting emaciated prior to the offering, as a religious duty; or, the bodies might have been offered to the wolves, if they died in their act of a solemn vow. It should be noted, in this connection that the Avesta mentions corpses being eaten by dogs, as by birds.[21]

Another ticklish account, which has dodged the efforts for satisfactory interpretation, is where the *vaikhānasa*-s are said to have been killed by a certain Rahasyu called Deva-malimluc. The account has a very restricted occurrence.[22] According to the account in the Jaim. Br., *vaikhānasas* are said to be "seers" (*ṛṣīkāḥ*) and beloved of Indra. The name of the "killer", however, is Rahasyu Mārimlava. Indra desired to see the *Vaikhānasa*-s, and approached Rahasyu. When he asked Rahasyu whether he saw the *vaikhānasa-ṛṣis*, the latter (pointing out to himself) said that "he" (meaning himself) killed them.[23] Indra was glad that Rahasyu owned the guilt. The plea of Rahasyu was that he would have acquired both the sin of killing and falsehood, had he told a lie; now that he had told the truth, he only had the burden of the killing (*sa hovāca anṛtam ca bhrūṇa-hatyāñ ca-ud ayāṁsam; tam anṛtam evāyāsīt*). The account goes on to say that Rahasyu was asked by Indra to choose a boon, for he spoke the truth. Rahasyu asked for a *brāhmaṇa* as his son. The boon was granted; and it is said, that the progeny of Rahasyu came to be Takṣu-s (or Takṣavas; there are two readings: *takṣavaḥ*; and *takṣavāḥ*). The gods questioned Indra, how in spite of him Mārimlava killed the ascetics.[24] Indra thought that the ascetics should be brought to life; hence he composed the *sāman*, which came to be known as Vaikhānasa, as he himself was Vikhanas (*indro ha vai vikhanāḥ*). The Vaikhānasa *sāman* is praised, here, as being a medicine (*bheṣajam*) and also an expiation (*prāyaścittiḥ*). The account at the Pañcavimṣa Br. is shorter; and, though it is about the same, certain details are different. Apart from the name of the killer appearing as Malimulc, the latter is said to have killed the *vaikhānasa*-s at a place called Munimaraṇa. The gods knew that the ascetics were dear to Indra; (and, not seeing them) they asked Indra what had happened to them. Indra went in search of the ascetics; but could not find them. He, then, cleansed the worlds by a single unabated effort,[25] and found them at (the place called) Muni-maraṇa ("Ascetics-Death"). He revived them by means of the Vaikhānasa laud. That was his sole desire at that time; hence, it is said that the Vaikhānasa laud[26] is the "Desire-fulfilling" laud.

It will be clear that the motive for the employment of the account at the two texts is different, being at one place called the *bheṣaja*, and, at the other, fulfilment of desire. Even so, the aim is the same viz. activating or setting to motion the ascetics. Nothing further is known about the ascetics; and there is no other appendage to the account to clarify the point. From the mood of Indra reflected in the account, the *yati*-s may be believed to have regained their (divine) life. The *sāman* is a *bheṣaja*; and its application would only prove the same point. There can be little doubt that the legend is ancient and independent of Indra, like the other one studied above (i.e. of the *yati*-s and the wolves). Indra is ushered in as a general emancipator, or hero, as is the case in the earlier account and at other places. Another point to be noted is that the place where the ascetics are said to be killed is named Muni-maraṇa in one account (Pañc.Br) though the other account is silent about it. The name suggests that the place is so called not because the ascetics were killed there, but because they died there. In the former case, we expect the name to be Muni-māraṇa. Again, the name appears to be indicative of a continued and known practice, rather than a solitary event.[27] The adjunct of the detail of the ascetics regaining their life (cf. *enān samairayat*, Jai.Br.; and *tān...samairayat*, Pañc.Br.) works two ways. In the first case it indicates the belief that such a death is only temporary, and a step to the next divine birth; and, on the other, it serves as a commendation of Indra and the laud.

Now, about the "killer" Rahasyu Deva-malimluc/ Mārimlava. The name Rahasyu occurs at both the places; but there is a difference regarding the other: Deva-malimluc at the Jai.Br., and Mārimlava at Pañc.Br. Even so, at both the places the gods appear to be keenly concerned about the death of the *vaikhānasas*; in one they directly ask Indra about the fate of the *vaikhānasas*; and, in the other, they gather round him to question how, in spite of him, they were killed.[28] The name Devamalimluc is explained by Śayaṇa thus: "surpassing the gods and rendering them lustreless"[29] where *mali* is taken as a noun, "dirt" or "blackness". But, the rendering has to be discarded, in view of the other word, *mārimlava.*[30] Both the words are connected with killing, as is clear from the passages.[31] There is no other variation of the name Malimluc in relation to the legend of the *vaikhānasas*; but we have another similar word, Malimluca, which refers to the extra month, which is also called Saṁsarpa, Sanisrasa and Aṁhasaspati.[32] The point is, why should the month be called Aṁhasas-pati, "Lord-of-sin"? The names Saṁsarpa and Sanisrasa (fr.√*sam+sṛp* and √*sraṁs* respectively, the latter being the frequentative) indicate swiftness of gait; and the extra month being the thirteenth, and coming once and vanishing for the next three years, is justly described by this epithet. A deeper thought shows that the name "Lord-of-sin" corresponds to the concept behind the word Deva-malimluc, "God-killer". The month is characterised, technically, by being side-tracked and crossed over by the sun,[33] which seems to be the reason why it is characterised as inauspicious (*aṁhasaspati*); and the epithet "God-killer", probably, is symbolic (as its having thus, avoided—"killed"—the Sun-god?). The surmise gets support from the later tradition, which mentions the ancient name Malimluca for this month, and ordains that no ritual auspicious to the gods or to the manes should he performed in this month; this is because this month is tinged with sorrow. Hence also, a vow named śoka-vināśana ("Destroyer-of-sorrow") is enjoined in it.[34] The suggestion of J. Narten, who has studied the word Devamalimluc along with Malimluc and Marimlu, that there is an indication of the extra month being regarded as a demon,[35] is acceptable. With the traditional belief regarding the Malimluch month, one feels that the Vedic Deva-Malimluc is only a personification of this month; and the name Rahasyu is symbolic of its mysterious behaviour of coming out of the set yearly norm. The later name Malamāsa for this month appears to be a corruption, or it may be a new name. There is no sufficient ground to believe that the original word *mali* (in Malimluc), like *mala,* indicated dirt; and the suggestion that *mali* is only another form of *mala* is unwarranted.[36] The epithet "poisonous" is also added to Malimluca,[37] which does not particularly support the suggestion of *mala*, but indicates killing. The belief about the anthropomorphism of the months is already proved by their being addressed in the texts mentioned above. Actually, the extra month was believed to be a vile person from whom the Soma-plant was to be purchased.[38] This reference to a month, called often Malimluca,[39] indicates an ancient originally prevalent practice of purchasing the Soma-plant in this particular month.[40]

The truth behind the account of the *vaikhānasa-s* and Rahasyu Malimluc (Mārimlava) appears to be that the *vaikhānasa-s* believed in giving up their life in the thirteenth month, with the hope of a new divine life. This is clear in the point that Indra brought them to life again; and the month is said to be *indrasya śarma*. The two accounts analysed here would have, then, to be taken as the earliest indications of religious suicide, the later forms of which were the *samlekhanā* of the Jains and the *Bhṛgupatana*[41] and other methods of the Hindus. The people following the Vedic sacrificial cult did not follow this method; and though they appear to be rather shocked by this terrible method they had no disrespect for the *yati-s* and the *vaikhānasa-s* who followed the life of the ascetics.

* * *

Bodewitz, H.W., raises a question,[42] "Are we supposed to assume that Indra acted as a helper of ascetics with suicidal tendencies?" The answer to this question lies in the fact that there are other versions of the account where, in the killing of the *yatis* by the wolves, Indra does not figure. This point has been accepted by Bodewitz himself. This means, that Indra is not an integral party to the myth. This also proves my suggestion that the *yati*-killing account is independent, to which Indra, as a hero, gets attached; this is a later phase. Further, Bodewitz points out that the *yatis* did not only consist of old men, but also of children (Pañcavimśa *Br.* 8. 1. 4 and 13.4.16) and that three young boys, from among the *yati-s*, sought the help of Indra who supported them (Jaim Br.I.185). As Bodewitz says, the instance is the "Sāmavedic treatment of the story" (p.67). Thus, he agrees that the treatment differs from the original; and, this is exactly the point. The story had become popular, and, like other popular stories in the Vedic times, it came handy for the sacrificer-thinkers to use it to praise various rites and objects used in the Vedic sacrificial context. In other words, the story got the status of a myth and was rubricated as *arthavāda* (cf. Charter). The version of the myth from the Jaim. Br., which Bodewitz has mentioned, is to extol the Traikakubha laud. Likewise, other texts have used the myth to extol the details at the *Uttara-vedi* at the Agniṣṭoma (Soma) sacrifice or Varuṇapraghāsa *parvan* of the Cāturmāsya. As has been made clear in Part I, there are two main stages in the history of a myth. The first is of its original nature; the second is of its use in various contexts, depending upon the purpose for what it is used. This is one more example.

Bodewitz says that at Kaṭhaka Sam. (25.6) where Indra does not play a role, the intention of suicide seems to be entirely absent. But, that is the case in almost all passages. Had there been a clear mention of the intention of suicide, there would not have been any problem. The problem, and the suspicion of 'religious suicide' arises due to other references, such as a place called Munimaraṇa, which I have referred to in my article, and which Bodewitz has left out in his disagreement to my suggestion of suicide. Though the context at Munimaraṇa is not that of the *yati-s* (it is of the Vaikhānasa-s), the name cannot be taken as indicating simply a cremation-ground (or burial ground), (for explanation may be seen Dange, 1980-81, p.117). The suggestion of Bodewitz that the expression: "'to surrender people to the *sālāvṛkas*' may originally simply have meant to kill people and leave them uncremated or unburied" is not happy; for, in that case what could be the fate of Purūvaras who lamented that the *sālāvṛka-s* would eat him (*ṚV* X.95. 14)? Should we believe that Purūravas would be killed and left unburied or uncremated ? And by whom ? As I have mentioned (*op.cit.*p.116) it had been a custom to offer the dead to the wolves, or dogs, though the Rgveda does not mention it as a regular one; and there need not be anybody to kill a person to give him to the wolves. There is hardly any passage where Indra is said to have "killed" the *yatis* to support the stylistic expression. On the contrary the *yatis* are actually said to have been devoured by the wolves. Where the expressed literal evidence (*vācyārtha*), is clear, there is no need to understand the implied one (*lakṣyārtha*). Thus, the position is clear:

(i) Indra does not figure in every instance of the story;

(ii) There is a clear mention of the eating of the *yatis* by the wolves.

This shows that the eating of the *yati-s* by the wolves is not caused by Indra, either literally or figuratively. Indra being a hero of multiple exploits, this detail came to be tucked on to him, in addition to the others like his being the paramour of Ahalyā, the *menā* of Vṛṣaṇaśva etc. Actually, the concept of Indra-*kilbiśa* (sin) got formulated later, and by that time this popular account had already a tuck on Indra. About the probable suicide of the *yatis* we have to take help from the detail of Munimarana.

The *yati*-wolf account does not mention any children as it occurs in other texts, except the Sāmavedic treatment;[43] and, there seems to be no doubt, the Sāmaveda brought in the three children (or boys) to suit the three elevations (*kakubh*-s) on the body of Indra where they could ascend to. It is to be noted that Indra is called Trikakup(bh) in the Ṛgveda (I. 121.4). In the context of the Traikakubha laud (*Jaim.Br.* I.185), in the idea of the three *kakubh*-s ("elevations") of Indra there is a mixture of ideas: the cosmic body of Indra, and his personal body.

The strain in both is that of *annādyam* ("nourishment"). If we remember that Indra is also conceived as an androgen—having both the male and the female characteristics in him,[44]—it seems that the three *kakubh*-s on his personal body are the three (not two, as usual) breasts. What else can be the nourishment (*annādyam*) on the body ? It is here that the image of the children comes in. The clinging to the three elevations on the body *trikakup*-s of Indra, to suit the name of the laud, and the epithet *trikakup* in respect of Indra, can hardly suit grown up men (among the *yati-s*). Hence, the *yati-s* are seen as children—may be milk-sucking ! The motif is present in a later myth involving Indra, that of Mañdhātṛ.[45] It is to be noted that the three children are held by Indra in between his shoulders (*tān antarāṁsay or adhyāsyata*), which means that the *kukubh*-s are all in between his shoulders. The moment the three children were thus held, the *kakubh*-s of Indra bent low to suit the children (i.e. their mouths). This solves the difficulty of the construction. Hence, the translation of Oertel, given by Bodewitz, is obviously unacceptable; for, it twists the original text: *ta asya tisraḥ kakubho 'lambanta* (Oertel : "They clung to his three points"; that is why, to him, "this and what follows is not clear"; (see Bodewitz, p.68). Oertel mistakes *tāḥ* (which obviously goes with the Fem. *tisraḥ kakubhaḥ*) for *te* (taking it with *kumārāḥ*.)! Hoffman takes the word *tāḥ* as rightly indicating *kakubhaḥ* (Bodewitz, *op.cit.);* but misses the point, as he understands them to bend towards Indra (*asya*?). Bodewitz's objection to these interpretations is understandable. But, he completely misses the imagery. His argument is that Indra is "already *trikakubh*" (*ṚV* I.124.4) before the arrival of the *yati-s*. But, that is exactly why the Sāmavedic text uses the point, and uses the Ṛgvedic image of the three elevations, adding that they are in between the shoulders of Indra to offer nourishment to the three *yati*-children who he gets close to the "breasts", the *kakubh*-s, that themselves bend for the "children". The correct translation would be "These three elevations of him (i.e. of Indra) got elongated (to the mouths of the boys)."

Bodewitz's statement : "In every passage where the *yatis* and the *sālāvṛka*-s occur together (with or without Indra) some of them are alive and escape from these wolves or hyenas (p.67)," is not quite correct. For example, the Maitrāyaṇī Sam. (I.10.12) refers to this myth, but there is no mention of some *yati-s* escaping (also Kāṭhaka Sam. XI. 10; XXXVI.7; Taittirīya Sam. II.49.2; VI.2.7.5; nowhere do have mention of escape). The escape motif comes only in the Jaiminīya Br. and the Pañcaviṁśa Br. (ref. to above); and, at Tait.Sam. (XXV.6) it comes to extol the *uttara-vedi*, where all have been said to run to the *uttara-vedi*. Are we to suppose that the escape-motif is absent in these other accounts because the story in all these is not given fully? But, then, where is the full account ? The probability is that, as the children-motif is introduced for the praise of the laud Traikakubha (and it never occurs in any other version), so is the escape to the *uttaravedi* brought in, to extol that *vedi*; and this is not true of other versions of the myth.

References

1. Kāṭhaka Sam., VIII.5.
2. Taittirīya Sam., VI.2.7.5
3. Ait.Br., VII.28.
4. Kāṭhaka Sam., XXV.6.
5. *Ibid.*, XXXVI.7. Here the *uttaravedi* is not that in the Mahāvedi at the Soma-sacrifice. It is one of the two additional altars,

but to the north. The other one is to its south; that is the Dakṣiṇavedi. Both are made to the east of the usual altars. Here the northern (*uttara*) altar is also to be raised; hence, *uttara*.

6. *Ibid.*, also XI.10.
7. ṚV X.136.7, *Keśī*; cf. AV VIII.6.17, *munikeśa*, epithet of an evil spirit.
8. Kāṭhaka Sam. VIII.5; cf. Bhavabhūti, *Uttararāmacaritam*, IV.26; *vikirati śakṛt-piṇḍakān āmramātrān*; this may give the idea of a miniature head of the size of a mango (*āmra*). The account of the ascetics occurs also at Jai.Br.I.185, for a different purpose.
9. Dange, S.A. *Sexual Symbolism from the Vedic Ritual*, Delhi, 1979, esp. pp. 51-82.
10. ṚV VIII.6.18[ab], *yá indra yátayas tvā bhṛ́gavo yé ca tuṣṭuvúḥ*; here the Bhṛgus are different from the Yatis; also *ibid.*, 3.9[cd]; X.72.7 for the praise of the *yati-s* for nourishing the worlds.
11. The reason is that this quarter is associated with the dead, and also with no return; cf. Śatapatha Br., III.1.1.2, *eṣā vai dik pitṛṇām; sa yad dakṣiṇapravaṇam syāt* (i.e. the altar) *kṣipre ha yajamāno amum lokam iyāt*; cf. also I.2.5.17; II.3.3.16; III.2.3.17.
12. Soma is described as *sahasra-nītir yatiḥ*, "going in thousand paths".
13. ṚV X.13.3.
14. *Ibid.*, X.95.15.
15. *Ibid.*, also 14.
16. *Ibid.*, X.95.15, *Sālāvṛkāṇām hṛ́dayāny etā́*.
17. *Ibid.*, 14, *ádhā śáyīta nírṛter upásthe ádhainam vṛ́kā rabhasā́so adyúḥ*.
18. *Ibid.*, VIII.6.18, *Yá indra yátayastvā... tuṣṭvúḥ*.
19. S.B. Deo, *History of Jain Monachism*, Poona, 1956, p. 431, where he cites from the *Bṛhatkalpabhāṣya*.
20. Hastings, J. *Encl. Rel.* and *Ethics*, vol. XII, p. 26, where a reference from the Jātakamālā, SBE, vol. I, occurs.
21. Vendidad, Fargard VII.3; see SBE, vol.4, *The Zend Avesta*, pt. 1, Delhi, 1988 (1887), p.75.

22. Pañcavimśa Br., XIV.4.7; Jaiminīya Br., III.190.

23. The expression is, *sa hovāca syo vai bhagavas tān amārayad iti*; also W. Caland, The *Brāhmaṇa of the Twentyfive Chapters*, Calcutta, 1931, on XIV.4.7, p. 358, note 2, where he refers to the Jai. Br., "It is I who have killed them, O Bhagavan".

24. *Mārimlavo amīmarat*; the verb is to the taken in the casual sense; cf. *ajījanat*, ṚV IV.53.2; V.83.10 etc.

25. *ekadhāreṇa*; Sāyana, *ekodyogena*; for Caland "the exact meaning of the purificatory process by one stream is difficult". Probably, *eka* has the sense of "mighty" or "excellent"; cf. Śat Br. I.16.4.12, *eko vīraḥ*; Jai. Br., II.156 (for Indra), *ayam na eko vīro bhūt*; also ṚV I.31.5, *eka-āyuḥ*, said of Agni; also X.103.3, *ekavīraḥ* (Indra); VII.38.5, *ekadhenubhiḥ*; *dhāra* (masc.) may be understood as indicating a unique method, fr. √*dhṛ*, "to hold"; cf also *dhārapūtāḥ* (Ādityas) at II.27.2; 9; *dhāra-vāka* at V.44.5. The expression *ekadhāreṇa* may also mean "by a sudden torrent of rain", Indra being the rainer.

26. The laud (*sāman*) is on ṚV VIII.31.17, *nákiṣṭám kármaṇā naśat ná prá yoṣan ná yoṣati*, and has the strain of excellence and non-separation; the latter suits the present context.

27. *munimaraṇe amārayat* and *munimaraṇe avindat*.

28. Pañca. Br. (*loc. cit.*) *tam edvā abruvan kva tarṣayo'bhūvann iti*; Jai. Br. *satas tavo* (=*tava*+u).

29. *devān mālinyam mlocayati iti devān atigaḥ*

30. Caland, *op.cit., loc. cit.*, does not read Mārimlava, when he provides his translation from the Jai. Br. in the note; but only Malimluc. His text and version of the Jai. Br. are not indicated.

31. Mārimlava is from Marimlu, the meaning not changing, the suffix (*aN*) being *svārthe*. Marimlu and Malimlu have the same root √*mṛ* ~ *mḷ*, relating to death or injury; the varieties would be Marimṛ, Malimḷ, Malimṛ, Marimḷ. The word *malimḷ* comes with *stena*, and has to be differentiated from the latter; hence, it does not denote only "thief" or "robber", but "dacoit" or "killer".

32. See Macdonell, A.A. and Keith, A.B. *Vedic Index of Names and Subjects*, under *māsa;* Vājasaneyi-Sam., 22.30; 7.30, Maitrāyaṇī Sam., III.12-13; AV V.6.4; Kāṭhaka Sam., 35.10; 38.14. The later

texts make a difference between Aṁhasaspati and Saṁsarpa; see Kane, P.V. *History of Dharmashastra*, vol. V-i, p. 672.

33. Cf. Skanda Purāṇa, V.1.60.33 (*sūryeṇa*) *asaṅkrānto yadā māsaḥ*; also Kane, *op.cit.*, p. 671, n. 1053, where he quotes from Laghuhārita, *tam atikramya tu ravir yadā gacchet kathañ cana.* This month is called Puruṣottama, according to certain Purāṇas (Kane, *op. cit.*, p. 672, where he refers only to the Padma P., VI.64); and some mention Puruṣottama as the lord of this month. The idea seems to be to do away with the evils attached to this month; the special ritual at this time requires the worship of Viṣṇu (Puruṣottama) with Lakṣmī; see note 34 below.

34. For this vow see Skanda P., *loc. cit.*, 19-21; 33-38.

35. Narten, Johanna *Malimlu-malimluca*, IIJ, IX-iii, 1966, pp. 203-8; *Schaltmonat Dämon.*

36. The name Malamāsa is explained as follows: "They say that it is the dirt of Time", *malam vadanti kālasya*, quoted by Kane, *op. cit.*, p. 671, 1052. Mahīdhara's comment, on Vāj. Sam., XI.78, *malimlūn*, as *malinā bhūtvā mlocanti*, is grammatically unsound; even granting that *mali* (*malin*= *mal+in*) is an adjective, it has to be an object of the verbal formation (*kṛdanta*) *mluc*. Actually, the word is *malimlu*, both here and at 79. Kane cites RV X.136.2, *múnayo Vātaraśanā piśáṅgā vasate málā, op. cit.*, 671.

37. Śāṅkhāyana Śr. S., VI.12.15, *malimluco'si sagaraḥ.*

38. Aitareya Br., III.1, *tam trayodaśān māsād akrīṇan*

39. Kāṭhaka Sam., 38.14, *malimluco nāmāsi trayodaśo māsaḥ*; *indrasya śarmāsi.*

40. Why the Soma-plant was purchased in this month is not quite clear; or, at least, why it is associated with the thirteenth month! Probably, the detail could be compared with the status of the Soma-plant in ritual-context. The Soma-shoots are arranged in the shape of a man, prior to their being pressed; and the pressing of the Soma-shoots is seen as the killing of King Soma; cf. Śat. Br., III.9.4.2; 17; Maitt. Sam., IV.7.7; 8.3 etc. The ritual-symbolism in Soma-pressing is of death and rebirth, the latter when the pressed shoots are placed in the Vasatīvarī waters (see Eggeling, *Tr.* Śat. Br., SBE, 26, p. 244);

and it is based on the monthly movement of the moon and the sun. The Sun-Indra is always the "Eater" and Moon-Soma is always the eaten, Śat. Br., I.6.4.12 ff. The nature of the thirteenth month as the Aṁhasaspati and Malimluc (-a) seems to have, in addition, the germ of new birth, taking into account that Indra brings the Vaikhānasa-s back to life. The killer and the new-birth-giver in one is also the nature of the sun; the same is true of the preceptor in relation to the disciple or the initiate; on this point, see Dange, *Legends in the Mahābhārata*, Delhi, pp. 171-90. This would show Malimluc(a) in a new light -- the beneficent month-demon — and would help the custom of religious suicide in it for a divine fresh birth.

41. Manusmṛti, VI.31-32; Yājñavalkyasmṛti, III.55, and the Mitākṣarā, on it.

42. "What did Indra do with the Yatis?" *Amṛtadhārā* (Dr. R.N. Dandekar Fel. Vol.), Delhi, 1984. pp. 65-72., where he attempts a critical assessment of my paper, "Religious suicide in the Vedic period (?)", *Indologia Taurinensia* (Vols VIII-IX) Dr. Ludwik Sternback Com. Vol. 1980-81, PP. 113-122. I have changed the title here to focus attention on the myth.

43. *teṣām adyamānānām trayaḥ kumārāḥ paryaśiṣyanta* etc. These Kumāras are said to have been taken by Indra to his three "elevations."

44. ṚV. I.51.13; cf. *Indische Studien*, III, p. 479, context of the *āsurī* Vilesteṅgā; Indra takes the form of a woman among women.

45. Mahābhārata, Vana, 126.30-31.

Seven

Bones of Dadhīci

There is a popular myth that the sage Dadhīci (Dadhīca) provided his own bones to Indra (or the gods) with which the latter vanquished the *asura-s*. The myth permeates various stages of the Hindu-mythology, including the Vedic and the Puranic. To start from the Puranic records: According to one account, (Skanda P.I.1.16.77ff-17.3ff) the gods made all weapons, including the thunderbolt of Indra from these bones. It is also said in another text, that once the gods approached Dadhīci and placed their weapons in his hermitage for safe custody. It was agreed that the gods would turn up soon and take back the weapons.[1] Now, over a thousand years went by; but the gods did not return. Dadhīci came to know that, due to the weapons deposited at his hermitage, the *asura-s* began to have hatred for him. So to preserve the weapons, and also to mitigate the hatred of the *asura-s*, Dadhīci merged (washed?) the weapons with *mantra-s* and drank the water.[2] So, now, the 'weapons' (i.e. the essence of the weapons) went into his body. When the gods arrived, they did not see the weapons, and requested Dadhīci to produce them. So, he produced them from his body, in the form of his bones; but, in that act he died (Brahma P.110.5ff). The Mahābhārata (Mb.) refers to this detail twice (Vana, 100.9-21; Śalya,

51.26ff). The gods knew from Tvaṣṭṛ that they could fashion a thunderbolt from the bones of Dadhīca. Hence they went to the hermitage of the sage on the other bank of the river Sarasvatī and requested the sage, who readily released his vital breaths from his body. The gods took his bones and went back to Tvaṣṭṛ who fashioned a thunderbolt for Indra. With this thunderbolt Vrtra was killed (Vana, *loc.cit.*). According to the account at the Śalya *parvan*, Indra is said to have got prepared many weapons such as maces, thunderbolts, discs and so on. With the thunderbolt, thus prepared, Indra killed as many demons as ninety-nine (v36 *jaghāna navatīrnava*), an expression borrowed from the Ṛgveda, I.84.13). At both the places the location for the gain of the bones is the river Sarasvatī.

A fuller reference to this mythical account, with the detail of the bones of Dadhīca (Dadhīci), occurs in the tradition recorded by the Śāṭyāyanas, as mentioned by Śayaṇa in his commentary on Ṛgveda (ṚV) I.84.13. According to it, the *asura-s* were afraid of the sight of Dadhīci. So, as long as he was alive they concealed themselves. But, when he died, the whole earth was filled with the *asura-s*. Being unable to exterminate these *asuras*, or to defeat them, Indra searched for the sage Dadhīc. Being told, on enquiry that he had died, Indra enquired if any part of the body of the sage remained somewhere (*kiñcit pariśiṣṭam aṅgam asti-iti*). He was told that there remained the *head of the horse*, fixing which on his own body Dadhīc had taught the honey-lore (*madhu-vidya*) to the Aśvins; but, the whereabouts of the head were not known. Indra requested the gods to search for the head of the horse. The gods searched for it, and found it at a place called Śaryaṇāvat, on the Sarasvatī, at Kurukṣetra. Having searched it out, with the bone of the head of the horse[3] (which the sage Dadhīc had donned), Indra killed the *asura-s*. Though the Ṛgveda has *dadhīceḥ asthabhiḥ* at v13, in the very next verse (14) it states that the head of the horse was concealed in the mountain (or hills, *parvateṣu*) in the Śaryaṇāvat. The statements in these two verses of the hymn from the ṚV, together, present the picture as follows -

(1) Indra killed the enemies (*asura-ṣ*), numbering ninety-nine, with the bones of Dadhīc (13, *indro dadhīco asthabhiḥ* etc.).

(2) (With the thought from the previous verse) Desiring the head of the horse that was concealed in the hills, he recovered it at Śaryaṇāvat (14, *icchann aśvasya yac cchiraḥ* etc.).

This would give the following equation:

> The bones of Dadhīc =The bones (from the *head*) of the horse.

This equation gets support from the myth of the Aśvins learning the *madhu-vidyā*, wherein the teacher, Dadhyaṅ, is identified with the horse as he dons the horse's head. The name of the teacher, Dadhyaṅ is only a variant of Dadhīc, and the two words are the same, grammatically.[4] According to the myth, Dadhyaṅ knew the secret of the head of the sacrifice - how the head of the sacrifice, which was cut, was to be restored; but he was warned by Indra, that, if he gave out this secret to anyone he would cut the former's head. The Aśvins heard of this, and went to Dadhyaṅ requesting him to divulge the secret to them. Dadhyaṅ, however, told them about his difficulty. So, they hatched a plan. According to it they would cut his head, and replace it by that of a horse; they would conceal the original head of Dadhyaṅ somewhere. Afterwards, they would replace the horse's head with the original head. Dadhyaṅ agreed, and taught the Aśvins about the secret, with the head of a horse which they provided. Indra cut this head, when he knew about it; and the Aśvins placed the original head on the body of Dadhyaṅ (Śatapatha Br. XIV.1.1.18-25).[5]

The difference in the accounts at the later (Puranic) tradition and the early (Vedic) tradition has to be marked. In the early Vedic tradition, Dadhyaṅ does not appear to die. It is only the head that undergoes immediate displacement; and this is the exploit of the Aśvins. The exploit of Indra is the cutting of the head of the horse that was placed on the body of Dadhyaṅ. The Śāṭyāyana Br. closely follows the ṚV in stating that, it is the *head of a horse* (and not the whole body-bones) that was found out by Indra that served to make the weapon for Indra. Though here Dadhīc is said to have already died, there is no 'suicide' for Indra, or for the gods. And it is clear that the horse's head was efficacious as it rested on the body of Dadhyaṅ for some time. The equation in this case is as follows:

Head of Dadhīc/Dadhyaṅ=Head of the horse.

Now, there is yet another myth - or, rather, a variation of the same myth—which is very popular and which occurs just before the Dadhyaṅ episode, at the Śat.Br. This is the myth where Viṣṇu's head is said to be severed as he rested it on the upper tip of his bow; the ants gnawed at the bowstring, and the tip of the bow darted up cutting the head. This head is said to be the head of the sacrifice, identified with Viṣṇu (Śat.Br., *loc.cit.* 6-10) (*sa yaḥ sa Viṣṇur yajñaḥ saḥ*). It is further said, that this head of Viṣṇu is the sun (Ib.10 *tat patitvā-asau ādityo'bhavat*). The rest of the body lay stretched to the east. In the ritual context this myth supports the rite of *pravargya*, where the typical '*mahāvīra*' vessel, having a semblance of three jars placed one over another, figures, and is conceived as the head of Viṣṇu, who is said to be the sacrifice (*Ib.*). The detail of the head of Viṣṇu became popular in later times in his aspect of Hayagrīva (Horse-necked, ie.-headed), Skanda P.III.2.15.32ff). The same Vedic account (as from Śat.Br.) occurs here with negligible variations; and it is Viśvakarman who is said to have placed the head of the horse on Viṣṇu's body (*Ib.*14.40-60;15.1-10). According to Mb. (Śānti, Adhyāya 347) Viṣṇu himself takes the form of Hayaśiras to regain the Vedas stolen by the demons, Madhu and Kaiṭabha; and, after the gain of the Vedas, he places this head of his in the 'north-eastern quarter in the sea' (Ib. *sthāpayitvā hayaśira udak-pūrve mahodadhau* etc.). Reading this later account with the earlier one (from the Śat.Br.), it is clear that the tradition retained the head of Viṣṇu as the solar disc. But, the head of the horse got various associations - Indra and Aśvins, on the one hand, as the recoverers and protectors of the 'head'; and, on the other, Dadhyaṅ (Dadhīci or Dadhīca) and Viṣṇu as those who wore the head. It is also clear that the head was the sun in the Viṣṇu-myth; also that it was the 'head' of the sacrifice. In the ritual context it remained as the *mahāvīra* at the Pravargya, but in the mythical context it changed from Dadhyaṅ to Viṣṇu; in the latter case it symbolized the sun. The position, now, is as follows:

Head < of Viṣṇu, the 'horse-head'
of Dadhyaṅ, the 'horse-head' in the earliest (ṚV) records.

Here, now, we are at a point to see if Dadhyaṅ - the sage - is likely to have been fused with the sun and the horse. This immediately reminds us of the word Dadhikrā or Dadhikrāvan, who is the divine horse. The sub-point that deserves attention is whether Dadhikrāvan and the horse at the horse-sacrifice are two aspects of the same concept, in essence!

In this context, there is clear proof in ṚV itself for the identification of the horse at the horse-sacrifice and the sun (I.162-163); the former hymn is for the sacrificial ritual itself; the latter praises the same horse in the garb of the sun rising from the primeval ocean. The latter, like the former, is enjoined to be recited at the horse-sacrifice, when the sacrificial horse is ready for the rite called *upākaraṇa*, on the middle day of the sacrifice.[6] It is clearly stated, that the head of this horse is seen (by the seer) in the form of the solar orb traversing in the sky (v 6[b] - *divā patayantam pataṅgam*; and - *siro' paśyam pathibhiḥ sugebhiḥ*). This would indicate the following:

(1) In the remote past, at a stage when, in the region of Śaryaṇāvat, the horse-sacrifice was believed to be the supreme sacrifice, the head of the horse had gained unique importance. This goes with the general belief prevalent among the Vedic people that the head of the sacrifice was cut, and was to be obtained somehow, and this was done symbolically, the example being of the Pravargya[7]-Mahāvīra, in the ritual-context. In the myth, it was supposed to be actually gained and placed on the sacrifice.

(2) On the mythical plane, the head of the sacrificial horse (=a Zoomorph of sacrifice) was placed on Viṣṇu's body, and also that of Dadhyaṅ, which indicates unique status of the latter.

(3) Chronologically, the myth of Viṣṇu Hayagrīva is later than that of Dadhyaṅ or Dadhīc; for, the latter occurs in the ṚV, while the former in the

last portions of the Śat.Br.

(4) On the cosmic level, the sun was considered to be the head of the horse, sacrifically killed, while, on the purely mythical level it was concealed, but was to be found out.

(5) Dadhīc is mentioned prominently in the later Ṛgvedic period (Maṇḍala I mostly)[8], which also corroborates with hymns about the sacrificial horse. But Dadhyaṅ (another form of the word dadhīc) occurs in the earlier ṚV (VI.16.14) as the sage who is said to be the (first?) one to have kindled the sacrificial fire. He, with his father Atharvan, was very famous in the Vedic tradition, and may be considered to be among the pioneers of the Vedic sacrificial cult. At the same place, earlier, Atharvan is said to have kindled the fire from (or in) the lotus leaf (v13), which detail continued in ritual in associating the *puṣkara* (blue lotus) with the rite of kindling the fire.[9] From the unique importance of Atharvan and his son Dạdhyaṅ, it is not improbable that the myth of the lost head of sacrifice was associated with Dadhyaṅ, indicating that he, indeed, wore the 'head of the sacrifice'— and, for that matter, the head of the horse in the heyday of horse-sacrifice. Thus, Dadhyaṅ was associated with an already set myth and, most probably, with a ritual, about the head of the sacrificial horse.

(6) The myth, about the sacrificial horse, indicates that bones from its head[10] were efficacious in removing all calamities, or destroying all enemies, if at all found, and for magical rites, later. This also presupposes a custom of concealing the head

at some remote place. The whole Vedic sacrificial tradition is silent about the head of the main victim at a sacrifice, which would indicate its being conealed or taken away, out of all bounds, lest it be used for magical purposes.

The probable fusion of Dadhyaṅ with the sun-horse Dadhikrā or Dadhikrāvan is another phase of the same concept. It is to be noted, that in the Ṛgveda there is no other personal noun that has *dadhi*, as the first or second member in its compound structure. Like Dadhyaṅ/ Dadhīc, who is so closely associated with the myth of the horse-head which ultimately connects with the sun, as noted above, the horse Dadhikrā (Dadhikrāvan) is the sun-horse himself. Moreover, Dadhikrā is directly associated with the horse-sacrifice. This is clear from the fact, that a verse from a hymn to this solar horse is well set in the ritual at the horse-sacrifice. Thus, after the priests recite certain verses having deep sexual overtone, when the symbolic union of the killed solar (sacrificial) horse and the queen is being enacted, a verse in praise of Dadhikrā (Dadhikrāvan) is recited,[11] as a purificatory charm. This would show that the deified Dadhyaṅ, with the myth of the horse-head associated with him, comes closely on par with Dadhikrā.[12] This, probably, is the reason why both have *dadhi* in their names.

It is not improbable that the very name Dadhyaṅ is symbolic, indicating his identification with the solar-horse, who gained the name Dadhikrāvan. The bridge appears to be the horse-sacrifice in whatever earliest form it existed. In any case, Dadhyaṅ and 'his' *head of a horse* is the earliest point in the myth of the bones of Dadhyaṅ. We are, now, in a better position to trace the development of the myth.

(1) Cryptic account from ṚV

Indra killed the demons with the bones from the head of the sacrificial horse, which had magical value in the ancient tradition of Vedic people. This horse was symbolically called Dadhikrā or Dadhikrāvan. He was called so, as he was the 'holder' (*dadhi*) of the secret of prosperity, fertility and longevity, as he signified constant energy and movement (*krāvan/krā* from √*kram*). As the head of the sacrificial horse was concealed somewhere (as it had magical value), nobody knew the whereabouts of the head, except for an ancient sage, who, himself had (gained) a name similar to that of the symbolic name Dadhikrā (as he was believed to 'hold' the secret knowledge; hence, he was called *dadhi-añc*=holding-the-secret 'mover'). He was the son of the great sage Atharvan. Indra resorted to him and was successful in knowing the location of the head of the horse. (At this stage Dadhyaṅ's knowledge of the secret head gave him the mastery over the head; and it came to be called 'his' head). Hence the expression at ṚV *dadhīceḥ asthabhiḥ*, which has been rightly understood by the Śāṭyāyana Br. as *dadhīceḥ aśvasya asthibhiḥ*).

(2) At a later period, as of the other Vedic texts, the Brāhmaṇas, the head of the sacrificial horse was totally identified with that of the sage Dadhyaṅ, which is a case of Zoomorphism gliding into Anthropomorphism. Here the Aśvins and Viṣṇu figure; but the motif of killing the demons is absent.

(3) At a still later period, of the Mb., the regular and popular later version is seen gaining currency. Here in place of the 'head' of Dadhyaṅ (now Dadhīca/Dadhīci) we have the bones from the body, mistaking the original context of *dadhīceḥ asthabhiḥ*, and taking the expression

too literally. Hence, as against the Vedic tradition of the head we have the sage committing suicide for a good cause; and all the bones of his body figure. Once this happened there were variations and innovations in the Puranic versions, as noted in the beginning.

From the analysis of the myth, it would be clear that the bones of Dadhīci are not of a human, but of the sacrificial horse; and, again the original myth centred round the head-bones of the sacrificial horse, the sage Dadhyaṅ - Dadhīci, holding the meaning of an ancient custom about these bones of the sacrificial horse[14] for success of all sorts, including the warding off of evil powers (*asura-s*) and the gain of prosperity. It is clear that the myth and ritual of the horse-head, and bones from it were tucked on to the sage Dadhyaṅ/Dadhīci.

References

1. The motif occurs at the Taittirīya Sam.(I.5.1.1), where the gods are said to have deposited their wealth with the fire-god (though not weapons) till they came back after defeating the *asura-s*.
2. The motif occurs at the ordeal called *kośa* in later times. In it the wash-water of an idol of a deity is asked to be drunk by the suspect. Cf. Kane, P.V., *Vyavahāramayūkha* (Ed.), Bombay, 1926, p.82; also Skanda Purāṇa I.2.44.2.
3. *tasya śiraso 'sthibhiḥ*, to quote the Śaṭyāyana; and Sāyaṇa - *asthibhiḥ aśvaśiraḥ-sambandhibhiḥ*.
4. *dadhi+√añc* gives *dadhyaṅ* (Nom.Sing.); *dadhi+ √añc→ dadhi +ac* (Pāṇ.VI.4.24)→*a* elided (Pāṇ.VI.4.138); with i→ī; cf. *prāc* (whence *prācī*) also *pratīc* from *prati+añc.*
5. Cf. ṚV I.116.12; 117.22; 119.9.
6. Āśvalāyana Śr.S.X.8 at Śayaṇa, Introduction to the hymn I.163. *Upākaraṇa* comprises the touching of the victim, after it is given ritual bath, with a blade of *darbha* (grass) or/and a leafy branch of the tree called Plakṣa *(Ficus Infectoria).*

7. Cf. Śatapatha Br. III.9.2.1 *yatra vai yajñasya śiro 'cchidyata*; earlier the *pravargya* is called the head of the sacrifice, Ib.III.4.4.1 *grīva vai yajñasya-upasadaḥ, śiraḥ pravargyam*; also for the severed head of Viṣṇu, Śat.Br.XIV.1.1.10 *yat prāvṛjyata tasmāt pravargyaḥ*; cf. also the head of the metre Gāyatrī cut by the vaṣat sound, Maitrāyaṇī Sam.II.5.7-8. For severed head, see Ms. Dange, S.S. "Severed Head in Myth and Ritual", *ABORI*, Vol.s LXXII and LXXIII for 1991-1992, Poona, 1993, pp.487-49b6.

8. ṚV I.84.13; 117.22; 119.9; Dadhyaṅ I.80.16; 116.12; only once at VI.16.14 and once at IX.108.4.

9. Taittirīya Br. I.1.3.6; also Taitt. Sam.V.1.4.4.

10. At the Old Testament, Judges 15.14, Samson is said to have killed his enemies with the jaw-bone of a donkey. The place where this happened is known as Ramath Lehi, which, in Hebrew, means "Jaw-bone Hill".

11. ṚV IV.39.6; Taitt.Sam.VII.4.19.15; Vājasaneyi-Sam. XXIII.32; the verse is *dadhikrāvṇo akāriṣam jiṣṇor aśvasya vājinaḥ* etc.

12. Macdonell, A.A., *Vedic Mythology*, under Dadhyañc, has already faintly suggested the similarity between Dadhyañc and Dadhikrā. However, he has not probed the point further.

13. Yāska, however, gives different etymologies, Nirukta II. 28; they do not fit in with the ritual and the myth about the horse; *dadhi* fr. *dadhāti iti*, fr. *√dhā+ki* (Pāṇ.III.3.92), though without an *upasarga* as a Vedic peculiarity. Even in *dadhat krāmati* (Yāska) *dadhat* is not an *upasarga*, to warrant Paṇini III.2.67 where the *anuvṛtti* of *upasarga* is to be taken! The same applies to *krā/krāvan* (*krāva*) with *viṭ* and *vanip*.

14. That the bone, especially the rib, of the horse was used as an instrument or a weapon is suggested at ṚV VII.83.1[b]- *pṛthu-parśavaḥ*; and Śayaṇa renders *parśu* as *pārśvāsthi*; cf. Taitt.Br.III.2.2.1 *aśva-parsvā barhir acchaiti*. The word *pārśva* (side) is from the context of the side of the body - i.e., of the rib, *parśu*.

Nṛsiṁha

Eight

Nṛsiṁha—The Man-Lion

In one of his incarnations, Viṣṇu is said to have assumed the form of a lion, in which half his body (head) was that of the lion and the other half was the body of a man. It is indicated that he had also the nails of a lion, wherewith he tore open the stomach of Hiraṇyakaśipu, the demon-king who was the father of Prahlāda, Viṣṇu's devotee. Prahlāda, though just a 'boy', was adamant in his devotion to Viṣṇu, while the father was averse to this god.

The popular version of this myth occurs in the Bhāgavata P. (Bhāg.P.VII.8.1ff), according to which, briefly, the *asura*-king, Hiraṇyakaśipu is averse to the devotion of Viṣṇu on the part of his son, Prahlāda. He tortures him variously, yet the latter does not deviate from the devotion to Viṣṇu. Ultimately Hiraṇyakaśipu asks Prahlāda, 'If Viṣṇu be everywhere, why is he not seen in this pillar?" (v13 *kasmāt stambhe na dṛśyate*). On being told that he was also in the pillar, the king smites the pillar with his fists (v 15). Immediately rushes forth from it the god with the terrible face of a lion (vv 18-21). He takes the king aloft and carries him to the threshold of the hall, places him on his lap and tears his stomach (vv, 14ff; 29 *dvāryura āpātya dadāra līlayā*). The Viṣṇu P. (300-500 A.D.) also gives the account of Hiraṇyakaśipu and his destruction by Nṛsiṁha Viṣṇu, but it does not refer to the *sabhā* (hall), nor the threshold as the place of killing (Viṣṇu P. I.17 and the following chapters). It mentions the various punishments inflicted on Prahlāda by his father; also that he kicks Prahlāda on the latter's chest (19.50), and not that he kicks or fists the pillar. The account cools off tamely; and then, suddenly, we have the expression, "when his father was killed by the god in the form of a lion" etc. (20.32).

Of the Purāṇas, the other important sources are the Matsya P. and the Brahmāṇḍa P., which could be assigned the same period,[1] both slightly earlier than the Bhāg. P. (200-400-600 A.D.). According to the Matsya P. (161.1ff) Hiraṇyakaśipu had gained a boon from Brahmā by severe penance that he would not be killed either by a god, or by a man, or by a demon, or by a *piśāca* (a ghostly spirit), or by any beast. Having obtained the boon he began harassing all, including the gods (a feature which is common to all the accounts). Hence, the gods approached Viṣṇu and complained to him about the roughings of this demon. Viṣṇu promised to help them and deal with the demon. Learning from them that his boon included the demon's non-death even by ordinary and usual weapons and that he would not be killed either by day or night (and in the dwelling or out of it, another feature common to these accounts, but absent here), he took the form half of a man and half of a lion (v 37 *narasya kṛtvā-ardhatanum Siṁhasyārdhatanum tathā*), having touched one of his hand with the other (indicative of a magic action !)[2] and went to the place of Hiraṇyakaśipu, taking with him *Om-kāra* (the auspicious and symbolic utterance *Om*, Ib.35). There he saw the assembly-hall of the demon. (It was filled with every thing including various trees, nymphs dancing merrily and demon-chiefs in their aircars!!). Among the demons and *asura*-s were almost all (usually described and mentioned in the Puranic texts), including Prahlāda, Virocana, Bali, Naraka, Vipracitti and others (vv 78,79). Viṣṇu (referred to here as *mṛgādhipa*, v 88) saw all this. Hiraṇyakaśipu's son, Prahlāda, with his divine eye, saw the god arrived as a lion (162.2 *siṁham apaśyad devam āgatam*). As all were astonished at seeing the unusual form he told his father that everything—all species of creation and even the assembly—was to be seen in the man-lion (v 11). On hearing this speech of Prahlāda, Hiraṇyakaśipu ordered the demons to catch that 'lord of beasts' (*mṛgendraḥ*) of unusual form. They tried hard attacking the creature, but were roughed up by him. The fight continued (Ib.5-38ff; 163.1ff). Ultimately, Hiraṇyakaśipu himself darted to him. And Nṛsiṁha, the *mṛgendra*, tore him (not his stomach) with the help of the *Om-kara* with his long sharp nails (163.94).

From the account it would appear that Prahlāda was quite grown up. Moreover, it would appear that Prahlāda, his son Virocana and his grandson Bali were in the same assembly. This is also the reason for there being no mention of the torturous tests of Prahlāda. The account is not in accord with the version at the regular Mb. (Ādi 65.17-20, though the regular Mb. does not narrate the episode of the conflict between Hiraṇyakaśipu and Nṛsiṁha) and other texts, according to which Virocana is the son of Prahlāda and Bali the grandson. If all these were in the assembly-hall, Prahlāda must be taken to be pretty old. This would also indicate that the Nṛsiṁha (Man-lion) account was not the same through the ages. From the version of the Matsya P., which is, by far, the oldest of the Purāṇas, it could be gathered that -(i) A mythical *asura* king (mythical, in spite of the genealogy given by the Purāṇas) known as Hiraṇyakaśipu came to be regarded as the father of Prahlāda, who started the worship of a Lion-man. Further, that, though an *asura*, Prahlāda was prone to accept the Vedic god Viṣṇu; or (ii) Prahlāda was a real son of Hiraṇyakaśipu, but not a child when he made known his devotion to Viṣṇu. To support Prahlāda's devotion to Viṣṇu and his behaviour, in contrast to the general pattern of the behaviour of the *asura*-s, the Bhāg.P.(VII.7.2ff) narrates that Hiraṇyakaśipu's wife was carried away by Indra when the *asura* was away for penance; Nārada heard the lamentations of the woman and rescued her; he brought her to his hermitage as she was pregnant with the would-be Prahlāda and kept her under his care till the birth of the child; as he entertained his mother in her pregnancy, and also the child after he was born, by telling the stories of Viṣṇu and giving him instruction about proper behaviour, Prahlāda got groomed different from the *asura*-s.[3] However, like Nārada (and Indra) the part of Hiraṇyakaśipu appears to be an embroidery in this account. Now, let us see what the Brahmaṇḍa P. gives us.

The Brahmāṇda P. (II.3.3.4-35) shows a trait of presenting etymological explanations at various places; and even in this case it is marked, though it refers to the myth very briefly. It does away with the tests to which Prahlāda was subjected; does not mention Hiraṇyakaśipu's boon of 'no-death' either in day or at night, nor in-or-out of the dwelling etc. It states that Hiraṇyakaśipu was so named as, in the state of the foetus, he dropped out from the mother's (Diti's) womb and sat on the golden (*hiraṇya*) seat (*kaśipu*) on the occasion of a Soma-sacrifice called Atirātra[4] (Ib.vv 4 and 5). But, just a bit later in the same place we are informed, that at the Horse-sacrifice of Kaśyapa (performed by Kaśyapa ? or, at which the sage officiated as priest?), performed at Puṣkara, the foetus sat on the golden seat (*hiraṇya-kaśipu*) meant for the Hotṛ priest and gave a narration (like the Hotṛ); hence he came to be called so (Ib.7-10). It is further said, that Viṣṇu was born from Nara (not 'man' here; Nara, the divine sage from the dual Nara-Nārāyaṇa); hence, in the NaraSiṁha form he is indicated as 'Nara' (Ib.26). But, why he is also called *siṁha* is not explained. Then it is told, that this Narasiṁha killed Hiraṇyakaśipu in the arm-fight (*bāhu-yuddhena*), using his sharp nails, which are neither dry nor moist (indicating the elaborate boon (Ib.29). It will be seen that the explanation of the name Hiraṇyakaśipu here is not only fantastic; it is also ridiculous, as Kaśyapa is said to have performed the Horse-sacrifice which is the prerogative of a king, which is not the case with Kaśyapa— a creator 'Prajāpati'. Like Nārada, who never appears in the Vedic sphere and is a ploy in the Hindu patterns of myths in the post-Vedic sphere, Kaśyapa is the common ancestor of the gods and the *asura*-s, birds and beasts, humans and sub-humans *et al.* The indication is that he was mythical or pseudo. The same is the case with Hiraṇyakaśipu on the *asura* side and of Manu on the human side, the latter seen as the Creator even of sub-humans[5]. For the explanation of the name Hiraṇyakaśipu the Brahmāṇda P. follows the Vedic details. The Vedic texts do not mention any person of that name; but, the word *hiraṇya-kaśipu* occurs twice in the AV and once each in the Ait.Br. and the Taitt. Br. The AV mentions *hiraṇyakaśipu* once (V.7.10) as an epithet of the goddess Nirṛti, the companion of the god of death, who is also equated with the enemy. This goddess is conceived as seated on a seat (*kaśipu*) of gold (*hiraṇya*). She is to be pacified with a bow and humility, lest she should harm. At another place *kaśipu* occurs independently and is indicative of a seat, where it is said to be made of the fibres of reed thrashed for the purpose (AV VI.138.5). In the ritual-context at the Rajāsūya sacrifice meant for royalty and the gain of a son, the Hotṛ priest narrated the legend of Śunaḥ-śepa seated on a golden seat *(hiraṇya-kaśipu*, Ait.Br. VII.18=33.6). The *Hiraṇyakaśipu*, as it is referred to in the Vedic context, does not appear to be a raised seat. The horse to be silenced (ritually killed) at the Horse-sacrifice was placed on a *hiraṇyakaśipu*; and the arrangement was as follows: a spread called *tārpya* (which is said to be a woollen blanket drenched in or smeared with clarified butter) was laid first; upon it was spread a carpet of leather and upon it was spread the *hiraṇyakaśipu* (Taitt.Br.III.9.20.1). The Brahmāṇda P. draws ideas from this sacrificial context, when it states that the foetus dropped out (from the womb of Diti) and took seat on *kaśipu* made of gold (or, golden, *hiraṇya*), to explain the name of the *asura*-king. Like Hiraṇyakaśipu, his wife Kayādhu also does not figure in the Vedic context. However, Prahlāda does. The Jai.Br.(I.126) mentions Virocana as the son of Prahlāda, the *asura*, in an account which states that Indra wooed Uśanas (the priest of the *asura*-s) to come to the side of the gods with the promise of the cows of Virocana (*virocanasya prāhladeḥ kāmadughāḥ*). All this would show that Prahlāda was a real person and that, though he was of the *asura* clan, he was not antagonistic to the Vedic faith, nor was Virocana.

Now to revert to the Viṣṇu P. slightly. We learn that Prahlāda comes home to his father's capital for a break in study. His father, Hiraṇyakaśipu asks him what he has learned and Prahlāda praises Viṣṇu as the omnipotent lord of the universe. Hiaraṇyakaśipu censures the preceptor, who has come along with Prahlāda, for this type of instruction and the preceptor tells him that such things were never taught by him. Prahlāda clarifies that he was instructed this way by Viṣṇu himself who stays in his heart and everywhere. Then follow the tests and torture (I.17.1-48). Then follows conciliation by the sons of Śukra, the family priest of the king. Now, Prahlāda teaches even other boys how great Viṣṇu is and how the worldly miseries could be avoided by devotion to Viṣṇu (Ib.49—end of the chapter). Another round of tests follows. There is no mention of Kayādhu (as the mother of Prahlāda). Every time Viṣṇu saves Prahlāda. Finally, Viṣṇu appears before him and would like to favour him. He asks the god to pardon his father for all his sins. Viṣṇu disappears; Prahlāda bows down to his father, who embraces him with his eyes moistened. There is nowhere any mention of the lion, except for the sudden mention, as noted earlier, that Nṛsiṁha killed Hiraṇyakaśipu (Ib.20.32). In this text actual death of Hiraṇyakaśipu is never said to have been accomplished, either in a regular fight or a battle, or in the *sabhā*. It would appear from the Viṣṇu P. that there was reconciliation between Prahlāda and his father (Ib.20.23-31), though the Purāṇa immediately refers to the killing (when?) of Hiraṇyakaśipu by Nṛsiṁha (Ib.32), as noted above. This would indicate that the myth about the Nṛsiṁha incarnation was in the making in the early years of the Christian era with stray details aloft; and by the period of the Bhāg. P. (4th to 6th century A.D.)[6], it got a regular fuller form. It does not occur in the same form in the other main Purāṇas, as we have noted. The regular edition of the Mb. does not mention the myth, nor the incarnation of Nṛsiṁha. It is only the southern version that mentions it, along with the details of the boon according to which Hiraṇyakaśipu was not to be killed either by a human or a beast, nor with a weapon, in the day or in the night, either in or out of the house and so on (like the Matsya and the Bhāgavata Purāṇas). So, Viṣṇu took the lion-form and killed him in the evening (joint of the day and the night) and with his nails (not regular weapons), placing him on his lap, but in a regular fight (Sabhā after 38.29, the southern version.)[7] Now, the point is, how do we have the detail of the pillar, (Bhāg.P.) whence the lion incarnation of Viṣṇu is said to shoot out? - a detail not mentioned by the Viṣṇu P. (A.D. 300-500) which is the text devoted to Viṣṇu himself! And even in the southern version from the Mb. (which can be taken as older than these Purāṇas) the detail is absent. Was the pillar a Simple one, or was it superimposed with the figure of a lion? We have clear mention (in Bhāg. P.)that the 'lion' Viṣṇu came out of the pillar, but did not kill the king there itself, on the spot. He brought him at the threshold to keep to the 'not-in–not-out' detail of the myth, which is obviously a gift from folklore, according to which all joints (including the evening which is a joint of the day and the night), are evil-infected and, hence, have to be worshipped or are associated with the worship or divinities, and avoided. Though the point is mute, one thing is pretty clear which is that a lion had continued to be looked upon as divine, and its figure might have been carved, superimposed or inscribed on pillars, receiving worship. The pillar in the hall (or, was it attached to the throne?) of Hiraṇyakaśipu, hence, might have been conceived, at this period, to be superimposed by a lion (not Viṣṇu) on the basis of an actual practice; and an older myth—god killing a demon—got associated with this type of lion-pillars.

In this connection, we may note two mythical accounts from Burma (Myanmar), regarding the worship of a virtually Nṛsiṁha (*nṛ*=man) figure, though it is called Manu-Siṁha (*manu*=man; and not the Law-giver). According to one account, the princess of Kalinga was married to the King of the Veng country. A girl was born to them. It was foretold that this girl would marry a king named Kesara (=lion). So, she was named Kesarī. Also, she was well guarded. But when she attained youth, she fled away into the forest, was carried away by a lion, and kept in his cave. There, from the lion, she gave birth to a boy who was named Siṁhabāhu and a girl who was named Siṁhasivali. Both these had the face of a human but the legs of a lion. After some years, when they attained youth, these children expressed the desire to visit Kalinga and meet their maternal grandfather. So, when the lion was away they set forth with their mother; but they got their lower bodies covered with leaves so that they should not look awkward in the lion-legs. Now the 'lion', not finding them in the cave, went wandering and reached the capital of Kalinga, where he roamed about causing much distress among the people. So, the king ordered the 'lion' to be killed. Nobody could do the job. Hence, Siṁhabāhu accepted it and killed the lion, pursuing him in the forest, not knowing that he was his own father. It took a very long period and much wandering. But, finally he killed him and carried the head of that lion to show to the king of Kalinga; but, by that time the king was dead. The ministers wanted to make Siṁhabāhu king of Kalinga (as the king had no son). But, he refused; gave his sister Siṁhasivali to the Commander-in-Chief, Anurakṣa, who had helped him and his mother and sister to reach the capital of Kalinga, and who was a distant brother of Siṁhabāhu's mother, Kesarī. He also gave Anurakṣa the kingdom of Kalinga. With his mother he went into the forest, some portion of which he cleared and established a new kingdom, the capital of which came to be called Siṁhapura, in memory of the original 'lion' - the father killed by Siṁhabāhu, who was sorry for the act when he knew the truth, and got severe headache. So, as advised by wise men, he built a temple. In the inner shrine he established the idol of the god (which, it is not clear); but at the entrance he established the Manu-siṁha, which he worshipped as his father. So, whosoever visited the shrine had to first worship the Man-lion and then the god. This was the origin of a custom of placing a lion-head with human body at the entrance and calling it Manu-siṁha.

According to the other account, 237 years after the demise of the Buddha, his disciple Moggalan sent two of his disciples—Sohana and Uttara—to Svarṇabhūmi in the Ramaṇṇa-deśa (Rāmaṇīyaka?) in the midst of the sea. There in the city Taykala, once a baby boy was born to the king. Now, a water-demoness regularly used to come into the city from the sea and devour new-born boy-babies. This time also she approached the delivery-room, with all her evil attendants. The two disciples came to know of it; and they immediately approached the place. By their power, they created the Manu-siṁha; and the evil powers ran away. From that time onwards, the custom of placing the Manu-Siṁha at the door-stead came into being.[8]

Now, both the accounts obviously show that the custom was very old; but to give it further sanctity, Moggalan and his disciples were associated with it in the latter, while a regular tale with the lion-motif was formed, as is clear from the names Siṁhabāhu etc. in the former account. This would mean that, like these accounts, the Hiraṇyakaśipu episode could essentially be an adjunct to the custom of erecting a 'Nṛsiṁha' at the throne, a pillar or at the entrance of a dwelling. Whether the custom was borrowed from Burma is out of question. But it might appear that the custom started somewhere by the early centuries of the Christian era in Kalinga or the east (cf. Veṅga=Vaṅga=Bengal) and spread from there becoming very popular in India earlier than the fifth century A.D. From a definite mention of the year (237th year after the Buddha) in one of the Burmese accounts, it would appear that the custom was already known in the region from which the disciples came. It was later followed at the new place.

These episodes show a striking resemblance to the Nṛsiṁha-Prahlāda episode and yet slight variation. In between themselves, the episodes from Myanmar (Burma) show a difference of purpose. In the first account the girl is said to have been named Kesarī because of the prophecy that she would marry a king who was a lion, Kesara (i.e. *kesarī* 'lion' in Sanskrit). Even though she was guarded, she fled to the forest and was carried away (so says the account) by a lion! The point is, have we here a mythification of a real event, or an attempt to explain a custom by a myth? In the first case the girl could have been carried by a tribal chief (with or without her consent), known as 'lion', probably, due to his insignia showing a lion, or the tribe itself being known as 'Lion-tribe'. Even today Singh (=*siṁha*) is a very prominent surname among the martial castes in India; also a district of Bihar (ancient Magadha), which is adjacent to the ancient Kalinga, is named Siṅgh-bhūm (i.e. *Siṁha*-bhūmi). The account says, that the son of this lion-king established the Manu-Siṁha (probably on a pillar, like the Aśoka-stambha; such pillars have been quite common), which he worshipped as his father. This could be according to the custom rather than any innovation by the son. The account differs from the myth of Nṛsiṁha and Prahlāda in the detail that the latter has the creature as neither a man nor a beast (Bhāg.p. *loc. cit.* vv 18-19 *na mṛgam na mānuṣam* and *nāyam mṛgo nāpi naraḥ*); yet, it is termed *Nṛsiṁha*. The general description shows that the head of Nṛsiṁha was that of the lion, while the son and the daughter of the lion-king in the story from the Myanmar account had the face of a human but the legs of a lion (like the Sphinx). Their names show 'lion' (*Siṁha*) as the first member (Siṁhabāhu and Siṁhasivali), though the figure, which represented the dead father has Manu (indicating a human) as the first member (Manu-siṁha). The second account indicates that the ManuSiṁha served as the protector of children (though of a child in the account proper); but, this could be taken only as a phase of his general character of Protector-deity. The child-protector phase tallies with the Nṛsiṁha, the myth about whom (and the only, for that matter) occurs in the context of saving the 'boy', Prahlāda.

With this, now, we turn to the Vedic records regarding the lion, and the symbolism regarding him in sacred rites, thus connecting the early and the later Hindu traditions, in ancient times.

The Ṛgveda (ṚV) mentions the lion (I.64.8; 95.5;V.83.3, where the resounding advance of the rain-god, Parjanya, is likened to the roar of the lion; also III.9.4. Agni, like a lion, in water). The Atharvaveda (=AV, V.21.1; 6.IV.36.6), also refers to him. However, there is no belief associated with this animal. He is said to be a strong and ferocious animal. The *siṁha* was a specific animal, with a definite connotation, unlike the *mṛga* which suggested just a 'beast', unspecified. This would show, that the expression, *bhīma mṛga* is not indicative of a 'lion'.[9] Like the lion, the lioness also is mentioned as a strong female animal (ṚV VII. 18.17, *siṁhī*, the form being *Siṁhyam*, in the Accusative). But, at the stage of the ṚV, yet, there is no belief associated either with *siṁha* or *siṁhī*. However, in the ritual texts there is a definite identification of the altar (called *uttara-vedi*, 'the raised altar' situated to the east) with the lioness (Vāj.Sam. , V.10-12; Taitt.Sam. I.2.12.8, 12 etc.). The altar is praised also as *mahiṣī* ('the great lady', 'the queen', or 'she buffalo'; Ib. *Siṁhīr asi, mahiṣīr asi*). By this period the equations that got settled were as follows:

(i) Altar = Woman ('great lady')[10]

(ii) Altar = Earth (as we shall see below)

(iii) Altar = Lioness.

or

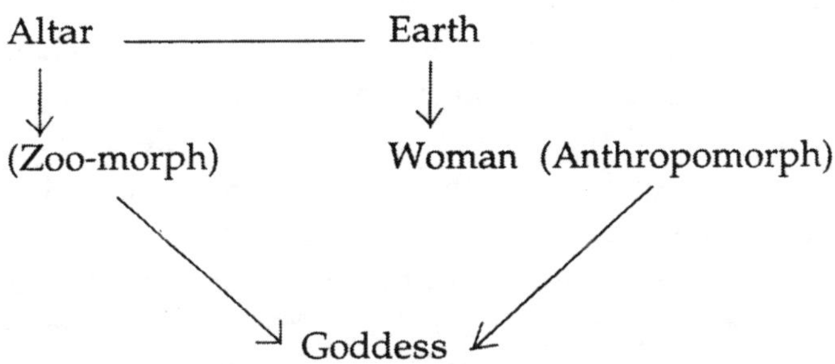

Here the lioness became a symbol not only for the altar but also for a goddess that represented the earth. The ṚV clearly states that the altar is the very limit of the earth, and the sacrifice is the 'navel' of the created world (ṚV I.164.35 *iyam vediḥ paro antaḥ pṛthivyāḥ, ayam yajño bhuvanasya nābhiḥ*). This symbolism entered later texts which say that the altar 'is the earth', and that the expanse of the earth is as that of the altar, symbolically spreaking (Śat.Br. I.2.5.7 *yāvatī vedis tāvatī pṛthivī*; Taitt. Sam.II.6.4.1; also 3). The ritual-texts have a regular myth regarding the lioness, who, in addition to being the symbol of the altar, is said to be the Speech, presenting a fresh equation as—

Speech=lioness=altar=Earth, anthropomorphosed. Thus, it is narrated that once there arose a competition between the Aṅgirases and the Ādityas as to who should be the sacrificers, the others being invited to officiate as priests (giving them a lower position). Finally, the Ādityas were successful in persuading the Aṅgirases to be their priests. Now, after the completion of this Soma-sacrifice called Sadyaḥkrī the Ādityas gave them speech as the sacrificial fee (*dakṣiṇā*). The Aṅgirases did not accept it. So, the Ādityas gave them the horse as the sacrificial fee, the horse being the symbol of the sun. Now, Speech got angry with (both of) them (and with all the gods) saying that she was insulted as the horse was preferred to her. Seeing that the gods and the *asura*-s were drawn at battle, Speech stood in between them taking the form of a lioness, and began seizing (and devouring) them. Both, the gods and the *asura*-s, tried to invite her to themselves in a bid to pacify her. She ultimately went to the gods on the condition that for her should be the first offering in a sacrifice. This was accepted. This offering to Speech is the oblation of ghee on the raised altar (*uttaravedi*) after it is prepared and consecrated, even prior to being offered to the sacrificial fire (which is carried on to this altar later); for, it is said, Speech and the raised altar are the same (Śat.Br.III.5.1.13ff; esp. *simhī bhūtva-ādadānā cacāra*; further *simhī*=Speech=altar, Ib.21,24,25). The symbolic identification of Speech, altar, lioness and the earth tends to indicate the deification of the lion (and the lioness) and it served as the basis for the later belief and myth about the goddess on the lioness, or the goddess being the lioness, as we shall see. However, in the Vedic period the lion does not occur as a vehicle or a zoo-morph of any god as such. The kernel of the Rām. and Mb. (as distinguished from its extant literary versions) cannot be placed later than about the tenth century B.C.; it must be taken as developed by that period, as Bhāsa, the first known Sanskrit dramatist (5th or 4th century B.C.) draws upon both having such expressions as Rājasiṁha. In the Mb. we have such other expressions as *rāja-siṁhān mahābhāgān* in the context of the *svayaṁvara* of Draupadī (Mb. Ādi, 184.24), indicating the 'kings' to be invited at the 'marriage by choice'; *vṛṣṇiSiṁha* (for Kṛṣṇa, Ib. Sabhā 40.8), and *Nṛsiṁha*, for the king of the Cedis, Śiśupāla (Ib.9). The Rām. speaks of Daśaratha as *rājasiṁha* (Rām., Bāla 13.24c; also of Romapāda, Ib.29).

Some of the dramas of Bhāsa end with *rājasiṁhaḥ praśāstu naḥ*,[11] which, though it does not specify for certain any particular king, does indicate the importance of *siṁha* in the expression, also suggesting a metaphoric concept of Man-Lion sans-myth.

The importance of the *siṁha* is to be noted also in some myths from the Puranic texts. Pārvatī is said to have produced a lion from her forehead (Sk.P.V.2.55.3ff); and she, herself, is said to have taken the form of a lioness, where (Ib.24) the same account says that she took the lion, produced from her forehead, as her vehicle, and sent him to Mahākālavana, the haunt of Śiva at Avantī (Ujjayinī). This would indicate the belief in the divinity of the lion on the one hand, and, on the other, the process of his identification with important god-heads. It is to be marked that the Purāṇa speaks of the place, where the lion was sent, as being named after the lion viz. Siṁheśvara, (cf. Siṁhapura established by Siṁhabāhu), which would indicate a shrine sacred to Śiva. The fact seems to be that an already existing place, sacred to a lion-divinity, came to be associated with Śiva and the Śiva-liṅga there came to be called Siṁheśvara. From another side, it is clear that Pārvatī, who had already been seen as the earth-goddess, Durgā, came to be associated with the lion.[12] In this case, the lion came to symbolize the power of the earth-goddess, Durgā=Pārvatī. The point is important, and has to be taken as reflecting a very old tradition of beliefs fostered by ritual context. Images of Gaurī=Pārvatī were very well popular through the long Hindu tradition; and in certain cases Gaurī was depicted as sitting on a lion or a wolf (Agni P.326.12 *siṁhasthā vā vṛkasthā vā*). The image of Gaurī seated on a lion was more popular than that seated on a wolf. Sometimes the lion gave place to a tiger. However the *siṁha*, as the vehicle of Gaurī, came to be very popular; and in a way the *siṁha* came to be her seat (*āsana*). This aspect of Gaurī=Pārvatī is seen in the post-Kuṣāṇa images of Mahiṣāsura-mardinī,[13] a very famous aspect of the goddess, noted by the Purāṇas, where she has been portrayed as seated on a lion. The Matsya P. (200 A.D. - 400 A.D.) gives a very vivid description of the Mahiṣāsuramardinī-- her right foot is placed on the lion, as she stands up to kill the buffalo-demon; her other foot rests on the shoulder of the buffalo-demon, whose upper half appears in the human form (Matsya P.259.64f). While on the one hand, the *Siṁha* came to be closely associated with the wife of Śiva, or, rather, the earth-goddess turned wife of Śiva, on the other, the most prominent male divinity that the lion came to be associated with was Viṣṇu. A question that may sound, apparently, unworthy of any attention, but is quite pertinent, is- why, among the incarnations of Viṣṇu, does the lion figure immediately after the boar? The ready reply may be that after the aquatic animals, the first earth-water moving beast is the boar; that, the next stage is of a purely earth-centred beast. But, then, why man-lion? The implication, without doubt, is of the conception, and identification, of the lion as the power of the earth. It is this conception, and a firm belief that the lion is the power - aspect of the earth, that gave rise to the earth-goddess taking over the lion (*siṁha*) as her vehicle (*āsana*), and also herself being seen in the form of a lioness! If we closely follow the mutual mythical relationship of Viṣṇu, Śiva and Pārvatī, surprising details and patterns present themselves before us:

1. Śiva never takes the form of a female for any god;

2. Viṣṇu takes the form of a female.

This is not only in the myth of the churning of the ocean, where he is seen as Mohinī, but also outside it. Śiva, as a male ascetic, takes Viṣṇu as his female associate in the pine-forest (*dāruvana*).[14] In this case, Viṣṇu as an androgen, comes on par with Gaurī-Pārvatī.

3. Śiva is usually associated with Bull; and, where he gets associated with the lion, it is through Gaurī-Pārvatī, as we have noted above. On the other hand, Viṣṇu's identification with the lion is unique among the male divinities; and the pattern of his incarnation is a proof in the case.

Viṣṇu— an androgen : male - lion (Nṛsiṁha)

: female - partly Śiva's consert.

Pārvatī — lioness, as Earth-goddess

Śiva's consort.

∴ Viṣṇu = lion is on par with Pārvatī = lioness = Earth.

Another trait of Viṣṇu, in connection with royalty, is, that the earthly king is an aspect of Viṣṇu (cf. *nāviṣṇuḥ pṛthivīpatiḥ*). If, then, the human king sat on the throne, and it came to be called *siṁhāsana*, the implication of the belief is -

1. The *siṁhāsana* is symbolic of the whole earth;

2. It suggests the seat of Viṣṇu, the 'lion'; and so,

3. The human king is Viṣṇu, and the 'lion'; also the Lord of the earth.

Royalty and prowess, together with the authority over the earth, thus, came to be symbolised by the lion, and the lion-seat. Howsoever subtle and soft the process may be, it has to be marked. Śiva has no place in this pattern, as he is never associated with royalty. In rituals a replica of a lion came to be gifted to a *brāhmaṇa* for obtaining prowess, indicating royalty (cf. Matsya P. 100.27; this was done at the vow called *Vīra-vrata*). The Vedic tradition indicates the ferocious aspect of the earth through its identification with the raised altar (*uttaravedi*), which itself was identified with Speech, as we have noted. The later tradition directly mentions the lioness as another form of the earth,[15] along with such identification through Gaurī=Pārvatī who is believed to be the earth-goddess in one of her aspects. In her mild aspect she is conceived as the cow, a trait that obtains in the Vedic as well as the post-Vedic tradition. The mythical presentation of this idea is in her getting 'milked' by Pṛthu, who appears as the king who was the first to teach the art of tilling and ploughing.[16] Could we say that, Viṣṇu, already a Vedic god, later came to be on par with her in her lioness-form and was seen as her controller, in the Nṛsiṁha? Viṣṇu, as Nṛsiṁha, strikes a balancing male position for the *siṁhī=mahiṣī* earth, his royal seat being termed *siṁha-*

āsana. However, the point requires more probe.

It is to be particularly noted, that, even with the well-developed symbolism of Speech=altar=lioness (indicating also the equation as lioness=altar=earth), it is difficult to find a clear equation between a king and the lion in the Vedic myth or ritual. The same is true about any god being equated with the lion. The lion is said to have been produced from the undigested juice of Soma that streamed out from the nose of Indra (Śat.Br. V.5.4.10). This would, conceptually, show a sort of an association of Indra and also of the juice (due to its colour) with the lion; the hair of a lion were also placed in the wine to be mixed with Soma-juice.[17] Yet, as has been said earlier, this cannot be taken as proof of a clear identification of the lion and Indra, nor of Soma, nor of any other god and the lion. The identification of Viṣṇu and the lion cannot also be seen in the expression "Like a terrible beast wandering at will in the mountain" (ṚV I.154.2 *mṛgo na bhīmaḥ kucaro giriṣṭhāḥ*) as it is not used only for him (cf.X.180.2, Indra); also the epithet *giriṣṭhāḥ* ('mountain-dwelling') never occurs for *Siṁha* in the Ṛgveda. Further to be noted is, that a lion does not roam exclusively in a mountain. Moreover, the expression shows only a comparison; further, as noted earlier, *mṛga* does not necessarily mean 'lion'. Thus, the point is, that Viṣṇu is never spoken of as 'lion' in the Ṛgveda. Even later, we hardly have a term like Nṛ-matsya, Nṛ-kūrma (or Nṛ-kacchapa) or even Nṛ-varāha, though archaeological evidence shows the Varāha as a mixture of the boar (upper part) and man. However, the case of the Man-lion from the Hindu incarnations is unique in the sense that it has parallels from the ancient world, even outside India. The most striking example is that of the double Aker from ancient Egypt, which was believed to guard the two ends of the earth. Aker was the earth-lion with a human head, the prototype of the Greek Sphinx who had a woman's head and the body of a lion(ess). The Sphinx, who guarded the entrance to Thebes, was verily an earth-goddess (though termed a dreadful creature) in the restricted sphere of Thebes, as contrasted with the earth's docile aspect in the form of the heifer.[18] According to another Thebian myth, the Greek hero Heracles shows a mixture of a man and a lion, as he is said to have killed the Thespian lion that roamed Mount Cithaeron, near Thebes, and donned the hide of the beast the head of the latter forming the hero's hood. In a way, Heracles became a man-lion ! This trait in the Heraclean myth became popular from the sixth century B.C. Before that the depiction of the hero shows only the armour and the usual staff. It is very much probable that the Egyptian human-lion motif seen in Aker and also in the sphinxes that guarded the underground abode of Sokar was borrowed by the Greeks. But, there is yet another point. The mix-up of the lion-head with others appears to be a prominent trait of the Middle East. In Assyria a form of the divine dress was a cap enclosed in horns, between which appeared the soaring lion-headed eagle.[19] This lion-headed eagle symbolised the god Ningirsu, especially at Lagosh.[20] When Gilgamesh carried the plant of life it was deceitfully stolen by the earth-lion who came in the form of the serpent, suggesting that both the serpent and the lion were symbols for the earth.[21] But, there is hardly anything here to suggest a human-lion (or, a man-lion) in one.

From what has been seen above, it is clear that the lion, or the lioness had come to symbolize the earth in the ancient Middle-east and Egypt; and there is every probability of the motif of identification between the earth and the lion-lioness being borrowed by ancient Greece from this source. The Greek myth of the Hercules-lion appears to be a version of the Aker Sphinx and an improved version of the Ningirsu cap or the lion-headed Tamuz. It may be noted in this connection that, though the royal chair of Tutankhamen (1350 B.C.) shows lion-heads in it[22] and the throne of king Solomon (about 1000-900 B.C.) shows the head of a lion at the two ends of each of the six steps[23], it is not known if these kings were also called 'king-lion' (*rāja-siṁha* of the Hindu scene), which term was quite popular in the Hindu epics (1000 B.C., as indicated earlier). The Mb. (not only its southern recension) has a number of names having *siṁha* as the first member—Siṁhaketu ('lion-bannered' Karṇaparvan 56.49), Siṁhacandra (Droṇaparvan 158.40) and Siṁhasena (Ib.16. 32f.;23.50), Siṁhapura (Sabhāparvan 27.20). These names compare with such names as Siṁhabāhu and Siṁhasivali from the Myanmar myth which locates them to Kalinga (and the vicinity of Magadha). We also have Siṁhikā as the name of Prahlāda's aunt.[24] Comparing the data from the Vedic records and that from this post-Vedic period, it appears that the man-lion motif was not so much the creation of a lion-man from the lioness-woman (altar=earth) as an independent development on the basis of the male wielder of power and royalty seen as a lion, though the earlier Vedic influence of altar=earth (=Speech) could not be denied altogether. Though the exact source of this man-lion motif might yet be elusive, there is hardly any probability of its being borrowed from the Middle East. Another pertinent point is, that the uniquely mentioned '*avatāra*' of Viṣṇu is more often referred to in the Puranic texts as *mṛgendra, mṛgādhipa* and *siṁha*, than Nṛsiṁha or Narasiṁha. The Matsya P. appears to pay more attention to the *mṛgendra-mṛgādhipa* rather than the genealogy of Hiraṇyakaśipu (and its order), fixing its attention on the position of the *mṛgendṛa*. It does not mention the pillar and its cracking up due to physical pressure from Hiraṇyakaśipu; but, it indicates the position of the *mṛgendra* as being at the entrance, wherefrom he is said to view the assembly. Hiraṇyakaśipu darts to him from his seat in the assembly. This corroborates the description in the Bhāg. P. that mentions the demon-king as being killed at the entrance of the hall (or, abode), though it is said that Nṛsiṁha came out of the pillar *(stambha)* indicating that the pillar was inside. In that case, the pillar could be adjacent to the throne, which was the *siṁha-āsana*. In any case, it was inside the hall (Bhāg.P.VII.8.18 *stambhe sabhāyām*). A glance at the designs and figures at the entrance of palaces shows, that by the tenth century A.D. the figure of a lion formed an important part thereof. There appeared *siṁha-cakra*-s (circles) and *siṁha-mukha*-s (lion-heads) on the entrance of a palace. The canopy (*toraṇa*) showed a figure which was called *siṁha-karṇa*[25] (lion-ears) and *siṁha-kumbha* (jar) and some palaces were termed *siṁha-pañjara* and Siṁha.[26] It is not improbable (rather, it is very much probable) that the hall of the palaces (said to be) of Hiraṇyakaśipu was contemplated as showing a siṁilar lion-figure at the entrance[27] or at the inner pillar. It is of interest to note that Hiraṇyakaśipu asks why Viṣṇu is not seen on the pillar, not speaking anything about any figure on the pillar. There is ground, hence, to believe that the lion-man who is said to have shot out from the pillar of the entrance, or the one that was inside, was an actual lion-figure (or, even a mixed lion and man figure) popular in the period when the myth was formulated. In that case, Hiraṇyakaśipu's question about Viṣṇu not being seen in the pillar has to be understood as his having no ignorance about the pillar having a figure of a lion or a man-lion. The Matsya P. has a plain and simple account, stating Prahlāda as being in the hall. The Viṣṇu P. and the Bhāg. P. mention Prahlāda as being a boy *(bāla)*, and yet put high-flown philosophical teachings in his mouth, which is a sign of the account being groomed and embroidered. The Matsya P. says that Hiraṇyakaśipu was killed by the *mṛgendra*, though earlier at a few places it mentions *nṛ-siṁha* or *nara-siṁha*. It refers to Viṣṇu promising to help the gods by killing the *asura*-king; but, from the arrival at the hall up to the end Viṣṇu is never mentioned. The god Hari (a word indicative of a lion, though also Viṣṇu and Kṛṣṇa in the post-Vedic literature) is said to have arrived at the entrance of the hall (*harir īśvaraḥ*, Matsya P. 161. 36). Prahlāda, with his divine eye, sees the god Lion (Ib.162.2 *siṁham devam āgatam*) and the *mṛgendra* kills Hiraṇyakaśipu with his terrible nails (163.14). It is to be noted, that Hiraṇyakaśipu is referred to as *daitya-siṁha* (Ib.161.87 *aiśvaryam daitya-siṁhasya*). So, one is the *daitya-siṁha*, while the other is *nṛ-siṁha* (or *narasiṁha*) stationed at the entrance. The reason for commotion seems to be that the lion at the gate got astir and menacing, a sign of displeasure. The Viṣṇu P. leans more to the Viṣṇu image. It does not speak of the 'god *siṁha*', but Acyuta (I.17.15), mentioning Viṣṇu at many places. In the raging battle Prahlāda, seeing the priests of his father getting destroyed by the evil power Kṛtyā and getting compassionate, implores upon the god saying, "O Kṛṣṇa, O Ananta, protect them" (Viṣṇu P. I.18;38). He requests the god, "O Keśava, be pleased" (Ib.20.16), as the latter presents himself when the former praises him (20.14). The occasion is of the binding of Prahlāda by the serpent-fetters (not of a pillar, when hit or kicked), and the god is described as 'Hari, wearing the yellow lower garment' *pītāmbara-dharo hariḥ*). We are told that Hiraṇyakaśipu was sorry for what he did to Prahlāda; he embraced Prahlāda, smelt his head and, with tears in his eyes, said, "Alive you are, O son!" (Ib.v 30). When he was killed "by Viṣṇu in the form of the man-lion", Prahlāda became the king of the Daityas (Ib. vv 32 - 34). The Bhāg. P. describes Prahlāda as *mahābhāgavata* (VII.8.15), which shows the influence of the Bhāgavata cult of the Vaiṣṇavite origin; but, in the account under observation we rarely have Viṣṇu. It is Kṛṣna, the son of Vasudeva, who is the Bhagavān (VII.4.36-37) Hari (Ib.5.5;30), who is Viṣṇu (vv 31,35). Earlier, a heavenly voice (not exactly Viṣṇu) assures the gods that the Daitya-villain would be killed if he tortures his pious son (Ib.28). In the actual scene of fight it is Hari, Nṛsiṁha, Nṛ-hari (Ib.8.20, 28-30) who, after killing Hiraṇyakaśipu at the entrance taking him away from the pillar, seats himself on the throne (v 34). When the Nṛ-Siṁha makes himself invisible, Prahlāda is installed on the throne by the family-priest of the *asura*-s (Ib.X.31-33).

From the story of Hiraṇyakaśipu and Prahlāda, and its variations noted above with embroideries, it is clear that here we have a sort of proto-history (as it is not possible to give the dates of the individuals, though traces of social and religious change could be noted). The very first observation is, that it follows the pattern of the Vedic conflict between the gods and the *asura*-s, who are believed to be from a common ancestor. This suggests reconciliation of societies (if at all they were in strife). Further, Prahlāda's was a definite attempt to cement the differing faiths, though, as is clear from the behaviour of others in his line, the strife continued. But, then, the nature of the strife had remained internal. This is clear from the account of a dispute between Prahlāda's son, Virocana and Sudhanvan, the son of Aṅgiras. The two youngster sons questioned the superiority regarding each other; so they approached Prahlāda for a decision. Learning both the sides, Prahlāda decided in favour of Sudhanvan. He said, "Listen son, Sudhanvan is better than you and his father is better than me; also, his mother is better than your mother" (Mb.Sabhā, 68.66-86). This shows, at the least, Prahlāda's partiality and desire for reconciliation with the '*deva*' people (if we could say so), which would indicate that the Devas and the *asura*-s were (=came to be regarded−regarded themselves as) phratries to each other (Latin, *frater* = Eng. brother). This is exactly their relationship even in the Vedic texts, both being 'sons of Prajāpati'. Their mutual relationship was of strife, deceit and yet efforts towards reconciliation, even leading to marital relationship. Thus, Viṣṇu contrives the extermination of Bali, the son of Virocana. This has to be taken as a pre-historical event couched in the mythical belief about the dwarf. However, Bali is famous for his benevolence and is respected in the Hindu tradition; he is even worshipped and offered choicest things on the occasion of the festival of lights. Bāṇa, son of Bali, agrees, ultimately, to the marriage of his daughter Uṣā with Aniruddha, grandson of Kṛṣṇa (believed to be an *avatāra* of Viṣṇu). Aniruddha and Uṣā were in love with each other and the former had arranged to take her away with him.

Finally, about the story of Prahlāda and Hiraṇyakaśipu the following observations could be made:

Hiraṇyakaśipu and Hiraṇyākṣa were the mythical brothers, like Madhu and Kaiṭabha, whose prototype could be seen in the Vedic Danu (or Dānu, ṚV). Like Hiraṇyakaśipu, we do not have Hiraṇyākṣa also as a person in the Vedic literature; the word *hiraṇya-akṣa* appears only once in the ṚV (I.35.8) and is an epithet of the god Savitṛ, indicating that his 'eye' was golden (=sun); this corroborates the concept of Savitṛ being the sun at the sunrise and sunset, when the orb could be seen as goldish yellowish red. The *asura*-s and *dānava*-s (the *a-deva* phratry, generally averse to the influence of the *deva* Viṣṇu) had already developed the lion symbol— depicted as a natural beast or as a man-lion— by about the tenth century B.C. (comparable with the ancient Egyptian mixed zoo-morphic or anthropo-zoomorphic deities like Anubis, Bast, Thot, Aker, or the Mid-eastern Assyrio-Babylonian Ningirsu and Tammuz, or the later Greek Sphinx, Centaurs which were believed to be half man half horse; cf. the Kinnara and *tumbaru* of Indian myths and the Greek minotaur, bull-headed man). This symbol (lion or the lion-headed man) was depicted at the entrance of a dwelling, or at a prominent place which may be even a pillar (at the entrance or inside), as a protector deity. The Vedic people also had the practice of fixing a pillar at the entrance of a dwelling (ṚV I.51.14); but there is no indication of its having any figure as such. The *asura*-king Prahlāda tried to identify it with the Vedic *deva* Viṣṇu and had to encounter some opposition. 'Hiraṇyakaśipu' stands for the traditional royal Dānavism (if we may say so!)—the anthropomorphosed seat, especially when the myth-teller was a person of the Vedic Deva tradition and was conversant with the ritual connotation of the *Hiraṇyakaśipu*, with the difference that he associated it with the king. So, the story is a mixture of proto-history and metaphor, the latter being an important support for a myth. The texture of the mythical account, thus, throbs with the strife between the Deva and the Siṁha symbol. The strife brings with it the patterned fight with all its varieties as the 'myth' grew.

References

1. The dates of the Purāṇa texts mentioned here are following: Kane, P.V., *History of Dharmaśāstra*, Vol.V, Pt. 2, Second Ed., Poona, 1977 (1962), pp.887ff.

2. This action of the hands is seen even in the case of Rāvaṇa, when he is said to have assumed a huge form to abduct Sītā; cf. Rām., Araṇya,49.1, where he is said to have clapped one of his palms with the other, *haste hastam sam āhṛtya.*

3. The same occurs at the Agni P.19, according to Vettam Mani, *Puranic Encyclopaedia*, Delhi 1975, p.595. However, the extant Agni P. is not the original one according to Kane, *op.cit.*, p. 887.

4. The sacrifice is so named as it is not completed in a single day; it takes the following night and even the next day. It is an independent sacrifice, but may form part of the Horse-sacrifice.

5. Ch. One, p.17ff. *infra.*

6. Kane, *op.cit.*, gives it a wider range, saying that the period of this Purāṇa could be before the 9th century A.D., which seems difficult to accept.

7. Gorakhpur ed., Gorakhpur, Gītā Press, Vikrama-Saṁvat 2013, p. 340ff.

8. These accounts are from Ram Newaj, *Vedic-Puranic sources and Burmese Myth and Ritual*, Thesis, Uni. of Bombay, 1994, pp. 279-84. Suvarṇabhū(mi) is generally identified with Burma. Varāhamihira mentions it in his *Bṛhatsaṁhitā* (XIV.31). Shastri, A.M., *India as seen in the Bṛhatsaṁhitā of Varāhamihira*, Delhi, 1969, p.101, n.5, thinks, after citing other opinions, that "it cannot but be Sumatra, including, perhaps, Java". However, Ramaṇṇadesa of which Suvarṇabhūmi is said to be a part, is a difficulty. It is variously identified. According to the present writer, it could be Nicobar (Nakrapuram); Dange, *Legends in the Mahābhārata*, p.348 f.

9. Macdonell, A.A. and Keith, A.B., *Vedic Index.*, Vol. II, under *siṁha*; here the creature is said to be lion; later at *A Vedic Reader, for Students*, p. 32, Macdonell renders *mṛgo bhīmaḥ* as "dreaded beast". The indication is, that *mrga* is not necessarily

lion. We shall see later that there is absolutely no support in the ṚV for the identification of Viṣṇu with the lion, nor for this incarnation.

10. Śat.Br. I.3.3.8 *yoṣā vai vediḥ*; cf. Ib. III.5.1.11.

11. Epilogue of *Svapnavāsavadattam*; also *Pratijñāyau gandharāyaṇam* etc.

12. She is mentioned as Śarvā, who is none else that Pārvatī. She is the wife of Śarva (=Śiva; *śarva* is from the root *śṛ*, "to injure") and is said to be the third body of Śiva, who is called *kṣiti-mūrti* (*kṣiti* is earth). She is also said to be earth; see Brahmāṇḍa p.I.2.10.39ff. According to the Varāha P. (which is to be placed before the 10th century A.D.) Brahmā created two girls. One of them was seated on a lion; she was Durgā (Varāha p. 28.23ff). The name Durgā suggests her association with earth and the mountains (*durgā*, 'difficult to reach'; she was the daughter of the Himalaya mountain).

13. *Siṁhopari sthitām*; the lion is to be shown in idols with blood at his mouth (after killing the demon). See Ch."Mahiṣāsura-mardinī".

14. For the account see Dange, *Encl.P.B.P.*, Vol.IV, p.1325

15. The Brahma P. (155.2-8), which gives the same account, says that the Ādityas gave the earth as the sacrificial fee.

16. *Vedic Index of Names and Subjects*, Vol.II, under Pṛthu; also the *Kumārasaṁbhavam* of Kālidāsa, I.2

17. Śat.Br.V.5.4.19; according to another opinion the hairs were to be thrown on the portions of meat-offering, Ib.18. The hairs of a tiger and/or a lion were to be placed on the right and the left wing of the altar at the Agnicayana sacrifice (Taitt. Sam.V.3.1) to give strength to it.

18. See Ch. Four; p.118ff. *infra*.

19. Mackenzie, D., *Myths of Babylonia and Assyria*, p.64. The cap enclosed in horns may be compared with the Vedic *śiprā*, which was a helmet with drinking horns at both its sides, for which see Dange, *Pastoral Symbolism from the Ṛgveda*, Poona Uni.Pbn., p.108ff. Tamuz had a lion-head, Mackenzie, *op.cit., loc.cit.*, in single use the word always appears in the dual as *śipre*.

20. Mackenzie, D., *Myths of China and Japan*, p.221.

21. Mackenzie, D, *Myths of Babylonia and Assyria*, p.165, 182; also by the same author, *Myths of Pre-Hellenic Europe*, p.304. A Cretan goddess is depicted as balancing a forward stretched serpent on one of her hands stretched forward. At her two sides stand a lion and a lioness. In one of the Akkadian cylinder-seals, in the context of the Etana myths, there appears a lion at the foot of a tree with another one on the tree, and the usual theme of eagle-serpent gives place to the new lion-lion (not serpent) theme. On the basis of the ancient practice of catching lions and destroying them by casting them into a pit, Kirk surmises that the hole of the serpent and the pit of the lion associate both with the earth, Kirk, G.S., *Myth, Its Meaning....*, p.128f.

22. Davies, H.A., *An Outline History of the World*, Oxford Uni.Press, London, 1937 (1928), Picture opp. page 32, p.33.

23. *Good News Bible* (Old Testament, Today's English Version), "Kings", I.10.18. This would indicate a borrowal, as idols of any sort were not favoured by the Israeli faith. Soloman is said to have turned against the faith and began worshipping Astarte, the goddess of Sidon and Moloch "the distinguished god of Moab", Ib.11.5-7. The borrowal could be from the dominant Assyrio-Babylonian practice.

24. Mb. *Ādi* 65.12, where she is indicated to be a wife of the sage Kaśyapa. Rāhu, who is the eclipser of the sun and the moon, is said to be her son. This is a case where a fact seems to be 'eclipsed' by myth, especially when his brothers are said to be Candra-hartā ('moon-usurper'), Candra-pramardana ('moon-mutilator') and even Sucandra, Ib. 31. As is usual with such mythicals, her husband's name is not exactly available.

25. *Samarāṅgaṇasūtradhāra*, ascribed to Bhoja, 18.39. It was like the *Brāhmī letter ṭha (ṭhakaro yaḥ)**, (which in the then script, must have looked like the ear of a lion. Such a depiction is seen also on other sculptures like a *vṛndāvana*, which is a raised quadrangular clay mound in which the holy Tulasi plant stands at the door of a Hindu house.

* 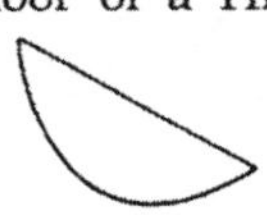

26. *Ibid* 49.10; 54.12;21;55.85;56.10; *siṁha-kuṁbha* , p.370 (no regular numbers, as the ed. mentions from other manuscripts).

27. Like the 'Kīrtimukha 'figure, which obtains from the 4th-5th century A.D.; for the myth see Dange, *Encl.P.B.P.*, Vol.IV,p.1312. In certain cases it showed the face of a lion; see Dhavalikar, M.K., "Kīrtimukha", Proceedings of the seminar on *Symbolism in Temple Art and Architecture,* Ananthacarya Indological Instt.. Series, No. XI Bombay, 1982, p.85 ff.

Nine

Some Unique Myths regarding Viṣṇu

Viṣṇu has been a very popular god-head in the Hindu pantheon; and, like Indra, he has a very unique personality. He is the killer of the demons, favourer of his devotees and also has a sort of cunning associated with his personality. Yet, the trait that we are going to focus our attention on is rather out of the way. This trait concerns sex, which is a very important aspect of the human, and also of the divine life. To speak precisely, we are focusing attention on the androgenic personality of Viṣṇu. This trait involves a combination of both sexes in one; and it is found to be present in important gods from all pantheons.[1] Coming to the Vedo-Hindu scene, Prajāpati was an androgen, being described as having breasts like that of a woman.[2] The river-goddess Sarasvatī was also seen as an androgen.[3] Indra was also seen as such, and could stay among women in the form of a woman, and among men in the form of a man[4]. The best known example of this trait is that of the Ardhanārī-īśvara, a combination of Śiva and Pārvatī.

The androgenic trait of Viṣṇu is known in his form of Mohinī; but there are certain other accounts to show how this god (and, for that matter, all important gods) is believed to be so. Now, the androgenic trait is one peculiarity of Viṣṇu, he being portrayed, in certain myths, as a girl or a woman. This, in itself, might seem to be awkward for a casual reader. However, there is also another trait that is (apparently) more awkward (of course, seemingly!) in Viṣṇu. He is a deceiver of his opponents by impersonating them and deceiving their wives. He would take their form and approach their wives to unite with them. The point is, what could be the probable meaning of such 'awkward' (-looking) myths ? We shall examine the question. Let us take certain examples.

According to one account, which shows the fusion of the Śiva and the Viṣṇu cults, or their lack of hostility towards each other, at the marriage of Śiva with Pārvatī, the former is said to have appointed Viṣṇu as the care-taker of Pārvatī; and Viṣṇu accepted the request, taking the form of a woman (Kūrma Purāṇa I.15.122[cd] *strii-rūpa-dhārī nityam sevate sma maheśvarīm*). In another account, which is associated with the sojourn of Śiva in the pine-forest (*dāru-vana*), Viṣṇu is said to have accompanied him in the form of a beautiful woman (Ib. II.37.9 *strīveśam Viṣṇur āsthāya...*), as Śiva moved naked. It has to be noted, that this trait is in addition to the Mohinī form of Viṣṇu; and it persists. Thus, in the *bhaga-liṅga* concept, where generally Śiva and Pārvatī are the partners, Viṣṇu is also seen as the female organ. Viṣṇu is said to be the *bhaga* and Śiva the *liṅga* (Skanda P. V.3.14.20[cd] *bhaga-rūpo bhaved Viṣṇur liṅga-rūpo maheśvaraḥ*). The Mohinī account has it that Viṣṇu took the form of a beautiful woman to outwit the demons; but, the motif goes further, adding some other details. According to one account, once when Śiva saw Viṣṇu in his Mohinī form, his semen fell. This was collected by the seven seers on a leaf. They inserted it in the ear of the daughter of Gautama, named Añjanī, who, in due course of time, gave birth to Hanūmant from it (Śiva P. III.20.3-7). In another variant of the same account, knowing from Nārada about the Mohinī form of Viṣṇu Śiva went to meet the latter, along with Pārvatī, and requested him to show that form of his to him. Viṣṇu did it immediately. But, on seeing that form Śiva got infatuated and ran after 'her'. Now, Pārvatī tried to check him, and clasped him; and he released his semen on the ground, and from it the god Mahābala was born (Brāhmaṇḍa P. II.4.34-76). The account occurs also in the Bhāgavata P. (VIII.12.1-37). According to it, Viṣṇu takes the form of a beautiful young girl and plays with a ball. While doing so, the wearing of this girl gets loosened, and falls to the ground. Śiva, who was with Pārvatī, not being able to control his emotions, runs after the girl, Mohinī, and catches her in his embrace, and his semen flows out getting spilt on the earth. The account is used to explain, further, the birth of the god Śāstā called also Ayyappan, the presiding deity at Sābarīmāl, saying that the god was born from the union of Mohinī and Śiva.[5] It may be noted, that herein there is a new discordant detail, which speaks of the 'union' of Mohinī and Śiva, while the regular Puranic accounts noted above do not mention an actual union. There the semen of Śiva is said to flow on the ground and give rise to a number of things. In the account from the Bhāgavata P. the things produced include gold and such others; and in the account from the Brahmāṇḍa P., the god Mahābala is said to have been produced from the semen away from the body of Mohinī=Viṣṇu. In yet another use of the Mohinī motif, we have the south Indian god Kuṭṭāṇḍavara involved. According to the myth popular in south India, especially in the Arcot district, the (Vedic) god Indra himself was incarnated in the form of this god; but, due to his sin of killing the *brāhmaṇa* (Vṛtra, the son of Tvaṣṭṛ, and also the elder brother of Vṛtra, Viśvarūpa) he had a curse in this incarnation as Kuṭṭāṇḍavara. According to it, his body would rot away except for his head. So, none was prepared to give him his daughter in marriage; because, if she was married to him in the morning she would be certainly a widow by the evening, when he rotted away but for his head! So, it is said, Śrī Kṛṣṇa (=Viṣṇu) took pity on him, and married him in his form of Mohinī in the morning; and when the god remained only in the form of his head, Mohinī broke her *tāli* (the auspicious necklace worn by a married woman), in the evening.[6] It is to be noted, that, though Kuṭṭāṇḍavara is a local south Indian deity, he is sought to be identified not only with the Vedic Indra, but, in actual practice, with Viṣṇu himself. This is clear from the fact that the idols of this god, showing only the head, show the Viṣṇu mark of *kumkuma* on the head[7]. According to the practice, there is a festival of this god in the month of Caittra (roughly April). In the morning, crowds of men dressed as women visit the shrine of this god, with *tāli*-s in their necks; and in the evening, they break them, as they become widows![8] There is no doubt that, in the origin, the account of Mohinī is independent of the accounts of Kuṭṭāṇḍavara and Ayyappan; but, the point is of the popularity of the motif of Viṣṇu becoming a woman. In the case of Kuṭṭāṇḍavara, the Viṣṇu-mark on the forehead of the god and his wife Mohinī indicate that they are aspects of the same whole divinity. Bereft of the Vedic-Puranic guise, it is clear that Kuṭṭāṇḍavara is an androgen. He marries his own female aspect. The period of the integration of the Mohinī myth and the south Indian Kuṭṭāṇḍavara myth, shows not only a cultural fusion but also similarity of the motif of the androgynous god-head. In all these myths, Viṣṇu is seen as a beautiful young girl or woman. But, we have also an account where he is said to have been born from the ear (which is the symbol of the female organ) of Śiva. This was in the context of the destruction of the demon Andhaka; and here Viṣṇu is seen in the form of a terrible woman (Skanda P. VI.122.7-52), which shows the influence of the Devī-cult, wherein such goddesses as Mahiṣāsura-mardinī, Caṇḍī and others dominate.

Now, we look to the other trait of Viṣṇu, that of the deceiver and crossing the limits of acknowledged morality. One of the myths of this nature is that of Tulasī, the wife of the demon Śaṅkhacūḍa. According to an account, it was necessary to defile the chastity of his wife, Tulasī. So, Viṣṇu went to Tulasī, in the guise of Śaṅkhacūḍa and had union with her; he also implanted his semen in her. When, in the war with Śiva, Śaṅkhacūḍa got killed, Viṣṇu showed Tulasī his original form. Knowing the truth, now, Tulasī cursed Viṣṇu to be a stone (called *śālagrāma*) on the bank of the Gaṇḍakī, which was her own river-form (Brahmavaivarta P. I.21.1-28). Viṣṇu blessed her to be one of the women in his *rāsa* (in his birth as Kṛṣna); and also said that she would become the Tulasī tree, the leaves of which would be formed from her hair (*ib.* 32-34). The Brahmavaivarta P. is a late text, and the influence of the Kṛṣṇa cult is evident. This myth does not obtain in other main Purāṇas. But, even here the myth is rather loose, as it says that Śaṅkhacūḍa was the friend of Kṛṣṇa (=Viṣṇu), named Sudāmā in his former birth, and that in her that birth Tulasī also performed penance to get Viṣṇu as her husband. This chronologically awkward gloss is to support the deceit of Tulasī by Viṣṇu. But, here is another myth; and this is about Vṛndā, the wife of the demon Jalandhara. The scene is again the battle of the gods and the demons; and Viṣṇu has to defile the wife of the demon to render his defeat easy. So, he takes the form of an ascetic and sits under a tree in the vicinity of the palace of Jalandhara, who is away in the battle. His wife, Vṛndā, sees an inauspicious dream about her husband; and she is advised to approach the ascetic. As she goes to him, she sees two demons following her with an unholy intention. The ascetic (=Viṣṇu), however, protects her from them; (they were created by Viṣṇu himself to impress upon her about his strength). Thus winning the confidence of Vṛndā, the ascetic is ready to answer her question about the whereabout of her husband. A monkey sitting on a nearby tree (he is a party to the plan of Viṣṇu) is sent by the ascetic to know about the matter. He goes and returns with the head of Jalandhara. Vṛndā implores upon the ascetic to revive her husband. So, the ascetic accepts, and disappears with the head, and reappears as a whole bodied Jalandhara. Vṛndā is overjoyed. She enjoys her life with this Jalandhara, with all sexual sports, for many years. One day, however, she marks a difference and knows that she was deceived. At that time, Viṣṇu shows her his own form. She curses him that he would also be separated from his wife in his birth on the earth; and, there too, monkeys would help him. This comes true; and Viṣṇu has to take birth as Rāma, get separated from his wife Sītā, and is helped by the monkeys in killing Rāvaṇa and regaining his wife (Skanda P. II.4.21.8-29). Cursing Viṣṇu Vṛndā enters fire (Ib. 30). In a variant of this myth, Viṣṇu is said to have taken to this course of deceiving Vṛndā, as her husband, Jalandhara, was trying to cheat Pārvatī, likewise, sensing defeat in the battle against Śiva. That account also ends in the curse to Viṣṇu and penance to death on the part of Vṛndā. The curse is that Viṣṇu's wife would also be deceived by an ascetic (Rāvaṇa) as he deceived her in the form of an ascetic[9]. However, the tit-for-tat course decided upon by Viṣṇu (and also not in his own interest) does not absolve him of the awkward step that he takes—a step against the normal moral behaviour. In the first of these two versions of the myth, it is said that Tulasī was Lakṣmī herself. This may appear as a gloss, and does not explain the behaviour of Viṣṇu satisfactorily. Now, we go to another account, where Viṣṇu is said to have made advances towards a girl. The account is as follows.

The king of Mathurā, named Puṇyanidhi, once went to Rāmeśvara, and propitiated Viṣṇu there. Lakṣmī desired to test Viṣṇu. So, she took the form of a girl, aged eight years, and approached the king where he was dwelling. Thinking that she was an orphan, the king kept her in his dwelling place. Once Viṣṇu saw her, and tried to catch hold of her, taking the form of a *brāhmaṇa*. Seeing that act of the *brāhmaṇa*, the girl cried aloud; this brought the king on the scene. He took hold of the *brāhmaṇa*, and tied him to a pillar in the temple of Rāmanātha (Śiva at Rāmeśvara). In the night, when the king was asleep he dreamt that the person at the pillar was Viṣṇu. The next morning he approached the *brāhmaṇa* (Viṣṇu) and asked pardon of him. Viṣṇu was pleased, and accepted to stay at that place for ever. This he did as Setumādhava (Skanda P. III.1.50.1-98). The age of the girl is symbolic; for, the Puranic tradition shows the belief that eight years or twelve years is the symbolic age of a goddess.[10] The intention of Viṣṇu is not clearly stated; yet, the punishment given to the *brāhmaṇa* indicates that it was a severe lapse of normal conduct. Now, we have a reversion of the account in another myth. This is the myth about one Subhadrā. It is said that once a *brāhmaṇa* girl, named Mādhavī, slept on the bed of Viṣṇu (and Lakṣmī) unknowingly. When Lakṣmī noticed this, she cursed her to be born as a girl with the face of a mare. And, (to make the matter sure and clear!) she told her that she would be the sister of the incarnation of Viṣṇu, Kṛṣṇa. Viṣṇu tried to pacify Lakṣmī saying that the girl had done so just without knowing that the bed belonged to Viṣṇu; so, she should be pardoned. But, the curse of Lakṣmī could not go in vain. When the girl was actually born, Kṛṣṇa and Balarāma took her to Brahmā, who restored the girl's original form and named her Subhadrā (Skanda P. VI.81.11;84.4ff). The account goes on to say, that Subhadrā became the goddess of fertility and fecundity, and came to be worshipped by barren women with the desire of a child.

Now, to recapitulate the various aspects of Viṣṇu mentioned above: (i) He becomes a woman; (ii) He deceives married women, who are wives of the demons; and (iii) He is sexually (though just faintly) attached with girls, the latter's age being roughly eight. Now, to take up the first aspect. This aspect, as we have noted, makes him an androgen, and falls under a general category. The idea in this concept is that the main god is a complete unit in itself having both the sexes inherent in him. In the myths of this nature, his female aspect is stressed, as his *śakti* (power), or *māyā*. The Vedic context has Indra as becoming the *menā* (girl) of Vṛṣaṇaśva (Ṛgveda I.51.13); and, as noted at the beginning of this chapter, he also becomes a woman among women. The Vedic period does not show any other god '*becoming*' a woman, though in the pair of Varuṇa and Mitra, Varuṇa is conceived, some times, as a woman Mitra casting his 'seed' in him.[11] The concept of a powerful goddess is not developed in the earlier Veda; and we have to come to the Upaniṣadic period for that concept, where an all powerful goddess is seen on the scene; this goddess excels all the gods (Kenopaniṣad 3.12) and is called Umā, the daughter of

Himavant (*sa tasminnevākāśe striyam ā-jagāma bahuśobhamānām umām haimavatīm*). Though Umā, here, is not the androgen and is a separate entity as a woman, she comes as a unique and powerful woman. Viṣṇu, as a constant companion of Indra in the Vedic scene and stepping further than him in the post-Vedic period, takes the former's androgynous nature and also the mild, yet powerful, aspect of the evolving supreme goddess that obtains for the first time in the Upaniṣad mentioned above. This is the stage set for Mohinī, whom we meet for the first time in the Mahābhārata. In a way, Mohinī is actually Māyinī (!); and the pattern set in his form of Mohinī is further embroidered in the myth of Bhasmāsura, where Viṣṇu is said to have taken the same female form and destroyed him with guile.[12] The Puranic accounts where Śiva desires to see the female form (Mohinī) of Viṣṇu and gets infatuated (as noted above) present only a merger of the aspects of Umā (from the Kenopaniṣad) and the Mohinī concept. This is clear from the detail in the account of Śiva's infatuation for Mohinī, according to which Pārvatī is also present. The subtle merger of the concept of Umā and Mohinī in the post-Mahābhārata period is clear from the fact that Viṣṇu accompanies Śiva in the form of a woman when he goes to the pine forest (*dāruvana*). A further step is seen not only in the attendance of Viṣṇu as a woman on Pārvatī but also as the female organ while Śiva is the male organ, as noted earlier. This is another aspect of the Pārvatī=*yoni* and Śiva=*liṅga* pair (cf. Śiva P. IV.12.37 *girijām yoni-rūpām ca... tatra liṅgam ca tatsthāpya...*). It is, thus, clear that Viṣṇu's female aspect is only the half of the concept of the complete self-sufficient divine primeval unit.[13] In the post-Vedic period when Indra fell to the background, and Brahmā (Prajāpati of old) was proclaimed as an old *pitāmaha*, only two of the old gods remained on the scene as active, viz. Śiva (in his new aspect from the old Rudra) and Viṣṇu. There is hardly any myth where Śiva is shown as taking the form of a female[14]; and he came to be rightly called '*bholā*' (innocent) in the later tradition. He is depicted as fully manly, with his *liṅga* (phallus) prominently described which could be cut away from his body (as is clear from the account of the Dāruvana) and could be restored again.[15] His usual female counterpart is Pārvatī, in her mild and also the ferocious aspect. But, the religious belief also needed the old androgynous concept of a god to supplement the manly aspect of Śiva. And that was provided by Viṣṇu, who, as a female, was depicted as a mild and seemingly guileless damsel. He, as a mild female power, was, hence, a complementation, from the old bold, to Pārvatī-Gaurī-Mahiṣāsuramardinī-Caṇḍī; but, he was also occasionally depicted as a fierce woman, as noted above.

The deceit of Tulasī and Vṛndā cannot be taken in the light of human relations. With the concept of the Śakti, a Śakti of the demons also was contemplated. Tulasī and Vṛndā, hence, are not to be understood as actual wives of the demons. They were their powers in the female form. Their defeat was equal to the defeat of the demons. Inversely, the defeat of Pārvatī was also the defeat of the gods, through Śiva. Hence, we have accounts like the demon Jalandhara trying to seduce Pārvatī, the supreme Śakti.[16] This defeat of the Śakti (female) by a male god, or a demon for that matter, takes the form of sexual insult in myths. Thus, the efforts of Viṣṇu to sexually insult Vṛndā or Tulasī,[17] even by guile, is symbolic of destroying the 'power' of their husbands. The same, inversely, is the case when the demons try to sexually insult the goddess. The awkwardness in such myths, hence, is only apparent; and it remains only till the symbolism and pattern therein become clear. A subtle point to be noted in this type of myths is that the account repeatedly suggests, that the wives of the demons were, *in fact*, the wives of the gods (here Viṣṇu), prior to their being the wives of the demons, and that they would revert to the god; also that they had performed penance to gain the god as husband. Yet another suggestion from such accounts is, that part of the divine *śakti* was controlled by the demons through austerity. And, yet, it had to revert to the divine domain. The sexual overtone on the part of the god is symbolic of this assertion of re-control.

In the case of the last aspect, where the god tries to catch the eight-year old girl, it looks like sexual overtone. But, the demon is missing. It has been already noted above, that the age is symbolic of the divine girl. Hence, the step to catch the girl is only symbolic of the control of his divinity in the female form on the part of the god; inversely, the girl's lying on the bed of the god suggests the same. It is to be noted, that the name of the girl that lies on the bed is Mādhavī, which indicates the Śakti of Mādhava (Viṣṇu). She is cursed to have the head of a mare, which makes her equal to Lakṣmī herself, who, in a variant myth gets to be mare-headed![18] In the case of the Setumādhava account, the girl is none else than Lakṣmī herself. These myths about Viṣṇu are not based on the concept of Viṣṇu being the god of fertility. That is a different topic; and it need not be touched here.

References

1. Thus, for example the ancient Egyptian god Hapi is depicted as having two breasts. He is the god of the Nile; see Donald Mackenzie, *Egyptian Myth and Legend,* London, no year, p. 27; also the primeval god Atum is the Great He-She, Rundle Clark, R.T., *Myth and Symbol in Ancient Egypt*, London, 1959, p.41. According to a myth among the Hopi Indians of America (South-west), the great vault of the firmament is He-She; cf. Suzuki, David and Kundston, Peter, *Wisdom of the Elders*, Bantam Books, New York, p. 31.
2. These breasts are in the form of the two lauds, Pañcavimśa Brāhmaṇa XIII.11.8; Jaiminīya Br.I.225.
3. Her male spirit is called Sarasvant in as early as the Ṛgveda, VII.95.3, and has the breast, VII.96.5 *sarasvataḥ stanam.*
4. This is in the context of the story of a demon woman, Vilesteṅgā; see Macdonell, A.A. *Vedic Mythology* (Hindi Tr., Ramkumar Rai), Chaukhamba, Varanasi; 1961, p.107. It is also said that the man in the right eye of a person is Indra, while that in his left is Indrāṇī, thus giving the first ever concept of Ardhanārīśvara in the form of Indra, split into two as an androgen, Śat.Br. X.5.2.9
5. See Vettam Mani, *Puranic Encyclopaedia,* p.*700,* where he mentions the source only as Kambar Rāmāyaṇa, without any further details of reference. The regular Purāṇas do not mention Śāstā or Ayyappan. Vettam Mani's Encyclopaedia cannot be taken as a reliable source, nor is it methodical. For the previous references, see Dange, *Encl.P.B.P.* (Vols I-V, 1986-1990); for the references mentioned here, see under Śiva and Viṣṇu, Vol. IV and V respectively.
6. Whitehead, H. *The Village Gods of South India*, Delhi, 1970 (1921), p.27.
7. *Ibid.*
8. *Ibid.*
9. This account is recorded by Vettam Mani, *Puranic Encl.*, pp. 496-98; but he mentions just the Padma Purāṇa, as the source, without any details of reference. To the best of the present writer's knowledge the Padma P. does not have it., nor any

other Purāṇa. The Brahmavaivarta P. does have an account of Vṛndā (IV.86.1-150); but it has no Viṣṇu. It is a different account altogether, though Vṛndā is said to be performing penance to win Hari as husband.

10. Cf. Dange, *Encl. P.B.P.* Vol.II,p.687f.

11. Śat.Br.II.4.4.9 *tad vaitām rātrīm mitro varuṇe retaḥ siñcati.*

12. The story of Bhasmāsura is not found in any Purāṇa text, and it has to be taken as a later one. However, the same story occurs with Mohinī and a demon of another name, which is Kālapṛṣṭha, Skanda P. V.3.67.3-76. The detail of the demon getting turned to ashes must have given currency to the easier name Bhasmāsura; *bhasman*=ashes.

13. The first such unit is that of Dakṣa and Aditi, who are said to be born from one another, Ṛgveda X.72.4.

14. In one myth demon Āḍi takes the form of Pārvatī and tries to have sexual union with Śiva, with the idea of cutting off his *liṅgam* with his vaginal teeth; but Śiva is the male; cf. Skanda P. I.2.29.21 *cakre bhagāntare daityo dantān vajropamān dṛḍhān*; this is the motif of *vagina dentata* common in folklore.

15. *Encl.P.B.P.* Vol. IV,p.1325, under 'Śiva'.

16. Śiva P. Yuddhakhaṇḍa 16 and 17; also Skanda P.II.4.17.8ff.

17. Later, there appears to be a fusion of the accounts of Tulasī and Vṛndā. The suggestion is already present in the Brahmavaivarta P. (Prakṛti-khaṇḍa 6.37), where Tulasī is said to have performed penance at Vṛndāvana and came to be called Vṛndāvanī. It may be of interest to note, that a four-cornered high stand, made of clay, wherein the Tulasī plant is fixed is called Vṛndāvana in Maharashtra.

18. This is a late myth. According to it Viṣṇu curses Lakṣmī to be a mare as she fixes her eyes on Revanta, who is seated on a horse. This is from Vettam Mani, *Puranic Encyclopaedia,* p.269a under Revanta(2), where he refers to Devī Bhāgavata Skandha 6.

Ten

The Myth of Dhundhu

As noted already, the exact meaning of a particular myth eludes the reader of the present day; for the tradition of the particular society never mentions how and why the myth got generated. Yet, in certain cases the myth gets transparent and one can go through the various layers to get at the 'meaning'. We take the myth of the 'demon' Dhundhu as it occurs in the Mahābhārata (Vana, Ch.s 201-204), studying its later versions.

The account tells that the king Kuvalāśva of the Ikṣvāku family got the name Dhundhumāra, as he killed the demon Dhundhu. It states that in the sandy desert (*marudhanvasu,* 201.11) the sage Uttaṅka had his hermitage, where he practised severe penance. Thereby he pleased Viṣṇu, who appeared before him. The sage looked at the god and praised him variously stating that the god pervaded the whole universe.[1] Viṣṇu, thus propitiated, asked Uttaṅka to choose a boon. The sage requested the god to keep him interested in the devotion for the god, in truth and control of senses. Viṣṇu granted all this readily, and further said, that he would also perform wonderful deeds for the benefit of the three worlds. Then, in the same breath, he informed the sage about the 'great demon' Dhundhu, who was performing great penance; that he would be killed by Kuvalāśva, the

Dhundhu and Dhundhumāra

son of the king Bṛhadaśva. He said "Kuvalāśva would acquire the strength of *yoga* from me, and command from you (i.e. from the sage) and will be successful in killing Dhundhu". Saying this, Viṣṇu got out of his sight (Ib.27-34). Now, Uttaṅka heard that the king Bṛhadaśva wanted to abdicate his kingdom in favour of his son, Kuvalāśva, who had twentyone thousand sons (202.5d *sahasrāṇy ekavimśatiḥ*), and to resort to the forest to dedicate himself to severe penance. Uttaṅka hastened to the king and convinced him that before he resorted to the life of a hermit he should save the people from the demon Dhundhu. He said, "Near my hermitage, in the desert, there is a sea of sand (v.16[C] *samudro vālukāpūrṇaḥ).* Its name is Ujjālaka, and it is many *yojana-s* in expanse (1 *yojana*=4 *krośas*=8 miles). The mighty demon Dhundhu is holed up in it, underground (*antarbhūmigataḥ*). He is the son of Madhu and Kaiṭabha *(madhukaiṭabhayoḥ putraḥ).* After killing him, you may take to the forest!" Uttaṅka also describes the demon, "He is unvanquishable by the gods, demons Nāgas, Yakṣas and Gandharvas. The demon stays dormant in the depth of the sandy desert, concealed under mass of sand; and his respiration at the end of a year, causes tremor in the earth and the forest-regions all over for seven days. Due to the vibrations of his breath a dust-storm gets arisen, mixed with flashes of flames fringed with fumes and smoke. This makes it impossible for me to stay in my hermitage". Uttaṅka urges the king to kill the demon looking to the well-being of the people at large (202.1-31). The king assures the sage that his son Kuvalāśva with all his sons (203.4 *putraiḥ parivṛtaḥ sarvaiḥ*), will accomplish the task, and that the sage should permit him to go to the forest as he had discarded the weapons. He instantly commissions his son to the desire of the sage (203-6).

The next chapter repeats that Dhundhu was the son of Madhu-Kaiṭabha (204.9) and adds that he performed penance standing on one foot. Remembering the death of Madhu-Kaiṭabha (his fathers) at the hands of Viṣṇu, he had defeated him and other gods (Ib.1-6). So Kuvalāśva went to where Dhundhu was lying; and there ensued a terrible fight (the description is exaggerated as usual; we take the main account). Kuvalāśva, being directed by the sage Uttaṅka, went where the demon lay. He was accompanied by the multitude of his sons. The king and his many sons caused the sea of sand to be dug (20[a] *arṇavam khānayāmāsa*). After digging for seven days (v 21 *saptabhir divasaiḥ)* they found out the demon with his expansive body lying in the western quarter, wholly covering it (v 22[d] *diśam āvṛtya paścimām*). The sons of Kuvalāśva thoroughly surrounded the demon, who ran here and there. Being thrashed and cudgelled by the sons of the king, the demon ejected fire from his mouth as was the case in bygone times when the sage Kapila showered fire on the sons of Sagara (vv 27-28); but ultimately as he was vanquished, profuse water oozed out from his body. The king, Kuvalāśva, drank the whole of the fire-mixed water due to the strength of his *yoga* (given to him by Viṣṇu). As he killed the demon Dhundhu, he came to be called Dhundhumāra (Ib. 34). It is further said that this *ākhyāna* is the praise of Viṣṇu (v 44[d] *viṣṇoḥ sam-anu-kīrtanam*).

On analysing the account we have the following parts—

1. Viṣṇu assures Uttaṅka that anybody who goes to destroy the demon, would be aided by his (Viṣṇu's) *yoga*. Ultimately the account gets the Viṣṇu-caption (*viṣṇoḥ samanukīrtanam*), through the sub-account of Uttaṅka, as intermediary.

2. The pure episode of the demon, who is vanquished by a king (Kuvalāśva) and the army of his sons, need not have Viṣṇu.

3. The account refers to the earlier account of Sagara's sons who were instrumental in digging the path for the Gaṅgā.[2]

Here, there appears to be a joint to the original account which starts from the later chapter. Viṣṇu's assurance is the joint, though placed in the earlier chapter, where it is stated that it is Viṣṇu, who, sort of induced Uttaṅka to go to king Bṛhadaśva (ch.201). We have no mention here of Dhundhu's hindrance in Uttaṅka's penance. And yet, in the next chapter the sage gives this as a reason. We, now, refer to some Puranic versions of the same account.

According to the Vāmana P. (52.13ff), Dhundhu was the son of Kaśyapa from the demoness Danu. He obtained a boon from Brahmā by his penance, that he should never be killed by the gods, along with Indra. Conquering all gods, along with Indra, Dhundhu himself gained the position of Indra (the account speaks of Dhundhu's conquest of such regions as Mahas, Janas, etc. He also performed the Horse-sacrifice and other sacrifices, Ib.-50). The gods resorted to Viṣṇu for help; and he agreed to help them. Having released his body in the water of the river Devikā (near Dhundhu's city) he came out as a dwarf, with his hair dishevelled. He again went down under the waters and came to the surface. Thus, he was showing that he was getting drowned. The *brāhmaṇa*-s, and Dhundhu himself, saw him. Dhundhu, the lord of the demons, got him out of the river, and asked him who he was. He told (to trim the long account), that he was Gatibhāsa, the younger son of a brahmin called Prabhāsa, and that his elder brother's name was Netrabhāsa. According to the narration, after the death of their father, Netrabhāsa told his younger brother (Gatibhāsa) that, as he was a dwarf, he could not have any share in the property. When Gatibhāsa argued, the elder brother lifted him up and threw him into the river. "I have been floating in the river for one year now; and you have brought me out", said Gatibhāsa. Hearing him Dhundhu said that he would give him as much wealth as he desired. But Gatibhāsa declined and said, "Looking at my height, give me only three steps. I am unable to protect any more land." Dhundhu granted the desire. Now, the dwarf Gatibhāsa took his two steps and covered the whole universe. But, when he saw no place where he could put the third step, he jumped on the back of Dhundhu, assuming a huge form. Thereby a depth measuring thirty thousand *yojana-s* (1 *yojana* = 4 krośa-s= 8 miles) was formed. Gatibhāsa, now known as Trivikrama, took Dhundhu out and again threw him in the expansive pit.[3] He also rained sand over the pit to fill it totally. Dhundhu, thus, got buried inside. Trivikrama (Gatibhāsa, originally Viṣṇu) took the form of the river Kālindī and became invisible there (-89).

The account serves as a sort of a fore-appendage to the pure account in the Mahābhārata, and ends in explaining how the demon was posited under the earth. It suggests that the sea of sand was created by Viṣṇu himself. The motif of 'three steps' and thrusting the demon under the earth is very much the same as in the account of Vāmana and Bali. There is a faint indication that the region where Dhundhu was buried alive is the Western region from the name Prabhāsa, the father of Netrabhāsa and Gatibhāsa. The river, Kālindī, whose form Viṣṇu is said to have taken while disappearing, cannot be taken as the Yamunā, also known as Kālindī, nor is this detail mentioned in other accounts.[4]

The Brahmāṇḍa P. (II.3.63.31-60) mentions the account in short. It starts with the desire of Bṛhadaśva, the father of Kuvalāśva, to abdicate the throne. Uttaṅka dissuades him, asking him to annihilate Dhundhu as he was the source of great trouble in his penance. Dhundhu is said to be the son of the demon Madhu (and not Madhu Kaiṭabha, as is mentioned at Mb.). Dhundhu is said to be staying concealed under the sea of sand (v 36 *samudro vālukāpūrṇaḥ)* performing severe penance. The other details closely follow the description at Mb., and even certain expressions are the same. However, there is no mention of the gods approaching Viṣṇu and the latter taking the form of a dwarf (as in the Vāmana P.), nor Viṣṇu himself telling the sage that the latter would work a wonder, and that Kuvalāśva would kill Dhundhu with the strength of *yoga* infused in him by Viṣṇu (as in Mb.). This text (Brahmāṇḍa P.) also refers to Viṣṇu in the speech of Uttaṅka to Bṛhadaśva— "Viṣṇu gave me a boon" (v 44[a]) and (earlier, 42[cd], when the sage tells Bṛahadaśva), "Your luster will be enhanced by that of Viṣṇu", and further (v 50), "Viṣṇu entered Kuvalāśva with his own lustre". Here also it is stated that Kuvalāśva caused the sandy sea to be dug (v 54 *samudram khānayāmāsa vālukāpūrṇam avyayam)*, and that Dhundhu was seized by the sons of Kuvalāśva in the western quarter (cf. v 55 *diśam āśritya paścimām*). Other details regarding the fiery water etc. are the same as in Mb. As at Mb., here also it is said that only three sons of Kuvalāśva remained unscorched by the fire. The demon is said to be a "water-demon" (v 59 *udaka-rākṣasa*).

Other Purāṇas give about similar details. Thus, according to the Brahma P. (7.61ff) Dhundhu was the son of Madhu. He was staying in a sandy sea and used to trouble people. So, being requested by Uttaṅka, king Bṛhadaśva sent his son Kuvalāśva to kill him. Kuvalāśva went with his sons, and began to dig the sandy sea. As they dug on and on, fire began to shoot from the mouth of Dhundhu, in which ninety-seven sons of Kuvalāśva perished. Kuvalāśva decided to finish the demon; but the latter now, attacked him with gushes of subterranean water. However, the king was a *yogi*; so, he drank off all the water that gushed towards him. He also extinguished the fire emitted by Dhundhu, the 'water-demon' (*udaka-rākṣasa*), and killed him (Ib.84). The same account occurs at Śiva P. (V.37.14-36), with the difference that Kuvalāśva's father is not Bṛhadaśva, but Yuvanāśva.[5] Here also Dhundhu is said to be in the western quarter (Ib. 31 *diśam āśritya paścimām*). Similar account occurs in the Vāyu P. (Uttarakhaṇḍa 26.31-58); and the Viṣṇu P. passingly refers to the event (IV.2.38-40), but giving the name of Bṛhadaśva's son as Kuvalayāśva. The Harivamśa also narrates the account in a systematic way, but unlike the Mb. account which is untrimmed. It straightway states that Kuvalāśva was the son of the king Bṛhadaśva (Harivamśa XI.22ff). He had a hundred sons, versed in all lores and skilled in weaponry. They were also performers of sacrifices and gave profuse *dakṣiṇā* to the priests. Now, Bṛhadaśva desired to leave for forest. Uttaṅka came to know of it and approached him (The rest of the account is very much the same as already noted above). The sandy desert is named here Ujjāṇaka (and not Ujjālaka, as in Mb. and other texts), indicating that it was devoid of habitation (*ut-jana*)—a total desert. Other details are the same - the demon blows out his breath at the end of the year, causing great tremors etc. (and even the expressions are the same), and that this sandy sea was in the western region,[6] where Dhundhu was spotted by the sons of Kuvalāśva. All but three of Kuvalāśva's sons perished in this exploit, which is a detail mentioned above in the Puranic records, and also by Mb. which gives their names as Dṛḍhāśva, Kapilāśva and Candrāśva (Mb. Vana 204-39-40) though it mentions the number of sons as twenty-one thousand.

Now, we analyse the various accounts structurally but not in various columns as Claude Lévi-Strauss would have liked[7], marking important points:

The sage Uttaṅka has his hermitage in the sandy desert, generally known as the 'sea of sand'. He performs penance and Viṣṇu appears before him. He asks the sage to choose boons. The sage does not want any thing for himself, except devotion for Viṣṇu. Viṣṇu is glad and, of his own accord, tells him that he would be a great benefactor. How? There is the king named Bṛhadaśva. His son is named Kuvalāśva. He would kill the demon Dhundhu staying in the same sandy desert. Viṣṇu himself would infuse Kuvalāśva with his *yoga* (Mb. Vana 201). The Puranic accounts and the one from the Harivamśa leave the portion noted above from the Mb. which is clearly an appendage to the main account. There are negligible variations; and we may note the homologues as follows—

1. Bṛhadaśva leaves for the forest, assuring help to Uttaṅka in subduing the 'demon' Dhundhu. He commissions his son Kuvalāśva to accompany Uttaṅka.

2. Kuvalāśva has many sons, well-versed and well-minded. Many - indicated by 'a hundred' or 'twenty-one thousand'.

3. The 'sea of sand', which is the abode of Dhundhu is in the western region of India.
4. The demon forces out his breath at the end of (each) year; and his weapons are fire, fiery-hot water and even *aṅgāra* (hot embers). His whole body is full of water, which gushes out at a specific period (by the end of one year). Otherwise, the whole sandy desert is waterless. When the event of the 'breathing' of the demon takes place for seven days (a specific time) there are tremors in the adjoining region.
5. The gushes of water and indications of heat (fire etc.) are a part of the body of the demon who is totally identified with the region, but is subterranean.

Now, as we come to the final nature of the demon (which is, now, almost obvious) we consider certain details in the account from the Vāmana P. The Vāmana P. is a Vaiṣṇava P., and right from the Mb. the supremacy of (Kṛṣṇa=Viṣṇu) is attestable. In the present narration also Mb. has a clear appendage of Viṣṇu's design to be at the back of the whole exploit. In other accounts also Viṣṇu plays an important role in asmuch as he is said to impart the yogic strength to the hero, Kuvalāśva. The Vāmana P. takes a further step not in the account proper, but in the pre-appendage, in the sub-story of Gatibhāsa. Here also, like Mb. it tries to stress the role of Viṣṇu; and the ancient motif of Viṣṇu-Vāmana (the dwarf)[8] comes handy. However, instead of placing his third step on the head of the king of demons - who generously favoured him (as is the case with dwarf Viṣṇu), the dwarf Gatibhāsa jumps on the back of Dhundhu, the demon king who is equally favourable to him. This change is on purpose, which has close relation to the change of the situation. Here the demon is known, in the current and popular account, to stand for the whole sea of sand. So, he has to fall flat; hence he has to be pushed from the back, by jumping on it. The fact that the fall of Dhundhu generated an expansive hollow indicates the expanse of Dhundhu's body, which is totally identified with the hollow. This was filled with sand. This account provides a backstage for the main and pure account that we have at Mb. and the other versions. The Vāmana P. would have us believe that, formerly, the region was not sandy; that there were two rivers (including the one called Kālindī), but both were lost in the sand-formation. Viṣṇu's taking the form of the Kālindī and disappearing would indicate the presence of a small river that got lost in the sandy desert, which was continuously changing as it advanced; and the formation was a case of seismic change. Reading this backstage account from the Vāmana P. with the others, it becomes clear that the huge demon Dhundhu is only a metaphor on the sandy desert that got gradually formed on land that had, in itself, scanty water. This is clear from the ficticious mention on his parentage. Later accounts do away with the awkwardness of his being the child of two fathers, and mention only one, Madhu. Danu is mother common for the *dānava*-s, while Kaśyapa is a common father for many. When the desert was getting formed, there were periodical quakes and tremors, and even mild volcanic eruptions. The constant mention of the western quarter in other accounts, that get balanced with the name Prabhāsa (Gatibhāsa's father) would indicate that this mythical metaphorical account centres round the region between the Rann of Kacch and the desert where the Sarasvatī got lost in the desert. This would be to the west of Ayodhyā, the capital of the Ikṣvākus. It also indicates efforts to dig in the vast sandy land, for the gain of subterranean water perennially. As such, like the feat of Sagara, also of the Ikṣvāku family, his sixty thousand (many) sons and later of Bhagīratha to tame the Gaṅgā and release her on a set course, this myth has to be seen as an ancient record of human effort, in the reign of the Ikṣvākus, in limiting the advancing sandy desert, digging it deep enough to get water pushed up for the benefit of the people. As the desert is superimposed by the 'demon'[9], the king who performed the feat has to be superimposed, or helped, by the popular god—Viṣṇu. The many 'sons' of the king need not be taken literally; they could be his subjects and army whom the king has to protect as sons. Thus, the mythical account has to be understood as concealing a historical incident.

References

1. The description, as it occurs here, reminds one of Ṛgveda X.90.1, the description of Puruṣa.
2. Rāmāyaṇa, Bāla, 40.6ff, the sons of Sagara are said to be sixty thousand, 19 *Ṣaṣṭiḥ putrasahasrāṇi*; 2nd ed., Chinnaswami Shastrigal and V.H.S. Shastri, Mylapore, Madras, 1958, Mb. Vana 106.7-16 for the number of sons; digging of earth 107.33.
3. For an earlier instance, cf. Taitt. Br. I.5.10.7, where the son of Prahlāda is likewise thrown; and a tank is created. Water from it was unfit for drinking.
4. One Kālindī river is mentioned also in the Ketumāla region, Vāyu P. 44.1-24 for rivers; see S. Muzafer Ali, *The Geography of the Purāṇas*, People's Publishing House, New Delhi, Ahmedabad, Bombay, 2nd ed., 1973 (1966), p. 97. This would show that the name is not to be taken very seriously.
5. Mb. Vana 202.3 mentions Yuvanāśva in the same context, but quite early in the dynasty, as the grandfather of Bṛhadaśva.

6. Harivamśa, XI. 50 *diśam āvṛtya paścimām*, which is the same as at Mb. noted above.

7. Claude Lévi-Strauss, *Structural Anthropology*, (Tr. in Eng., Clair Jacobson and Brooke Grundfest Schoft), Penguin, London, 1969 (1963), p. 214.

8. Cf. Śat.Br. I.2.5.5 *Vāmano ha Viṣṇurāsa*, which is the earliest mention.

9. We may compare such cases as of Gayā and its association with the demon; also Gayaśiras; another demon is Karṇāṭa, giving his name to Karṇāṭaka. See Dange, *Encl. P.B.P.*, Vol. II, New Delhi, 1987, under "Demons", 'Karṇāṭa', p. 407ff; for Gaya, Gayaśiras, Vol. III, p. 794.

Eleven

Sabardughā and Kāmadhenu

One of the prominent pastoral-agricultural images that found place among the Hindu myths is that of the Kāmadhenu, 'the cow that fulfils all desires!' Actually, the very word *dhenu* (or *dhenā* in ṚV along with *dhenu)* indicated a 'store' (fr. the root √*dhā;* cf. Yāska in Nir. VI. 17 for *dhene* dual of *dhenā*) mixed with the idea of 'drink' (fr. √*dhet=dhe)*. This mixed concept of 'store' and 'drink' gave rise to the concept of the 'food on feet' (ṚV X.169.1[d], *padvat avasa)*. The image of the cow is extended further to the river, which is believed to be a cow. Thus, the Sarasvatī is visualized as a cow (ṚV VII.95), and the deity, Apām-napāt ('son-of-waters') was believed to be stationed at the confluence of the rivers Sarasvatī and Dṛṣadvatī. This god has his own 'cow' in his watery abode (ṚV II.35.7). The identification of the river and the cow forms a regular, and a very popular, motif in folk-lore.[1] The rain-clouds giving the much desired rain were also seen as cows. A consolidated result of all these ideas formed a base for the kāmadhenu. The earliest indication of the 'desire-yielding cow' is to be seen in the cow called *sabardughā*, mentioned at various places in ṚV. The word has two parts: *sabar* and *dughā*, the former has the sense of 'milk' and, at some places, 'nectar', while the second part means 'cow' (lit. 'milking', fr. √*duh*, 'to milk'). But,

Sabardughā is not restricted to the gifts relating to milk alone. She is said to 'milk' all types of wealth (ṚV I. 134.4). The masculine form, *sabardugha,* occurring only once, is for Soma (IX.12.7), as its shoots give out the 'elixir' of the juice when pressed. The juice is *sabar,* which Soma 'milks'; hence, he is *sabardugha.*

Though at various places, the Sabardughā is associated with rain, and Sabardugha with juice, the concept goes beyond these perceptible things. Sabardughā is invoked to 'milk' what is totally absent with the invoker (ṚV X.61.17 *a-svam duhadhyai).* She is desired to be activated even where there is no context of rain-water, or of the normal milk (ṚV VI. 48. 11). She is said to arrive with desired blessings *(Ib.* 12^{d} *sumnair evayāvarī).* Sabardughā provides the seed for the concept of the mystic cow in later myths. Though ṚV mentions *pṛśni* (Pṛśni) as a cow, at various places, indicating the cloud-cow and also the mother of the Aśvins, in this latter sense, she has to be taken as slightly different from the Sabardughā, conceptually. Later, Pṛśni is associated with the Aṅgirases (Taitt. Br. II.1.1.1). This Pṛśni has to be taken as a phase of the Sabardughā, though she is described as *gharma-dhuk* ('milker of the warm fluid'='rain' or providing milk for the ritual of Pravargya'); because, she is not restricted to this concept alone. As a matter of fact, Sabardughā seems to be the forerunner of Nandinī, the special cow of the Vasiṣṭhas, in the later literature, who is said to provide not only the sacrificial requirements and objects of enjoyment, but also even armed and armoured warriors. According to Mb. (Ādi 99.9ff), this cow, Nandinī, was born to Surabhi (the celestial cow, mother of all celestial and mythical cows), who is said to be the daughter of Dakṣa; her 'father' was Kaśyapa (the common ancestor of all creatures and of anyone of uncertain origin). Nandinī was given to Vasiṣṭha by the gods. Her distinguishing epithets are *homa=dhenu* (sacrificial cow), *sarvakāmadhuk* ('milker of all desires'); and, it is indicated that she would help keep all diseases away from one who drank her milk. This is sought to be supported by a mythical narration. According to it, once Pṛthu and other Vasu-s (*vasu* is a category of divine persons) came to the forest where the hermitage of Vasiṣṭha was located and Nandinī moved freely. They were with their wives. One of the women saw the cow and told about her to her husband, Dyo. He told her that a person who drank the milk of the cow would live for ten thousand years. She asked her husband to obtain the cow from Vasiṣṭha, because her friend named Jitavatī, the daughter of king Uśīnara, was born as a mortal woman and that she wanted this friend of hers to drink the milk of the cow so that she could be devoid of oldage and diseases. To please his wife Dyo, with other Vasu-s, stole the cow. Later, not finding the cow anywhere, and knowing that she was carried away by the Vasu-s, Vasiṣṭha cursed them. However, when the Vasu-s came to know of the curse, they approached Vasiṣṭha for the removal of the curse. Vasiṣṭha did so, except in the case of Dyo, who had to be born as a mortal. This one became Devavrāta, Bhīṣma.

The account would show that the original myth regarding the mysterious mythic cow is used for bestowing divinity on Devavrāta. This is clear from another myth regarding her, where Viśvāmitra figures. Viśvāmitra and Vasiṣṭha were traditional rivals of each other (and their rivalry goes back to the Ṛgvedic period, due to contest at chief priesthood in the family of Divodāsa and Sudās).[2] This account occurs at *Mb.* (Ādi 174), which calls it a very old story (v 2 *ākhyānam purāṇam*). It says, that once, while hunting in the forest, Viśvāmitra happened to arrive at the hermitage of Vasiṣṭha. The latter welcomed him with various things his *kāmadhuk* cow released. They included medicines from wild and cultivated herbs (v 10 *grāmyāraṇyāścauṣadhīś* ca), milk, nectar-like compound accomplished from six juices, all sorts of eatables, costly jewels and varieties of cloth (Ib. vv 10-12). Being pleased, and amazed by the mysterious faculties of the cow, Viśvāmitra, the Gādhi king, requested Vasiṣṭha to part with the cow for any number of other cows and even in exchange for his whole kingdom (vv 15-16). Vasiṣṭha did not agree. When all his entreaties proved to be of no avail, Viśvāmitra seized the cow with the help of his soldiers and tried to carry her by force, even as she was bellowing pitiably. She cried to Vasiṣṭha why he was not cursing and restraining the soldiers of the king from taking her away. Vasiṣṭha replied that he was a *brāhmaṇa* and the strength of a *brāhmaṇa* lies in pardon, not injury (v 29); but, he assured her that he has not left her by himself. Knowing that, and being satisfied, the cow, now assumed a terrible form and created many soldiers from her own body: the Pahlavas from her tail; likewise Yavanas (Ionians), Siṁhalas, Śabaras, Kirātas, Pauṇḍras, Pulindas, Cīnas, Hūṇas, Mlecchas, and the Keralas (vv 36-37). These soldiers attacked the soldiers of Viśvāmitra, who, ultimately admitted defeat and said, "Fie upon the strength of the *kṣatriya;* power is that strength which is of the lustrous *brahman* (possessed by a *brāhmaṇa*)" *(Ib.* 45)[3]. It does not require much effort to see, that the nucleus of the concept of the *kāmadhenu* is used in two different contexts in the two myths told above, though the common point in both is that the cow was taken by force, as she was unique. The latter account occurs also in the Purāṇas (cf. SK.P.VI.167.31ff). In a variant of this motif, we have an account that once Brahmā asked the *kāmadhenu* to provide the *brāhmaṇa-s* with attendants. So, she caused a large dent in the earth with the forceful flow of milk from her udder; then she bellowed; from the bellow came out men with pig-tails, having holy threads on their shoulders running across their upper body (SK.P.III.2.10.4ff). The belief in the *kāmadhenu* fulfilling any desire is clear. However, the trait of the creation of soldiers and men from her body is prominent in the account, and its variations, of the strife between Viśvāmitra and Vasiṣṭha. The Rām., giving the account elaborately (Bāla, Ch.s 52-55) is the source of the account. Here, Viśvāmitra is said to arrive in the hermitage of Vasiṣṭha, who expresses his desire to welcome him and his soldiers with the usual 'guest-honour' (*ātithya).* Viśvāmitra, however, says that he was quite satisfied with the adoring speech of Vasiṣṭha and the fruits he offered. But, Vasiṣṭha insists on offering a more spacious welcome. Viśvāmitra agrees. So, Vasiṣṭha calls his cow. The name of the cow is not Nandinī; it is Kalmāṣī and Śabalā (both meaning the same thing) indicating that the cow was having dark spots (first word) or spotted (second word)[4]. The rest of the account is practically the same as noted above. The cow creates all sorts of eatables and drinks (*Ib.*Ch.53). Vasiṣṭha pleaded that the cow, Śabalā, was every thing for him. She was the source of all offering in the daily rites, such as Agnihotra (where an offering of milk is to be poured into the sacrificial fire) and the domestic offerings, and even of his sacred lores (vv 11-14), also the half-monthly sacrifices (Darśa and Pūrṇamāsa; v 24). The arguments give place to quarrel and then ensues the fight. Making sure that Vasiṣṭha did not desire to give her away to the king, and hearing from

Vasiṣṭha that he was helpless before the mighty king, the cow requests him to appoint her to the task of smashing the army of Viśvāmitra. Vasiṣṭha consents and the cow produces a multitude of flying creatures (*paplavāḥ*, monkeys?) that began to destroy the army of the king. But, the king destroyed the creatures. The cow, now, produces various human races including Śaka, Yavana and others (*Ib.* Ch. 54, whole of it). The fight then involves various missiles; the cow produces them for Vasiṣṭha. Ultimately, Vasiṣṭha gets the *brahmadaṇḍa* (the staff of *brahman*-power) in his hand, which gives him victory (*Ib.* Ch. 56). Accepting defeat, Viśvāmitra agrees that it is the *brahman*-lusture that is real strength (v 24, Fie upon ...; the verse is the same as noted before from Mb.). Used in the context of the rivalry between Vasiṣṭha and Viśvāmitra, the concept and myth about the *kāmadughā* take the form of a charter for establishing the superiority of the *brahman* power over that of the *kṣatra*. Flatly it may appear to extol the *brāhmaṇa* at the cost of the *kṣatriya*. But, the fact that Viśvāmitra decides to go in for penance later makes clear that, according to the original practice, the status of these two classes (*varṇa-s*) was interchangeable. The constant mention of the cow as the sacrificial cow (*homadhenu*, or the source of Agnihotra etc.) would show that the Ṛgvedic concept about the *sabardughā*, and that behind the *kāmadhenu*, is commissioned here for praising the sacrifice—which is just little short of the equation between sacrifice and the desire-yielding cow. The offshoot of this equation is that it is the sacrifice that gives real power, and that weapons and army, together with the royal authority, are subservient to sacrifice. This smybolic equation of sacrifice and the cow, that gives all that is desired, forms a basis for the divinity of the ordinary cow, in whose body the gods are believed to stay. With this, we revert to the original imagery about the *sabardughā*.

ṚV mentions the exploits of the Ṛbhus, who were three brothers; they performed some wonderful exploits which gave them the status of semi-divinities. They are said to have been the sons of Manu (=mortals); but, they obtained immortality on the merit of their varied wonders. In essence, they appear to have been deified artisans. One of their exploits concerns the wonderful re-creation of a cow. This cow is 'sabardughā' (ṚV I. 20.3). She is said to have been created in a whole from the mere skin. She is also said to have been dead and remained only with bare skin. But, the Ṛbhus protected her, put flesh on the skeletal remains (ṚV I.161.7; cf.I. 110.8; IV.33.4), and this was done every year. The myth says, "Every year did the Ṛbhus protect the cow; every year they fashioned flesh on her; every year they added and secured lustre upon her (body) ..." (ṚV IV.33.4). The rejuvenation and structural completion of the 'cow' is closely associated with the flood of waters. Says the myth: One of the Ṛbhu brothers causes blood, like water, to flow (or, following the exact reading *śroṇām eka udakam gām avājati,* 'One leads the lame cow to water')[5]. Another one arranges the flesh with the tools...". They also create grass and water everywhere, when they sleep in the house of one Agohya (I.161.10-11), the duration of this sleep being for twelve days (IV.33.7). There are two parts of this myth about the Ṛbhus. The first is the production of the whole 'cow' from the bare skin, protecting it and nourishing it. The second is the creation of foliage, grass etc. and the flow of rivers, i.e. enough water everywhere. To take up the first. The *sabardughā* cow is an independent entity, as we have noted above. This mystic and symbolic concept regarding the *sabardughā* is employed in the mythical and mysterious exploits of the Ṛbhus to extol them. However, the *sabardughā,* here, has some added traits. It is said to be famished, almost dead, only the skin remaining. Along with the concept about the *sabardughā* we have examined earlier, ṚV uses the epithet *sabardughā* for the earth and heaven (dual *sabardughe* in view of the two, earth and heaven, III.6.4; 55.12). The reason is that both, earth and sky, give produce and rain respectively, both being nourishing. The nature of *sabardughā* gets clearer when she is called also *viśvarūpā* (IV.33.8; also I. 161.6), 'multiformed'. This epithet compares with the Nandinī cow, and more particularly with the *kalmāṣī* and *śabalā* of Vasiṣṭha. The epithets śatarūpā, kalmāṣī and śabalā go well with the sky-cow (one *sabardughā)* and the earth-cow (the other *sabardughā)*; because, both are spotted with multi-coloured clouds and multi-coloured corn-stalks, respectively. The imagery of the sky-cow is well set in the Vedic tradition, which has also another name for her, viz. *pṛśni.* The spotted cow figured also in ritual to be given away as *dakṣiṇā*, or is to be immolated as a symbol for the sky (cf. *sthūlapṛṣatīm anaḍvāhīm ālabheta).* The earth-cow, the other *sabardughā*, connects directly with the Pṛthu myth, noted earlier.[6]

The second part of the myth tells about the growth of grass and other types of foliage (including vegetation); but it is associated with the sleep of the Ṛbhus. They are said to have stayed and reposed and slept in the house of Agohya ('the one who cannot be concealed'). In the meanwhile the world got covered (with dark clouds) and the Ṛbhus asked Agohya "Who knew this wonderful exploit of ours?" Agohya replied in symbolic language, saying, "it is the 'goat' who told me that the 'dog' knows it. This is a known exploit during the year". Traditionally, this is taken to be the exploit of the annual rain[7], apart from what the 'goat' and the 'dog' signify.[8] Though the *sabardughā* is not mentioned in the context of the sleep of the Ṛbhus, the yearly drenching of the earth that was parched and the generation of the foliage appear to be only an expression and explanation of the symbol of the dead cow (earth-symbol) getting fleshed up. The sleep of the Ṛbhus and the advent of rain have parallels in the Hindu mythical tradition, though the Ṛgveda does not apparently have a parallel of this type. However, there is a myth regarding the Aśvins. They are said to have generated milk in the cow of one Śayu (the name indicates 'a person who sleeps', fr. √*sī*, 'to sleep'). This cow also was sterile, very weak and with scanty flesh on her body (ṚV I. 116.22); she was a 'non-cow' (so to say; I.117.20 *adhenu* is the word used). This exploit forms an important part of the Aśvin myths (cf. also I.118.8; 119.6; VI.62.7 etc.), and the protege, at all places, is Śayu. Śayu does not appear to be a real person, or a king as he is supposed to be,[9] if we look to other places. It is not improbable, that śayu' ('sleeping') has some ritual-and-mythical importance, as the word is contrasted with *caran* (moving) in an important context, where the meaning gets connected, ultimately, with the gain of rain (ṚV IV.18.12-13)[10]. In any case, the strengthening of a weak, or a sterile, cow is common to the myth of the Aśvins and that of the Ṛbhus. And, with the key-word *sabardughā* mentioned in the myth of the Ṛbhus for the cow (I.20.3, noted above), it could be extended to that of the Aśvins as the concept and the symbolic pattern seem to be the same. The difference is that in the myth of the Ṛbhus they sleep, while in that of the Aśvins the person who sleeps (śayu, fr.√*sī*) owns the 'cow'. The ultimate meaning in both cases, however, is the same. It is the fructication of the earth-cow, through rain.

From what has been said above, it is possible to trace the development of the concept of the 'desire-yielding cow'. The first stage of the concept was that of the 'cow' that gave the nourishing fluid. This fluid was not exactly milk; it was the very essence of vitality. The concept was, initially, based on the cow that gives milk. The divinity attached to the earthly cow transplanted her to the celestial plane, with the result that she was imagined to be a supranatural cow that gave not only the nourishing rain but also all the essentials required in life. Her 'milk' came to be nectar (=*sabar*). A further stage was that of the belief, according to which this cow contained everything related to sacrificial offering in her body. This is the stage when she was seen as the *homadughā*, the sacrificial cow (of the Aṅgirases and Vasiṣṭha) providing milk for all types of sacrifice. Mythologically she was the source of all types of objects of pleasure. This was the stage when the *sabardughā* gave place to the *kāmadhenū*. Employment of this myth in the context of the rivalry between Vasiṣṭha and Viśvāmitra added a further trait; this was the production of weapons and soldiers from her body. The additions rendered the *kāmadhenu* to develop on the lines of the holy grail,[11] sans the shape of the cup. The *kāmadhuk* of individuals like Aṅgiras and Vasiṣṭha have their origin in the cow of Śayu in the myth associated with the Aśvins, with the difference that, in the case of Aṅgiras and Vasiṣṭha the cow is not said to be famished or skin-bare. The famished and skin-bare cow getting fattened, and set in the imagery of rain and the abundance of sprouting vegetation, is the symbol of the summer-parched earth getting drenched and fruit-bearing, after rain.

With the *sabardughā* syndrome getting gradually extended on the lines noted above, a further pattern developed regarding the *kāmadhenu*. On the one hand the usurpation of the special cow served as a pattern of vengeance on the line of the Vasiṣṭha and Viśvāmitra strife involving the cow of the former and, on the other, a whole family of *kāmadhenu-s* arose. As an example of the first, may be taken the case of the Haihaya king Arjuna, the son of Kṛtavīrya. According to an account once Arjuna, the son of Kṛtavīrya (=Kārtavīrya), was hunting in the forest adjoining the river Narmadā. When he, and his attendants, roamed enough and had killed many wild beasts they got thirsty. After they had quenched their thirst with the waters of the river and had moved further, they saw the hermitage of Jamadagni. Jamadagni received him and requested him to accept his welcome. The king said that it would not be possible for the hermit to serve his whole army as he lacked resources. However, Jamadagni insisted and the king stayed with his army. The sage had his cow (not called *kāmadhenu*), Dogdhrī ('milker') whom he called and requested her to serve the king and his army as was suitable for a king. And, in an instant the humble hermitage of Jamadagni got transformed into a palace like that of Indra, the king of gods. It was endowed with all types of pillars and apartments studded with gold, silver and jewels. Various types of highly furnished seats (*siṁhāsana* and other seats) showed themselves. Varieties of eatables and drinks and all pleasures were ready at hand (Brāhmaṇḍa P. II.3.26. 35-62). (The description of the palace and the objects of enjoyment continues). Seeing all this being produced by the cow, Dogdhrī, the king requested Jamadagni to part with her in his favour. He said he would give any thing and even the costliest things in exchange for her. But, the sage was firm and would not be ready to part with the wonderful cow. So, the king took leave of the sage and started for his capital. But, the thought of the cow would not vacate his mind. Knowing this, his minister, Candragupta, said to him, "O King! As we were returning I saw another wonder. All that was created by the cow got assimilated in her body afterwards, within a moment! So, it is absolutely necessary that you should possess the cow of the sage at any cost". But, the king said, that it was not proper to usurp the things belonging to a *brāhmaṇa*. This thought of the king was supported also by his priest named Garga. However, the minister, cutting the speech of the priest, insisted that the king should have the wonder-cow at any cost; but, then, the king advised him to take the cow as he thought fit and bring her to him. The minister agreed and went to Jamadagni. The sage refused to be budged and there ensued a tussle. The minister seized the cow along with her calf (*Ib.* II.3.28.19-75). Jamadagni repeatedly warned him against taking away a *brāhmana's* belonging per force; but, he did not pay heed. Jamadagni had become sober these days (so says this Purāṇa; -29.13) and had left his characteristic anger since his son, Paraśurāma, had pacified him in the incident concerning his mother (Reṇukā; see Ch. on "Reṇukā and Yellammā"). He only held fast the cow at her neck; but, he was beaten by the attendants of the minister and fell dead. As the cow was being dragged, along with her calf, by the minister and his men, she got herself loose from the fetters. Now, she hit the men of the minister very hard by her hooves, her tail and her horns. Having scattered them and, even as they were watching with dread and amazement, she shot up to the sky and became invisible (Ib.-29.14-21). This account matches the one from Rām. in length; but, whereas the Rām., and the other texts mentioned above, are woven round the rivalry between the families of Viśvāmitra and Vasiṣṭha having its roots in the hoary Vedic past, this account is grafted on a new family feud. Actually, here we have a sort of inversion. What Vasiṣṭha suffered on account of the *kāmadhenu* at the hands of Viśvāmitra is now the fate of a close relation of Viśvāmitra; because, Viśvāmitra was the maternal uncle of Jamadagni (Mb. Śānti, 49.18-31).

The mythical tradition puts Surabhi at the starting upper end. Nandinī is said to be her daughter. Other *kāmadhenu-s* mentioned in the Puranic tradition are Sunandā, Sumanā, Susīlā and Kapilā. Except the last name which shows the influence of fire (*kapila* is the reddish tawny colour), other names are all indicative of good nature and benevolence; which is why these cows are all conceived as helpful,[12] a quality that goes well with fulfilment of desire. This has to be understood as the final and a broader phase of the *sabardughā-kāmadhenu.*

References

1. Dange, *Glimpses of Puranic Myth and Culture,* Ajanta Publications, Delhi, 1987, pp. 118ff.
2. H.D. Velankar, "Viśvāmitra and Vasiṣṭha in the Ṛgveda", *Dr. Mirashi Fel. Vol.,* Nagpur, 1965, pp. 1-7; Dange, "Sasarparī and the Horse of Sudās", *VIJ.* Hoshiarpur, V-1, March 1967, pp. 25-32.
3. The account accurs also in Śalya-parvan, in short, Ch. 40.16-24.
4. Monier-Williams, *A Sanskrit-English Dictionary,* Delhi, 1990 (1899) records Kalmāṣī as the speckled cow of Jamadagni with ref. to Mb., which information is doubtful, Jamadagni's cow is called Dogdhrī at Mb.
5. Sāyaṇa on I.161.10; actually the word is *śroṇām,* which he understands as *śoṇam* and renders as *śoṇavarṇam udakam rudhiram.* Félix Nève, *An Essay on the Myths of the Ṛbhus* (Eng. Tr. Ms. G.V. Davane, Ajanta Publications, Delhi, 1985, p. 150)

renders as, "One makes blood flow like water". Geldner does not approve of Sāyaṇa's gloss regarding *śroṇam* as *śoṇam* (blood-water).

6. See Ch. IV; p. 125 also n 19 there.

7. See Sāyaṇa's comments on the verse, 13, *varṣaṇarūpam karma.*

8. Sāyaṇa takes *basta* (the hornless goat) as *vasta* (a case *b* interchanging with *v*), and understands *vasta* as the sun; further, 'dog' (*śvan*) as the wind (*śvānam śvasantam vāyum*). Agohya is taken to mean the sun by Nève.

9. Sāyaṇa; also Macdonell, A.A. and Keith, A.B., under Śayu. In the Hindu tradition Viṣṇu sleeps at the start of the rainy season. So do all gods. The sleep of Viṣṇu is recorded in Kālidāsa, Meghadūta (cf.II. 50). But, the Purāṇas are informative regarding the sleep and the dates of the sleep, for various gods. The duration is from Aṣāḍha, bright 12th to the 11th of the bright half of Kārttika. The period cover, the rainy season. The is no record of sleep of all gods, or even of *Viṣṇu* in the Vedic texts; but Rudra is sent away to sleep at the end of the four-monthly sacrifices, when the rains cease; cf. Śat, Br.II.6.2.17. If this is connected to the sleep of the Ṛbhus, it would appear that sleep and rain, as a mystic association goes back to the ṚV and the Ṛbhu myth is the basis for the later sleep-motif. For gods' sleep, see Dange *Encl.P.B.P.* Vol. II. p. 663f.

10. Dange, *Sexual Symbolism,* p. 162ff.

11. Cf. Richard Cavendish (ed.), *Legends of the World,* pp. 240; 244f; for examples of this motif see Dange, *Legends in the Mahābhārata*, pp. 305f.

12. For examples see Dange; *Encl. P.B.P.*, Vol.II, p. 354f.

Twelve

Urvaśī—The Weaver of the Life–Web

Urvaśī has certain interesting traits in the Vedic and the post-Vedic mythology.[1] Even as the woman who is the beloved of Purūravas, her nature is that of a fleeting woman that would arrive at a ritual, or occasionally, only to favour an important person, not getting to be his permanent wife. This is in line with the concept of the *apsaras*. But, in addition to this she occurs in a different light altogether; and this is as the lady at the weaving frame. Though this happens only once, the aspect is important. In the hymn of the Vasiṣṭhas (ṚV VIII.33), Vasiṣṭha is said to have been born from her; and this birth is typically mytho-folkloric, where there is no corporal contact at all, thus showing the first Vasiṣṭha as a semi-divine mortal. He is born from the waters of a sacred jar into which the semen of Mitra and Varuṇa falls on seeing Urvaśī, who, thus, gets to be the external cause for the birth of Vasiṣṭha, and (hence also) his mother. This is one phase of the relationship between Urvaśī and Vasiṣṭha. But, there is another phase. This is where Vasiṣṭha is said to elevate his whole later clan (Vasiṣṭhas) as taking part in the weaving of the web of life. They are said to know the very secret of life, and conversant with the weaving frame spread by Yama, the first mortal turned divine (VII. 33.9 *yamena tatam paridhim*

The Birth of Vasiṣṭha

vayanta apsarasa upa sedur vasiṣṭhāḥ; and 12, *yamena tatam paridhim vayiṣyann apsarasaḥ pari jajñe vasiṣṭhaḥ*). Both these expressions convey the same belief, viz.; the many *apsaras-es* know the secret of the 'weaving' of the threads of life (a concept which later develops into that of the *saṁsāra*); and the One lady that is similarly associated with this 'weaving' is Urvaśī. The first Vasiṣṭha, being born of Urvaśī, knows the secret of such weaving of the threads of life, obviously from his mother, Urvaśī. Now, this association with the web of life is unique for Urvaśī[2] and also for the first and later Vasiṣṭhas. There is no other occurrence in the Vedic and post-Vedic literature involving either Urvaśī or Vasiṣṭha with the web of life. This means that the seer of this hymn has tried to float a myth that was not accepted by posterity. However, this mythical detail is not special to the seer of this hymn. There seems to be no doubt that he used this detail from a floating mass of folk-beliefs that particularly became prominent at his time, like another Vasiṣṭha who used the then popular belief in the efficacy of the frogs to usher in rain (VII.103).

The unique concept of the lady at the 'weaving frame' which occurs only here, with Urvaśī and the Vasiṣṭhas, for the first and the last time, inasmuch as the weaving is transferred to 'the web of life', may appear to have been suggested from a number of references in the Ṛgveda to the act of weaving managed mostly by women in that period; but, scrutiny shows that it is less probable. We do have such references. Thus, the dawn and the night are said to 'weave', spread and rewind the spread up threads (ṚV II.6.9 *tantum tatam sam vayanti*; contrast IV. 13.4 where the Sun is described, *yāsi tantum ava-vyayan*). The *tantu* (thread) came to be symbolized as the continuation of life on the one hand, and, on the other, it symbolized also the progeny, and also sacrifice with its many details. Thus, one seer vouches, that he certainly knows not to 'weave' the threads (VI.9.2, where the word *tantu* occurs as the *Singular* standing for the many sacrificial details, *nāham tantum na vi jānāmy otum*), which would indicate his humility in accepting that he does not know how to offer the sacrifice with all its details. That *tantu* came to symbolize the sacrifice is clear from the word *saptatantu*, which is quite famous (cf. I. 164.5 *sapta tantūn vi tatnire kavayaḥ*, which has the germ of the later concept of sacrifice being *sapta-tantu*). The same is the case in the thought, that the seers (or, the wise) stretch forth new threads out of the one that was made by the ancients (I. 159.4). And when the seer says that the thread should not be broken as he is 'weaving' a prayer with the mental faculty (II.28.5 *mā tantuḥ chedi vayato dhiyam me*), the implication is that his faculty of poetry should not be thwarted; also, impliedly, that his family-line should not be cut away (and he is confident of that, because he is praising the god who, he knows, is generous). The 'weaving' lady appears as the night that rewinds her spread of threads that formed the darkness (II. 38.4); and the seer also knows that mothers weave the cloth for their children (cf. V.47.6 *vastrā putrāya mātaro vayanti* where *putrāya* need not be taken to exclude the daughters). These references to the thread(s) and weaving, factual and symbolic, indicate that the stretching of a thread from the mass of wool (in the period of the Ṛgveda) or silk (in the later Vedic period, when cotton was yet unknown) was thought as a great wonder. The thread symbolized continuity and activity; and the weaving of the thread to create new cloth was a unique wonder. In the mythical context, the spinner, or the weaver, came to be regarded as a wonder-worker as giving rise to new form of life. However, even with the idea of the night 'weaving' the cloth of darkness and so on, as noted above, the lady that controlled life was the mythical concept of the seer of the Vasiṣṭha family, as mentioned above, who presented it for the first time in the Vedic context, in the form of Urvaśī.

The lady that weaves the web is seen in the later period, prominently, in the account of Uttaṅka, who sees her while bringing the ear-rings for the wife of his preceptor. As he was bringing the ear-rings, Uttaṅka is deceived by the serpent Takṣaka, who enters a fissure in the earth. Indra widens the fissure for him to enter the underground kingdom of Takṣaka. Uttaṅka praises Takṣaka and the serpents, but does not become successful in regaining the ear-rings. At that time Uttaṅka sees two women weaving a cloth out of the black and white threads spread on the weaving apparatus, a wheel with twelve spokes and also he sees six boys. This vision is explained further. The women were named Dhātā and Vidhātā, which speaks of their nature as the creator. The threads are night and day, the twelve spokes the months of the year, and the six boys the six seasons. The whole vision indicates new creation and the spread from the static (Mahābhārata, Ādi, 3. 126ff; esp. 144, and explanation at 166). This is the evidence from the earliest text on the Indian side, together with its variation at the period of the Mahābhārata, where we have a regular myth based on the concept of the lady with the weaving apparatus. However, this concept is not restricted to the Indian scene, the earliest pictographic evidence being from ancient Egypt. The Egyptian goddess Neith held in her hand a shuttle, which was the symbol of weaving; and, in this particular context, the weaving symbolized the continuity of life.The Syrian goddess of similar nature had a distaff (a cleft stick) used at weaving. In the Greek mythology we come across three sisters, weaving the life-web in the abyss of Demogorgon; and the word Demogorgon means 'Start of Life'. The names of the three sisters are Clotho, Lacchasis and Atropos. Clotho is the weaver.[3] The Aztec goddess of love, named variously—Tlacolteotle, Ixquina, and also Tlaelquani—had her male attendants dwarfs, hunchbacks and so; but, her female attendants were shown as spinning and weaving[4]. Her dwelling place was called Tamohuan Ichan, or Xochitle Ichan, or Itzehzcayan; all these meant 'The House of the Descent of Birth.' In Japan the star-goddess, also known as Amaterasu, the daughter of the sun, was a 'weaving girl'.[5] The secluded image of the weaving woman being grafted on the well known figure Urvaśī, who is unfamiliar with it in the whole of the Vedic and later tradition, appears to have been borrowed by the Vasiṣṭha seer from a floating concept of a similar nature, though much before the Egyptians and the Greeks.

References

1. See Dange, "Urvaśī, the water-belle", *J.Ori.Instt.*; *Baroda*, Vol. XXV-i, Sept. 1976, later incorporated in his *Sexual symbolism from the Vedic Ritual*, Delhi, 1979, pp. 177-208; see ch. 13 on "Purūravas", *supra*, pp. 332-341.
2. *apsarasaḥ* at 12 is taken as plural by Geldner. Prof. Velankar understands the plural as indicative of respect for Urvaśī.
3. Edith Hamilton, *Mythology*, Boston, 1942, p.49. Demogorgon is a mysterious terrible infernal deity, first mentioned in A.D. 450, acc. to *Chambers Twentieth Century Dictionary*, Indian ed., 1983.
4. Donald Mackenzie, *Myths of Pre-Columbian America*, p.217.
5. *Ibid*, p. 219.

Thirteen

Purūravas

The legend of Purūravas is so famous that it might be felt unnecessary to probe the matter further. His relationship with Urvaśī has been sufficiently studied and discussed.[1] Yet certain details in connection with his behaviour need further consideration; and they would throw welcome light on the social status of a royal person (if we accept the tradition) vis-a-vis the position of the *brāhmaṇa*-s at that time. Purūravas is a famous person in the Hindu tradition, right from the Veda touching the Purāṇas, through the Mahābhārata. From the Veda we know that he was an infatuated lover of Urvaśī (ṚV.X.95), whom he gained and lost, as he could not abide by the conditions laid down by Urvaśī. At the same time, the ṚV. evidence has a clear indication of the relationship between Urvaśī and Purūravas being that of the performer of a special type of sacrifice, wherein the divine water-nymph Urvaśī was controlled for the gain of timely rain, she being called *apyā* (ṚV.X.95.10).[2] At another place in the ṚV., Purūravas is said to be the *sukṛt*, the performer of a ritual (ṚV.1.31.4 : *Purūravase su-kṛte*). Another interesting detail about the relationship between Purūravas and Urvaśī is that the former is said to have struck her with the cane-rod (Ib.5 : *śnathayo vaitasena*), which is a double-meaning word, indicating the male-organ (Sāyaṇa) and also the churning rod to produce fire from the lower wooden slab. There is also another detail in the ṚV., in the same hymn, where Urvaśī is said to be regularly (or yearly) arriving at the sacrificial assembly being invoked by Purūravas (*Ib.* 16) when she is said to be present for four nights in the Autumn. This would show that Purūravas was a royal sacrificer-seer, who invented a special ritual; may be he was also a clan-leader, which also goes well with his being taken to be a king in the later tradition. In the ṚV, he is only the 'king of the body of Urvaśī' (*Ib.* 5). The tradition of the Śat. Br.(XI.5.1.1ff), which gives the elaborate legend of the marriage of Purūravas and Urvaśī and the loss of the latter to the former, also stresses the motif of Purūravas learning a new method of sacrifice from the Gandharvas who give him a fire in a fire-pan to sacrifice with for a whole year, at the end of which he would again meet Urvaśī; this again suggests an yearly ritual and the gain of a new method of sacrifice by Purūravas. Two points emerge from the Vedic version of the account of this couple: (i) Purūravas was a wonderful sacrificer; and (ii) He innovated the ritual, the Gandharvas being mentioned to give a mystic tinge to the whole account;[3] also, he employed a woman in the ritual to represent the cosmic woman that controlled the cosmic waters (*apyā*) and was called Urvaśī. The second motif is supported by the whole sexual complex of the Vedic ritual-tradition.[4] In the later tradition, this motif was transformed so as to make the divine Urvaśī the 'wife' of the mortal man, Purūravas. The first motif percolates in the later tradition in an interesting way. We shall probe it further.

That Purūravas had been a famous sacrificer is recorded by the Brahma Purāṇa (151.3-27), where it is stated that he was advised by the sage Vasiṣṭha to perform many sacrifices so that he would get Urvaśī back. This he did at the bank of the Gautamī, whereby the place came to be called Yajñadvīpa (Ib.21). At these sacrifices, it is said, Urvaśī came regularly on the night of the Full-moon days (*Ib.*22: *paurṇamāsyāṁ tu śarvaryāṁ tatra-āyāti sadā-Urvaśī*). As at this place Urvaśī came down from her upper abode in heaven, it came to be called Nimnabheda (*Ib.*27). This would show that Urvaśī was not the real wife of Purūravas; she was only a ritual help in the form of a woman, representing the divine nymph also called *svarveśyā* (heavenly prostitute) in the tradition (cf. Vāyu P. Pūrva. 22.12-19, where she is so called). In the face of the fact of Purūravas being a perfect sacrificer, as is seen from the tradition of the Veda noted above, the Mahābhārata and the later (*Purāṇika*) tradition shows a clash between Purūravas and the *brāhmaṇa*-s. He is said to have been endowed with superhuman powers, though himself a human, and yet he is said to have clashed with the *brāhmaṇa*-s (Mb. Ādi. 75.20: *vipraiḥ sa vigrahaṁ cakre vīryonmattaḥ purūravāḥ*). There were efforts on the part of the brāhmaṇas to win him over: yet they were futile. The *brāhmaṇa*-s (called here "great sages") cursed him ; and he perished. He is said to be greedy and maddened with power. The sequence of the narration in the Mahābhārata would indicate that, after clashing with the *brāhmaṇa*-s, he brought the fire from the Gandharvas, which was the triple fire (v 23 : *ānināya kriyārthe' gnīn yathāvad vihitāns tridhā*). This would mean that he was not destroyed by the *brāhmaṇa-s* so as to cause his death, but was only ruined; but he regained his status by following the method of the Gandharvas, which indicates an innovation upon the usual method of *brāhmaṇa*-s. What is the authority for the Mahābhārata to record this shift ? The motif of the gain of the new fire from the Gandhravas is clear in the Vedic tradition: but the clash with the *brāhmaṇa*-s, and with the usual tradition, is a new point. And the poet of the Mahābhārata cannot be taken to have added it on the basis of his own imagination. The probability is that it was already handed down in the tradition, though the Vedic texts do not think it necessary to note it.

The Purāṇas take the motif of the Mahābhārata and add some more details. According to one account, the *brāhmaṇa*-s in the Naimiṣa forest (*naimiṣīyāḥ*) were performing a *sattra* (sacrificial session for a period of one to twelve years). Purūravas took part in it, along with Urvaśī, the *svarveśyā*. As the *sattra* went on, the river Gaṅgā gave out gold from her waters, which rose in size like the mountains. Viśvakarman prepared a sacrificial ground from the gold thus come out. Purūravas saw the wonder, demanded the whole gold and the sacrificial ground. The *brāhmaṇa*-s declined, and there ensued a quarrel. The *brāhmaṇa*-s then smote Purūravas, and ultimately killed him with the thunderbolts prepared from the sacred *darbha*-grass (Vāyu P. Pūrva. 2.12-21; 21[ab]: *kuśavajrair viniṣpiṣṭaḥ sa rājā vyajahāt tanūm;* Brahmāṇḍa P.I. 2.2.15-23). According to the Brahmāṇḍa P., Purūravas came along to the *sattra* as he was hunting about (20b: *mṛgayāñ caran*); it also states that he was greedy about the golden sacrificial ground (21[a]: *lobhena hatavijñānaḥ*; and earlier 15ab : *tutoṣa naiva ratnānām lobhād iti naḥ śrutam*). Here also Urvaśī does not seem to be his actual wife, and she is actually said to be the heavenly prostitute (*svarveśyā*). Though the texts noted above say, that, when Purūravas was killed, the *brāhmaṇa*-s made his son Āyu the king, it is not clear if he was his son through the marriage with Urvaśī. Again, why Purūravas should take Urvaśī on a hunting expedition is doubtful. The fact seems to be that this detail is added later. The main motif is the clash between Purūravas and the *brāhmaṇa*-s; also that the *brāhmaṇa*-s did not actually kill Purūravas (and the version of the Mb. is clear on this detail). The Brahmāṇḍa P. states, at another place, that there was only one fire formerly, but Purūravas contemplated three (II.3.66.19 : *eko' gniḥ pūrvam āsīd vai ailas tam trīn akalpayat*). Now, it is to be remembered that the ṚV. does not mention the ritual-fire, namely *Gārhapatya, Āhavanīya* and the *Dakṣiṇa*. Out of these names indicating fire, only *Gārhapatya* occurs in the ṚV., and that too only thrice; but, at no place does it indicate the ritual-fires of that name (ṚV.I. 15. 12; X.95.27; -36). The ṚV. mentions that it was the clan of the Bhṛgus that established the earthly fire (II.4.2) for the benefit of men: but that fire is also said to be one, for the purposes of ritual. Does it mean that the concept and ritual of the three fires was really invented by Purūravas? If that is the case, why does not the Ṛgveda refer to it? The answer, probably, is that the innovation was not fairly accepted at the Ṛgvedic period, though Purūravas was acclaimed to be a great seer-sacrificer as noted above. It has also to be noted that Purūravas is mentioned in the later Ṛgveda (I.15.12 and X.95), a marked characteristic of which is the introduction of sexual rituals, another pronounced ritual-hymn in this context being that of Yama and Yamī (X.10), which employs the motif of incest. This may be the reason why he was rather unpopular with the orthodox ritual-practisers. This was the era of innovations, as is also clear from such hymns as that of Vasukra (X.27). In the older Ṛgveda, such innovation is noticed in the Vāmadeva-hymn (IV.18).[5] Though the dislike for Purūravas is absent in the Vedic tradition, it is clear in the later tradition, as we have noted.

There is another detail in the Purūravas legend, which helps explain the *brāhmaṇa*-s' dislike for him. Though the Ṛgveda does not say clearly that he was a king, the later tradition mentions him as such. The Vedic age does not restrict seerhood to persons who are born-*brāhmaṇa-s* ; and there are examples to show that others, who were not born-*brāhmaṇa-s*, also came to be recognized as *brāhmaṇa*-s, the case of Kavaṣa Ailūṣa[6] being only one such. Kṣatriyas are known to have become seers of hymns (cf. III.23, the seers of which are Devavāta and Devaśravas of the Bharata clan). At this period, seers from the Serpent clan are also seen as composing hymns (Jaratkarṇa X. 76; Arbuda Kādraveya X.94 etc.). This new trend in the then society speaks not only for a broad-based religious upheaval; it also indicates a natural tendency of strife between some of the old orthodox seers, the born-*brāhmaṇa-s*, on the one hand, and the new seers that came forward to 'usurp' the designation of 'brāhmaṇa', because they saw a new method, or ritual, along with the necessary hymn, both being *brahman*.[7] The clash of the *brāhmaṇa-s* with Purūravas is, hence, to be taken as an example of this new socio-religious change. The point gains support from the fact that at some places in the Purāṇic tradition Purūravas is said to have been a *brāhmaṇa*, but that he had lost his brāhmaṇahood, or that he was a *brāhmaṇa* aspiring to become a king. Thus, according to the Matsya P. (114. 10ff) he was a *brāhmaṇa* staying in the place called (very significantly, indeed !) *Dvija-grāma* ("Village of the *brāhmaṇa-s*"). He aspired for a kingdom and got one after he worshipped Viṣṇu on the 12th bright day of the month of Kārttika; but, since he took bath applying unguents to his body on the day of the *ekādaśī* (the previous day), he lost his form and became ugly. According to the Vāmana P. (I. 53. 11ff) he was a *brāhmaṇa* in the country of Śākala, having been a *vaiśya* in the former birth in the Madra country. In his birth as a *brāhmaṇa* he is said to have been ugly to look at (Ib. 78: *vikaṭarūpo 'sau sarva-śāstra-pāragaḥ*). But, due to his propitiation of Viṣṇu at the river Irāvatī, he became a king in the next birth; and he was the same as Purūravas (Ib. 79-83). According to the Brahma P. (227.98ff) he was a foolish *brāhmaṇa* in one of his former births in Vārāṇasī. In that birth he desired to have Urvaśī, and took a vow that he would not "enjoy a cart" (Ib.117 : *na bhokṣye 'dyaprabhṛti vai śakaṭam satyam īritam*). Once Urvaśī came to bathe in the Matsyodarī, and this foolish *brāhmaṇa* saw her. He expressed his desire to have her. She, however, told him to wait there alone and disappeared. After a month she returned with a *sakaṭa* covered with (or made of) sugar (*śarkarāvṛta*) and asked him to have it. But the *brāhmaṇa* was true of word. Urvaśī said that the *śakaṭa* was not of wood, but of sugar; so he could accept it ! He declined saying, that once the decision was made it applied to all types of *śakaṭa*. Urvaśī, then, revealed her own form and took him to the Rūpatīrtha (Holy place that restores form), where he was asked to take a dip. He did it and got a handsome form. He also attained the region of the Gandharvas, and was born as Purūravas, being a king.

The Puranic accounts noted above show a curious mixture of the Vedic legend and certain later-recorded details. But, all have the same motif, i.e. the mixture of brāhmaṇahood and royalty in the case of Purūravas. Though he is said to be a *brāhmaṇa*, he is ridiculed and is said to be ugly. Brāhmaṇahood came to be from the real Vedic tradition, and the abuse from the hatred of the born-*brāhmaṇa-s*, who seem to be reluctant to give him the supreme status of a real *brāhmaṇa*!

Now we come to the last point in the discussion. That the innovation of Purūravas was the three fires and his employment of a sex-ritual has been hinted at above. We fix our attention on another detail, we have referred to above, namely that he used the cane-rod to press Urvaśī. The sexual implication of this expression is already made clear by Sāyaṇa, who renders the word *vaitasa* as the male-organ. It should be remembered, however, that the word indicates the mid-region fire at one (and the only) place of its use (ṚV.IV.58.5 : *hiraṇyayo vetaso madhya āsām*, "the golden cane-rod is in their midst", speaking of the cosmic waters). Urvaśī being pressed by "this" rod presents a peculiarly sexual picture in the human relationship, and suits well in the context of the hymn. But, in the context of the knowledge of the new fire-cult said to have been learnt by Purūravas from the Gandharvas, it indicates, probably, an innovation on the method of producing fire. If we remember that the lower *araṇi* and the churn-rod (which formed the lower wooden slab and the upper rod) to churn out fire are constantly identified with Urvaśī and Purūravas in the ritual-texts, we could appreciate how Purūravas could be taken to have invented a new method of churning fire.

The reference to Urvaśī as the lower *araṇi* (made of the slab of the Śamī tree) and to Purūravas as the churn-rod (of the Aśvattha tree) would fairly indicate the status of this couple in the ritual-tradition (Vāj. Sam. V.2; Śat.Br.III.4.1.22; Kātyā. Śr.S.V.1. 28-30). Even in the accounts from the Purāṇas, it is seen that Purūravas goes to the sacrifice of the Naimiṣa-*brāhmaṇa*-s with Urvaśī; and, Urvaśī being the heavenly (or cosmic) female at all such places she must, in practice, indicate the ritual-woman most probably a prostitute.[8] The birth of a son from Urvaśī could not be from the vague cosmic woman, but from a woman who would impersonate her in ritual-practices, such progeny being considered as that of the sacrificer. We may compare the cases of Dhṛṣṭadyumna and Draupadī, whose mother is not known. The arrival of Purūravas at such places, along with 'Urvaśī', could indicate his propagandist intention, which the yet orthodox *brāhmaṇa*-s revolted against. Yet the name of Purūravas gained importance and the ritual of the kindling of the sacrificial fire by the drilling method was identified with the union of this couple, along with the placing of two *darbha*-blades signifying the testicles.[9] Hardly any other couple is so spoken of. The Śat.Br. specifically says that, when the fire-pan containing the fire given by the Gandharvas was lost in the forest where Purūravas had placed it, the Gandharvas asked him to prepare the upper *arani* from the Aśvattha and the lower from the Śamī; they also suggested another set both from the Aśvattha. He prepared the latter set. This is the reason, they say, that both the *araṇi-s* should be prepared from the Aśvattha tree (X.5. 1. 15-17). The drilling method is known from the ṚV. (III.9.5; —23.2; VI.16.13 etc.); but the specific method of drilling from the Aśvattha has to be taken as the innovation of Purūravas, on the authority of the Śat.Br. What was the earlier method? It is not clearly stated. Probably we have an indication in the words "pressed with the cane-rod". Actually the original words are *śnathitā vaitasena*; and the latter word would indicate not only cane, but also a bamboo or a stout reed. Does Urvaśī resent this method, when she complains that she was thrice pressed with the bamboo-rod, indicating the lower *araṇi* being rubbed with the bamboo ? The Brāhmaṇa text provides the answer in suggesting, that thereafter Purūravas employed the new method of the Aśvattha-rod and slab.

It may be of some use to note, in this connection, that the old method, or the aboriginal method, appears to be the use of the bamboo or the stout reed, along with the motif of the sexual union of the Bamboo and the lower slab. We note the example of the Central Indian tribe called the Baiga. In one of their myths dealing with the creation of fire, it is said that once Bhainsasur (Mahiṣāsura?) glanced at Pārvatī and got enamoured of her. He tried to kill Mahādeo, her husband, and ran after him. Mahādeo, being afraid, ran to Bhagvān for help. Bhagvān himself took the form of Pārvatī to deceive the evil one. But, now, seeing the beauty of the pseudo-Pārvatī, Mahādeo became sexually excited, and released his semen. Bhagvān caught the semen in his folded palms (still in the form of Pārvatī) and poured it into the hollow of the bamboo. Since that time the Baiga could produce fire by drilling the bamboo-stick on soft wood. As the semen was hot, when poured into the bamboo, it produced fire.[10] In the Vedic context, some similar method seems to have been supplanted by Purūravas by the Aśvattha method for the easy kindling of fire, together with the sexual motif as a charm for the easy birth of Fire.

References

1. Schroeder, L.V., *Mysterium und Mimus im Rigveda*, Leipzig, 1908; Geldner, K.F., *Der Rigveda*, HOS, Cambridge, Massachusetts (Vol.s I-III), Second Print 1978 (1951), Vol.III, pp.298ff; Kosambi, D.D., *Myth and Reality*, Bombay, 1962; Wright, J.C., "Purūravas and Urvaśī", BSOAS, Vol.XXX, 1967, pp.526-47; Goldman, R.P., "Mortal Man and the Immortal Woman", *J.Or.Instt.*, Baroda, Vol.XVIII, No.4, pp.273-302, to mention a few.

2. Dange, *Sexual Symbolism from the Vedic Ritual*, p.190f.

3. At Kāṭh.Sam. VIII.10 it is said that she went back to the gods, not to the Gandharvas; also that Āyu was born while she was among the gods.

4. Dange, *op.cit.*, pp. 51-115

5. For a detailed discussion, *ibid.*, pp. 161-74.

6. He is the seer of ṚV X.30-34; for the legend, see Ait. Br. II.19; Kau.Br. XII.3

7. Dange, *Hindu Dharma āṇi Tattvajñāna* (Marathi), Shri Lekhan Vachan Bhandar, Pune, 1973, (for Maharashtra Universities Book Production Board, Nagpur, 10), pp. 124-27; for *brahman* being 'prayer' and also 'ritual', see Dange, *Divine Hymns and Ancient Thought*, Vol.I, Navrang, New Delhi, 1992, pp.39, 139; Vol.II, 1995, p.8f.

8. The position of the prostitute in ancient India (and even today) was unique. See Gonda J., "Ascetics and Courtesans", *Adyar Library Bulletin*, Vol.XXV, Nos. 1-4, 1961; Dange, *Encl.P.B.P.*, Vol.IV, pp.1129-31.

9. Śat .Br. III.4.1.21-22

10. Stephen Fuchs, "The Baiga understanding of Ultimate Reality", *Ultimate Reality and Meaning*, Vol.I, No.3, pp.166ff.

Fourteen

Kṛṣṇa - 'The Eighth'

Kṛṣṇa was the eighth son of Vasudeva. A probe into the matter reveals that names of only two are known. In addition, we have some mythical details. Hence, it is necessary to investigate, if the word 'eighth' has some symbolic meaning.

According to the Bhāg. P.(X.1 and further) Kaṁsa, the king of Mathurā, himself sat as a charioteer in the chariot at the procession on the occasion of the marriage of his sister Devakī with Vasudeva. As the procession meandered its way there was divine proclamation from the sky, "O Kaṁsa! Harken, the eighth foetus of this your sister will be your destroyer" (X.1.34).[1] Hearing this, Kaṁsa tried, later, to kill his sister. But, her husband entreated upon him not to kill her, as she was at no fault, herself. Kaṁsa agreed; but he imprisoned both Devakī and Vasudeva and decided to kill the 'eighth' issue, as soon as she delivered it. But, being afraid that any one of the issues might cause his destruction, he began killing each as soon as Devakī delivered the child. In this way, he destroyed six children. The text tells us that Devakī gave birth to eight sons and one daughter each a year (totalling nine; v.56).[2] After six sons were destroyed this way, the seventh (known later as Balarāma) was dragged out of the womb of Devakī by Yogamāya (a divine female power) who then placed him in the womb of Rohiṇī, another wife of Vasudeva who was in Gokula.[3] As he was dragged out' *(saṅkarṣaṇāt)* he was also called Saṅkarṣaṇa (Ib.2.4-15). A similar account occurs in other Purāṇa texts, with some details. Thus according to the Harivaṁsa (Viṣṇuparvan, II.1) Nārada tells Kaṁsa that the 'eighth' issue will cause his death. Kaṁsa kills six male children of Devakī. These sons are said to be killed because in their former life as demons, they incurred wrath of their grandfather (father's father), Hiraṇyakaśipu; because, they approached Brahmadeva to request him to render them immune to death, without his consent. So, he cursed them that they would be born, one after the other, from the womb of Devakī and would be killed by Kaṁsa (Ib.11ff). As already planned, Viṣṇu tells Yoganidrā (not Yogamāyā here) to take out the seventh foetus from the womb of Devakī and place it into the womb of Rohiṇī. He tells her that he would, himself, be born as Kṛṣṇa and that she should enter the womb of Yaśodā, the wife of the cowherd Nanda, who would be in Gokula (Ib. vv.24-35). Accordingly, Kṛṣṇa and Yoganidrā were born, respectively, to Devakī (in Mathurā, in the prison) and to Yaśodā (in Gokula) in the eighth month of their pregnancy (b.37 *aṣṭamasya māsasya).* Viṣṇu had told Yoganidrā, that Kaṁsa would smash her on a slab of stone, as soon as she was born; then she would fly to heaven and Indra would take her as his own sister, whereupon she would acquire his *gotra*. She would, thus, be Kauśikī (of the family of Kuśika Indra). She would also be called Ārya. This was according to the plan as detailed by Viṣṇu, prior to his *avatāra* as Kṛṣṇa on the earth. There is no mention of the divine voice here, the purpose of informing Kaṁsa being taken up by Nārada. The Harivaṁśa, thus, shows a difference in Yoganidrā from Yogamāya of the Bhāg.P. which is, a later text. The detail of the divine speech alerting Kaṁsa of his death at the hands of the eighth son of Devakī is the same in both texts. The Viṣṇu P. (V.1.60ff) has the same account. However there are certain details which differ from the two sources mentioned above. Here also Kaṁsa is alerted by Nārada; not by the divine speech as in the case in the Bhāg.P. Again, though Hiraṇyakaśipu figures as cursing the six sons in their previous life, he is said to be their father; not father's father as is the case at the Harivaṁsa (v 70 *hiraṇyakaśipoḥ putrāḥ ṣaḍ garbhāḥ).* Kṛṣṇa is the 'eighth' (v 64 *aṣṭamo garbhaḥ*), who would be the *avatāra* of Viṣṇu. The plan is that of Viṣṇu and, in it, he is helped by Yoganidrā, as is the case with the Harivaṁśa. She is to take birth from the womb of Yaśodā in the rainy month of Bhādrapada. On the same night Viṣṇu would take birth from the womb of Devakī. However, the night would have a joint of the eighth and the ninth dates *(tithi)* month. On the eighth Kṛṣṇa would be born, while Yoganidrā would show herself out as soon as the ninth started. Vasudeva would exchange them. He would take Kṛṣṇa near Yaśodā and bring Yoganidrā from her bed to that of Devakī. The Brahmavaivarta P. (Śrīkṛṣṇa-janma-khaṇḍa 7.1ff) has practically the same account, with the difference that Kṛṣṇa gets born when ten months have been completed (c.44 *saṁpūrṇe ca daśame māse).* There is no mention of Nārada. Like the Bhāg.P. here the divine speech figures.

It will be seen that these accounts generally follow the pattern of the Harivaṁsa, straying away from it only in some details. The usual Mb. does not have this account. It, however, occurs in its southern recension (Gorakhpur ed. Sabhā, 22, after v 36, p.316ff). The speech is said to be of 'certain divine messenger' *(devadūta).*

There is no mention of the first six sons being related to Hiraṇyakaśipu. Kṛṣṇa is the 'eighth' and Balarāma, the seventh, is dragged out from the womb of Devakī and placed in that of Rohiṇī; but this was not done by Yogamāyā nor by Yoganidrā; it was done by Yama, the god of death, by his magic power called *yāmyā māyā*. The girl is not born from Yaśodā. She is said to have been purchased (on the same night?), as soon as she was born, from some cowherd woman (*upa-jahre parikrītām sutām gopasya kasya cit*). This version does not clearly say that this girl was smashed on a slab of stone by *Kaṁsa*. It just states that she was killed. As she flew into the sky, she uttered the word *'ārya';* hence, she came to be known as *Āryā*. It is also stated that, in all this, Vasudeva deceived Kaṁsa *(evam tam vañcayitvā ca).*

Keeping aside details that are not very important, we fix attention on the main points. It is very clear that Vasudeva devised a regular plan to save his children and particularly Kṛṣṇa. The point that is present in the narration of the southern recension of the Mb. is eloquent. Which is that the girl, to substitute Kṛṣṇa was purchased and was placed with Devakī. Though it is not specifically stated, the probability of Nanda and his wife, Yaśodā, procuring a fresh-bron cowherd girl to substitute Kṛsṇạ, according to an early plan, is open. In that case there will be difficulty about a wet-nurse for Kṛsṇạ, if not Yaśodā herself. Another point that deserves note is regarding the transfer of Balarāma, who is transferred to the womb of Rohiṇī, another wife of Vasudeva who was staying in the Gokula as noted above, along with Nanda and Yaśodā. The part played by Yogamāyā (or Nidrā) is, obviously, to give some sort of a halo to the whole plan. This is clear from her description as a regular goddess.[4] Balarāmā is said to have been born prematurely, in the seventh month of pregnancy and it was given out that it was a case of miscarriage (*garbha-visraṁsa*)[5], which put Kaṁsa off the guard, while in reality, he might have been smuggled out, though not by Vasudeva himself. He was nurtured by Vasudeva's other wife, Rohiṇī. He is said to be the seventh. But, this is in view of the general belief that Kṛṣṇa was the 'eighth'. It might be necessary to modify it when we go deeper into the meaning of *aṣṭama. Actually,* a child born in the seventh month has more chances of survival than the one born in the eighth month of pregnancy as is said to be the case with Kṛṣṇa. It is necessary to prove the nature of birth in the case of Balarāma, Kṛṣṇa and the 'girl', as they are the main issues in the account, from the four texts that we have taken as representative -

Mb.: Balarāma was the seventh foetus and was transferred as a foetus (*garbha*) by Yama by his *yāmya* magic from the womb of Yaśodā to that of Rohiṇī (wife of Vasudeva) (*loc.cit., yamo rājā... akṣipat*).

Hari V.: Devakī conceived the seventh foetus. This was carried to Rohiṇī by Nidrā (Yogamāyā) in the *seventh month* (cf. *loc.cit.* 2.31). It is further said, here, that (Rohiṇī) herself began taking out her foetus at midnight as she saw blood coming out from her womb (though she was pregnant?). She fell into a swoon and did not see her foetus that came out. But Nidrā consoled her saying that this foetus of Devakī (which she had brought) would be her foetus; also that, as it was drawn out, it would be called Saṅkarṣaṇa). This will mean that (i) Rohiṇī herself was pregnant and released her foetus in her seventh month; but, it did not survive. (This is absent in other texts). That foetus was substituted by the foetus of Devakī; or (ii) that Balarāma was born to Rohiṇī herself in the seventh month; the foetus was about to become lifeless; but it survived. This may be compared with Mb. which credits this act to Yama, the god of death. If we take the Hari.V. as correct, it will mean that the swoon of Rohiṇī due to intense pain was metamorphosed as Nidrā, and later 'goddess' Yogamāyā or Yoganidrā. In the first alternative, which is popularly believed to be true, the difficulty is, who carried the prematurely born frail child out of the prison in person? Hence the miracle of Yogamāyā is inserted. With the second alternative this question does not arise, as it was never born to Devakī. The detail that Rohiṇī tried to draw out the foetus as it was slipping out due to miscarriage (cf. 4.3 *garbham pātayantī),* suits the name Saṅkarṣaṇa well. The expression that due to fear Devakī's foetus fell out (*Ib*.2.33) has to be taken in view of the first alternative explanation and a later version of the account that got currency and which even the Hari V., indicates to be confused. The reason for this is, that superficially reading, in this text, all the children would appear to be born just one after the other (cf. *Ib*.8 *tasya garbhasya mārgeṇa garbham ādhatta Devakī).* Also to be noted is, that if in the seventh month (*Ib*.2.31 *saptame māsi*) Balarāma was born to her, the words "in the eighth month (33 *aṣṭame mayi*)" in respect of Kṛṣṇa would mean that he was born in the eighth month of the same year, and he would be not only the 'eighth' but also born in the eighth month of pregnancy in the same year. We shall place these expressions side by side. Kṛṣṇa says to Nidrā:-

Hari V.- "The seventh foetus of Devakī is my elder brother. That should be transferred to Rohiṇī in the *seventh month*" (2.31).

"In the eighth when I shall be in the womb (*aṣṭame*

mayi garbhasthe), Kaṁsa will try hard, thinking that the seventh foetus of Devakī fell off due to fear" (33; even if we understand *aṣṭame mayi garbhasthe* as "when I, the eighth am in the womb...", a verse coming later creates confusion -)

"In the eighth month when we two are born" (37; we two, i.e. Kṛṣṇa and Nidrā - *aṣṭamasya tu māsasya jātāvāvām*).

Before this verse and after 33, we have Kṛṣṇa saying to Nidrā that she should be the foetus of Yaśodā; that she would be brought from her to Devakī, after Kṛṣṇa is born. And thus she would be the ninth foetus of Devakī, born to our family (2.35).[6] The subsequent narration tells that the 'girl' was *born* to Yaśodā on the same night as Kṛsṇa was born to Devakī and that both these women gave birth to the respective children in the eighth month when the foetuses were not even complete (4.11).[7]

In the whole account there are the following corresponding data:

(a) Balarāma: *seventh month* of pregnancy in the case of Rohiṇī;

'*seventh foetus*' of Devakī (born in her seventh month of pregnancy?)

(b) Kṛṣṇa : Eighth month, in the case of Devakī; and her 'Eighth foetus' transferred to Yaśodā.

(c) 'girl' : eighth month in the case of Yaśodā; ninth foetus in the case of Devakī, after transfer.

In all these cases the word *garbha* indicates the child, as is clear; not the unborn foetus.

Viṣṇu P. - In the short account here, the detail of Balarāma being born in the seventh month is totally absent; so is the case with the birth of Kṛṣṇa in the eighth month. Kṛṣṇa is said to have been born in the rainy season in the month of Nabhas, (which is Bhādrapada). This is a new point, along with that he was born on the dark eighth of this month (V.1.78 *prāvṛṭkāle ca nabhasi kṛṣṇaṣṭamyām),* and that Nidrā was born to Yaśodā on the ninth. Then Vasudeva transferred them. Another new detail here is that Balarāma is an aspect of Kṛṣṇa and is named Śeṣa, serpent.

Bhāg.P.- This text tries to clear (but adds to) the confusion that appears at the Hari V. by saying that Devakī gave birth to eight sons and also a daughter, each in a separate year that followed (X.1.56 *anuvatsaram*). Following the Viṣṇu P. it states that Balarāma was the seventh and was called also Ananta (Serpent Śeṣa)[8]. But, here also his birth in the seventh month is absent; so is absent the detail that Rohiṇī started bleeding after trying to get her foetus released in her seventh month. What we have is, that Yoganidrā carried away the foetus of Devakī and placed it in the womb of Rohiṇī (X.2.8-10) and that this led people to grieve that the foetus of Devakī was lost. There is no mention of the exact month (of pregnancy in the case of Devakī), nor of the month being *Nabhas*, nor even of the day being the dark eighth *(aṣṭamī)*. However, there is mention of heavy rain and the flooding of the Yamunā (3.49-50). Kṛṣṇa is said to be the eighth (1.34; 60). Both the Viṣṇu P. and the Bhāg. P. mention that Śeṣa warded off rain from falling on the body of Kṛṣṇa, with his spread up hoods. (cf. Viṣṇu P.V.3.17); but while the Viṣṇu P. states that, when Vasudeva reached the other bank of the Yamunā, he saw Nanda and other cowherds on it, ready to pay the usual tax to Kaṁsa, the Bhāg.P. is silent about this detail. Both, however, are one in mentioning that Yaśodā had gone to sleep under the power of Yoganidrā (Ib.20; Bhāg.P.51).

The Brahmavai P. (Śrīkṛṣṇakhaṇḍa 6.277-278) - This text mentions the killing of six sons of Vasudeva by Kaṁsa and that the seventh was Śeṣāṁsa. It mentions Kṛṣṇa as the eighth and that he was born after ten months (7.44), also that he was born on the dark eighth, when the half-moon was in the sky (7.64). Vasudeva took Kṛṣṇa to Yaśodā in Nanda-vraja, saw all in deep sleep, placed the child there, brought her daughter and placed her by the side of Devakī. In all this Vasudeva took Devakī in confidence (7.106-111). But, Kaṁsa here gives the girl back to Devakī and Vasudeva on the advice of a divine voice. This sister of Kṛṣṇa was named Ekānaṁsā (7.124-130).

In the different versions Yoganidrā, Yogamāyā or even the *māyā* of Yama are closely developed on the fact of sleep *(nidrā)*, which figures with almost all except Vasudeva. This sleep *(nidrā)* is the basis for the myth of *yoga* or *māyā* who is described as goddess who was popular at that period.[9] In the expression—"The seventh foetus of Devakī should be placed in Rohiṇī in the seventh month" (Hari V., Viṣṇuparvan 2.31) the seventh month appears to be that of Rohiṇī's conception (and not Devakī's) if we take into consideration that she was trying hard to get the foetus released *(pātayantī)*, being *rajasvalā* (letting out blood, Ib.4.3) and that she saw it released (v r, *garbham niḥsṛtam ātmanaḥ)*. Further, we have Vasudeva referring to Balarāma as *rauhiṇeya* (5.4; and 6 *rauhiṇeyam mamātjam)*. The 'seventh' foetus of Devakī (2.31 *saptamo devakīgarbhaḥ*) has to be taken only in view of Kṛṣṇa being called *aṣṭama* ('eighth'), while it was neither actually 'seventh', nor did it belong to Devakī, though it was from Vasudeva and, thus, the elder brother of Kṛṣṇa. For this we have to again, examine the 'six-garbha' myth. These six appear as a unit and also as separate, making Balarāma the seventh and Kṛṣṇa the eighth. These two are saved, while the 'girl' is killed. So are the 'six'. But, there is a difference between the six' and the girl who is said to be the ninth, though actually third. She is a substitute for Kṛṣṇa, while the case of the 'six', in a way, resembles that of the 'seventh' foetus. We have seen how the 'seventh' foetus of Devakī, said to have been extracted, presents difficulties in view of Rohiṇī's own foetus, unlike the exchange of the full born two children. The exchange does not present any problem, as there is a human agent, Vasudeva, to accomplish it. In the case of Balarāma, born prematurely, there is no such mention and the case of one-way transfer, if at all it was, depends entirely on a divine agent. Further, Hari V. clearly states the premature delivery with Rohiṇī. Moreover, one could be expectant of the time of a delivery (in the case of Kṛṣṇa and the girl), which can hardly be the case with premature delivery. A question may be asked about Kṛṣṇa's birth in the eighth month of pregnancy (as is the case at Hari V.) also not being abnormal. The answer is that it was actually not in the eighth, nor even after the tenth month was complete (cf. Brahmavai P.), but in the normal course. As is already pointed out above, Hari V. appears confusing in the case of the birth and the order of delivery - seventh Balarāma in the seventh month; eighth Kṛṣṇa in the eighth month. The eighth month, though not the eighth *tithi* of that month is, no doubt, under the influence of the belief in the number eight, as we shall presently see. It is to be noted that Bhāg.P. does away with the month of the birth. On this, it may be said that it does away also with the premature delivery of Rohiṇī and that, in that case Balarāma's being actually born to Devakī could also not be doubted. But, then, how could one explain the pre-born child's transfer and placement in the womb of Rohiṇi[10]. To credit it to the divine power will be explaining it away! Apart from the confusion regarding the births appearing one after the other as if, in the same year, the case of Rohiṇī in Hari V. appears natural enough - the foetus causing pain, her desire to get it out *(pātyantī)*, her swoon due to intense pain, and her solace after seeing the immaturely born (her own) child, believed to be given her back by divine favour, which was interpreted in variant accounts, later, as being the seventh child of Devakī herself, like the 'six', to make Kṛṣṇa the eighth - *aṣṭama.*

The extant accounts in all these texts, including the Hari V., can hardly be the purely original ones. All of them, in the form as they are, cannot but be taken as embroidered with bits of narrations fused together. In any case, the case of the six foetuses (*ṣaḍgarbha*) is more imaginary (and more mythical) than such details as Śeṣa holding an umbrella of his hoods on the child Kṛṣṇa, and the floods of the Yamunā keeping their height only as far as the ankles of Vasudeva,[11] or that Yamunā cleared the way for Vasudeva "as formerly the sea gave the way to Rāma"[12], which is a clear indication of patternisation on earlier accounts.[13]

Now about '*ṣaḍ-garbha*'. The names of these six are not mentioned. The name of the first occurs at the Bhāg.P. (X.1.57) as Kīrtimān; those of other five do not obtain. There is also variation regarding their father's name, once as Hiraṇyakaśipu and then as Kālanemi, Hiraṇyakaśipu being their father's father (as noted above). The Hari V. says that they were all formerly kept secure in water in a *garbha-gṛha* ('house of foetuses' as if in one unit), which is clearly a symbolic expression for a 'womb', but generalised. They were asleep. They were then placed in the womb of Devakī, now particularised.[14] According to the plan of destroying the demons that took birth on the earth, along with Kaṁsa who was also a demon, Kālanemi, in his former birth (Bhāg.P.X.1.68), Viṣṇu is said to have gone to the nether region *(Pātāla)*. He saw these demons sleeping in the water. Extracting the life-principles from their bodies, he gave them to Nidrā to be placed in the womb of *Devakī* (Hari V., Viṣṇuparvan 2.11-28). The Viṣṇu P. gives this account in short, but says that these demons were the sons of Hiraṇyakaśipu (V.1.70-72). The *Bhāg*.P. does not have it. This will show that these 'six' are clearly fictitious and their account is a supportive ploy to make Kṛṣṇa the eighth. The seventh position of Balarāma is also in view of Kṛṣṇa being the eighth. The *ṣaḍ-garbha* ploy appears to have been suggested from the star-myth and the six women, wives of six sages, who became pregnant and from whose combined sixfold foetus was born the god kārttikeya with six faces.[15] In the present case there is twofold inversion of the old myth—(i) a unit of six breaking into its individual parts; and (ii) the god giving place to demon (*asura*).

From what has been said above, it would be clear that the children who actually figure in the account are only three—Balarāma, Kṛṣṇa and the girl, called variously[16] and with the probability of her being purchased (Mb.). In that case, Balarāma is the first son of Vasudeva from Rohiṇī (for the reasons given above), Kṛṣṇa the second from Devakī and the girl (from *Yaśodā* or from a cowherd woman) 'adopted' by Vasudeva for Devakī (if we may so so). But, then, why should Kṛṣṇa be the 'eighth'? For that we have to probe the original word *aṣṭama*, which will also throw light on the continued association of *aṣṭama* (month and day) with Kṛṣṇa. It should be remembered that mythical ideas have a mutual association, which often develops into symbolism pulsating on various levels, in the same tradition, or even in different traditions in certain cases. It is necessary to place such ideas side by side. Right here, we have a subtle indication of the symbolic significance of *aṣṭama* in a version of the account itself. According to the Hari V. Viṣṇu tells the girl that, when Kaṁsa dashes her on the stone-slab she would fly to heaven, where Indra would receive her as his own sister (2.48);[17] *atraiva tvām bhaginyarthe grahīṣyati sa vāsavaḥ* and that she would be of the same *gotra* as of Indra (Ib.). In the account, this is exactly the relationship between Kṛṣṇa and the girl. They are not actual brother and sister; they come to be brother and sister. This strikes equality between Indra and Kṛṣṇa, who is the *avatāra* of Viṣṇu according to the mythical element in the account. This suggestion of equality is not isolated. It goes back to the Vedic period[18] and the old mythical association is used here, along with the concept behind *aṣṭama*. Though the concept of *aṣṭama* is not seen prominently in the association between Indra and Viṣṇu in the Vedic period, Indra is associated with the concept of *aṣṭama* in the Veda. The line of association extended to Kṛṣṇa is as follows -

> Indra is *aṣṭama*;
> Viṣṇu is (associated with) Indra
> ∴ Viṣṇu is *aṣṭama* as seen in his aspect of Kṛṣṇa.

This will be clear in Viṣṇu (and Kṛṣṇa) being called *upa-indra* (*upendra*).[19] It is to be noted that the word *aṣṭama* or *aṣṭa* indicates not only a number, but pervasion on the basis of etymology (fr. the root *aś*, 'to pervade')[20]. The

Jaiminīya Br. (II.155) has a striking passage, "The gods had eight (*aṣṭau*) associates. They were called Abhi-yugvānaḥ (co-joined); the manes had eight associates; men had eight, the demons (*asura*-s) had eight. Among them all, Indra was the *aṣṭama* on account of his magic power when he desires to kill Vṛtra (Jai.Br.II.155 *māyayā aṣṭamo bhavatī vṛtram jighānsan)*. The symbolic significance behind this expression is that Indra becomes the cardinal among the groups of eight. Extended to the present content, Viṣṇu places himself in the *aṣṭama* position - the chief position that pervades all associates in his aspect of Kṛṣṇa. Thus, the human Kṛṣṇa is placed in the position of the divine, through the symbolic value of *aṣṭama*. And, as Viṣṇu helps Indra in killing Vṛtra, (symbolising the enemy), here Kṛṣṇa (Viṣṇu) on the terrestrial plane kills the enemy Kaṁsa. The *mayā* (power) for this comes through his being *aṣṭama*. A further probe shows that the faculty of being *aṣṭama* in the case of Indra, is originally seen in the case of Agni, the fire-god, the most important in the Vedic pantheon. One verse about him has,

> "In whom, the leader of sacrificer, seven bands *(raśmayaḥ;* rays; here flames) are tucked, Him, the divine *aṣṭama* (the eighth), may we make congenial to us" (ṚV II.5.2).

The 'seven bands' are symbolic for a group of seven, including the priests. Elsewhere there is mention of seven priests (X.61.1), the fire-god suggested as the *aṣṭama* (X.114.9). The quarters and the priests are seven; but the main quarter is the east[21] which is indicated to be the eighth though not mentioned (ṚV IX.114.3). Out of the eight sons of Aditi, Mārtāṇḍa (Sun) is the eighth (ṚV X.72.8). That the eighth had a very special connotation is clear when the seer asks, "Whom, among the priests, they say that he is the brave *aṣṭama*?" (X.114.9). In this connection, we may note an explanatory passage from the Ai.Br.(I.3.1). The gods purchased Soma. As it was being brought to the place of sacrifice, he lost the knowledge of the quarters and his strength failed him. To restore his strength the gods (here, the priests who were believed to be the gods on the earth)[22] recited a verse; but to no good. They went on reciting and recited up to seven; but they were not effectual. So, they recited eight (*aṣṭau*) verses. Immediately the knowledge of the quarters and the strength was restored for Soma (esp. *aṣṭābhir aśnuvata, tad aṣṭānām aṣṭatvam).* Here, it is clear that the *aṣṭama* has the concept of 'fullness' and pervasion. Soma is believed to be 'king'. Hence, he has to be *aṣṭama.* The eight quarters envelop *(aśnuvanti)* all sides; hence they are *aṣṭa.* That is why the sacrificial pole has eight angles.[23] In later symbolism, this idea is seen in the gods and goddesses having eight hands[24]; four hands indicate control over four main quarters, while eight hands are indicative of the four main and four sub-quarters. This being the tradition regarding *aṣṭa* and *aṣṭama*, Kṛṣṇa, though the second son of Vasudeva, is said to be *aṣṭama* (the all-pervading, all-encompassing). With this in view the *ṣaḍ-garbha* myth and the seventh position of Balarāma are fashioned to make Kṛṣṇa 'the eighth' - *aṣṭama.*

References

1. Bhāg.P.X.1.34 *asyās tvām aṣṭamo garbho hantā*
2. *Ib.* 56 *putrān prasuṣuve cāṣṭān kanyām caiva-anuvatsaram*
3. *Ib.* 2.7 *rohiṇī vasudevasya bhāryā-āste nandagokule;* Viṣṇu P.IV.15.18; V.1.74.
4. Hari V. Viṣṇu-parvan, 2.40ff; *triśūla* (three-spiked lance), sword with golden handle, having a saucer filled with honey

in the hand, the other holding a yellow upper cloak, serpents decorating her arms, armlets having peacock-feathers, holding a staff surmounted with peacock-feathers, holding a staff surmounted with peacock-feathers. She is referred to as Vindhyavāsinī, to be propitiated with wine and flesh; to be worshipped on dark 9th or 11th, 3.9.92; also 2.52.

Viṣṇu P., V.1.84, she is called Āryā Durgā, Ambikā, Bhadrā, Bhadrakālī; 86, offered wine, flesh etc.

5. This has to be contrasted with exchange (*garbha-vyatyāsa)* in the case of Kṛṣṇa and the girl, Hari V., *loc.cit.*, v 37.

6. Hari V., *loc.cit.*, 2.35 *tasyāstvam navamo garbhaḥ kulesmākam bhaviṣyasi.*

7. Ib. 4.7 *garbhakāle tu-asampūrṇe-aṣṭame māsi te striyau.*

8. Bhāg.P.X.2.5; called Śeṣa v.8; Viṣṇu P.V.1.73. The earliest reference to the concept of *ananta* as circular, indicating the end as invisible, occurs at the Jai.Br.I.257, where Prajāpati (with whom the Agniṣṭoma-Soma-sacrifice is identified) is said to "sleep (or lie), becoming a circle, the *ananta*". Imitating his shape, even other divinities are said to be of a circular shape; these include, the sun, the moon, sky, mid-region, earth etc. (*parimaṇḍalo bhūtva-ananto bhūtvā śaye ...)*

9. See note 4 above; Mb. *loc.cit.* mentions the name Āryā in this context; but does not describe her as a goddess. However, at Vana 228.10 it enlists Āryā among *śiśumātaraḥ*, 'child-mother' - protectors.

10. Hari V. loc.cit. 2.31 *saptamo devakīgarbhaḥ,* also 4.3.

11. Bhāg.P. X.3.49f; also Mb., loc.cit.; Viṣṇu P.V.3.18 compare here Moses crossing the Red Sea, which divided itself, *Old Testament*, Exodus, 14.21-23.

12. Bhāg.P. X.3.50.

13. Cf. the account of the 'demon' Dhundhu, Ch. Ten, pp. 301-312 *infra* and the mention of the Gaṅgā and Bhagīratha.

14. Cf. the myth of the birth of the Kauravas, sons of Gāndhārī, Mb., Ādi. 114.9-22.

15. As we have it in the account of the birth of Agni as Skanda Kārttikeya, Mb., Vana 24.30ff-42; 25.1-18; for Puranic records, see Dange, *Encl.P.B.P.* Vol.II, New Delhi, 1987, p. 673, under

"Gods", Kārttikeya. Six has also a symbolic significance associated with life. It is in the sixth month of pregnancy that the foetus is believed to be endowed with life; cf. the goddess Ṣaṣṭhī.

16. She was called Eakānṁśā, as noted above, at Brahmavai.P. but Ekānaṅgā at Mb., Sabhā after 38.29, Southern recension.

17. Hari V., Viṣṇu-parvan, 2.48 *tatraiva tvām bhaginyarthe grahīṣyati sa vāsavaḥ.*

18. Indra invokes Viṣṇu, calling him friend (*sakhe viṣṇo*), for help at the killing of Vṛtra, ṚV IV.18.11; VIII.100.12.

19. Mb. (Gorakhpur), p.344; also Anuśāsanaparvan 149.30 for Viṣṇu; Hari V., Viṣṇuparvan, 19.59 *mahendram ca-upendram ca,* at Kṛṣṇa's victory in the Govardhana episode.

20. Nir.III.10 *aṣṭau aśnoteḥ;* for the association of *aṣṭa* with divinities, Taitt.Br.III.1.2.6 *aṣṭau devā vasavaḥ;* Taitt. Ār.I.12.4 *aṣṭau digvāsaso'gnayaḥ;*

    Cf. the account of the eight Vasus, drowned by the river Gaṅgā, Mb. Ādi., ch.96-98.

21. This is clear from the fact that, in ritual, the main altar, the Āhavanīya, was established in the east of the sacrificial altar-premises; cf. also ṚV X.101.2 *prāñcam yajñam nayata;* also fire to be established in the three fire-places was always carried eastward from the Gārhapatya and east-south for the Dakṣiṇāgni. This way it was never taken to the west.

22. Śat.Br.II.4.3.14 *dvayā vai devāḥ ...ye brāhmaṇāḥ te manuṣyadevāḥ.*

23. Śat.Br. V.2.1.5 *aṣṭāśrīr yūpo bhavati*

24. For hands indicative of quarters, see Skanda P. Viṣṇukhaṇḍa 24.42 as mentioned in Dr. Janardan Mishra, *Bhāratīya Pratīka-vidya,* Bihar Rashtrabhasha Parishad, Patna, 1959, p.58; also other references to that effect. Actually the concept goes back to the Ṛgveda cf. X.121, 4 *yasya-imā pradiśo yasya bāhū...;* and Sāyaṇa on it, *bāhū vacanavyatyayaḥ, bāhavo bhujāḥ, bhujatva-prādhānyayuktāḥ pradiśaḥ,* i.e. quarters including sub-quarters are the arms of the god Ka (Prajāpati in later texts).

Ancestors in the canyon

Fifteen

Ancestors and the Canyon (*garta)*

At least in two allegorical accounts from the Mahābhārata there is a close association between the ancestors and the canyon. Ancestors are seen hanging in a canyon (*garta*), and the spectacle gets to be symbolic. It is said that, the sage Jaratkāru practised severe penance and was averse to getting married. He wandered visiting various holy places. During these wanderings once he came to a place where, in the canyon of the earth (*garte*) he saw some persons hanging head-down-feet-up. They were totally supportless but for a frail blade of straw that was somehow maintaining its fixture in the wall of the hollow. A rat was gnawing at its root. The persons who were solely dependent on the support of that straw looked emaciated and lack-lustre, as if drenched in grief. Jaratkāru approached these persons and asked who they were and how they got to this precarious state. They replied that they were his ancestors. "Yes", said they, "you could help us only if you desire". However, they made it clear that their plight would not vanish simply by his penance. "You see," said they, "in our family-line, now, only one male has remained and he too is averse to marriage, devoted to penance as he is! If you happen to meet him in your wanderings, tell him that his ancestors are hanging supportless in a canyon—

Well, his name is Jaratkāru. Tell him that he alone is our support. Ask him to get married and help continue our family line" (Mb.Ādi, ch.s 45 and 46).

The Mahābhārata, which records this account explains further as follows—the blade of straw was Jaratkāru himself. The rat symbolised Time. Taking hint from the speech of the ancestors, Jaratkāru is said to have married a *nāga*-girl of the same name as his. She was the sister of Vāsuki, the *nāga.* A son was born to them. He was the famous sage Āstika.

A similar account occurs in the Vana *parvan* of Mb. (96.14-19) and concerns Agastya. Here also the ancestors are hanging head-down-feet-up in a canyon. The account is not elaborate and there is no mention of the rat nor of the blade of straw. The ancestors tell Agastya to get a son produced so that the family-line may not be cut off. The rest of the account says that, having the good of the ancestors in mind, Agastya thought to himself, 'How could I produce a son?'. Thinking marriage as a necessity towards this end, he searched for a bride suitable to himself, but could not see anyone to come to match him. He, then collected the best portion of various animals and therefrom shaped a young 'woman' (*striyam,* v20). On knowing that the king of Vidarbha was practising penance for the gain of a son, and thinking that he should favour him, he gave her to him, though he had produced her for himself (v.21, *nirmitām ātmano'rthāya muniḥ prādān mahātapāḥ*). Thus, the 'woman' was born to the king like a lightning. As soon as she was born, the king was overjoyed. This girl was named Lopāmudrā. Later, even though she attained youth, nobody dared to marry her being afraid of the sage (v 28 *mahātmanaḥ*). However, Agastya arrived on the scene and requested the king to offer the daughter to him as wife. The king was disturbed; but, Lopāmudrā pacified him saying that she would marry the sage. And Lopāmudrā became the wife of Agastya (Ib.97.7; the account goes further, with which we are not concerned here).

Before we take another account it is necessary to point out certain things. The mention of Agastya and Lopāmudrā as a couple occurs in the Ṛgveda (ṚV I.179.4); but there is no reference to the other details in the account.[1] This would mean that the prelude of the *garta* episode, as also the account of the 'King of Vidarbha' was a later addition. The whole of the narration is far from convincing and not free from contradictions. Why should Agastya give to the king of Vidarbha a 'woman', when the latter was practising penance to obtain a son (*putrārtham*). Again, when the 'woman' was readily meant for the sage himself, and hence young, how could she be given to the king and be 'born' (cf.v 23, *jātamātrām*) afresh requiring the sage to wait till she became young? Was she born to the king at the place of penance or at the palace? Born to him; but what about the part of the queen? No name of the queen appears. All this cannot be explained simply by saying that in a myth such things are common.

In yet another account we have a man (a *brāhmaṇa*) wandering alone in a dense forest with fierce beasts roaming at ease. The forest itself is said to be resting between the arms of a terrible woman. The man cannot get out of the forest nor is he at peace of mind in it. It is surrounded on all sides by venomous cobras. There is also a deep well (*vāpī*) covered with creepers at a place; and, before knowing what is happening to him, the man falls in it. But, he does not reach its bottom as he gets entangled in the mass of creepers. To his horror he sees a big serpent in the well below him and, as he casts his glance up, he sees a huge elephant standing above. Half of the body of the elephant is white, half is dark. He has six heads and twelve feet. The man notices that the elephant is slowly approaching the well. On the edge of the well rests a tree, in which honey-bees have made a comb. Drops of honey drip through it and the man swallows them as they reach his soliciting tongue. However, his thirst for these drops does not ebb; on the contrary, it flames up. Rats, some white, some dark, gnaw at the tree (*Ib.*Strī-*parvan* 6.3ff). Here there are no ancestors nor is there any indication of the family-line. This is a simple allegory on the human existence, as the Mb. clearly states (it calls it *upamāna,* v 4) and explains it. Accordingly, the forest is the spread of creation (*saṁsāra*) in the arms of Destiny. The various wild beasts are ailments that torture the creatures, here symbolised by the man entangled in the mass of trees. The serpent in the well is Time, while the elephant above is the Year (*saṁvatsara*) with the six seasons as its mouths. The twelve feet of the elephant are the twelve months of the year. The white-dark colour of the elephant's body symbolises white and dark half-months. While the honey stands for sustenance, the rats stand for the days and nights. The account forms part of a dialogue between Vidura and Dhṛtarāṣṭra. The well in this narration, in any case, comes on par with the canyon (*garta*) of the two earlier accounts both being excavators of the earth.

But the point made by the Mb. explaining the allegory is that the Well here stands for the body of the creatures (*ib. 7 yas tatra kūpo nṛpate sa tu dehaḥ śarīriṇām*). Such an explanation does not obtain at the other two accounts involving the *garta.* The explanation, put in the mouth of Vidura here by the narrator, making the Well the very body of Creatures, does not go well with the case of the man in the narration itself. A well being the symbol of the body does not get support also from the series of accounts in which this particular narration is set. An account, which immediately precedes, has an important suggestion. The allegory of the Well in the forest is closely connected with the earlier chapter. The chapter immediately preceding (i.e. Ch.4) deals with the development of the foetus, its animation and final position prior to actual birth. It is explained that the foetus, fully developed, gets stationed in the womb in the 'head-down-feet-up' position. This is exactly the position of the ancestors in the *garta*. The *garta* is, in effect, an inversion of the concept of actual birth due to the only remaining male source being averse to seek a female partner through marriage. The position of the ancestors is that of the foetus, that is ready to get born, yet there is no opening - all is dark!

Another belief that works here is, that the ancestors like to get born in the family-line. This will show that the *garta* appears in these accounts as a blind womb. The case of the well in the third account is about the same, though the man is not specifically termed 'ancestor' (*pitṛ*). In any case, the Well is not the same as the body (*deha*); it is the socket for the body. The forest-well allegory is crudely presented with apparent contradictions and duplication. Thus, the single serpent below in the well is Time while the huge elephant with six heads and all is just a *saṁvatsara* (year), which is a fraction of Time. Again, while the rats as the single days and nights are a proper portrayal, the dark and white halves of the single elephant (year) is an unclear image. This would indicate that the picture, here, is a less creditable imitation of the earlier two. We now take up yet another account, that of the King Nṛga. As will be seen, the account is not strictly factual. It is laudatory and stresses the importance of the gift of a cow.

According to the account some people saw a large Well, in the vicinity of Dvārakā, bordered with foliage and creepers. Desirous of water from it they approached it; but they saw in it a lizard, huge like a mountain. They tried to take it out with the help of ropes and leather-bands; yet they could not. So they approached Śrī Kṛṣṇa for help; When Kṛṣṇa went to the Well, the lizard spoke to him in the voice of a human. He said, "I was King Nṛga in my former life and performed sacrifices. Once a cow of an *agnihotrin brāhmaṇa* (who keeps fires and propitiates them day by day) strayed away from his house and got mixed with my thousand cows that were specified to be given away as gift." When the cows were given, this cow also was taken away by the donees. When the owner *agnihotrin* returned he did not find the cow at his residence. As he went on searching her, he found her in the house of a donee; and he demanded it back. But now the other *brāhmaṇa* said that, since it was a gift to him, he owned it. Arguing over the matter, both approached me. I was in a fix. I told the original owner and the other one, in turn, that I would give any number of cows and wealth for the loss of that particular cow; but they would not accept. And they left. In the meanwhile death took me away. When I was led before Yama, the king of the dead, I expressed my desire to atone for my sins before enjoying the fruit of my merit. So, I was sent back onto the earth in this well 'head-down-feet-up' (Mb.Vana 70.1ff., especially 27 *kūpe-ātmānam adhaḥśīrṣam apaśyam patitaśca ha)"*. The account ends with freedom of the King from that state due to the favour of Kṛṣṇa, with the aetiology that, while the gift of a cow is meritorious, her transfer is sin, though through oversight.

These various accounts have the canyon common among them, though apparently, they differ in their message. In the last account, the fall from heaven to earth, due to sin, does not terminate at a variation of the canyon itself and logistically serves as a womb for rebirth, or restoration of the earlier state. But, by far, the most intriguing detail that obtains in the first account and persists in the second is that the canyon (or well) is associated with the ancestors (*pitaraḥ*). The concept goes back to the Vedic period. Thus, in the context of the erection of the sacrificial pole the pit for fixing it (called *kūpa* (well) or *avaṭa* here) is said to be the region of the ancestors. A blade of grass placed in it with ends to the east and another pointing northward is addressed, "You are the seat of the ancestors" (Vāj. Sam.VI.1 *śundhantām lokāḥ pitṛsadanāḥ* and *pitṛsadanam asi*; also Śat.Br. III.7.1.6). The same is the case when the pit for fixing the branch of the Udumbara tree (*audumbarī*) is addressed, and the water that remains after sprinkling the *audumbarī* is poured into the pit. The Śat.Br. (*loc.cit.*) says that the pit has the ancestors as the deity (*pitṛdaivatyo vai kūpaḥ khātaḥ*). The part of the sacrificial pole with bark on (as against the upper whole that is chiselled out), placed in the *kūpa,* is also said to belong to the ancestors. This would show that the pit with the blades of grass had come to be associated, in ritual, with the ancestors (*pitṛ-s*). It is clear that, in myth, the canyon in the first two accounts, comes on par with the *kūpa* or *avaṭa* for the sacrificial pole; or, we could say that, according to a popular belief in some quarters of the Vedic people, the pit or the canyon in the earth was symbolised as the region of the ancestors. The same belief, in myths, came to hold actual ancestors. The blades of grass which were the seat for them came to be the flimsy support for the helpless ancestors who are now seen as falling head-down into the blind darkness of son-lessness, in contrast to their usually assured seating posture in ritual, as the sacrificer-son is a married householder assuring them the continuity of the line. The next stage in the symbolism is when the pit gets to be a blind uncertainty, as the whole creation is in the hands of Destiny. A point to be considered in this connection is a shift in the belief regarding the abode, or region, of the ancestors. The general Vedic view is that the manes (ancestors) stay in heaven.[2] Heaven is conceptually located in the upper region, above the mid-region and far above the earth. How come, then, that in the later Vedic ritual texts (as noted above) themselves, this region is believed to be located on the earth—and in the pit? The explanation is that this lower subterrestrial region is suggested from the practice of burying the urns containing the bones, that are collected after the cremation of the body.[3] This would give a double-phased region of the ancestors - visually under the earth; and, conceptually up in heaven where they are even seen as enjoying drink in the company of Yama, the first mortal-turned divine.[4] The allegorical myths seen above have basis in the first phase. The concept, in these myths, then, is that until the family-line is assuredly hoped to be continued, the ancestors stay in the subterrestrial region. In that case, the number of ancestors in this lowly region cannot be more than three, who immediately precede the lone living one; because, the unit of ancestors is said to be three - father, father's father and father's father's father - in relation to the recently dead male who is the fourth. When this fresh dead (fourth) is joined to the earlier three, the upper first goes beyond the unit, which accommodates this fresh one as the third in respect of the living who has performed the ceremony for the fresh-dead father.

References

1. The hymn starts with a dialogue between Agaṣṭya and Lopāmudrā. Finally it says, that (= Agastya) desired progeny, and strength. He was 'digging' with a hoe (or sharp shears). We do not have any further details of this story in the Vedic literature, as such.
2. ṚV X.15.14[b] *madhye divaḥ.*
3. Cf.Āśvalāyana Gr.S.IV.5.7-10.
4. ṚV I.135.1, together with X.14.6.

Sixteen

Triśaṅku's Ascent to Heaven

Triśaṅku is, rather, a notorious name in the Hindu mythical context and there is a popular expression—'like Triśaṅku'—in some of the Indian languages, indicating undestinated status. Ancient Hindu texts - Epics and Purāṇas - mention Triśaṅku as the father of the Ikṣvāku king Hariścandra. He desired to reach heaven bodily. Reaching heaven bodily is an abnormal element in the account, while the reality of the Ikṣvāku family and of Triśaṅku is undoubted. Hence the accounts regarding Triśaṅku fall into the category of legend, which is a mixture of the mythical and real. The Vedic literature does not show knowledge of Triśaṅku as a popular figure and there is no elaborate account of him. Only the Taitt. Up.(I.9.1)[1] just mentions him as a sage. The Mb. indicates him as the father of Hariścandra as is clear from the latter mentioned as Traiśaṅkava (not the regular version, but the Southern recension, after the regular - Mb. Sabhā 12.10. Prior to that he is mentioned only as a king in the Ikṣvāku dynasty; but, again, only the southern version). At the Ādi-parvan (southern), after the regular 71.44 there is mention of Triśaṅku being sent to heaven by Viśvāmitra. This will show that, in the period of the Mb.Triśaṅku being sent to heaven was known in south India. However, even here the recension did not have the full account.

Triśaṅku

But, the Rāmāyaṇa (Rām.) has a fairly elaborate account of the ascent of Triśaṅku to heaven. The reason, probably, is that the Rām. is a chronicle of Ikṣvākus. The account here occurs against the background of the traditional feud between the families of Vasiṣṭha and Viśvāmitra, that goes back to the Ṛgveda.[2] According to the account, as it occurs here, King Triśaṅku wanted to go to heaven, bodily. So, he expressed his desire before Vasiṣṭha and asked him to help perform a sacrifice to that effect (Bāla, 57).[3] But, Vasiṣṭha declined, saying it was impossible. When Vasiṣṭha refused to help him, he is said to have gone southward; but, where exactly is not mentioned. Earlier we are told that Viśvāmitra had himself travelled and settled there due to insult and the refusal on the part of Vasiṣṭha to give his cow to Viśvāmitra. Triśaṅku, however, went to the south to the sons of Vasiṣṭha, who were practising penance. On approaching them Triśaṅku bowed to them, praised them and requested them to help him fulfil his desire to reach heaven, bodily. He also told them that he had to approach them, as their father refused to help him. But these sons of Vasiṣṭha, it is said, got angry with him, may be, because he dared to believe that they would act contrary to their father's treatment of him. Suddenly they cursed him to become a *cāṇḍāla*[4] (a low-born person)', even when he politely said, "O ascetics! Be it so; I shall have to attain some other status (if I do not go to heaven bodily). I wish you well." And, lo! within one night the king got transformed into a *cāṇḍāla*. The colour of his cloak changed to black. His appearance got terrible and the hair on his head porcupined, getting dishevelled. His body got covered with ashes from the funeral pyre and his ornaments turned into iron (Rām.Bāla 58.9-11). (Though this did not happen in his capital; or was the southern region not far from the capital ? Because...). Now, his ministers left him. His subjects ran away from him due to fear. Seeing this, the king left the place and approached Viśvāmitra (going again to the southern region as the latter had already taken resort there—?). Viśvāmitra received him with compassion and the king related to him all that had happened. Viśvāmitra assured him saying, "Even though your appearance has changed to that of a *cāṇḍāla,* I shall help you sacrifice in this same form of yours; also in the same form you will reach heaven; be not gloomy!" Thus assuring Triśaṅku, Viśvāmitra summoned all his sons, disciples and all priests. He ordered them to invite the knowers of rituals and sacrifices from all quarters to attend the sacrifice to be performed by Triśaṅku under his chief priesthood. He, however, asked them not to invite Vasiṣṭha and his hundred wrathful sons (*Ib.*59.1-12). But the sons of Vasiṣṭha came to know of the sacrifice and they appeared at it, uninvited.[5] They questioned the wisdom of the priests and ritualists in participating in the sacrifice. They said to them all, "Here the chief priest at the sacrifice is a *kṣatriya* - not a *brāhmaṇa.* The sacrificer (Triśaṅku) is a *cāṇḍāla* (outside of the four recognised *vārṇa-s*). You will officiate and participate in such a sacrifice (being *brāhmaṇa-s*)!! And, will you attain heaven yourself, after death, after partaking of food at such a sacrifice?" Hearing this speech of the sons of Vasiṣṭha, Viśvāmitra thundered, "Oh! These ones who splatter me with blemish, though I am blemishless, - they will themselves be reduced to ashes! These sons of Vasiṣṭha will be divided into seven hundred castes; they will subsist on dog-flesh and will be called *muṣṭika.*[6] Verily, Vasiṣṭha, himself, shall attain the status of a *niṣāda* by censuring me, the censureless."

Having rendered the sons of Vasiṣṭha pale and vanquished with his words, Viśvāmitra started the sacrifice, with Triśaṅku as the sacrificer in the status of a *cāṇḍāla*. He invoked the various gods to arrive at the sacrifice, as the priests and ritual-masters whetted their vigour for the performance of their respective duties. But, the gods did not arrive! Displeased at this, Viśvāmitra lifted his hand, that held the ladle (*sruva*)[7] up in the direction of the sky and said, "This Triśaṅku will attain the (usually) unattainable. He will rise to heaven, bodily." Turning to Triśaṅku he said, "Rise heavenward, Triśaṅku!" At this command of the sage, and with the force of his speech, Triśaṅku started getting lifted up - high-higher. And, straight into the precincts of heaven he got almost planted. Seeing this miracle, the gods, Indra at their head, ordered him to stop, saying, "Unworthy of heaven you are. Get going down". At this Triśaṅku began being hurled down, head-down-feet-up. He cried to Viśvāmitra for support and compassion. And, Viśvāmitra checked him midway, in the mid-region. He immediately created a new set of 'seven-stars' (Ursa Major) and other new stars. He proclaimed, "I shall create even a new Indra; or, I shall render the whole universe - devoid of Indra". Hearing these words of the sage all priests got confused; and now, they tried to convince Viśvāmitra that Triśaṅku was stained by the curse of the elders; that, hence, he could not attain heaven. But Viśvāmitra rejoined that he would not tolerate his promise fall wasted. Said he, "I have promised heaven to Triśaṅku. He must attain it. Also the stars and constellations created by me must remain as they are". The gods agreed, but with certain modifications - that the new stars will be there as they are; however, they will be out of the course of Vaiśvānara; that Triśaṅku will not go down to the earth, but he will remain midway with his head down and feet up, as a demi-god (*amara-sannibhaḥ*): All constellations will go round him (*Ib.*60.1-34).

Before we analyse this account, it is to be remembered, once again, that the Mb. does not have it. But it occurs at the Harivaṁśa, which is the remainder (*khila*) of the Mb. According to this text, Triśaṅku was an acquired name of Satyavrata, who was an Ikṣvāku prince. He was the son of king Trayyāruṇa and was very naughty. Once he abducted a rightly married (*kṛtodvāhā)* wife of another person and a daughter of a citizen of his kingdom. So, his father, the king, drove him out of the kingdom saying, "Get gone hence and stay among the *cāṇḍālas,* who cook the flesh of dogs. Henceforth you are not my son, nor am I your father". Satyavrata went and wandered in the wilds. About that time there came a spell of severe famine that lasted for twelve years. Viśvāmitra (who had his hermitage in the same kingdom) had left his wife and three sons in the kingdom of the Ikṣvākus and had gone away in the vicinity of the sea to practise penance. Seeing no means to maintain the family, his wife put a rope round the neck of the middle son[8] and prepared to sell him for a hundred cows. When Satyavrata came to know of this, he came to the rescue of the family. He set the child free and took upon himself the responsibility of maintaining them all. Living in the forest as he was, he maintained himself by hunting and eating flesh of beasts. He would also keep flesh for the family of Viśvāmitra tied to a tree near the hermitage. So that, the family had nothing to worry about. Moreover, he had been nourishing anger for Vasiṣṭha, who was the royal preceptor, as he did not try to abate the wrath of the king when the latter ordered him out. But, Vasiṣṭha only wanted him to expiate for the sin he had committed. He remained silent but had decided to install him on the throne after his expiation. However, Satyavrata thought otherwise. In the meanwhile the king also had gone out of the capital for penance and Vasiṣṭha's word was supreme in the kingdom. Satyavrata observed the *Upāṁśu* (silence) vow for twelve years during the famine. Once when flesh of other beasts was not available, he stole the cow of Vasiṣṭha, that was famed for fulfilling all desires (*sarva-kāma-dughā*),[9] killed her and took her flesh for the family of Viśvāmitra in the forest; he also ate the flesh. When Vasiṣṭha came to know this he got wild and summoned Satyavrata. He told him that, had he not committed these two fresh *śaṅku-s* (i.e. sins), he would have pardoned him for his first *śaṅku* in abducting others' women; but now that he had totally committed three *śaṅku-s* he would be declared 'triśaṅku'. Hence Satyavrata came to be named Triśaṅku (Harivaṁśa, I.12.11-24; 13.19). After the famine was over, and when Viśvāmitra came to know how Satyavrata helped his family, he asked him to choose a boon. Satyavrata (=Triśaṅku) said that he should attain heaven with the same body. Viśvāmitra agreed. He installed him on the throne of his father. He also made him perform a sacrifice at which Viśvāmitra himself officiated, even as Vasiṣṭha and the gods watched. And he sent Triśaṅku to heaven as desired by the latter (*Ib*.22-23).

In this account there is no direct clash between Vasiṣṭha and his sons on the one hand and Viśvāmitra on the other. In both the accounts the cow of Vasiṣṭha figures; but the details are different. At Rām. Viśvāmitra tries to take away the cow forcibly, while here Satyavrata kills her to sustain himself and the family of Viśvāmitra. Whatever be the symbolic status of this cow, we are not concerned with it here. The rivalry betwene Vasiṣṭha and

Viśvāmitra goes back to the Ṛgveda and it is closely associated with the gain of priesthood at the Ikṣvākus (Divodāsa - Sudās in the Ṛgveda). The striking variations between the versions of the Rām. and the Harivamśa are as follows:

(i) According to the Rām., due to the curse of the sons of Vasiṣṭha, Triśaṅku got transformed to the state of a *cāṇḍāla* within a night; and the cause of the curse was simply his request to the sons of Vasiṣṭha to lead him to heaven, bodily, even when this was not accepted by their father. According to the Harivamśa Satyavrata came to be called Triśaṅku due to his sins, which are not specified by the Rām.

(ii) According to the Rām. Triśaṅku was stopped by the gods from settling in heaven; he was sent back and remained midway between Heaven and Earth in the form of a constellation. According to the Harivamśa he was settled in heaven. The Rām. is not specific about the cause of Triśaṅku's non-settlement in heaven - whether it was because he was a *cāṇḍāla* or because no mortal could think of bodily reaching and staying in heaven. Yet, it is fairly clear that bodily transplantation into heaven in his lifetime was not believed to be possible in the case of a mortal.

Now, let us take the accounts as they occur in the other Purāṇa texts. The Viṣṇu P. mentions the account in short (IV.3.21-24). According to it Triśaṅku was the son of Trayyāruṇi (not Trayyāruṇa). His real name was Satyavrata; but he was called Triśaṅku as he committed sins. He became a *cāṇḍāla.* He helped the family of Viśvāmitra during the famine which lasted for twelve years. To get rid of the state of a *cāṇḍāla* by sustaining the family of Viśvāmitra he tucked some flesh on a Vaṭa-tree (*nyagrodha*) that stood on the bank of the Gaṅgā.[10] This account corresponds to that from the Harivaṁśa even in the detail that Viśvāmitra installed Satyavrata on the throne. The Bhāgavata P. (IX.7.4-7) mentions it just in three stanzas, like the Viṣṇu P. Here he is said to be the son of Tribandhana (and not of Trayyāruna). He became a *cāṇḍāla* due to the curse of the preceptor (not due to that of the sons of the preceptor). He was sent to heaven by Viśvāmitra, but was sent back to the earth head-down-feet-up. Viśvāmitra stopped him midway. He is seen even this day.[11] Though it is not specifically mentioned, it could be gathered that he is seen in some constellation.

The accounts noted above are almost similar to one another; the variations are slight and do not harm the main narration about Triśaṅku. However, the order of events has to be sorted out. The Rām. has Triśaṅku itself as the name of the prince, while in other texts it is Satyavrata, from which it could be believed that Satyavrata was the original name in the popular oral tradition. When it was recorded in the Rām. the original name was dropped and Triśaṅku was retained. The Rām. does not say how Triśaṅku was so named, nor that he had abducted a married woman or a maiden daughter of a citizen. Moreover, here Triśaṅku appears to be a fully coronated king (cf. Bāla 58.10 *rājā cāṇḍalatām gataḥ*). He is not given to insult his priest or his sons. On the contrary, it is the sons of the preceptor who insult him. His only fault was that he desired to reach heaven with the same body. It is clear that the account from the Rām. is subservient to the rivalry between Vasiṣṭha and Viśvāmitra; because, there is no mention of the father of Triśaṅku, nor of the family of the Ikṣvākus. It is a general back-drop for the story of Rāma and jots down incidents that are relevant to that aim. The popular and authentic account has to be taken as from the Harivaṁśa, which mentions the name Satyavrata, which occurs also in other (Puranic) accounts, which give reasons for the name Triśaṅku. The Harivaṁśa, the Viṣṇu P. and the Śiva P. have the same name for the father of Triśaṅku (Satyavrata), with a slight variation (Trāyyaruṇa - Trāyyaruṇi), though the Bhāg. P. has Tribandhana. All these accounts start from the earlier life of 'Triśaṅku', the youthful Satyavrata, who, somehow, could not go well with Vasiṣṭha. In the version from the Rām.Vasiṣṭha is hinted to be superior to Viśvāmitra, while in the other accounts Viśvāmitra is seen a step ahead of Vasiṣṭha. The detail at the Rām. that Triśaṅku turned into a *cāṇḍāla,* dress and all, in one night is fantastic. What appears to be a historical fact is that Satyavrata, who was modest and good-mannered for all practical purposes, did commit a crime in his youthful days in abducting a woman (Harivaṁśa I.12.13). Whether he took her for himself is not clear. It seems, however, that by abducting her he spoiled her act of taking the necessary seven steps, as part of the marriage-ritual by the couple (Harivaṁśa I.12.12 and also 13.7). The motive of abduction is described by this text in uncertain terms as, "may be out of childishness, out of desire, out of misunderstanding, out of fun and frivolity".[12] Further he also tried his trick at a maiden (or were they the same?). But it is said, he observed a vow for twelve years in silence (or, secrecy; cf. 13.3 *upāṁśuvratam āsthāya dīkṣām dvādaśavārṣikīm;* also v 13). A further probe into the narration indicates that this vow was suggested by Vasiṣṭha himself to Trāyyaruṇa for Satyavrata as an atonement for the act of abduction;

for the sage's words to Satyavrata are, "Had you not committed the two more darts of sin, I would have destroyed your first dart of sin" (namely, the abduction). The three darts were - (i) not being agreeable to his father and displeasing him by his act of abduction; (ii) killing the preceptor's cow; and (iii) eating the flesh without getting it ritually consecrated by 'sprinkling' with water (*aprokṣitopayogāt*) (*Ib.*13.17-18). The spell of famine gets closely associated with the sequence of these incidents. It is said, that due to the displeasure of the king about the act of his son, Indra did not send rain for twelve years. Which would mean, that the famine and the dry spell were believed to be the result of a misconduct on the part of the prince. Hence it would appear that the king, in consultation with Vasiṣṭha, sent his son out. And himself went out to forest for atonement, as it was believed that a flaw in royal behaviour causes calamity - especially a dry spell.[13] Another point is, why should the young prince live like a *cāṇḍāla?* The account from the Rām. where it is said that Triśaṅku got transformed into a *cāṇḍāla* in one night cannot be relied upon too much; because, in it Triśaṅku is already a king and is said to be punished simply for requesting bodily attainment of heaven. But, even the accounts from the other sources, we have mentioned, say that he was asked to go to the forest and stay among the people who ate dog-flesh (i.e. *cāṇḍāla*-s). There is no indication that he went of his own accord. This would indicate that it was for the atonement of his wayward behaviour; and this *vrata*[14] lasted for a considerable number of years. It would appear that, when the prince completed the years of the vow he came back as a chastened heir to the throne, being the only son of his father. He was accepted by the subjects and was crowned as king. This forms the first part of the life of Satyavrata.

The desire to go to heaven bodily is the second part and is subsequent to his being recognised as king by one and all; but not by Vasiṣṭha and his sons. The Rām. account has to be taken as mixing, and messing up, these two parts; for, there is no banishment of Triśaṅku (the former Satyavrata) in it. He is already a king. It is also probable that when he returned, he was accepted by Vasiṣṭha also as king due to the need of time and the will of the subjects. However, the Vasiṣṭhas declined to accept his desire to perform a sacrifice wherewith he could reach heaven. This led the king, now married [15] (which means that this request came after quite some time subsequent to his return and coronation) and well established, to seek the priesthood of Viśvāmitra for the sacrifice. It may be noted, that it was the sacrifice that was necessary to 'reach heaven'. It is, normally impossible for any one to reach heaven bodily. Hence the reaching of heaven has to be taken as symbolic. And here a historical fact takes a mythical turn. We have to look for a sacrifice wherein 'reaching heaven' occurs, though symbolically. This is the case at the Vājapeya sacrifice. In it, there is a ritual-detail according to which the sacrificer imitates reaching heaven, not only by himself but, along with his wife. Vājapeya is a unique and interesting Soma-sacrifice, beset with colourful ritual-events. The 'reaching heaven' ritual is associated with the sacrificial pole. The pole is symbolic as sort of ladder and also represents the cosmic tree (*axis mundi*). That part of it which is in the earth, when fixed, represented the region of the manes (ancestors).[16] The middle portion symbolised the terrestrial world and thereafter, up to the rounded top-piece (*caṣāla*), the mid-region.[17] Above that was 'heaven', starting up from the *caṣāla*. The sacrificer goes up the ladder, which is rested against the pole, calling upon his wife, "come along, we shall ascend to heaven". The wife replies, agreeingly. This agreeing reply includes her in the ascent, though she does not actually ascend. The sacrificer, then, touches the *caṣāla,* saying "we have reached heaven, O Gods!" Then (after some other details of rites, with which we are not concerned here) he comes down.[18] Ascending to heaven and getting back was enacted in the sacrificial context. This was called *dūrohaṇa* ('ascending the difficulty') and it was said to be 'ascending heaven' (Ai.Br.18.6), which was seen as being through the orb of the sun (cf. 'This one is the *dūrohaṇa,* he that shines'). This 'ascent to heaven' for the sacrificer was accomplished in another context, symbolically with the chanting of a *mantra,* with pauses to show that the sacrificer ascended in grades. The start was with one-quarter (i.e. one line of a four-line verse; and quarter is the *pāda,* 'foot'; so he goes foot by foot i.e., step by step); then a pause; then the second- quarter; pause; third-quarter, pause; fourth-quarter. With each quarter the sacrificer is said to rise up. The second stage is of reciting the (same) verse in halves, totally two halves. This sets the sacrificer in the mid-region. Then three-quarters at a stretch; pause and the remaining quarter. The last phase is to recite the whole verse at a stretch. This lifts the sacrificer and, with the termination of recitation, he is believed to have settled in heaven. Then starts his return from heaven. In this first, three-quarters are recited at a stretch; and the sacrificer is believed to start to decend. Then pause; then one-quarter; then two quarters are sung; then pause; then two-quarters; then pause; lastly quarter by quarter with a pause after every quarter. With this last he sets himself back on the earth. (The pattern will be clear from the diagram). Ascent is also termed *roha,* while descent *pratyavaroha* (Ai.Br.loc.cit. *dūrohaṇam rohati* and *pratyavarohati*). The 'ascent' is accomplished with the verse that starts with the word *haṁsa* (ṚV IV.40.5 *haṁsaḥ śuciṣad* etc.), while for one who

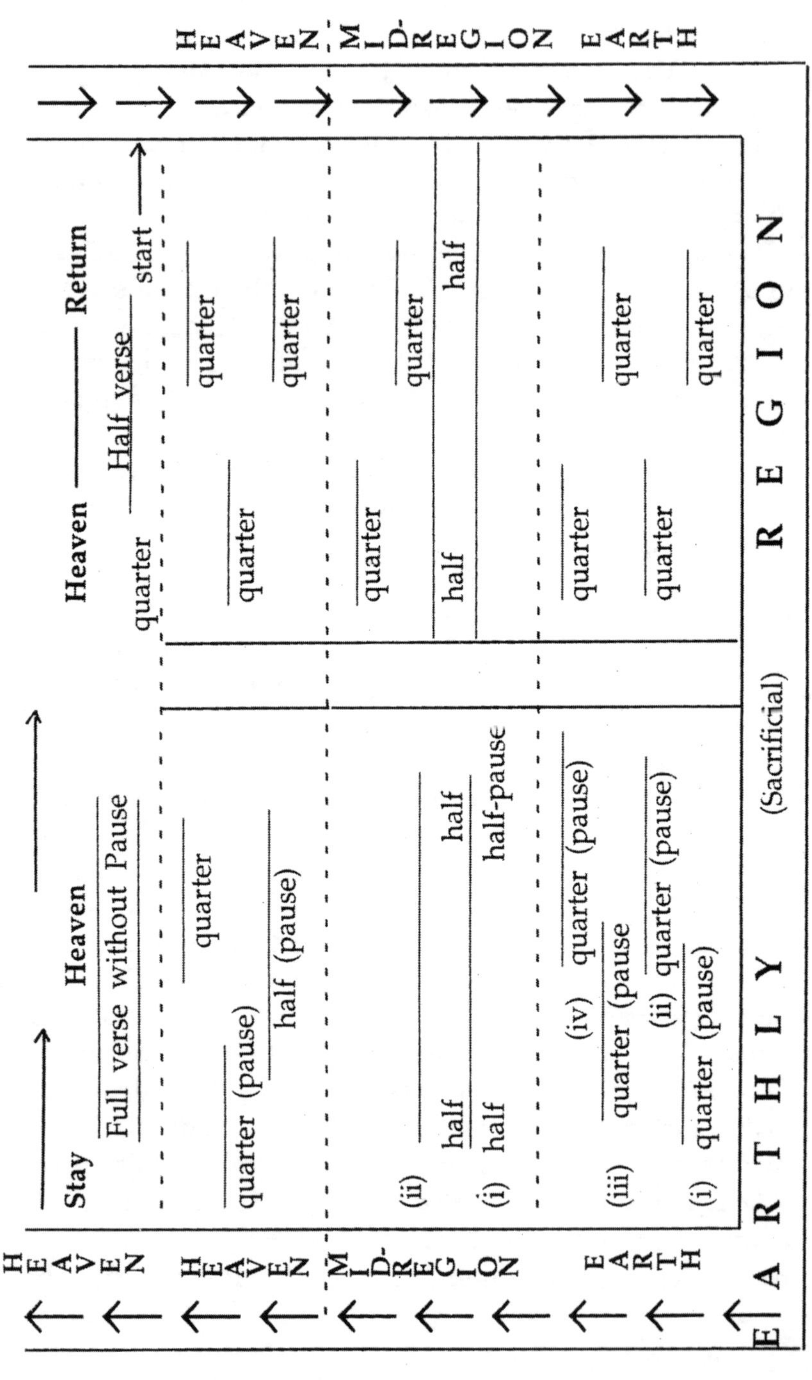
HEAVEN
HEAVEN
MID-REGION
EARTH
Stay
Heaven
Full verse without Pause
quarter (pause)
quarter
half (pause)
(ii)
half
(i) half
half
half-pause
(iii) quarter (pause
(iv) quarter (pause)
(i) quarter (pause)
(ii) quarter (pause)
Heaven
Return
quarter
Half verse
start
quarter
quarter
quarter
quarter
quarter
half
half
quarter
quarter
quarter
quarter
EARTHLY REGION
(Sacrificial)

wants to settle in heaven (even being on the earth, but without symbolically returning to earth), one should recite the verse having the word *tārkṣya* (*ṚV* X.178.1); but, in that case, these sacrificers would not stay in this world for long (they would die soon). The desire to attain heaven, on the part of Satyavrata-Triśaṅku has to be understood in this way, in the context of the sacrifice. And, in all probability, the sacrifice was Vājapeya, which was marked by the ritual of 'heaven-ascent'. It will be useful to note that the words of Viśvāmitra reflect those used in this ritual.[19]

Vasiṣṭha's reluctance to allow Satyavrata to perform the sacrifice indicates the orthodox opinion. Even after coronation, Satyavrata was just Triśaṅku ('tripple-sinned') for the Vasiṣṭhas. So, he could not avail himself of the sacrifice which facilitated 'heaven-ascent'. On the other hand, Viśvāmitra is known for his reformist attitude.[20] He, not only helped install Satyavrata on the throne but also, helped him 'reserve' his place in heaven (conceptually), by officiating at the sacrifice towards that end. It is difficult to know the reason why the name Satyavrata does not occur in the Rām. Probably, it was due to the fact that the Vasiṣṭhas had been finally and firmly established as royal priest by the period of Daśaratha, or even earlier in the period of Dilīpa, the Viśvāmitras getting only due regard. Hence the bards of the Ikṣvāku tradition maintained the Vasiṣṭha version of Triśaṅku, Vālmīkī never disturbing it, or never knowing the other one. Whatever may be the case, it is clear that the acclaimed royal priests, the Vasiṣṭhas, did not favour the sacrifice for 'heaven-ascent' (the Vājapeya) in the case of Triśaṅku - may be, because prior to the full expiation of the first *śaṅku* (abduction), he committed the other two, as Vasiṣṭha said. But, even on the general plane of the performance of the Vājapeya, there occur divergent views. A section of ritualists were of the view that Vājapeya should not be allowed to be performed; for, one who performs it, wins everything, as he wins Prajāpati himself. The result will be that he will keep nothing for his people; the people would perish (Śat.Br.V.1.1.9f). In the vein of this argument throbs the plea of the Brāhmaṇa ritualists and priests that the Rājasūya should not be a speciality of the royal families; but that the Vājapeya should be kept only for the Brahmins. The view is clear in the statement, "In fact, this sacrifice is the *brāhmaṇa*'s own sacrifice; for, Brāhaspati performed it" (*Ib.*1) and "Then (as a second or subsequent claim) it belongs to the *kṣatriya (rājanya)* as Indra performed it."(*Ib.*); "even then, the Rājasūya is for the *ksatriya* alone" (*Ib.*12). And, finally, it is said, "the Rājasūya is lower; Vājapeya is higher in status" (*Ib.*)[21] The Vasiṣṭhas obviously maintained the difference. The Viśvāmitras were of an open mind.

This would indicate that the 'heaven-ascent' of Satyavrata (Triśaṅku) was a fact of history, inasmuch as it was ritually and symbolically accomplished, though it appears as a myth. The portion which speaks of the fall of Triśaṅku from heaven gives a turn of a star-myth to the whole episode. Though it is not quite possible to locate the constellation, as no constellation bears the name Triśaṅku, it may be noted that the fall is described in a pattern known in the epics and Purāṇas. It is "head-down-feet-up", which, in the case of the star-myth, would be like a meteor. When the ritual turned into a myth, the *avarohaṇa* was described in the pattern of the 'falling star', which has not fallen to the ground. Now, though the evidence may be late (as it occurs in the Puranic literature), its roots could be taken to be far back.

According to the classification of the constellations in the Purāṇas certain of them are named 'Adhovaktra' (down-faced). They are Rohiṇī, Ārdrā, Puṣya etc. (Garuḍa P.I.59.16), as against those that are called Ūrdhvamukha (up-faced). Triśaṅku comes nearer the *adhovaktra* constellation in his fall. However, it is not clear which exact constellation represented Triśaṅku.

References

1. According to Swāmī Dwārikadasa Śāstrī ed., *The Twentyeight Upaniṣads,* Prācya Bhārati Prakāśana, Varanasi, 1965; according to the Gītā Press, Gorakhpur ed. I.10.1; the expression is *iti triśaṅkor vedānuvacanam.*
2. See H.D. Velankar, "*Viśvāmitra and Vasiṣṭha in the Ṛgveda", Dr.V.V. Mirashi Fel. Volume,* pp.1-6.
3. Rām., Bāla 57.12[ab] - *gaccheyam svaśarīreṇa devānām paramām gaṭim.* The exact rendering would be "may I attain the highest state of the gods."
4. Ib. 58.9[ab]-*śepuḥ parama-saṅkruddhāś cāṇḍālatvam gamiṣyasi.* At Divyāvadāna 33, he is called a *cāṇḍāla*-king.
5. This practice of going to a sacrificial session, uninvited and putting a challenge obtains. We may compare Air. Br.35.1.ff for a dispute between Rāma *mārgaveya* and Viśvantara Sauṣadmana as regards the ritual drink; and *Śat.Br.*XII.9.3.1 for a debate regarding the offering of wine into the proper fire, at the Sautrāmaṇī.
6. The word *muṣṭika* is rendered as *ḍomba* in Monier-William's and Apte's Sanskrit-English dictionaries, which has the connotation of a supervisor at cremation grounds.
7. *sruva* is a ladle with one small opening, or two half openings at one end. It is a sort of a dipping spoon, as against other ladles that are used for offering; see *Yajñāyudhāni*, ed. by T.N.Dharmadhikari, Vaidika Samshodhana Maṇḍala, Pune, 1989, p.12.
8. The sale of the middle son occurs also at the Ai.Br.33.3, in the context of the legend of Śunaḥśepa. Śunaḥśepa was the

middle son and was sold by his father for a thousand cows; cf. also Bhāsa's drama, *Madhyama-Vyāyoga*, where Ghaṭotkaca takes the middle son of a *brāhmaṇa* for being eaten by his mother for the release of her fast. Bhīma goes in his place, being himself the 'middle' of the Pāṇḍavas. The social implication is of a belief that the funeral of the parents, or any auspicious rite, is to be performed by the eldest or the youngest. In the present case, the middle son is Gālava, who became famous later as a sage. The name is sought to be explained by his being tied at the neck, *gala*.

9. The *Kāmadughā* has her prototype in the *Sabardughā* in the Ṛgveda, I.20.3 and many other places. The cow of Vasiṣṭha is a symbol for the 'all container' and 'all producer' as various accounts show. She is named Nandinī, Mb. Ādi 174.8-12ff. See Ch. Eleven.

10. This Nyagrodha appears to be the tree that still stands at the confluence of the Gaṅga and the Yamunā at Prayāga, modern Allahabad. It is called *akṣaya-vaṭa*, Mb. Vana 84.85; 95.14.

11. cf. also Brahma P.VIII.18-19; Śiva P.V.37.48-59.

12. Harivaṁśa I.12-13. However, it is said that he abducted her prior to her taking seven steps; Ib.13.7-

    In that case Satyavrata abducted her before the mariage.

13. We may compare the case of Devāpi, the elder brother, and Yāska, Nirukta II.3.10; as Devāpi went to perform penance and his younger brother took the kingdom, "Indra did not send rain for twelve years; because it was *adharma* for Śantanu. However, Devāpi acted as Śantanu's priest at a rain-bringing sacrifice and it rained; cf. the due to the *vyatikrama* on the part of Romapada, Rām.Bāla.9.7-11. 'Twelve Years' in such accounts is a pattern of expression; it does not indicate the exact period.

14. cf. the vow called *avakīrṇi-vrata*, to be observed by a student who commits a sexual act. He has to sacrifice a donkey where four roads meet, or outside the locality, to the goddess Nirṛti and wear his hide for a period of one year, Manu Sm.XI.118-123; for more information P.V.Kane, *History of Dharmaśāstra*, Vol.IV, second ed., Poona, 1973, pp.112-13; also for living as a *cāṇḍāla* among the *cāṇḍālas* in the case of a *sannyāsin* who reverts to the life of a householder, Ib., p.113.

15. His wife's name was Satyavatī, the daughter of the king of Kekaya, Mb., southern reading after Sabhā 12.10; according to the Harivaṁśa, I.13.24, it was Satyarathā, daughter of the king of Kekaya.

16. See Ch. Fifteen, "Ancestors and the Canyon".

17. It was made from wheat-dough in the Vājapeya (Śat.Br.V.2.1.6; Taitt. Br. I.3.7), while in other cases it was made of wood, of the same tree from which the sacrificial pole was fashioned.

18. Śat.Br. V.2.1.9-11; the *mantra* is *svar devā aganma*. According to the Kāt. Ś.S.XIV.5.8 both go up, while according to the Apa. Ś.S.XVIII.4 the husband alone.

19. Cf. Ram., Bala 60.27; with this cf. Śat.Br. *loc.cit.* 10; Taitt. Sam.I.7.9.1 and Mait.Sam.I.11.8.

20. He accepts Śunaḥśepa as son against all odds. Ai.Br.33.5-6. He sacrificies for Mataṅga, though he was born to a non-brahmin from a brahmin woman; Mb. Ādi.71.31 with Anuś. 27.8.

21. The point of the mutual status of the two sacrifices obtains even later, cf. Kāṭ. Ś.S.V.1.1-2; Āsv. Ś.S.IX.9.11.

Seventeen

Reṇukā and Yellammā

The earliest references to Reṇukā occur in Mb. at two places. At one place Paraśurāma does not figure; but at the second place she is the mother of Paraśurāma ('The wielder of the axe'). Though perfectly human, she has somewhat of a mystery attached to her personality. According to one account, when her husband, Jamadagni, was practising the art of archery he gave her the job of fetching the arrows shot by him. Once when she was at this job, and went to fetch the arrow, she was a bit late in coming back. Jamadagni, notorious for his quick-at-brow wrath, sought from her the cause of her delay. She said, that as she was tormented by the heat of the sun—her head reeling and the palms of her feet getting scorched—she had to wait for a while under the shade of a tree. Hearing this, Jamadagni got furious at the sun for torturing his wife. He fitted an arrow to his bow and pointed it at the sun ready to shoot. The sun got afraid. He took the form of a *brāhmaṇa* and came down to the enraged shooter. He said, "O wise one! What will you gain by shooting at the sun, who is so important for the whole world?" He also gave various proofs of the sun's benevolence to humanity and other creatures, asking further, "How would you be able to shoot at the sun, who is never stable at one place?" Said Jamadagni, "You,

O you, Brāhmaṇa, the sun does stay still for a while at midday, which is this time! See how I dot him with my arrow, so he falls!!" The sun now left his form of a *brāhmaṇa,* afraid that Jamadagni would surely do what he said, and pleaded guilty for causing trouble to Reṇukā and solicited protection. Jamadagni was satisfied and pardoned him. The sun gave to Jamadagni a pair of leather-sandals to protect his feet and an umbrella to ward off the heat of the sun (Anuś.95.18.96.8ff). The context shows that the account has a definite purpose, which is to extol the practice of making gifts suitable to the season. As such, the account has the status of a charter. This would also show, that the characters here are of secondary importance. The mythical part is seen in the coming down of the sun, which also tends to suggest[1] the halo attached to the humans mentioned. The perfect harmony of marital relationship between the husband and the wife, a marked oriental trait, could have been shown even with the inclusion of another couple; but, the wrath and cooling down of Jamadagni are legendary in the Hindu mythical tradition (a trait seen further in the behaviour of Paraśurāma himself and attested by the Hindu epics) though etymology has not been taken as a support to explain his name (which would mean 'The fire that eats' or 'eating-fire', fr; √*jam,* 'to eat' and *agni,* 'fire').

Here is another account. It is a more popular one. According to it, Jamadagni had five sons from Reṇukā: Rumaṇvant, Suṣeṇa, Vasu, Viśvāvasu and Paraśurāma. Once it so happened, that all the sons had gone out to collect fruits and flowers from the forest, away from the hermitage. Reṇukā, who was following a vow, took permission of her husband and went to the river to bathe. While returning after bath, she was struck by a scene which, obviously, was uncommon for her experience. She saw that Citraratha, the king of the Mārtikāvata country (a part of India) was sporting in the water of the river along with his wife. This aroused in her mind a desire to, likewise, sport. However, the very next moment she came to her own, her face turning pale due to shame. This was a sin against her husband, indeed, though only mental. In the same out-of-mind condition of hers she reached the hermitage, the obvious effect of the 'sin' being that the cloth she wore remained wet (actually "soaked in water", *klinnāmbhasi).* Jamadagni noticed it, and, seeing her lack-lustre, flew into rage; for, he now knew the sin of faithlessness *(vyabhicāra)* she committed. As the sons returned, he ordered them, one by one, to behead their mother. All the four sons disobeyed. When it came to Paraśurāma, he readily obeyed the father's command and severed the head of his mother from her body. Jamadagni was satisfied and was also pacified. Pleased with Paraśurāma, he asked the latter to choose whatever he desired. Paraśurāma said. (i) My mother should come back to life; that is the first boon; (ii) His four brothers, who were cursed by his father to turn into non-human creatures for disobeying him, should regain their human form and faculties; (iii) All should lose the memory of the whole incident; (iv) He should be free from the sin of matricide; (v) No defeat in fight, ever; and (vi) Long life (Vana, 116, the whole ch.). All this was granted.

These are the two mythical accounts regarding Reṇukā and Jamadagni that obtain in Mb. Now, let us have an account from another source.[2] According to it, once Jamadagni and his other sons had gone out of the hermitage to collect flowers and fruits (a common ploy with which we are now familiar). Having finished all her household work, and keeping Paraśurāma to guard the hut, Reṇukā went to the river to fetch water (after her usual bath?). Here the river is said to be Narmadā, thus localizing the account in central India. As she was about to collect water in her jar (made of clay), she noticed that Arjuna, the son of Kṛtavīryya (not the Pāṇḍava, obviously), was sporting in the river with his wives and women. She decided to wait till the king finished his sportive dalliance. When he had finished and the whole group had left, she descended to the water. She saw that the water at that place had got turbid. Hence, she walked to the upper (eastern) side of the stream. But, now, she saw there the king of the Śālvas, Citraratha by name, sporting with his wife. The beauty of the king and his wife bewitched her; and she said to herself, "What a handsome couple! I have never seen such a handsome couple in my life!!" She got fixed to the spot, as it were, and let her sparkled eyes drink the whole scene oblivious of the rapid throbs of her heart. When she came to her own, it was too late; she realised it; hastened to the water; filled the jar; darted to the hermitage. And, she beheld her husband, who had been waiting for her, having reached earlier. She saw him flaming with anger; her body bent down to bow to him; her hands placed the jar down at his feet;—all too spontaneously for any thought. With a sense of guilt she explained why she was late, telling exactly what had happened. Jamadagni ordered his sons, one by one, to sever her head. (The rest is as is found at the second Mb. account). The account generally tallies with the one from the Mb. If we look under the expressed account for any special message, we could say that we have here the reflection of the approved code of conduct for a wife: (i) She should be entirely submissive to her husband; and (ii) Even a thought of pleasure, away from that from her own husband is sin for her. One more point could be, that the husband has to be adored and respected even if he be of an extreme temperament. But, all these points could hardly be taken as special for the account in both its variations. The wrath of Jamadagni (like that of Durvāsas) had to be taken as a characteristic of the person and has nothing to do with the meaning of the account. Though the whole account could be taken as a myth, actually the myth centres round the severance of the head and the coming back to life. Closely associated with this is the complex nature of Reṇukā. She is (as is expected to be) extremely devoted to her husband and is piously true in her confession. This is why the sons do not hesitate to disobey their father's command. Even when Paraśurāma obeys, he is anxious to get her back to life. Even the husband is pacified, once the 'punishment' is meted. This would mean that Jamadagni is an embodiment of order and that his wrath is not due to lust, or jealousy; it is due to the normal behavioural order being cracked. Hence, it has the edge of expiatory punishment. The point in the desire of the killer, Paraśurāma, that all the concerned parties should lose even the memory of the incident, is quite eloquent.

The account from the Mb. is short but simple, and it has only one king sporting. In the latter account, said to be from the Brahmāṇḍa P., there are two such kings with their own separate groups. But, this is a negligible variation. However, the Mb. account does not mention the name of the river, while in the other account the river is said to be Narmadā. The reason is, that Arjuna, the son of Kṛtavīrya, was the king of Māhiṣmatī situated on the northern bank of the Narmadā. Citraratha is said to be the king of the Śālvas. Now, the Śālva region was near the Matsya region which roughly corresponds to modern Punjab.[3] However, the variation in the regions is not important from the point of the meaning of the mythical account, though it shows that the account was popular round about the Narmadā and, later (?) also up to the Śālvas. Another point is that there was a clash between Jamadagni and Arjuna Kārtavīrya, the latter's sons killing him, and a miracle bringing him back to life (Mb. Vana, 116.194; Brahmāṇḍa P.II.3.26.41-II.3.27.59) would indicate a sort of rivalry between the two.

Let us now see a version of the account current in south India. Here the mother of Paraśurāma is not named Reṇukā, though his father is said to be the same, Jamadagni. According to this version, the mother's name was Mariammā (Māriammā). Māriammā was a very chaste woman and, due to her power of chastity, she did not require any container, like a jar or so, to fetch water. She could hold water on her palm like a big (crystal or snow) ball. After bath her wearing cloth would flutter and get dried in the air above her head, following her as she walked. Once, having taken her bath in the river, she was walking as usual to her house (hermitage?). Her cloth canopied overhead, gently wafting in the agreeable breeze, and the round mass of water sparkling on her palm in the bright sunlight. As she went along the road, she was suddenly taken aback by a reflection in the massed ball of water in her hand. She saw reflected a few couples of the Gandharvas (semi-divine humans) sporting in the mid-region. Immediately she looked up and again at the reflection, a tremor of infatuating desire running through her body. Only for a moment! The next moment she saw the solid ball of water diminishing by trickles, getting sprinkled on the ground. The cloth overhead stopped getting dry; it slugged down on her body—moist—wet! She had lost the special power, as there happened a dent in her chastity!! She reached home crestfallen. And, there stood before her husband, Jamadagni, seething with anger. He asked her what the matter was and how that unusual happened with her—the cloth, wet; the water-ball missing! She narrated everything. Jamadagni ordered Paraśurāma to take her into the forest and behead her. Accordingly, as he was leading his mother along the forest-path, the latter saw an outcaste woman passing nearby. Desiring her to have pity on her and protect her, Mariammā clung to her. Paraśurāma tried to separate them; but was unable to do so. Ultimately, lest he should be guilty of not obeying the order of his father, he dealt a severe blow of his axe on the neck of his mother. The result was that the heads of both the women got severed. Paraśurāma was horrified to see this and went straight to his father whom he told what had happened. Jamadagni was glad that his son obeyed him and asked him to choose a boon. Paraśurāma asked for the rejuvenation of his mother. Jamadagni agreed and gave to him in a vessel some water, duly consecrated with chants, and a cane-stick. He advised him to place the head sticking to the body of his mother, sprinkle some water on the joint, then to lightly strike the joint with the cane. Taking the water-jar and the cane, Paraśurāma went back to the place of the incident. He desired to bring both the women to life; so, he joined the heads and the bodies. But, in haste (so says the account), he joined the heads on wrong bodies, i.e., his mother's head onto the body of the other woman and the other woman's head onto the body of his mother. He sprinkled water on both these units and touched them with the cane. Both stood alive. When the news reached the people in the locality, all were gladly surprised and worshipped the women as goddesses. The one with the head of Mariammā was named Mariammā, while the other one came to be known as Yellammā.[4] In essence, they came to be believed as two aspects of the same goddess. Mariammā came to be pleased with the sacrifice of goats and cocks, while Yellammā with the sacrifice of a he-buffalo. One detail, which does not obtain in both the accounts of Reṇukā mentioned above from Mb., is of the divinity of Reṇukā as the wife of Jamadagni and mother of Paraśurāma, though, independent of the accounts mentioned above, Reṇukā obtains as a goddess in Mb. and the Purāṇas. A detail common to all the three accounts is that, in all of them, the mother has her head severed and joined later. This trait tallies with that of the goddess famous later as Chinnamastā (*chinna-mastā*, 'Goddess with the severed head'),[5] but not known from the Mb. and the main Purāṇas. It would also appear that the myth of Mariammā-Yellammā noted above is popular in south India, while that of Reṇukā comes from north India. From Mb., in the accounts noted above, it is located at two places: one at the north bank of the Narmadā, while the other at the Śālva region, which is near modern Punjab. It is to be noted that Mariammā has her status independent of Reṇukā in south India. She is known also as Marī; also that not in all cases this mythical account is told about her. Obversely, from Mb. Reṇukā appears to have been mostly located in northern India. Mb. Vana 83.159-160) mentions a Reṇukā-tīrtha (holy water-place) at Kurukṣetra (modern Haryana; former Punjab), which corresponds to the Śālva region mentioned earlier. Another one of the same name is said to have been on the way that was north of the Narmadā dotted by holy water-places, the last being Reṇukā before Pañcanada (Panjab) and the river Vitastā (*ibid.*82.52-88; Reṇukā at v 82). In the post-Mb. period, a change in location is indicated.

According to the Skanda P.(II.1.9.60ff), there was a shrine of Reṇukā on the bank of the river Suvarṇamukharī, where king Toṇḍamāna is said to have seen her. But, she was not anthropomorphic; she was in the form of an ant-hill (Ib.v 60 *valmīkākāra-samsthitām*). She is said to have been worshipped by him on the 9th of Caitra (which is the beginning of Summer; or, rather, the Spring). Here she is a regular Mother-goddess, who was offered beasts as victims and hundreds of jars of wine.[6] According to another version she was called Kāmalī, was the daughter of king Suveṇu of the Ikṣvāku dynasty and was married to Jamadagni (Vāyu P.Uttarakhaṇḍa 29.86-87). Toṇḍamāna is a king of the south (India). The first Puranic reference mentioned above would show that Reṇukā was then seen in south India as the goddess of the ant-hill. The process of identification seems to be as follows:

Ant-hill = Goddess
Reṇukā = Ant-hill (a part of earth)
∴ Reṇukā = Goddess, i.e., Earth-goddess.

On the one hand, the ant-hill is worshipped as a veritable mother-goddess even this day in the Bellari and other districts on the border of the districts of Āndhra-Pradeśa and Karnataka in India.[7] It is supposed to be an aspect of the goddess Durgā and, according to one mythical account, somebody is said to have seen the goddess Durgāmmā (southern name of Durgā: Durgā+ammā, 'Mother Durgā') coming out of the ant-hill.[8] On the other hand, the ant-hill has been seen as having a special importance throughout the Hindu tradition. As the home of the serpent it is important and is offered worship on the 5th of bright Śrāvaṇa, with the desire to please the cobra, expected to be present in it. Going back to the Vedic period, the ant-hill is said to be the earth; also that it is the ear of Prājapati and of the earth; also that it is the breast *(stana)* of the earth.[9] This will show that right from the Vedic times, through the Puranic period, the ant-hill was believed to be an aspect of the earth. This was the basis of the identification of the ant-hill as the goddess, which obtains even in south India. Though the ant-hill had not attained the status of an earth-goddess in the Vedic times, its ritual use, especially of the particles from its interior (called *valmīka-vapā)*, obtains widely.[10] It will be pertinent to note, in this context, that a particle of earth is termed *Reṇu.* Actually the ant-hill *(Valmīka)* had already come to be looked upon as a wonderful source of birth, as attested by the myth of the birth of *Vālmīki* ('born-from-ant-hill'), the famous poet of the Rāmāyaṇa. A faint reflection of the idea occurs at the Ṛgveda, when a certain 'son of Agru' is said to have emerged from the *ukhā*, after breaking it *(ukha-cchit)*, which doubtlessly indicates the ant-hill due to its shape; the only point is that this *ukhā* (an earthern vessel), in the form of the ant-hill, is seen as placed in the bottom-up position. This 'son-of-Agru' is said to have been in the process of being eaten by ants, which leaves no doubt about the *ukhā* being the ant-hill (ṚV IV.19.9). Toṇḍamāna's experience of Reṇukā being in the form of an ant-hill is, thus, as interesting as it is important. It is not clear if an actual image of a goddess was worshipped at the Reṇukā-tīrtha mentioned in Mb., noted above, or whether Reṇukā was worshipped in the form of an ant-hill, as is the case with the southern Reṇukā-ant-hill. But from south India there is yet another instance of identification in the case of the ant-hill. It is with the goddess Yellammā, and is supported by a ritual. According to the custom followed in the case of Devadāsīs, a girl to join that order is 'married' to an ant-hill. The explanation is, that the ant-hill is the symbol of the goddess Yellammā.[11] As this is only a symbolic marriage, the question of a marriage between two females does not arise. This is a 'marriage' (so called) which serves two purposes: (i) The *devadāsī's* identification with the goddess; and (ii) she should have no contact with a male (in principle). As the instances of identification between Yellammā and the ant-hill (not recorded by any Purāṇa but current in folk-tradition) and between Reṇukā and the ant-hill (recorded by the Sk.P. mentioned above) are both from south India, it is clear that the Reṇukā myth came to the south from the north and got assimilated into the Yellammā cult, creating variations. In between Māriammā and Yellammā, it is observed that the former has a diffused aspectual application. There are various Marī-s[12] while Yellammā's personification is fixed. There is no other goddess sharing any part of this name. This would mean, that originally Māriammā and Yellammā were mutually separate; further, that both were separate from Reṇukā. The first proposition is clear from the fact that Māriammā and Yellammā have mutually different types of beast-offerings. The second is clear from the account itself which states that two different women clasped each other. To believe that these three are the aspects of the same original goddess would be not only knave; it would also be unscientific. There is another point. Yellammā has a fixed status in the myth from south India noted above, while Māriammā takes the account of Reṇukā, husband, sons and all, sans the name Reṇukā. This trait is marked also in yet another case. According to a myth that obtains in about the same south Indian region (Tamil-Karnataka border), once there lived a sage named Piruhu. He had a wife named Nāgāvalī, who was extremely beautiful.

She was famed to be a model of a faithful wife. So, to test her chastity, one day, the "Trimūrti" (a term used here, which stands for the gods Brahmā, Viṣṇu and Śiva) approached her when her husband was out. Not knowing who they were and disliking their intrusion, she changed them into children. Ashamed, and also angry, they cursed her. As a result, she lost her beauty. She also immediately got afflicted by smallpox. When, after the gods had left, her husband came home, he was shocked and a sense of repulsion seized him. He drove her out of the house cursing that she would be born as a demoness in the next birth. Because of this change, she came to be called Marī. As she wandered away from her house, a washerman took pity on her and cared for her. As she stayed with the washerman, she gained also a new name, Uppai, which has the connotation of 'washerman's oven'.[13] This would show that Mārī was a fluid term applicable to any goddess subjected to a transformation, though the inherent concept behind the name Mārī is that of power. A similar myth is told about Anasūyā and her test by the same gods. She was the wife of the sage Atri. The Hindu epics (Rām., Ayodhyā, 117 and Mb., Anuś.14.95-98) mention her as the wife of Atri; but this account is absent in them. It is absent also in the Purāṇa texts. It is current in the Maharashtra region of India and appears very late; but, the account says, that the three gods asked her to serve them after stripping off her clothes. This she did; but, prior to that she changed the gods into innocent children. The point is: borrowal and change of name, the account being practically the same. In the case of the myths of Māriammā-Yellammā and Nāgāvalī-Māriammā the source seems to be in the north, the other names providing the clue. In the first case, the names of the males are just the same as in the case of Reṇukā, while in the case of Nāgāvali Piruhu is the south Indian corrupt pronunciation of Bhṛgu, who is wrongly mentioned here in place of Atri. The Nāgāvalī (Anasūyā)-Mārī myth has no severance of the head; yet, the three myths (Reṇukā, Mārī and Yellammā) have one thing in common: female chastity. This will be clear from yet another variation of the Mārī-Yellammā myth, which obtains in a Purāṇa located at a place called Alampur. Such local Purāṇas are called *sthalapurāṇa* (which could be termed 'Local sagas' or *'Ortlich sage'* like *Göttersage*). According to it, after being severed, the head of Yellammā (identified as Reṇukā) falls in an unholy place. As such, it is thought to be improper to get it joined to the trunk. Hence. it is left there and worshipped as (that of the goddess) Yellammā. The myth is said to be of Reṇukā; yet it boils down to be of Yellammā, the popular female deity of the place. The myth tells, that Reṇukā had gone one day, as usual, to the river to take bath and fetch water. Also, as usual, she had collected water in a jar made of mud; but, this jar was not baked; also, that Reṇukā had no cloth on her body, as she was observing a vow. This was her usual practice. The river in this account is Tuṅgabhadrā, the famous southern river that skirts Hampi the past capital of Kṛṣṇadevarāya. As she was returning, she saw a king and his wife sporting in the river Tuṅgabhadrā. She saw them and got attracted to their sport. Instantly the jar which she was carrying got dissolved and the water oozed out. The rest of the account is the same as in the other variations. However, there is one important variation here. When Paraśurāma severed the head of Reṇukā, Jamadagni asked Paraśurāma to choose a boon. He asked the rejuvenation of his mother. But, his father said that it was not possible;

because, the head had flown and had fallen in the big jar of a cobbler. Impure as it had become, said he, it could not be re-fixed to the rest of her body. It is said, that the head came to be called Yellammā, and was worshipped as such. The trunk came to be worshipped as the earth-mother. This is exactly opposite of the tale from south India noted above. However, the point common to both is that both, Māriammā in the tale mentioned earlier and Yellammā, here and earlier, are originally not Reṇukā; further that it is the impure head (of the woman from a low caste in the Māriammā tale, and the head of Reṇukā that fell in an impure place) that came to be called Yellammā. There is yet another point. In the Reṇukā-tale proper there is no permanent severance of the head and the trunk, though severance is the most important point in that tale associated with even the slightest loss of chastity. In the Māriammā-Yellammā tale the motif of severance brings with it the whole tale of Paraśurāma and Jamadagni except the original mother, Reṇukā; there is also re-fixation of the head and the trunk, though wrongly. In the Alampur tale there is severance, but no re-refixation. But, it is the head (without the trunk) that is actually worshipped at Alampur; also that the trunkless head is (of) Yellammā, the main goddess of the place which is a corrupt form of the name Yellammā-pura (Ellammapura—Alampura). That the trunk is not Ellammā is clear also from another evidence. A headless nude figure of a goddess is worshipped at one place called Navaliṅgeśvara in the vicinity of Yellammāpur (Alampur), while, according to localites, the head of the same figure is believed to be at Savadatti (Saundatti) in Belgaum district in Karnataka.[14] Yellammāpur, noted above, is located at the border of Mehboobnagar and Kurnool in Andhra.

From what has been said uptil now, it could be gathered that the myth of Renuka's severed head came handy to be used as an explanation for the custom of establishing only the head of a local goddess. This appears especially in south India. As a step further, we see temples of Reṇukā, Paraśurāma and Jamadagni at Savadatti; this, in addition to that of Yellammā. In certain cases severance of head gets associated with sexual shyness and sexual guilt. The latter is evident in the case of the Reṇukā-myth. For the former there is an interesting myth from south India. It is as follows: Once Śiva wanted to have fun at the cost of Pārvatī. He asked Pārvatī to keep his rug made of used cotton cloaks, which she did. Later, he took the form of a rat and cut holes into it. When Pārvatī saw the damaged rug she was distressed. Śiva, now, took the form of a darner and approached her to offer help if she had anything to darn. She readily gave him the rug asking him about the wages for the work. The 'darner', obviously, was mischievous. He said, "If you offer yourself to me... ." Pārvatī contemplated for a while, but agreed to what he desired, thinking not to annoy Śiva for being careless about his rug. When she was having union with the 'darner', the latter assumed his real form. And, Pārvatī was ashamed to the deepest vibration of her feelings, with the result that her head got severed from her body.[15] Here there is actual union; but, the person is her own husband. Nevertheless, the fact, that she was available for 'another' person is now known to her husband, creates a situation of tension in her mind. Though the element of fun in the case of the husband (and his, expected, mischievous glance) might take out the sting from the situation, rendering it un-guilty for her, the characteristic faithfulness in the wife deals a psychic blow, rendering her 'headless'. In the myth this takes the form of the severance of the head. Here the husband is free of tension; so, he does not ask for the severance; but, the myth uses the motif of marital faithfulness and sexual tension seen in the popular Reṇukā myth. In other words, at both the myths the severence of the head is psychological, rather than actual. This is clear from the fact that in the Reṇukā-myth, and also in that of Māriammā-Yellammā, there is rejuvenation. This is as far as the myths are concerned, leaving out actual cases where an angry husband might kill his wife. The non-actuality of severance being final, in addition to there being an indication of psychic tension, the act becomes symbolic; this also, in addition, serves the effort of explaining the presence of only the head of the goddess and also the headless body, or, better, the part lower from the navel pit.

We have seen above, that in the Reṇukā-myth proper, the head does not lie away from the body eventually. The head belongs to the same body. In the Māriammā-Yellammā myth the heads leave the original body even if they are re-fixed. In the Alampur myth, it is the head itself that is said to be Yellammā though it is said to have fallen in an unholy place. Conversely, the headless (and, essentially nameless) goddess near Alampur does not give her name to the place. Though local mythical tradition connects the nude headless goddess and the head (Yellammā) with the Reṇukā-myth from Mb., obviously because the Mb.Reṇukā-Jamadagni myth was popular and came handy, the place is not called Reṇukā-pura. This being the case, it cannot be said that Reṇukā and Yellammā are one and the same, nor that "Yellammā was the Prākṛta name of the goddess whose Sanskrit name was Reṇukā."[16] This would involve a fundamental error; for. what we have here is the case of two different goddesses being identified. Identification presupposes mutual difference. If people's belief is not tested on scientific and historical data, there will be a fallacy like accepting as truth that the various incarnations (Kṛṣṇa, Rāma, and even the Man-lion) were, in fact, the same person! It is also difficult to believe that, "Figures of the same goddess, whose (bodiless) head was worshipped, were made (headless) with prominent sexual organ".[17] It is the weakness of such an argument that sets aside the reality of the head (without body) being called Reṇukā by the faithful by arguing that Reṇukā, who is said to be 'Pṛthvī' is, in fact, the headless and nude goddess:[18] The fact of history has to be seen as the 'head' (without body) being sometimes called Reṇukā (as at Mahur) and in some cases as Yellammā (Alampur). It is clear that the headless goddess, not having a clear single name, and hence taken as the earth-goddess, came to be called Yellammā and further as Reṇukā,[19] a familiar name from the popular myth that travelled from the north. As we have noted earlier, there is hardly any reference in Mb. to Reṇukā, or *Reṇukā-tīrtha,* as located in south India. The Vāyu P., referred to above, mentions her as being also called 'Kāmalī,' being the daughter of the king Suveṇu of the Ikṣvāku dynasty. This detail is not available in Mb.; but, the Harivaṁsa (which is an appendage to Mb.), which is one of the oldest of the Purāṇas and has close familiarity with the Vāyu P., mentions that Reṇukā, called also Kāmalī, was the daughter of the king named Reṇu (not Suveṇu, as mentioned at the Vāyu P.). There is no reference to the myth of Reṇukā and Jamadagni including Paraśurāma and the matricide in both; but the verse about Reṇukā is almost the same; actually the first line differs slightly, while the second is just the same (Hariv. I.27.38-39; cf.

Vāyu P. Uttara 29.86^{cd} - 87^{ab}). The date of the Vāyu P. is about 350 to 550 A.D. The Harivaṁsa has to be dated about 300 A.D. (The common line is *tasya kanyā mahābhāgā kāmalī nāma Reṇukā*). The Sk.P., as noted earlier, says that Reṇukā was seen by Toṇḍamāna in the form of an ant-hill. These two details, viz. Kāmalī and ant-hill indicate the embroidery to the original Reṇukā of Mb. The Sk.P. belongs to a period not earlier than the seventh century A.D., and then went on gaining in size, the later limit of the recognized and extant volumes being not later than the tenth century A.D.[20] The word kāmalī has the connotation of a 'lusty' woman; it also means 'sandy land', indicating particles of solid earth. This word, not used for Reṇukā earlier (Mb.) and appearing by about the fourth century A.D. for her, appears to have been suggested from: (i) The Mb. account where she is said to have harboured, though momentarily, a 'desire' for enjoyment (Kāma) outside and in the absence of her husband, when the tradition expected her to be the norm of perfect chastity; and (ii) Her name, which has *reṇu* ('particle of earth', or sand). The graph of connotation could be as follows:

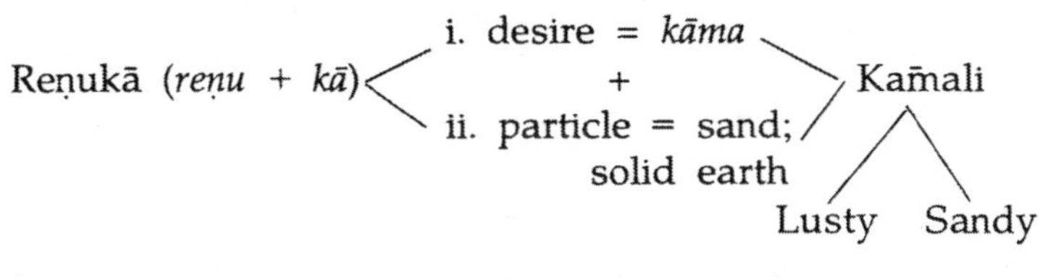

There is no definite geneological ground for Reṇukā; and the name of her father, Reṇu (Hariv. not to bother about Suveṇu at Vāyu P.) is suggested, without doubt, from her own name, Reṇukā. The name at Mb., is totally different; it is Prasenajit (Mb. Vana, 116.2). The Harivaṁśa and the Vāyu P. both differ from the Sk.P. in the additional point of identification of Reṇukā with the ant-hill which the latter introduces (and drops the word *kāmalī*), along with Toṇḍamāna. This gives a specific southern touch to the myth, which gets variously refashioned. The ant-hill has been known as having a unique importance since the Vedic period, as we have noted earlier. But, in the south it had gained the status of the mother-goddess. This is the position that appears in the detail of Toṇḍamāna. The divinity of the ant-hill, even as a male god, had already gained voguish importance in the early Pallava period (550 A.D. onwards) and gods previously worshipped in the form of the ant-hill came to be installed in temples. An example is that of the famous temple at Tiruvarur, which arose from the worship of Valmīkantha ('Ant-hill God').[21] The Pallavas and the Pāṇḍyas instituted a blend of the local Hindu faith and the Vedic Hindu gods in a bid to unite the various Hindu cults to thwart the Jain-Buddhist influence that was gaining ground.[22] This also brought about a fine blend of relationships between the northern mythical personalities and the southern, a fact reflected in the Reṇukā-Māriammā, Nāgāvalī-Anasūyā myths with the original northern male characters retained. Southern goddesses were married to northern gods as is seen in a number of myths.[23] About the myth of Reṇukā it appears clear that she, Paraśurāma and Jamadagni, got associated with Yellammā and Māriammā, and the region is prominently such a border of Karnataka and Andhra that also adjoins southern Maharashtra. The religious context was of the local goddesses who came to be associated, and later identified, with Reṇukā and her myth. The social need was of the emergence of the decadent Devadāsi cult, a diluted residue of the young girls termed *viralī* and *mātaṅkī* (=Mātaṅgī in Sanskrit indicated also as a goddess) that were dedicated to the king, as the human god, and were believed to be endowed with miraculous power. These girls now dedicated to the god or a goddess got Yellammā as their goal and also prototype. When the 'head'-goddess (having only the head) and also the headless goddess of no definite name but seen as the earth-goddess, were seen as Yellammā, and both got identified with Reṇukā, on the basis of the popular myth of the latter's severed head, the *devadāsī* softly came to be associated with Reṇukā. This is clear from the fact that, the girl to be initiated as a *devadāsī* has to be 'married' to Yellammā. She is, now, regarded as a 'boy'. But she has also to carry a basket in which the images of Reṇukā and Paraśurāma are placed; also, she has to wear a garland of cowri shells, (which is symbolic of the mother-goddess, cowri symbolizing the female organ). They go from house to house and ask alms of flour, which is called *jogavā,* at five houses. This is done every day. The vessel in which this *'jogavā'* is collected is called *'jog'*[24]. This shows how Reṇukā got to be associated with the customs which were, originally observed for the southern goddess Yellammā. In the earlier texts, Mb. and the regular Purāṇas, Reṇukā is not associated with such *jogavā*, or alms.

The identification of Yellammā with Reṇukā resulted in the transfer of the latter's myth of the severed head to the former due to only the head (or, only the body) being taken to be that of Yellammā, as we have noted earlier. The association of practices in connection with Yellammā to Reṇukā was a natural next step. But, we have also myths, originally in respect of Yellammā, tucked on to Reṇukā. One such myth may be referred to here. According to it, Reṇukā was once cursed by Jamadagni (Why? Was it because she happened to arrive late at the hermitage? No reason is given, which shows that this is not her regular myth), to suffer from a skin-disease. So she went to the *siddha*-s (persons having miraculous power) by name Ekayyā and Jogayyā, who were camping at Saumdatti (Savadatti) near a well called Jogul-bāvī. They advised her to apply turmeric powder to her body and take bath in the well (stepped well?). This she did over a period and got fully cured. She became lustrous. She expressed a desire that all who took bath likewise should attain cure of skin-diseases and gain lustre. Then she went to her husband.[25] This mythical account may be compared with another one, which is as follows: Once a rich man was staying at a place called Ugurugalla. Yellammā was his daughter. As she grew into youth she got afflicted by a skin-disease. Once she went to a place where there were the *pādukā*-s (wooden sandals) of Ekayyā and Jogayyā. (At holy places such sandals are made in stone and are installed). As she did penance there, rain-water that streamed from the *pādukā*-s drenched her, with the result that she was completely cured of the skin-disease. The place where this happened, and the *siddha*-s themselves appeared before her, was Jogul-bāvī. It came to be known as an important holy place. This myth is popular among the Vīra Śaiva sect. It is said, that males and females who get initiated in this Śaiva order get called Jogayyā and Jogammā, respectively, and can live together without marriage. The females *(jogammā*-s) get the status of a *devadāsī*. Yellammā also got a boon from the *siddha*-s that she would thereafter be worshipped by devotees who would arrive with jars filled with water, dance before her and pour the water there.[26] In other words, she remained there for good as a goddess. In this aspect her name is said to be Satyākkā ('True or reliable Sister'). This would indicate that she was not married or that she never went back to her husband. In the earlier account she is said to have returned to her husband. The variation is easy to explain. In the earlier account it is Reṇukā who, in keeping with the northern and original account about her, is married, and, in tune with it, has to return to Jamadagni. The second account, which is just a variation of the first, betrays the difference between the females. This is really a myth about Yellammā; it is tucked on to Reṇukā; but, it ill-suits the latter and, the original detail in her own myth could not be discarded. In the case of the Yellammā account, mentioned above, it is further said that her shrine became a holy place for the *devadāsī*-s. This explains why Yellammā is said to be the daughter of a rich man and without marriage. This suits the status of a *devadāsī.* According to another mythical account, as one head was severed by Paraśurāma, Reṇukā got another one in its place; and the chain continued. But, each time a head was cut a disease spread till there were a number of such diseases. So, Reṇukā got disgusted and decided to stay at that place (of the severance of the head) permanently. So, she stayed away from her husband, and also away from her sons. That is why, it is said, there are separate temples for Jamadagni and Paraśurāma at Savadatti. This is clearly an explanatory myth which serves to account for the separate temples; it is a 'charter'. In essense it has nothing to do with Reṇukā. It only serves to account for a goddess of diseases that is always out of the locality (cf. note 19). It does not state if she stayed with her fresh head, or without any head whatsoever. However, the indication is that some head stayed on and Paraśurāma did not cut it. But, this will not suit the original myth about Reṇukā and Jamadagni. This also will not suit the headless goddess, the so-called Lajjāgaurī, unless we assume that the last (?) head was cut (to conform to the original account of Reṇukā from the north), but Paraśurāma did not join it (which will go counter to the original account about Reṇukā). All this is because the two goddesses in question are originally different and are sought to be identified on the basis of the practice of worshipping only the head at one place, and the headless body at another. The crux of the whole discussion is that, though the Mother-goddess is essentially the earth-goddess and also a goddess of fertility, without being restricted to any one place or country, she has different connotations and varying functions in different places, in different periods, depending upon the beliefs prevalent there. Though these various goddesses are aspects of the general concept of the Mother, each of them could not be taken as being the same as the one that obtains at another place. So, Reṇukā could not be taken as the same as Yellammā, or Māriammā. Similarity in concept acts as a cause, or need, for the transfer of the myths of one to be capped on the other. But, similarity is not sameness. In such cases there is an effort to equate, which might result in identification. But, again, identification is a process wherein one assumes, or is made to assume, the characteristics and behavioural pattern of another, which only presupposes mutual independence and difference. In the present case, as the myth of Reṇukā got getting popular in the south of the Narmadā, various local goddesses got getting identified with Reṇukā due to the similarity between the severance motif in the myth and the twofold sculptures, or images of the goddesses, viz. 'trunkless head' and 'headless lower body' with prominent generative organ (*yoni*), the latter being also nude. In the same way, the nude goddesses of the later period may have a concept similar to that of the Vedic (earth) goddess (?) Mahānagnī but they can hardly be taken as the *same* as Mahānagnī, simply because of the word *nagnī*.

In the same way, the nude goddess without the head appears close in concept to the special vessel called *ukhā* used in the Vedic sacrifice as the 'mother of the fire god'; but, it has no other marks that characterize the headless nude goddess of later times, except teats on its four sides; at the brim it has something like a belt showing a *veṇī*-type (intertwined hair design).[27] A jar, or a pot, as the symbol of the Mother-goddess obtains universally.[28] As such, it is difficult to say if the 'below-the-waist' figures with prominent *yoni* have evolved directly from the Vedic context. The earliest such figure comes from Ter, in south of the Narmadā (actually in the present Maharashtra) and is attributed to the seventh century B.C.[29] If that was the Reṇukā, contemplated by Mb., some indication of that is expected in it. On the contrary, Mb. does not mention Reṇukā as nude. On the other hand, there has been a trend to believe that Yellammā and Reṇukā, who have been taken to be idolized in the 'headless' and the 'only-head' figures in Maharashtra and the border of Andhra with Karnataka, were nude. But, the 'only-head' goddesses are out of question as per nudity is concerned, as in their case the part lower than the face is not shown. In the case of the 'headless' figures, as we have observed, identification with Reṇukā is merely a surmise; because, there is hardly even a single clear reference to the nudity of Reṇukā.[30] This is not indicated even in the context of the *devadāsī*-s, who are generally taken to be associated with Yellammā and very rarely with Reṇukā. A myth from Maharashtra, which would *appear* to support the nudity of Reṇukā, might be referred to in this context. We have indicated the trend to identify local female divinities with Reṇukā for the reasons mentioned above. In the present case it is the goddess called Yamāee (Yamī of the Vedic tradition, the sister of Yama? Probably). The tradition prevalent in this region believes that Yamāyee is only another name of Reṇukā. So, in the context of her praise and worship, the popular myth about the severance of the head of Reṇukā is told; not without the usual expected embroidery! It is said, that after Paraśurāma severed the head of Reṇukā, Jamadagni was pleased with him. On suggesting that Paraśurāma should choose a boon and on knowing the desire of Paraśurāma that his mother should be rejuvenated, Jamadagni told him to cast the body (head and the rest of the body) into the sacrificial fire; that thereby she would attain a divine body and lead Paraśurāma to the place desired by him to go to along with his mother. This place is named Wadi-Ratnāgiri in the Kolhapur district (and not the Ratnāgiri on the western coast of India). Accordingly, Paraśurāma took the body of Reṇukā and cast it into the sacrificial altar. Reṇukā came out of it with a divine body and asked her son to lead so that she could follow. She warned him, however, that he should not look back and that, if he did, she would stop there and then, and never thereafter would meet him. As the twain went along the road, Paraśurāma was pinned by a strong urge to see if his mother was following him. He turned his head back to cast a glance (a common motif in such tales) at her.[31] Reṇukā got angry and stopped there. She was out only up to her umbilicus (navel-pit) and would not come out further. She said, "Hereafter I am not able to go...with the nude body". As she stayed there itself, the place came to be called Mātāpura, which is the same as Māhur[32] (Dist. Nanded,

Maharashtra). The point is, what could be gathered here about the form of the goddess called here Reṇukā? She was out up to her navel-pit. From the sentence, "I am not able to go, hereafter, with the nude body", read together with the sentence that she had come out up to her navel-pit, it would mean that she would not mind if this portion which is out is exposed to the public, but that hereafter if she came out she would be nude, as her lower portion will be out. This would also suggest that the image that is seen at Mahur is *not nude*. This exactly tallies with the image as it is; it is only the head. We have seen above, that the images of Mother-goddesses that are installed in temples are in the form of a head. This is true in the case of the image of the present idol of the goddess at Mahur, called Reṇukā, and also in the case of Yellammā. This is true also in the case of the myth of Māriammā-Yellammā, which does not support their being nude; after rejuvenation, they are whole, not just from the navel below to the feet. If we believe, and this against the actual image that is present at Mahur, that she came out and stayed nude, how do we contemplate her upsurge from the altar (or even from the earth)? If with head up, we have to accept the present position of the goddess. And there seems to be no reason to disbelieve the actual and lapse into a dark hypothesis. If one ignores the actual, and were to suppose that she came up feet first (to negate the existing 'head-up'='only head' position), it is expected that the idol be tapering (feet) up with a broad base (waist and navel). But, even this position would not tally with the 'headless woman with prominent sex-organ'; for, in these images the legs are seen, though folded at the knees and rested below. These difficulties would show that these figures are special Mother-goddess figures, and, not finding an exact mythical support, or any other record, they were tucked on to a popular myth about a popular figure. The fact is, that in the ancient Paraśurāma myth Reṇukā never appears as a nude woman. And, in the Yellammā myth, which is characterized by the head, the head is associated with such castes as the Madiga. This shows that, we have to look at the myth of Reṇukā, in its original form, shedding off her identifications, as we have noted the insecurity of the identifications in understanding the real meaning of the myth. Passingly we may note that, like other goddesses, Ekavīrā is also taken to be Reṇukā and that the latter is described as being nude. The point is, that nudity is not a distinguishing characteristic even of Ekavīrā, as there are cases where Ekavīrā is not nude;[33] she is shown with the 'head-only' pose. A comparative study of the homologues from the various accounts noted above would show the following:

1. Reṇukā, as she appears in the Jamadagni accounts from Mb. is a mortal woman; there is no indication of the Reṇukā-tīrtha being named after her. It is not improbable, that there was a popular goddess named Reṇukā and that the mortal Reṇukā was named after her, as the names of divinities are given to the mortals. The practice is seen even today.
2. This Reṇukā had acquired fame due to her chastity (and later became a centre of a pattern of myths involving the severance of head, which had become symbolic).
3. It was usual with her to go for bath to the river, away from the hermitage and fetch water. As she carried only one wearing on her body, she got it dried after bath at a quiet place, not frequented by others; she waited till the cloth got dried and immediately returned. Thus, for a short span of time

she remained naked feeling assured that nobody saw her.

4. Once, however, she saw a couple (royal; couples) that had come for a pleasure-trip enjoying a love-sport in the water of the river. This was a striking change from her usual secluded life, and she was attracted by it. She tarried a bit long, thorned by a desire for such fortune; but when she came to her own, she saw herself terribly upset and weak and pale. Her only cloth got soaked (with water that streamed out from the jar as she lost her balance? - cf. Mb. Vana, 116.8 *klinnā-ambhasi;* or perspiration due to a stroke of neurosis?).[34] The point deserves explanation.
5. She hastened home. Jamadagni saw her through and through, and gave his order.
6. Accordingly, her 'head was severed'. BUT, it was restored.

The last point raises the otherwise mortal Reṇukā to the status of a superhuman, setting her into the halo of divinity. It is not the case of an immortal woman being the wife of a mortal; for, in that case, she would control the fate of her husband. Here, as the myth goes, it is the husband who controls her life—he punishes her; chastises her. In the myth 'wet cloth' acts as a symbol; it suggests 'desire' and lack of chastity. It is also linked with temporary nudity. It contrasts with 'dried cloth', indicative of chastity. The same is the position when the myth is used in connection with Yellammā (=pseudo Reṇukā); but, here, in one case nudity is more clearly presented; for, the cloth is said to be flying overhead as she walked. With the mental unchastity, the 'ball of water' streams down and the cloth drops on her body getting wet. In the Alampur account, the jar is said to be made of fresh mud every day, and yet it held water.

There is no mention either of the cloth or if the woman (Reṇukā?), who is sought to be the same as the headless nude image, was wearing any cloth which got wet as the unbaked jar slushed out draining the water it miraculously held, due to the power of chastity in the person who held it. However, lack of chastity and the draining of water (causing wetness) are associated.

Like wetness that appears to be symbolic of the loss of chastity, the oozing or breaking (slushing out) of the jar symbolizes the same thing. In addition, it appears as the symbol of the head itself. In many places the head of the goddess is suggested by a jar, or the jar stands for the goddess herself;[35] and it is not improbable that the original concept behind the 'only-head' figure of the goddess was of a jar itself. In all such cases, the head is just round, without the neck, but with eyes shown with in-laid silver pieces with a black dot. The concept of a jar symbolizing the head goes back even to the Vedic period. Thus, the jar called *gharma* in the Pravargya rite was a triple round jar (i.e. looking as if three pots were placed one upon the other); and it was called the 'head of the sacrifice' and 'head of Viṣṇu'.[36] It was also called Mahāvīra. The wooden vessel used for keeping the juice of Soma was believed to be the 'head of Vṛtra'.[37] It is also said, that when Indra chopped off the head of the 'demon' Namuci, it contained the juice of Soma mixed with blood.[38] In the myth of Reṇukā, retold in south India, in one case the place of the water-jar is taken by the water-ball; but, thereby it does not lose its status as the container-jar. In all variations and modifications, it will be clear by now, that the breaking or vanishing of the container (of water) equals the severance of the head of the woman whose chastity is closely associated with the lack of blemish in the jar (container) she holds. This will mean, that the severance of the head cannot be actual. It is symbolic. The moment the severed head is rejoined to the body, the woman revives. The severance of head in this case, then, has a double symbolic value: (1) It stands for the tension at the thought of lack of chastity, which amounts to death for an emotional woman; and (2) It indicates atonement, and death as means to gain a new superior birth. The myth revolves on the point of contrast between mortal fallibility and the gain of divinity through torture and symbolic death, the same principle as obtains in initiation.[39] In addition the myth acts as a bridge between the mortal Reṇukā, wife of Jamadagni,[40] and the goddess Reṇukā—in all probability, a Mother-Goddess who had her *tīrtha*-s in the early B.C. period. As the myth travelled south, this chastened wife of Jamadagni came as the goddess Reṇukā, and was used to support the divinity of the 'only-head' and the 'head-less' goddesses; she was also used, through her myth, to heighten the status of Yellammā.

References

1. Examples of this type occur; cf. Mārk.P.16.25, ff., where a woman named Anasūyā does not allow the sun to rise; also Sk.P.VI.136.4-18; see Dange, *Encl. P.B.P.*, Vol. V., p.1614.
2. Vettam Mani, *Puranic Encyclopaedia*, p.340; this is said to be from the Brahmāṇḍa P., 60; the present writer could not find it in the standard edition of the said text. However, the myth is useful for study, as a variant.
3. S. Muzafer Ali, *The Geography of the Purāṇas*, New Delhi, 1973 (1966), p.138.
4. Henry Whitehead, *The Village Gods of South India* p.116f.
5. This is a very late aspect of the goddess, though; it is under the influence of Tantrism of a developed form.
6. Sk.P.II.i.9.87f. The practice was prevalent even earlier, cf.

Rām. Ayodhyā, 52.89, Sītā's promise to the Gaṅga. Rām. does not have Reṇukā.

7. Whitehead, *op.cit.*, p.74f.

8. *Ibid.*

9. Taitt.Br.I.1.3.4; **Kāṭhaka** Sam. 19.2

10. *Ibid.*; also **Mait. Sam.** I. 6.3 Śat. Br.VI.3.3.5 etc.

11. Saskia C. Kersenboom-story, *Nityasumangalī-Devadāsī Tradition in South India,* Delhi, 1987, p.197.

12. They are seven in number: Bīsalmāri, Guṇalmārī, Kelmārī, Vīraṇgere-mārī, Hiridevathī, Chammandammā and Uttahanahalliammā. Out of these Bīsalmārī is said to be the power of the sun, while Kelmāri is seen in the form of an earthen pot; see Whitehead, *op.cit.*, p.80

13. Whitehead, *op.cit.*, p.115; Bhṛgu, according to the Tamil language will be phṛhu; the labial sign stands for all the non-nasals in the class. The next step is pṛhu, as the aspiration shifts always from the first letter; and the conjunction almost always gets a vowel inserted; so *pi-ru-hu.*

14. Pandurang Desai, "Alampur" (in the Kannada language), *Prabuddha Karanataka,* Mysore Uni., Mysore, 25.2.1943, pp.25-30; also ref. to by R.C. Dhere, *Śaktipīṭhañcā Śodha* (in Marathi), Kolhapur (Maharashtra), 1973, p.28f. (The present author has retained the name Yellammā, as that is the pronunciation obtained among the folks. Ellammā is a bit refined; but, Yellammā is preferred also by Whitehead).

15. R.C. Dhere. *op.cit.*, p.20, where he refers to the *Kannada-Marathi*-Kośa, p.166.

16. R.C. Dhere, *op.cit.*, p.30

17. *Ibid.*

18. *Ibid.*, p.40f.

19. The Matsya P. (A.D.200-400), which is of the same period or earlier than the Vāyu P.(A.D. 350-550) and mentions over one hundred eight goddesses along with their places, does not mention Reṇukā (or Yellammā) though it mentions Ekavīrā in

Sahyādri (13.40), Mahālakshmī at Karavīra (v 41) and Piṅgaleśvarī aṭ Payoṣṇī (river; v 44). It should be noted, that, though the Matsya P.22.30ff. mentions many holy places, and Elāpura, it also mentions Alampura, suggesting that they are two separate places. They are mentioned immediately after Rāmeśvara, which is mentioned after Traiyambakeśvara (Tryambakeśvara), v 50. It also mentions Mātṛgṛha (v 76), the Prākṛta form of which will be *māu-ghara* and further *māu-hara,* which will give Māhur. However, the Purāṇa does not associate these places with the myth of Reṇukā (or Ellammā). Elāpura indicates a goodess named Elā, who, in the southern style would be Elā-ammā, the slang being Yellammā. The period of the Matsya P. is roughly 200-400, according to Kane, P.V., *History of Dharmaśāstra,* Vol.V, Pt.ii, Poona, 1977, p.900. Dates of the Purāṇa texts followed by the present author are those proposed by Kane, the said Vol., said place. Actually Elā or Ellā would indicate the 'boundary'; cf. Ellai-kal, Ellai-Karapu. In that case Elā (Ellā)-ammā would be outside the locality. The myth of her head at an impure place gets a new meaning, this way.

20. Kane, *op.cit.*, p.912; for Vāyu P., p.907.

21. Kersenboom-story, *op.cit.*, p.16 f.

22. *Ibid.*

23. *Ibid.;* cf. also Mīnākṣī and Somasundara, the latter being an aspect of Śiva; also Padmāvatī, near Tirupati, who has a temple, is said to be married to Śiva. The present author attended the yearly festival of this 'marriage' in November 1981.

24. Kersenboom-story, *op.cit.*, p.195f. However, *jogavā* is not restricted to the goddess Reṇukā or Ellammā. The present author, whose fourth generation ancestor was associated with the Ekavīrā temple at Amarāvatī (Maharashtra, Vidarbha) as chief priest by right (*vatana*), did beg the *jogavā* in a particular period in his boyhood, in the name of the goddess, though not at Amarāvatī.

25. *Kannada Viśva-kośa,* Vol.3,p.99. The present author is indebted to Shri Nadkarni, A.S. for this and the subsequent bits of information from the Kośa. Shri Nadkarni is a Kannaḍa writer.

26. *Ibid.*

27. Tait.Sam. V.1.6.4 where it is prescribed to be having two, four, or eight teats; it may be square or circular in shape. For a picture, see *Yajñāyudhāni*, Ed. T.N. Dharmadhikari, Vaidika Sam.Mandala, Pune, 1989, p.72; also, Dange, "Ukhā", *Proceedings of the All India Oriental Conference* (32nd Session), Pune, 1987, pp.151-57.

28. Sk.P.VII.1.167.97-98; for the south Indian context, see Whitehead, *op.cit.*, pp. 65; 77; 80 etc. Among the Aztecs, the jar was at once the Mother-goddess and the source of creation; see Mackenzie, D., *Myths of Pre-Columbian America*, pp. 167.170; 175; In India even to-day the goddess called Āṭhavī (i.e. the goddess of the eighth bright) is worshipped in the form of a jar.

29. H.D.Sankalia, "The Nude Goddess Or The Shame-less Woman", *Artibus Asiae*, Vol.XXIII-2, pp.111-23.

30. Even in the portion of the commentary *(bhāṣya)* of Bhāskaracāya on the *Lalitāsaharsranāma*, quoted by Dhere (*op.cit.*, p.36), the goddess at Alampur is not named Reṇukā.

31. Genesis, 19.12-13 Lot's wife looked back, against the instruction and got turned into a pillar of salt. According to one account, which was told to the present author, a person looked back and saw two serpents following him to attack him.

32. Dhere, *op.cit.*, p.41. Dhere proposes that the idol in question is nude, and that it is "not from the head to the navel-pit; it is from the feet to the navel-pit" and that "it is clear from the speech of Reṇukā that she cannot go ahead with the nude body". The point is, that the goddess was *believed* to be Reṇukā and even the folk-singer sings it that way. As has been already stated earlier, this is a case of identification and people's faith; it does not stand the test of historical analysis. Dhere admits that, "In such types of explanatory tales some openings of doubts do remain". To fill them historical details are more helpful.

    According to variant a account of this goddess, when Jamadagni was killed by Arjuna, the son of Kṛtavīrya, Reṇukā burnt herself on his pyre, assuring Paraśurāma, who was full of grief at this act, that Jamdagni and herself would again come to life; but that he should wait for a month, and then call her. However, due to impatience, as the month was almost over, but for a few days, he called her. At once Reṇukā came up from the place of the pyre, only with her face up and stopped. That is why, they say, only the face (*tāndaḷā* in Marāṭhī) is seen. This would indicate that she was not nude and cannot be identified as a nude goddess. For this variation see Moreshvar Tryambak Joshi, *Marāṭhavāḍyātil Śakti-darśan*, Igatpuri, 1979, p. 45.

33. This is at Amarāvatī in Maharashtra; see note 24 above. Photocopies of this 'Ekavīrā' are available.

34. Cf. the myth of Pārvatī and the rug of Śiva, mentioned above (p. 396). The severance of the head of the wife (here Reṇukā) is taken as the expression of sexual tension of the husband (Jamadagni). The release of this tension is acted by the son; see O'Flaherty, *Sexual Metaphors and Animal Symbols in Indian Mythology*, Delhi, 1981, p.89. O'Flaherty does not explain why the son acts in place of the father. Probably, the explanation is to be seen in the belief that the son is the 'father re-born', cf. Ait; Br.VII.13 (=33.1), *gāthā* 6th, "The father becomes the foetus and enters his wife, the mother; getting renewed in her (womb) he gets re-born in the tenth month". There is a folk-song current in Maharashtra, a line from which says, "lime is applied to the leaf of the plantain tree; (the result is) the wife delivers the husband, the tiny babe". 'Lime to the leaf' is symbolic of sexual union. The plantain tree is looked upon as a woman in folk-belief. In myths of this sort, beheading is said to be equal to castration, O'Flaherty, p.46, where she refers to Carstairs, G.M., 1958, *The Twice-born*, London, p.86.

35. See *n* 28 above.

36. Śat. Br. XIV.1.1.10f.

37. *Ibid* IV.4.3.4.

38. *Ibid*. XII.7.3.4

39. On this point see Dange, *Legends in the Mahābhārata*, pp.201-18, where he gives instances from various sources.

40. According to an embroidery of the ritual associated with Reṇukā, the goddess (the *devadāsī?*) breaks her bangles on the full-moon day; after one month, on the next full-moon day, she

wears new bangles. This is said to be done at Saudatti (Saumdatti). This is the enactment of the myth, according to which Jamadagni was killed by Arjuna Kārtavīrya, and was brought back to life. This is an account we have referred to earlier; Brahmāṇḍa P.II.3.26.41-II.3.27.69. At the account from Saudatti, Reṇukā is said to be the sister of Arjuna Kārtavīrya, *Kannada Visvakośa, loc.cit.*

Eighteen

Goddess and the Buffalo-'Demon'

The goddess (Devī) who subdued and then killed the demon called Mahiṣa (buffalo) is regarded as an important aspect of the goddess Gaurī, known also as Kātyāyanī and Durgā, the wife of Śiva. The account of the Devī and the destruction of the demon, Mahiṣa at her hands follows the set pattern in the Devī-mythology, which could be divided into three major parts: (i) The creation of the goddess from the powers (*śakti*-s) of various gods, as it is they who want her to destroy the demon, being powerless individually; (ii) The demon approaching the goddess with a desire to marry her; or he is enticed by the goddess to approach her; and (iii) The fight and the destruction of the demon. In the present case, Mahiṣa is introduced in the exploits of the Devī, directly, in the post-Mahābhārata period, though Mb. does mention the various goddesses. In Mb. these various goddesses are said to have accompanied Skanda, the son of Śiva, to destroy Mahiṣa (Śalya-parvan, 46.1-42). These goddesses were of various appearances and knowing various languages (*Ib.* one 'having a girdle of a hundred mortars', v 10; another 'a female cock', v 15; 'having the face of a hare and that of an owl' 22; 'having the ears of a cow', v 25; 'having the face of a she-buffalo', *Mahiṣānanā* v 25); yet, it is said to be Skanda Kārttikeya (the son born from the semen of Śiva, but outside the womb of Pārvatī; he was named Kārttikeya, as the six Kṛttikā-stars nurtured the semen), who killed the demon (Mb. Anuśāsana 14.214; Vana 231. 88-96). In the period later than that of Mb., the Devī is directly involved in the destruction of the demon, Mahiṣa, and not indirectly through Kārttikeya as the latter's follower in the battle. About the nature and birth of Mahiṣa we have interesting accounts. According to the Skanda P. (about the 7th-8th century A.D., VI.119.4ff) Mahiṣa was the son of the famous demon Hiraṇyāksa. He was in the habit of roaming, mounted on he-buffaloes of various types. As he was wandering this way, once the hoof of his mount injured the sage Durvāsas who was penancing. Getting angry, the sage cursed him to get turned into a buffalo for ever. On comprehending the calamity, this son of a demon, solicited the favour of Śukra, the preceptor of the demons. Śukra directed him to Śiva, being himself unable to undo the curse of the sage. When he approached Śiva, the latter also told him that the regain of his natural old form was impossible; but, he said that the son-of-the-demon would enjoy all pleasures. When he requested for the gift of the boon of immortality, Śiva said that he would not meet death at the hands of any male; but, that only the goddess Kātyāyanī (Durgā) would be able to kill him. So, the son of Hiraṇyākṣa was turned into a he-buffalo and, later, was killed by the goddess. According to an account from the Vāmana P. (about 600-900 A.D.[1] 18.42.ff), he was the son of the demon Raṁbha and Mahiṣī (*mahiṣī,* meaning a 'she-baffalo' and also 'queen'); but, Raṁbha was in the habit of taking the form of a he-buffalo, while Mahiṣī was a real she-buffalo. At another place the Skanda P., which places this myth against the background of the battle between the gods and the demons—a motif common with the other sources noted above—says that Diti (the mother of the demons, *daitya*-s as they are, hence, called) when she knew about the destruction of her sons at the hands of the gods, called one of her daughters and asked her to practise penance for the gain of a son who would vanquish the gods (the sons of her co-wife and sister, Aditi). Accordingly, this daughter took the form of a she-buffalo and did penance. Once, as she was getting through her penance, a sage named Supārśva approached her, and, on knowing the purpose of her penance, he gave her a boon that she would give birth to a son who would have the head of a buffalo and the rest of the body of a man. He also took her to his hermitage where she gave birth to the son as described above. According to the boon itself, this son, called Mahiṣa as he had the head of a buffalo, grew to be very powerful and started against the gods. The gods, afraid, approached Brahmā who gathered all the gods to devise a plan to control Mahiṣa. The gods, including Śiva, Viṣṇu, Brahmā and Indra got angry and their faces blazed forth with excessive energy. The mass of all this energy got fused into one and thence was produced the Devī, named Durgā. When the gods told her of the impending danger from the demon Mahiṣa, she assured them of her resolve to destroy him (to cut the long account of the gifts bestowed upon her by the various gods). She, then, went to the mountain Aruṇācala to practise penance. She posted four youthful boys on the four peaks of the said mountain with instructions not to allow anybody to the place of her penance; the only exception was that of a traveller who might be thirsty or hungry. Now, the buffalo-demon, Mahiṣa, was roaming in the vicinity of the mountain, hunting in the surrounding forest. His followers and servants chased the wild animals, who ran to the mountain and entered the hermitage of the goddess. The demons, chasing the beasts, followed in close pursuit; but, they were prevented by the boys. The demons, now, took, the form of birds and swiftly entered the place. They seated themselves on the branches of the trees and began looking for prey. Their chiefs got a full view of the beautiful goddess, deep in penance. They forthwith went to Mahiṣa and told him what they saw. Tortured by desire to see her, on hearing about her beauty from the chiefs, he took the form of an old man and approached the boys. He asked them the reason for this severe penance on the part of the young maiden. They told him, that she was desirous of a nine-fold ritual of marriage with Śiva; so she was in penance to please Śiva, who was not yet pleased. She would offer him a new-born wild cock, with the (season's) new fruits, pots of cooked rice and other such fresh and newly collected things, if her lord, Śiva, would be pleased and presented himself before her. On hearing this, Mahiṣa went to the goddess and showed his real form and told her that she should take him for husband; that he would obtain any thing in the world with the help of his nine treasure-houses. The goddess, however, told him that she was performing asceticism to obtain a mighty husband; that he should prove his might by fighting with her, if he wanted to marry her. Then there ensued a terrible battle, wherein the Devī took the form of blazing lustre and held various weapons in her numerous hands. The demon was terribly afraid and fled. Then he again challenged her, as he was instigated by the goddess to return for the fight. For this, she sent a sage named Sura-guru ('preceptor of the gods'). It is also said, that the face of this sage was that of a monkey. When the goddess killed the demon, she noticed a Śiva-liṅga in his throat. It is said, that, in fact, Mahiṣa was a devotee of Śiva; but, under the influence of the followers of the Jain or Buddha faith (the *kṣapaṇaka*-s), he had left worshipping Śiva; eventually, he tried to eat the Śiva-liṅga itself, which got stuck in his throat. Though she held many weapons in her hands, the goddess is said to have killed the demon with her short sword (*khaḍga*; the word originally has the meaning of the horn of the rhinoceros; the short sword was, obviously, curved). On noticing the Śiva-liṅga, and feeling sorry that she had killed a devotee of her lord, she went to the seer Gautama for some atonement. He asked her to worship Śiva at the Śiva-ȳaga (sacrifice in favour of Śiva), which was going on, on the mountain Aruṇādri ('Tawny mountain', the same as Aruṇācala). A celestial voice proclaimed that the place where the goddess killed the demon with the *khaḍga* would be known as Khaḍga-tīrtha (Skanda p. I.3.10.23ff).

It is to be noted in this context, that Mb., or earlier texts, do not mention the goddess as Mahiṣāsura-mardinī, nor do we have there such fuller mythical accounts of the goddess. On the contrary, Mb. has a prominent figurage of the demon, including his name, Mahiṣa, as noted earlier; but the stories regarding his birth and parentage are absent there. From the Puranic accounts it becomes clear, that Mahiṣa has, or is caused to have, infatuation for the goddess. This may appear to fall in the general pattern: 'To win the enemy seduce his wife', which obtains in such cases as of Tulasī and Viṣṇu, Sītā and Rāvaṇa and so on. Here the demon is not entirely anthropomorphic. On the contrary, he is mainly zoomorphic. This is clear from the account that occurs in the Vāman P. noted above. Even at the account from the

SK.P. (VI.119.4ff), we have referred to earlier, though he is said to be the son of Hiraṇyākṣa, an anthropomorphic demon, he gets transformed to the zoo-morph for good, and dies as a buffalo. Here is an account from the Varāha P. (about 1000 A.D. 95.3ff). According to this account, he was born from Māhiṣmatī who was the daughter of one Vipracitti. Though she was a human, once she assumed the form of a she-buffalo to frighten the sage named Sindhudvīpa. But the sage had already anticipated her mischief. So, as soon as she took the buffalo-form, he cursed her to have it for good. However, being entreated by her to help regain her original form, he told her that she would be a human again when she gave birth to a son in her present form of the she-buffalo. Later, it so happened that, as Sindhudvīpa was taking bath in the river Narmadā he happened to see a *'deva-kanyā'* (a divine maid; or, the daughter of a god) also taking bath in the river, just at some distance. Seeing her naked the sage got passionate and his semen got ejected. Lest it should go waste, he hurriedly collected it into a cupped stone, placed it there and went away. At about the same time, Māhiṣmatī happened to come along. she saw the liquid in the cupped stone and swallowed it, whereby she conceived. The result was that she gave birth to a son. He was Mahiṣa. Another detail in the account is that Sindhudvīpa is said to be staying and practising penance near the city Māhiṣmati, which is also the name of the maiden. The account would indicate that Mahiṣa was born to a buffalo mother from his human father; so, he was half buffalo and half human. This tallies with his iconographical representation according to which he was to be shown with the human half from the head to the chest, the lower part being that of a buffalo. Vipracitti occurs as the name of a demon chief in Mb. and

Māhiṣmatī was known even at the period of Mb. The account seeks to localize the myth at the city and on the bank of the Narmadā. That Mahiṣa is the son of Māhiṣmatī should be suggestive in this case. In any case, the relationship between the demon and the Devī appears to be twofold: (i) Zoomorphic demon wishing to marry an anthropomorphic goddess; and (ii) The slaughter of the 'loving' demon who could be taken as a pseudo god.

The twofold relationship mentioned above is to be seen in all the myths of Mahiṣa and the Devī. The iconographical representation of the demon and the Devī who kills him has continued from about the second century B.C. Matsya P. (third century A.D.), says that the demon should be shown with two (heads *dvi-śiraskam* 260.61). There is hardly any other demon, any goddess is said to have killed, who is so fortunate (!) to be shown with the Devī in icons with a beast-head, and for such a long time-span. The idols of the Devī killing the buffalo-demon are very common in India on the occasion of a nine-day festival of Durgā that marks the beginning of the reaping season (Autumn, October-November), and the cult has no ebb; it is growing in popularity. This would show, that the buffalo (apart from its association with the demon, here) has been as important as the goat (symbol for the fire-god), the bull (symbol and vehicle of Rudra-Śiva), the horse (symbol of the sun, and for victory)—all domesticated beasts—and the lion (aspect of Viṣṇu in his Nṛsimha *avatāra*, and the vehicle of the Devī herself). The importance of the buffalo-demon (Mahiṣa; in fact, the buffalo) is clear from the fact that, in the fight with the Devī, he is said to have assumed the form of a lion, leaving that of the buffalo.[3] Though the demon Mahiṣa appears in this myth, as the enemy of the gods and is killed by the Devī, in another context he appears as the vehicle of the goddess Cāmuṇḍā (Agni P. 135.7), diluting the monopoly of the god of death (Yama) whose popularly known vehicle he is! As an extension of his association with the god of death, it was customary to make a gift of a she-buffalo in favour of a dying person, the belief being that she would lead the soul of the dead to the region of Yama, whose vehicle her 'son' has been (Garuḍa P.II.21 15-16). Even otherwise (apart from the context of impending death) the gift of a she-buffalo was prescribed to please Yama (Agni P.211.5;6, where she is addressed as 'mother of Mahiṣāsura). This would show that the she-buffalo, as the 'mother' of Yama's vehicle, or of the demon *Mahiṣa,* was thought to be as important as the cow. In this connection the following reference is of particular importance. It is said that, once, the king Kuru came to the place where the river Sarasvatī streamed through the Plakṣa tree (*Ficus Infectoria*; a type of the Indian Fig-tree) in his wanderings. (It is implied that he was wandering with a band of followers for settling somewhere, say, like the Greek king Cadmus).[4] He liked the place and decided to till the land there. He made ready a plough and to it yoked the bull of Rudra on one side, while on the other he yoked the buffalo of Yama. He, then, produced various types of corn from his own body and sowed them. The place where this happened came to be called Kurukṣetra (Vāmana P. 23. 11-33). Though the myth refers to the bull as of Śiva and the buffalo as that of Yama, the fact is that Kuru used the common bullock and buffalo for the act of ploughing, a practice not uncommon in India and elsewhere.[5] Though the buffalo is the vehicle of Yama, the demonized buffalo has been associated with the myth of the Devī and Mahiṣa through the latter's association with land, in ploughing. A point to be marked is, that the buffalo is never mentioned as a sacrificial beast in the Vedic period, though Indra is said to have been honoured by Viṣṇu and the god Pūṣan by cooking a hundred buffaloes for him, and keeping ready three big containers (*sarāṁsi,* 'lakes') of the intoxicating juice of Soma for him to drink (ṚV VI. 17.11). Indra is also said to have cooked a *mahiṣa mṛga* (buffalo-beast; ṚV VIII.69.15) for (his?) father and mother (*pitre mātre*). Though the context is of the gain of rain from the cloud (as is clear from the previous verse, 14, "he broke open the moist food being cooked, with speech" i.e. mid-region speech, which is thunder), we may not underrate the actual practice that might have set afloat the image in the expression. Yet, the adjectival status of the word *mahiṣa* (in respect of *mṛga*) raises a doubt if the *mahiṣa*, here, is denotative of the common black buffalo. It should be noted, that Indra is addressed as *mahiṣa* (ṚV III.46.2) and is referred to as such (Ib. IV.18.11); so is the fire-god (I.95.9) and Soma (IX.82.3). Though the word *mahiṣa* appears at places as indicative of a domesticated beast (for IX.95.4, '*mahiṣa* being washed at a raised place'), the fact remains that there is no mention of its being *sacrificially* killed in the Vedic practice; and the reference to its being cooked could only be taken as indicative of special hospitality. Another point that deserves to be noted is that in the Vedic texts there is hardly any support for the practice of using a he-buffalo for agriculture, or for ritual-ploughing. This being the case, the Puranic mention of a buffalo along with a bullock (or, bull of Rudra), as noted above cannot be taken as reflecting the Vedic practice, though Kuru, and Kurukṣetra, are mentioned in the Brāhmaṇa texts. It is clear, hence, that the buffalo of Kuru, mentioned by the Vāmana P.

(600-900 A.D.), along with the bull is indicative of a post-Vedic practice. It is also very clear, that the buffalo-Devī relationship entered the Hindu pantheon after the Vedic period. In the post-Vedic phase of the Hindu religion, however, the Mahiṣa-Devī myth became very popular, the myth being a later vocal version of an earlier ritual involving the sacrifice of a buffalo to the Devī.

Various scholars have studied the images of the Devī in the act of killing Mahiṣa, marking also the difference in the presentation of the motif. These images appear from the early (or, pre-Kuṣaṇa period) i.e. the second century B.C. In the earliest of such sculptures the Devī is represented as seated and she kills the demon, in the form of the buffalo, holding him on her lap, pressing his spine to break it and pressing his neck.[6] It is this action that would suit the name of the goddess:—*mathinī/mardinī*. She holds a short trident in her hand, but it has nothing to do with the act of killing. In some cases of this period, the goddess is seen as pulling out the tongue of the buffalo. The goddess is shown with two or four hands. Lion is not shown as her invariable vehicle. In the later Kuṣāṇa period, however, lion appears as her vehicle. From the Gupta, and in the later, period the goddess is shown as having more than four arms. In one sculpture from the eighth century A.D. the face of the goddess is shown as that of a she-buffalo. This sculpture, from Gujar-kheri in Haryana (formerly part of Punjab) is unique. The goddess with the head of a buffalo and the buffalo-demon, form, as it were a couple.[7] We might recollect here, that one of the goddesses mentioned in Mb. is called *mahiṣānanā* (Śalya, 46.25), though she is not the 'killer of Mahiṣa'. In almost all of the early Kuṣaṇa sculptures the goddess is shown as killing the buffalo-demon by pressing her hands round his neck, though she has her weapons. The narrations from the Purāṇas have it that the goddess strikes the buffalo with her trident; then from its fore-part comes out a man with a dagger, the rest of the body remains as that of the buffalo; the goddess pulls him by the hair and cuts his head with the short sword (=dagger) in her hand (cf. Vāmana P. 21.48-49). In the sculptures from the early Kuṣāṇa, or the Gupta period, there is hardly any clue to the peculiar relationship between the goddess and the demon. What appears is only an act of the Devī killing the buffalo—and a tender one for that matter—which would indicate an offering of the buffalo to the goddess who herself kills it. As we have noted earlier, in Mb. the exploit of killing Mahiṣa is directly associated with Kārttikeya, though the goddess(es) accompany him. However, Kārttikeya is not termed *mahiṣāsura-mardana* (or *mahiṣāsura-mathana*), nor is the goddess so termed. In a later appendage to Mb. (Virāṭaparvan, ch.6.29) the goddess Durgā is called *mahiṣāsuranāśinī*. Though it is difficult to see what exactly the concept behind the demon Mahiṣa was in his enmity with the gods, it is fairly clear that, in the killing of the buffalo-'demon' by the goddess we have the concept of the sacrifice to the earth-goddess, as will be seen in our discussion later. As it is, Mb. refers only to the demon being killed at the hands of Kārttikeya. The myth of the birth of Kārttikeya (Mb.Śalya 44.5ff) and his consecration to the post of the commander of the army of the gods, leading to the destruction of Tāraka and Mahiṣa (Ib.Ch.s 45 and 46) would suggest that, as soon as he was born, and was nurtured by the Kṛttikās (the stars in the constellation of that name), he was taught all lores and was appointed to destroy the demons. The name would suggest the autumnal season (the month of Kārttika). Another indication, though subtle, is that the army under the leadership of Kārttikeya appeared like the sky in the autumnal season (46.56 *śāradī dyaur iva*). This corresponds to the festival of Durgā, which has a long tradition, in India and which is held in October; it also marks the period of some new crops and the sprouting of some other crops. The festival goes on for ten days from the first day of the white half of the month of Āśvina to the tenth. The tenth day is called 'The tenth of victory' (Vijayā-daśamī). The very next month is called Kārttika. One of the most important aspects of the goddess Durgā is of fertile earth, who is worshipped also in the form of sprouted seeds and is called Gaurī. Like the ninth, the tenth day, mentioned above, is marked by animal offerings to the goddess; but on the tenth a he-buffalo is slaughtered. Looking to the continued practice of installing the idols of the goddess during the autumn season, which is also referred to in the Purāṇas with the detailed instructions about the depiction of the goddess and the buffalo-demon, it could be safely admitted that the sculptures of the Devī and the buffalo were symbolic of the earth-goddess being propitiated with the sacrifice of the buffalo, which was a major factor in the ploughing of the field. A question may be asked: 'When both, the bull and the buffalo, are associated with the ploughing of the land (as is clear from the myth of Kuru, and also from actual practice in some parts of India) why is it that only the buffalo is sacrificed?' The answer is, that the Vedic practice of sacrificing a bull to Rudra (in Śūlagava) came to be rejected in the period that followed the end of the compilation of the Gṛhya-sūtras in view of the practice of releasing a black bull (*vṛṣotsarga*) which was already in vogue. The sanctity for the cow and the resultant sympathy for the bull (bullock) also account for the general extinction of the sacrifice of the bull. Even so, myths (of the charter type) got to be told and heard, as a ritual, on important occasions connected with the sprouting of the crops, wherein there is clear indication of the discarded practice of such sacrifices.[8] Equal sanctity was not bestowed upon the he-buffalo, whose sacrifice was adapted later in the case of the Devī from some non-Vedic source. The mention of the cooking and even eating of buffaloes in ṚV does not support ritual-killing, or sacrifice, as we shall see later. The sculptures are mute about the relationship between the buffalo and the Devī (and naturally so); but, the accounts in the Purāṇas show the buffalo-demon as being desirous of marrying the Devī, or having infatuation for her. In the context of vegetation, as indicated above (and shall be further probed) the relationship between the buffalo and the Devī is twofold: (i) As a seeder; and (ii) as a victim. For the first we may refer back to the myth of the Rathva, where Nandyo is the substitute husband of the earth, the wife of Ābh Kaṇbi; and for the first and the second, taken together, we can compare the Horse-queen couple at the Vedic Horse-sacrifice and the Vṛṣākapi-Indrāṇī in the myth from ṚV noted earlier[9]. The difference is that, in the case of Vṛṣākapi-Indrāṇī and the Nandyo-Earth 'wife', the male who is to be substituted for the husband is not a demon; and, in between Vṛṣākapi and Nandyo the latter is not sacrificed—that is, there is no evidence in the myth to that effect. The demoniac status of Mahiṣa falls in line with a pattern that developed in the post-Christ (=Puranic) period when a god's rival who coveted the god's wife came to be looked as a demon. Conversely, a god is seen as taking the wife of a demon deceitfully; but, the situation came to be explained by stating that the woman was, in fact, the wife of the god himself in her former life (cf. Tulasī).[10] In the case of

Mahiṣa it is also said that he was, in fact a devotee of Śiva; but that he became a demon as he came under the influence of some Buddhist or Jain sages and swallowed the very *liṅga* of Śiva (Sk.P.I.3.10.23ff) This element is introduced, obviously, due to the social status that these non-Vedic faiths had gained by the eighth century A.D. (Sk.P., period about 700-900 A.D.). The fact seems to be that the element of sexual advances of the 'demon' Mahiṣa towards the Devī had by that time come to stay as a very important part of the myth,[11] and it had to be explained away. However, thus also, the fact remains that the Devī and the 'demon' buffalo were believed to have a unique relationship with the double aspect: seeder-victim. This placed the buffalo in line with the victims that act as a scapegoat and stand for, not only the sacrificer but also the god. In the myth of the Devī and Mahiṣa (and other such myths), the sacrificer is absent; but, the victim does stand for the god, whose wife the former tries to appropriate, getting sacrificed ultimately. We can draw the following parallelism:

Instance	**Husband**	**Pseudo-husband**	**Wife**
Vṛsā-kapi	Indra	Vṛṣakapi (killed)	Indrāṇī
Horse-sacrifice	Sacrificer (king)	Horse (killed)	Queen (called Mahiṣī)
Rathva-myth	Ābh Kaṇbi	Nandyo (-)	Kaṇbi's wife

In the case of Mahiṣa the *liṅga* in his throat is for suggesting that he is divine (or, at least, the cruel aspect of the divine), here Śiva (though not directly created from the anger of Śiva). The unique relationship between the 'demon' Mahiṣa and the Devī tends to make Mahiṣa the alter ego of the Devī's husband. In the present case, as the Devī is Durgā (Pārvatī), Mahiṣa becomes the alter ego of Śiva. The *liṅga* in his throat makes the point clear. That the buffalo was not looked upon as a demon appears to be indicated from the fact, that in the pre-Kuṣāṇa sculptures the beast is shown as of a tender age; in the instruction for preparing the idol of the 'Devī killing the buffalo' the beast is prescribed to be looking three year old. In certain sculptures of the early Kuṣāṇa period the Devī is seen as looking affectionately at the buffalo.[12] In an interesting tradition from Orissa about the myth, noted by Parpola, the buffalo (Mahiṣa) was allowed to kiss the generative organ of the Devī when he was about to die.[13] This would indicate that Mahiṣa was not conceived as just a demon, or a rival for the fortunes of the gods; he was seen as a virtual pseudo husband of the Devī, who would marry him if he was capable of defeating her. The myth, in all its variations, is clear on this point. Even outside the Purāṇas, the motif is seen. Here is a myth from among the Baiga tribe residing on the border of Madhya-pradesha and Orissa in India. According to it, the god Bhainsāsur (='buffalo demon'; *bhains* is from *mahiṣa→mhains→bhains*) has his abode in water-reservoirs like tanks, i.e. where the water is stagnant. The Baigas keep she-buffaloes, on which their tribal economy depends; for procreation of buffaloes they keep also he-buffaloes. As the procreator of the wealth of buffaloes, the beast is held in high respect. Whenever any she-buffalo gets a calf born to her, the owner of the buffalo propitiates the god in a unique way. The god Bhainsāsur is offered a sacrifice of a pig. A young one of a pig is held by its hind legs and it is dashed and killed in between the horns of the she-buffalo that delivered. The myth about Bhainsāsur is as follows: Once Mahādeva and his wife, Pārvatī, were having their usual round of the earth. On the way, they saw in a field a mock-he-buffalo placed to serve as a 'sacrecrow'. They went near and invested it with life. When the buffalo rose up with life, he was infatuated on seeing Pāṛvatī, whom he decided to marry and ran after Mahādeva (-Śiva) to kill him so that he could have Pārvatī for himself. Afraid of Bhainsāsur, Śiva ran for help to Bhagavān, the chief god of the Baiga. On hearing from Śiva about the danger, Bhagavān took the form of Pārvatī; he deceived Bhainsāsur and ultimately killed him. In this myth, which is incensed with the popular Hindu myth, the buffalo (not a demon here) is killed by the tribal high god Bhagvān in the form of Pāṛvatī (cf.Viṣṇu-Mohinī killing Bhasmāsura). Yet, Bhainsāsur has his unique importance; because he is believed to be still present as a presiding deity of the buffalo-progeny.[14] This would indicate that the buffalo-god (demon?) was uniquely respected in this tribe, and it is not improbable that it was so with other tribes where the buffalo was the centre of their economy and even was used in agriculture. An example in this case is of the Toda tribe from the Nilagiri region in South India. Among the Toda there is a regular worship of a buffalo (both the male and the female). According to a belief current among these people, the soul of the dead gets an opportunity to serve the buffalo if the person took proper care of the buffaloes in his lifetime.[15]

The sacrifice of the buffalo to the Devī at the autumnal festival, the depiction of the Devī and the buffalo-demon as per the myths at the Purāṇas at this festival and the special relationship between the Devī and the buffalo (=god/demon), Mahiṣa, make it clear that, in essence, the myth has the fertility of the earth (tillable land) as the main theme. The battle-motif is a pattern fitted to it as an extension of the god-demon fight. Though the myth may be seen as a step in the development, or evolution, of the Bhakti-cult[16], it could be safely taken as an embroidery to the original content, viz. the sacrifice of a pseudo-husband, in many cases a zoomorph, for the gain of manly power to the real husband (=sacrificer; cf. Indra at the Vṛṣākapi) or for the fertility of the field and royal glory, or a son (cf. Horse-sacrifice). The sacrifice of the buffalo is current throughout India. In south India, at the said festival (called Navarātra[ī] at all places, throughout India) there obtains the following practice, even today. When the buffalo is sacrificed, its head is severed; its front right leg is cut off and it is placed in its opened mouth. On the head, placed before the goddess, the fat of the buffalo is arranged and, in it, a wick is lighted.[17] The lighting of a wick is common in the north also, but not the placing of the foot in the mouth. Another practice that obtains in the south is that, after the head is severed, its blood is mixed with the rice that is already cooked and kept ready earlier. This mixture is sprinkled along the street as the procession is taken out later. While the mixture is sprinkled a person goes on shouting loudly, "*poḷly poḷly*", which words means, "food", "prosperity".[18] This would make it clear, that the sacrifice of the buffalo was for prosperity in crop. This practice obtains from the Karnataka region and in some places in Tamil Nāḍu adjoining Karnataka. A practice from the Andhra province is yet more suggestive. At a festival which is celebrated in the last month of the year, and at the end of it, which is the time of the gathering of the crops, or in the Spring season, the goddess Nukallammā and other six goddesses, which are her attendants, are to be worshipped and propitiated with the sacrifice of a buffalo, with the usual method of severing his head. Its blood is collected in a large hollow plate and it is kept in front of the goddesses. In it nine types of corn, whose seeds show two parts (*dvidala*), like the pulses, are dropped. Then the door is closed. None is allowed to open it and disturb the plate for three days. On the fourth day the door is opened; the seeds of the corn are traced and taken out with care, washed and examined. The corns whose seeds show sprouts are believed to be in plenty for the ensuing year.[19] The last month of the year is Phālguna, and the month immediately preceding it is Māgha. Like the autumnal season (Āśvina-Kārttika), this season is believed, in the Hindu tradition, as very auspicious. This latter one is seen as the period when the earth gets ready to be 'seeded' by the sun-god.[20] It is about this period (Phālguna, bright, 8th onwards) that the ancient Vedic Horse-sacrifice started and, after one whole year during which the horse was led to roam through various regions, the next year (in the month of return) he was sacrificed. This buffalo is sacrificed to the Devī; and, if we connect the ritual with the popular myths, told above, it would mean that it was sacrificed as her male-partner, in her aspect of the earth. This also explains why the buffalo is called 'Devara-konā' or 'Devara-poṭu,' bestowing divinity on it.

There is another myth current in south India, out of the context of ritual, but involving the motif of the Devī and the husband, though real here. Before we take it up, we would better recollect that the demon (buffalo) Mahiṣa is on a lower level than the Devī, though he is said to desire to marry her. Now, the myth that we are to examine concerns humans; but, the wife is of the *brāhmaṇa* caste, while the husband is of a very low caste though he is as educated as a *brāhmaṇa*. The myth occurs in two versions. According to one version, there was a sage of the *brāhmaṇa* caste who had a beautiful daughter. This girl happened to be seen by a youth belonging to the *cāṇḍāla* caste, who was struck by her beauty and decided to marry her. So, he decided to go to Kāśī (Vārāṇasī) to learn the *śāstra*-s. Having reached Kāśī, he arranged to stay with a learned *brāhmaṇa* and learnt various lores. After staying away from his native village for many years, he returned a changed man. As he was away for a considerable length of time and now acted as a *brāhmaṇa*, with knowledge enhancing his personality, nobody recognized him (the point whether he originally belonged to the village of the girl, or was from a different village, is of no consequence here; because such reasoning is out of question for a myth). He contacted the girl, who had remained unmarried (for reasons not to be questioned), and won her love. He expressed his desire to marry her and she consented. When she asked the permission of her father, he did not show any objection. On the contrary, he was glad as he would get such an educated son-in-law! The girl and the youth were married and had children. Time rolled on. The children grew in age and everything went on smoothly. Once it so happened, that the man saw his sandal broken as he was about to go to the river to take bath. So, he sat down and started mending the sandal with easy skill. One of the children watched this curious act on the part of his father; he was amused and reported it to his mother. She was taken aback by the skill of her husband, which was unusual for anyone other than a cobbler. As she was the daughter of a sage, she saw through her innate power that the man, her husband, was really from the cobbler caste. Getting angry at the thought that she had been deceived, she cursed him saying that she would become the goddess Mārī and that her husband would become a buffalo, who would be sacrificed to her every year; also; that her children would become goats and hens to be sacrificed to her. This came to be true in an instant. The myth is prevalent in the Tamil region and also in Karnataka.[21] According to another version, current in some parts of Andhra and Tamil Nadu, there lived in a village a poor man who had been a petty revenue officer (*karṇam*). He had retired and had lost his sight. He had a daughter of marriageable age. At about the same time a young boy, well versed in *śāstra*-s came to stay in that village. Though he gave himself as a *brāhmaṇa,* nobody knew that he belonged to the *parāyā* caste (which is considered to be lower even than the *śūdra*). He influenced people by his erudition. They thought, that he could make a good husband to the daughter of the *karṇam*, who was blind and poor and could not move out to find any suitable boy for his daughter. They convinced the *karṇam* and he gave his daughter in marriage to the youth. The couple lived on happily in the village, as the youth had nowhere to go. They also begot children. After a length of time, a person from the village of the young man came to this village and recognized him. But, seeing that the young man was enjoying confidence of the residents of the village, he maintained silence about the real caste of the youth. He went home to his own village, where the youth's mother was residing and did not know for long where her son had gone. This man told her that he saw her son. As she desired to see her son, he directed her to the village where her son now lived. She went to the village and stayed in the locality of the people of her caste. Once the young man, the hero of the myth, chanced to pass by the locality and was struck with amazement as he saw his old mother sitting by the side of a well there. He hesitated, but decided to bring his mother home. However, he got her changed completely, without anybody getting to know of his plan. As she was a widow, he shaved her head as is the practice in the case of the *brāhmaṇa* women. He also attired her in clothing suitable to a *brāhmaṇa* widow. He did not forget to warn her that she should never utter any word anywhere; not in the house, specially! Once in the house, he told his wife that the old widow was his mother; but, he specifically told her that the old lady was dumb, which was a precaution against the betrayal of her caste due to her language. The wife was also glad and so were the children. After a few days, the wife prepared a special delicacy, vermicelli milk-soup (*sevigeyi pāyasam*), popular among the higher class people. When the old lady sat for meals along with his son and grand-children, she was delighted to see the special dish which she had not known earlier. In her excitement she exclaimed, "O! How nice; it looks like the entrails of animals we are used to!". Her son, his wife and the children were shocked to hear this. While wrath was added to shock in the case of the wife, it was a sense of shame that seized the husband. The old woman had betrayed her caste not only through her taste but also through her speech. But, the wife kept quiet. When, after all had taken their meals, the husband went out for work and the children to school, the wife decided to atone for the sin that she had committed by marrying a *parāyā*. She remained without food, closed the door of her house and set herself on fire. When her body was completely destroyed, she appeared in the centre of the village with the power of her virtue but as a goddess! (She was called Mārī, or Māriammā). She loudly censured the people for being instrumental in getting her married to a *parāyā* and proclaimed that she would destroy them all for this sin on their part. But, they wept and entreated her to pardon them and stay on in the same village. By and by she was pacified. she accepted their request on the condition, that they should seize her husband and bring him to be beheaded before her. This was done. On seeing that, her children began to abuse the people. The goddess, however, looked lovingly towards the children and told them that, in the next birth, they would be her specially favoured worshippers. This was done. They became the people of the Asadi sub-caste of the Mālā caste. That is why only people of this caste are chosen as the special priests for the goddess. Her husband, when beheaded, came to be born as a buffalo; he came to be sacrificed every year before his wife, who became the Devī.[22] (A further version of this myth is recorded, which will be examined later, below).

It will be seen that both these versions use the motif of the annual ritual of the sacrifice of the buffalo to the Devī, and they also reflect the peculiar relationship between the Devī and the buffalo-victim. A point to be noted is that the Devī is not Durgā, Pārvatī or Kātyāyanī as is the case with the Mahiṣāsura myth. Yet, the essentially lower status of the husband is exactly the same as Mahiṣa. There is an important difference. Here there is marriage between the parties, while in the Mahiṣa myth it is not so. Also marriage is in the earlier phase; not when the female gets the status of the Devī. The goddess Mārī in this myth is due to her being the popular goddess in south India. We may compare the case of Reṇukā, who is replaced by Māri in that myth. It is very clear that this new myth is fashioned on the Devī-Mahiṣa myth, as a meta-myth, as the characters in it are changed with an apparent purpose in view. The purpose appears to be manifold. While in the case of Māriammā and Yellammā the status of the goddess is sought to be elevated by making them the wives of a person of a higher caste (Paraśurāma, *brāhmaṇa*), in the case of the *brāhmaṇa girl* in the present meta-myth she is shown to regain her original status and even to improve upon it by a fire-ordeal. Reversely, her husband is made to throw off the garb of a higher status and revert to this original status; but, he improves upon it by his sacrifice to the goddess, thus keeping the unique relationship and contact through ritual. Thus, this meta- myth and the original myth of other Devī and Mahiṣa have the pseudo marital relationship in common. Though this pseudo relationship might appear to have been borrowed from the Devī-Mahiṣa myths, the source of which is in the agricultural belief about the plough or the buffalo (bullock in other cases) being the 'seeder' victim—also maintained in the present metamyth—the function has a shift. The function here is primarily to bestow status on the Āsādis who are privileged to be functionaries at the festival of the Devī. Though the Devī in this case is not Pārvati-Kātyāyanī, Mahiṣa is substituted by the husband of the girl and, later, is actually the buffalo. This would indicate that the Mahiṣa-Devī relationship is not restricted to Pārvati-Kātyāyanī and the buffalo. The main characters have to be taken as a general Devī (=earth; ploughable field) and a buffalo, not necessarily a demon. This is exactly the position in the early Kuṣāṇa sculptures, when an elaborate myth of Mahiṣāsuramardinī was yet to have any shape. The myth is absent in the Mb., though the text refers to the Devī at one place (Virāṭaparvan 6.15, Gita Press Ed.) as *mahiṣāsuranāśinī*; but, even the authenticity of that reference is doubtful as the chapter is not found in the early manuscripts.[23] Once the myth became popular, it came to have versions and variations. However, the meta-myth from south India appears to have less influence of the popular myth from the Purāṇas. On the contrary, it appears to be directly influenced by the practice of sacrificing a buffalo to the Devī, the latter being the ploughable field requiring the blood of the buffalo for the sprouting of the grains placed in her (cf. the Andhra custom noted above).

x x x

In this context it is necessary to consider some points made by Parpola (*op.cit.*) though it is not possible nor is it required to attempt a full appreciation of his paper on Mahiṣa and the metamorphosis of Prajāpati. However, we may mention that he has tried to prove that Prajāpati and even Varuṇa have some trait of the myths about Mahiṣa. According to him the Devī-Mahiṣa myth current in south India (not the one we have recorded; he does not mention it) is one among such as have been tampered with and changed by the later Brahmanic ideology imported from north India. This influence eliminated the particular idea of the god's death, which marked the original such myths, projecting it into the goddess's fight with the demon. He proposes that the original motif was of the "divine marriage" and the murder of the male spouse for his rebirth (his paper, p.276). Looking from this angle the myth of the low-caste husband and the *brāhmaṇa*-girl from south India, though a very late one and not having the status of the strictly divine marriage, would support Parpola's observation (following Shulman, Davis Dean). Following Heesterman, J.C. and Rolland, P., he suggests that myths and rituals like that (of the buffalo and the Devī and) at the Horse-sacrifice having the sexual element in it were borrowed from the Vrātyas by the Vedic people and that they were associated with the raiding expeditions that started after the rainy season and were marked with festivity. Alternately, they also marked the return from the raiding season by Spring (p.277). This could be borne out by the present day practice of the festival of Durgā in the Autumn and the Śabarotsava (which has mostly become extinct) associated with it to be preformed with sexual language (*bhaga-liṅga-kriyā-śabdaiḥ*), while the Spring festivity is attested by the Horse-sacrifice, which was performed also in Jyeṣṭha-Āṣādha (i.e. Summer). Though the texts (Taitt. Br. 1.8.4.1. and Śat. Br. V.5.2.3-5) do not clearly prove the point of "raids" to "appropriate the barley harvest in the east", we have indication of a military march starting after the rainy season, in Autumn, with the practice of advancing to the east on the first stretch (cf. Raghuvaṁśa of Kālidāsa, IV.24;28). Now if the march was for raid, one wonders why there was sexual element in the festivities that marked the Mahāvrata, and even the Horse-sacrifice that is taken as originally belonging to (or developed under the influence of) the Vrātyas. Even the Durgā feast, it is argued, has the same function as the (pre-) Vedic Vrātyastomas, as it is connected with war expeditions (p.277). That sex and sexual abuse is a marked trait of these Vedic sacrifices and of the Devī-festivals is accepted by Parpola, and others who have written on the topic and whom Parpola follows. We have mentioned above a myth from south India about the low-caste person marrying a *brāhmaṇa* girl. Here is another one, and associated with the ritual at the Devī-festival. According to it there were two sisters, named Dayāmāva and Durgāmāva, daughters of a *brāhmaṇa*. A person of the Holaya or the Mahar caste fell in love with Dayāmāva, seduced her into believing that he was a *brāhmaṇa* and married her (as is the case in the myth we have already seen). Years rolled on and they had children. One day the mother of the Holaya came to dinner to them. In fact this mother was Mātaṅgī (this is the name of a goddess, and the word indicates also a low caste; in Maharashtra it is called Māṅga, whose profession is to skin dead animals). While eating sweet cakes she told her son that they tasted like roasted buffalo-tongue. Dayāmāva was horrified to hear this and came to realize that her husband was of the Holaya caste. She put all her children into the house of Mātaṅgī and set it on fire. She ran after her husband to seize and kill him. But, he fled taking the form of a buffalo. However, Dayāmāva caught him and killed him.[24] This is the myth.

In practice and ritual Dayāmāva and Durgāmāva have their shrines near each other's. This would show that Dayāmāva is originally a south Indian goddess, while Durgāmāva is north Indian. Mataṅga and Mātaṅgī do not occur in the Vedic period. According to Mb. (Anuś.27.8) Mataṅga was the son of a *brāhmaṇa* woman from a non-*brāhmaṇa*. According to a mythical pattern current through the Hindu tradition from Mb. and through the Purāṇas, Mataṅga was a *ṛṣi* who had become a *vyādha* (hunter) due to some curse; but he performed a Soma-sacrifice in which he was helped by Viśvāmitra (Mb.Ādi 71.31-33), indicating that he was admitted into the Vedic fold. Mātaṅgī also occurs in Mb. but not in the Veda. Here (Mb.Ādi 66.61 and 66) she is said to be born from the anger of a cruel goddess named Krodhavaśā. In the later period (Purāṇas) she appears as a formidable goddess. This would indicate the gradual integration of the Vedic and the non-Vedic and also the southern and the northern cults to form a Hindu society. In shrines, and when they are in a *yātrā* (ritual procession), the idols of Dayāmāva and Durgāmāva, prepared from several pieces of wood, are carried close to each other, the former painted red while the latter green. Once every third or fourth year a special festival is held in May in honour of Dayāmāva and at the close of every fair (*yātrā*) a fine male buffalo is sacrificed to her. Though the festival is said to be for Dayāmāva, Durgāmāva's idol is also given prominence. Prior to the sacrifice, the buffalo is washed; turmeric and *kumkum* (red in colour) is applied to his forehead; he is also decorated with sandal-paste marks and a garland of margosa (*neem*) leaves is placed round his neck. The head-man of the village is given two necklaces (called *maṅgala-sūtra*), which he puts round the neck of the two sister goddesses; also two nose-rings are placed in their noses (these are the special decorations for a bride and a married woman in India; *maṅgalasūtra* is the term used in Maharashtra; its meaning is 'auspcious thread'. It is cut away when the husband dies and also the bangles of the woman are broken). Thus decorated, the goddesses are brought out of their shrines. Here a person of the *mādigar* (also called *mādigā*) caste (tanner) comes on the scene. He represents the brother of the husband (who is said to have concealed himself as the buffalo) of Dayāmāva. He advances to the front of both goddesses, holding a handkerchief-tucked and bell-tied stick in his hand. He faces the goddesses, especially Dayāmāva, and calls aloud the names for her private parts continuously till the carts of the goddesses are taken away out of the village. This is the ritual for the morning till noon. In the evening people of the Āsādi caste (a subdivision of the Mādigā or the Māṅga, cf. *mātaṅga*) dance before the goddesses, wearing fantastic clothes. They beat the drums and play music, while the 'brother-of-the-husband' (he is called *ranigia*) continues to shout filthy words and sexual abuses relating to the private parts of the goddesses*. Eventually the buffalo, who represents Dayāmāva's *mādigā* husband and is called *paṭṭaḍakoṇa* ('holy buffalo'; cf. *devarakonā or devarapoṭu* as he is called in the Andhra-Karnataka region; Whitehead, p.78, 56, 82) is sacrificed by severing his head, which is kept in the hut said to be of Mātaṅgī. The bangles and the *maṅgalasūtra*-s of the goddesses are broken.[25]

Though in the myth mentioned above there is hardly any trace of a raid, the element of sex is very prominent. So is the case with the Horse-sacrifice, a point noted by Parpola and others. and, even if we accept the hypothesis of raid, the element of sex has to be explained; or, should we suppose that all such instances of raid are to be believed as culminating in orgies and sex? There is certainly a close similarity between the Devī festival and the Horse-sacrifice; but, whereas in the Mahiṣa-Devī myth and ritual, as it obtains in south India, there is a clear motif of marriage, there is nothing of that type in the Horse-sacrifice nor in the Devī-Mahiṣa ritual as it obtains in the north and in the ritual and myth as it obtains in the Purāṇas, unless we believe that even here there is some tampering. But even if tampering is accepted in the case of the relationship between the Goddess and the buffalo in the north and the Purāṇas, the bloody aspect of the sacrifice of the buffalo is present. Moreover, the detail of the Śabarotsava shows that even in the sexual overtone there is no tampering! If Mahāvrata and the Horse-sacrifice be taken as being originally from the Vrātya source due to 'the 'intercourse' at the horse-sacrifice' (Parpola, p. 279ff; may be, because it is not found in ṚV?) in the post-ṚV texts having a counterpart in the Mahāvrata, what should be said about the hymn to Vṛṣākapi (ṚV X.86, we have already discussed in the earlier chapters), where ritual with sexual overtones is clear. One cannot bypass it simply because, in later times, the sacrifice of a virile monkey is not seen.

Parpola's suggestion that the rudiments of the Devī-Mahiṣa myth are to be found in the Veda (i.e., the post-ṚV Vedic portions that show influence from the Vrātya rituals) is difficult to accept from the examples that he has chosen. Let us examine. At the Rājasūya there is a rite in which a piece of lead is placed on the hind part of the skin of a tiger. This represents the head of the demon Namuci. The king consecrated for the Rājasūya, and symbolizing Indra, has to kick it away. The myth says, that when Indra kicked the head of Namuci, a demon came out from it. Parpola surmises that this is like the demon Mahiṣa showing his human body from the front part of his buffalo body. Further, Indra (-the king in the ritual) steps upon the tiger's skin. In this he sees, "in somewhat disguised form" Mahiṣāsuramardinī, the tiger-riding goddess (p.282). The point is, when (at which period) does the Devī get to be associated with the tiger as her vehicle? In the earliest icons of the Devī, that date from the early Kuṣāṇa period, she has no vehicle; she kills the buffalo taking him on her lap. At this period (about the second century B.C.) there is no room for the fight between her and the buffalo-'demon'. The earliest text that mentions the lion as a vehicle of the Devī, together with the fight motif, is the Matsya P. (200-400 A.D.), the Mārkaṇḍeya P. coming next (400-600 A.D.). Sometimes, she creates the lion from her forehead and then uses it as her vehicle (Sk.P.V.2.55.3f). She herself takes the form of a lioness (*Ib.*24). Sometimes she is said to have even the wolf as her vehicle (Agni

P.326.12). Lion as the vehicle of Durgā is well settled in the Hindu tradition after the Kuṣāṇa period; and even up to the seventh century A.D. there is no trace of the tiger, being her vehicle; it appears much later.[26] It is, hence, difficult to see how (i) Namuci-tiger-demon=Mahiṣa, with the half of his body showing a man; and (ii) King-tiger (skin)-Indra=Mahiṣāsuramardinī on the tiger, are similar in concept. The anthropomorph coming out of a zoomorph is not restricted to the Devī-Mahiṣa myth, nor could the demon coming out of the head of Namuci be taken as a "disguised form (with the war-god Indra substituted for the Goddess)". Though the fight motif is common to both, the emergence of an anthropomorph from a non-human creature is not restricted to this motif. Another example is of Vāc (Speech) being with the Asuras. According to a passage from the Śat.Br. (III.2.1.18ff) Speech was with the Asuras, while Mind, and through it, sacrifice was with the gods. The gods desired Speech and asked the sacrifice to allure her. When they won her over from the Asuras, they enveloped her with the (sacrificial) fire and offered her into the fire with a verse in the Anuṣṭubh metre. When Indra saw that the sacrifice united with Speech, he thought that a great Being (*abhva*) would be produced from the union. So, lest it should be better than him, he entered their union as a foetus. He was born after a year (in place of the great *abhva*; i.e. himself as the *abhva*). This is a myth with a common motif. However, it is used here, as a charter, to explain the use of the horn of the black antelope, which is fixed into the girdle (*mekhalā*) of the sacrificer. The girdle is made of a kind of grass held as sacred, (it is called *śaṇa*). The horn is said to be the womb from which Indra was born. Parpola's comment is that this "... suggests that Indra, the Vedic war-god, was identified with the war-god of the Asura mythology, namely Rudra (Kumāra Skanda), for Rudra was born of the union of Prajāpati (represented here by the sacrificial victim) and Vāc" (p.285). Just earlier, following Witzel's view, he says, the chief interest of this passage lies in the author's confession that originally the goddess Vāc was worshipped by the Asuras, i.e. 'demon-worshippers' speaking a Māgadhī-like Prakrit (thus also Witzel, Michael, 1989, Tracing the Vedic dialects, In: Colette Caillat (ed.), *Dialects dans les litteratures indo-aryennes*)." Is that so? The point is, have these statements from the Brāhmaṇa texts to be taken as actual historical evidences? If so, what should one understand when the same text (Śat.Br.) says, in the context of the purchase of Soma, that the gods decided to send Vāc to the Gandharvas in barter for Soma (III.2.4.3 *vācam evaibhyaḥ prahiṇavāma* and *tebhyo vācam eva prāhiṇvan)?* Are we to suppose that Vāc was initially with the Asuras; and that this statement is to be taken as being after Vāc was appropriated by the gods from the Asuras and had full control on her, and was again sent? Actually, such statements indicate structures of mythical expression. In the present context the statement is to suggest, that even the gods had to strive for everything. Otherwise, when it is said that metres and the whole sacrifice were in the body of the demon Vṛtra,[27] it might be taken as indicating that the science of sacrifice was learnt by the gods from the demons (*asura*-s). Such expressions have the value of an *arthavāda* (recommendation, or disapproval of a particular rite or object). The indication in the present case is that, in reality, the *asura*-s used such a language which was unintelligible to the gods (i.e., the followers of the Vedic cult); this was *because* Vāc went away from them (mythical). In the same way, it is difficult to contribute to the surmise that, from the union of Vāc and Prajāpati (mythical) a "great monster" will spring (*Ib.*, following the translation by Eggeling, which is itself not free from doubt).[28] The word *abhva* has both the senses: (i) good; (ii) bad, because, primarily the word has the meaning of something extraordinary. The connotation of the myth in question is: "Certainly some extraordinarily powerful person is to be born from such a unique union. Why not I?", thinks Indra. So, he sets himself in its place. And the statement that "Rudra was born from the union of Prajāpati (represented here by the sacrificial victim) and Vāc" remains unattested (*Ib.*; no reference appears here; is it ṚV X.61.7? But, there the female, Prajāpati's own daughter, is said to be kṣmā, which means 'Earth', not Vāc).

The identification between the *uttaravedi* (high altar) and Vāc, both being addressed as *simhī* (lioness) and both identified with the earth is well attested. This is the germ of the later association of the Devī and the lion[29] (as we have noted earlier). Though Vāc=*uttaravedi* is addressed as lioness and *mahiṣī*, the point to be marked is that while she is addressed as *simhī* continuously (six times), she is addressed as *mahiṣī* only once, just in the beginning (Taitt. Sam. I.2.12.2). While this reference, just once, occurs at the Black Yajurveda, in the Śukla (Vāj. Sam.V.12; Śat.Br. III.5.1.22-23 and –5.2.9) the address *mahiṣī* never occurs. If this single reference is to be understood as meaning 'she-buffalo', the pointer would be disastrous; because, in that case, what could the similar (actually the same) word, used for the sacrificing king's chief wife, at the Horse-sacrifice indicate? (Śat.Br. XIII. 5.2.5. *atha brahmā mahiṣīm abhimethayati*). This would show, that *simhī* and *mahiṣī* are not on the same level in the *mantra* addressed to the altar (=Vāk). This would also be supported from the fact, that in the myth associated with the Vāk=altar-goddess it is the *simhī* that is said to go about eating every body; not the *mahiṣī* (Śat.Br. III.5.1.21); because, a she-buffalo cannot go on 'eating' creatures. It should be noted, that, at another place where the Taitt. Sam. has the myth, with the same *mantra* addressed to the *uttaravedi* as *simhīr asi mahiṣīr asi* it specifically says that it is in the form of a lioness that she stood between the gods and the Asuras (VI.2.7.1-2 *simhīr asi mahiṣīr asi-ityāha simhīrhyeṣā rūpam kṛtvā...*) This will show that *mahiṣī* here, as in the case of the queen at the Horse-sacrifice, does not indicate a she-buffalo. The word has to be taken as meaning 'great' (You are a lioness; great *[mahiṣī]* you are'). The passages from the Veda could be taken as a source for the later (Puranic) concept of the Devī riding a lion, or being herself a lioness (as noted earlier); but they cannot support the Devī's association with the buffalo, or that she is the female counterpart of Mahiṣa. The same is true about the argument that Rudra, as Kumāra, is the masculine counterpart of the Kumarī (Pārvatī=Devī) of the Śākta mythology (of the Purāṇas), because Rudra is born for the "cruel" aspects of the gods (this is in the myth from Ait.Br. III.33) to punish the incestuous Prajāpati and Devī is born from the combined prowess of the gods to punish the lusty Mahiṣa (Parpola, p. 285), or that Prajāpati, taking various forms while mating with his daughter (which formed the first couple) is equal to Mahiṣa who also takes various forms, including that of a lion and an elephant, and that the Vāc-Prajāpati coupled is the prototype of the Devī-Mahiṣa couple of later times, and that Vāc and Durgā are identical (p.287). Multi-phased metamorphosis and the creation of a powerful being from the combination of parts of various entities is an important folklore motif[30] and such similarities can hardly be taken to have a similar meaning in all cases. Moreover, there is also the point of the nucleus and the embroidery. It will be seen that in the most original shape the Devī-Mahiṣa myth does not have a multiplicity of forms taken by the parties. The same is true of the Prajāpati-Daughter myth, of which the Vāk-Prajāpati is a very late variation,[31] further showing the parties as Brahmadeva and Śatarūpā/ Sarasvatī. The form remains the same, while the pattern changes if we compare the Prajāpati-Daughter syndrome with the Mahiṣa-Devī one. Pattern would go to the meaning while form is a cover. If this is not taken note of, one myth appears to be like another; and the content, and intent, would slip away! Moreover, chronology and embroidery introduce a difference, as has been amply noted in earlier chapters.

From what has been said above, it is difficult to believe that the whole Devī-Mahiṣa myth (and ritual) has its source in the Vedic myth of Prajāpati and his daughter, or Vāk (which is only one of the aspects of the Daughter). Further it is also not quite clear if the sexual rituals were really borrowed by the Vedic people from the Vrātyas, though the Atharvaveda shows a remarkable inclination towards respecting the Vrātyas (cf. AV XV), in the face of the fact that ṚV has clear indications of such rituals (X.86; cf. also I.126.6-7;-179: X.102.12. The last one forms part also of the ṚV Khila hymn V. 22, which has ample references to Mahānagnī and Mahānagna).[32] There could be very little comparison between the relationship between Prajāpati and his daughter on the one hand and the Goddess devouring her husband on the other; because, in the Vedic relationship there is never any marriage between the said parties, nor also between the horse and the queen-Mahiṣī at the Horse-sacrifice (as Parpola says; pp.283,288, 299). There is no "sacred marriage" between the horse and the queen. In fact, in the Horse-sacrifice and at the ritual reflected at the Vṛṣākapi hymn (ṚV X.86), the principle involved is that of the 'Ritual-husband' (a point the present author has made clear way back in 1969 and later elaborated in 1979).[33] On the other hand, the south Indian sources show marriage and slaughter of the husband for the Goddess as a marked motif. Here again, the form is the same, but pattern differs. This being the case, the myth from the Vādhūla-śr.su., which speaks of the various forms taken by Prajāpati and Vāc and finally the form of the porridge (*odana*) by the former being swallowed by the latter cannot be taken to be equal in meaning to the wife (slaughtering and) eating her husband (Parpola, p.287). The final part of the myth is that Vāc enters (the mouth of) *puruṣa* (man) and makes the teeth of the man serve as defence walls (*puraḥ*) against Prajāpati who has been pursuing her. Prajāpati takes the form of the rice porridge. To attract her and enhance her lust he 'decorates' himself with melted butter. Now, Vāc cannot restrict herself and swallows the porridge-Prajāpati. In this Parpola sees the identity of Vāc with Durgā. His course of identification is as follows:

Teeth=*puraḥ*=durga; Vāc in *duraga* is Durgā

Prajāpati=porridge; Vāc=tongue is Durgā

Prajāpati swallowed (by the tongue?)=Mahiṣa sacrificially killed and eaten by Durgā

Decoration by melted butter=decoration with flowers at marriage and sacrifice; the latter in the case of the buffalo.

(∴ Prajāpati=Mahiṣa and Vāc=Devī) (p.288).

At the outset it has to be pointed out that, the northern

myth and ritual do not attest the belief in the marriage, or even the relationship of bride and bride-groom between the Devī and the buffalo. Hence, the Devī-victim relationship in the north and the one in the south is not the same, though, apparently and formally, it is felt to be so. Further, the relationship between Prajāpati and Vāc (or, any aspect of the Daughter) is never of a victim for the Daughter. Though the archer (ṚV), who is turned to be Śiva later (Ait.Br.; Śat.Br. etc.,) shoots Prajāpati, in the myth or the ritual that progresses, the Daughter has no part, nor is she associated with the sacrifice of Prajāpati or eating any portion of his body (say, the *prāśitra* mentioned in an earlier ch.). Hence, the swallowing of the porridge-Prajāpati by Vāc cannot be taken as being equal to the Devī killing her husband; the implication is just of assimilation, as is the case with Śukra-Śiva or Kaca Śukra.

This detail cannot be explained by saying that it is also a case of the "purification" of the "pre-classical ritual" (of the Vratyas) by the orthodox Brāhmaṇas, who used abstract symbols (Parpola, p.276, following Heesterman, J.C., 1962, "Vrātya and Sacrifice", *Indo-Iranian Journal* 6.1:1-37). The question is, is there any other reference to support swallowing as murder or killing, in the myth involving Prajāpati and his daughter or even Vāc independently? The reply would be emphatically "No". Even in the myths relating to Vṛtra and Indra, swallowing indicates that the former was made the food by the latter; and, when the reverse occurs, it is not killing; it indicates new birth for the gain of something or rain-water (said to be nectar), as is the case in the myth where Śuṣṇa is said to swallow Indra, who entices the latter by taking the form of a lump of honey (*madhvaṣṭhīlā*). The case is similar to that of the Prajāpati-porridge and Vāc, both showing oneness through swallowing. The Śuṣṇa-Indra myth, further, acts as a symbol for rebirth in initiation. Where swallowing is set in a myth relating to opposite sexes, it indicates sexual action indicative of oneness. This is seen in the post-Vedic (=Puranic) myth where Kṛtyā 'swallows' Śukra by her vagina, on the order from Śiva.[34] In the present myth Vāc swallowing the porridge is the metaphor for Vāc 'swallowing' (sexually uniting with) Prajāpati. This is just the pattern of the Father-Daughter myth when the symbolic cover of swallowing is scratched. This is not to question if the walled fort (or city) was the speciality of the non-Vedic people (Vrātyas?), or if Durgā was not a goddess introduced in the later Vedic pantheon from such a source. But, let us examine the position of the buffalo in the Veda, and a myth from the Mait.Sam. (Parpola, p.293).

About the buffalo (*mahiṣa*). ṚV is well aware of it and it refers to the animal at a number of places. From the scrutiny of all the places where *mahiṣa* is mentioned in ṚV it becomes clear that: (i) The animal was admired for its huge form and strength. This is the reason why Indra, Agni, Soma (the plant revered as a god) and even Varuṇa, Aśvins and the Maruts are compared with, and addressed as *mahiṣa*. On the other hand, the lower *araṇi* (fire-kindling apparatus), or the queen or the wife, is referred to by the term *mahiṣī*; (ii) *mahiṣa* had become a symbol for the rain-cloud; and (iii) one or many *mahiṣa*-s are said to be cooked. The first point would also suggest that *mahiṣī* is also indicative of power, which has to be taken also in connection with the single identification: *uttaravedi*=*Vāc*=earth. The singular usage of *mahiṣa* occurs only once in ṚV, apart from its being associated with any god, where Indra is said to cook a *mahiṣa mṛga* (beast; VIII.69.15) for his 'father' and 'mother'[35]. This is the second point. Here, the preceding verse is suggestive. It says, that Indra goes beyond (vanquishes) all evils (hatreds, *dviṣaḥ*) and breaks open (*bhinat*) the *odana* by speech (*girā*) supreme as he is (*paraḥ*), and the *odana* is being cooked. By a well set symbolism in ṚV the 'speech that breaks' is the thunder, the mid-region speech as Sāyaṇa has very aptly said, and there is no reason to discard this interpretation which has a very strong basis of traditional imagery (cf. ṚV I. 164.41 where the thundering cow is the mid-region Speech, *mādhyamikā vāk* Sāyaṇa; So Geldner, *Der Rigveda*, I.P.235, who compares VIII. 100.10-11 and leads us to Tait. Br.II.4.6.11). Read with this, the *mahiṣa mṛga* cannot be an actual one (whether it be 'great beast' or 'buffalo beast', the latter less probable in view of *mṛga* of which *mahiṣa* is the epithet). It is the dark, waterful, cloud that is at the back of the veil of the metaphor. It is not necessary to go further to VIII.77.10 to understand the meaning of the verse in question (VIII.69.15) through the imagery of the *odana* that is broken open, while it was being cooked by speech; because, the *odana* at the latter place (VIII.77.10) is actual and brought to Indra along with a 'hundred' buffaloes, while the *odana* and *mahiṣa mṛga* in the present context form one whole image, which is of the cloud cooking the nourishing rainwater (not actual rice, or rice cooked in milk, *ksīrapākam odanam*, as a gift to Indra, as is the case in VIII.77.10). To take up the third. Apart from the singular usage of *mahiṣa*, which we have examined, there is no other one. In the plural the word always occurs as indicating the buffaloes (actual beasts) offered only to Indra. An interesting point has been raised in this connection (Parpola, p.295). Though the Ṛgveda has references to the sacrifice of the buffalo (and buffaloes) to Indra (and to Indra alone), the Brāhmaṇas (and also the later Samhitā texts dealing with ritual) have them "wiped out". This is, according to Parpola, because "the buffalo was too conspicuously associated with the *main* god of the enemy" (Emuṣa, the boar as he mentions earlier on the same page; "There cannot be any doubt that in the Ṛgveda the boar Emuṣa is an enemy slain by Indra"). The word *emuṣa* occurs only once in ṚV. and it is here. Now, if *varāha* here is a real boar, and if Emuṣa is also the real boar, one wonders if we can take the tale about the Emuṣa *varāha* as an actual account of the fight between Indra (the anthropomorphic god, or leader of the Vedic Aryans) and the boar. ṚV mentions *varāha;* but, it appears, the word, like *mahiṣa* at many places as noted above, indicates a symbol for power. In other words, it is metaphoric in use. Thus, Rudra is said to be the *varāha* of heaven (I.114.5 *divo varāham aruṣam kapardinam*). Trita is said to have smitten the *varāha* with his metal-tipped finger (X.99.6). The myth quoted by Parpola (as from Mait. Sam. III.8.3) is quite well known in the Veda (it occurs also at Taitt. Sam. VI.2.4.2-3), with the name Emuṣa, appearing as an epithet with the variation: *vāmamuṣa/vāmamoṣa* ('stealer of desired things'). This *varāha* is said to be staying behind twenty-one citadels (*puraḥ*, Parpola from Mait. Sam. or beyond seven mountains, Taitt. Sam.). At ṚV the details at hand are as follows:

VIII.77.10 : Viṣṇu brought (*ā-abharat*) a hundred buffaloes, the milk-cooked *odana* (rice) being impelled by Indra; and Indra brought (*ā-abharat*) the *varāha,* Emuṣa. (*ā-abharat* may also mean 'seized' and carried.)

I.61.7 : Viṣṇu robbed (the *varāha*) of his sustenance (*pacatam*) and smote the *varāha* (when Indra drank the sacrificial elixir [*pitu*] at his mother's Soma-pressings), beyond the mountain (*tiro adrim*), the archer (*astā*) as he was.

VIII.77.6 : Indra wielded his stretched bow and smote (the mountains); from the mountains (*giribhyaḥ*) he held (*dhārayat*) the cooked rice (*pakvam odanam*).

VIII.96.2 : Even without the weapons, Indra cracked the thrice seven (twenty-one) well-knit tops of the mountains (*girīṇām*)

(On this, again, Sāyaṇa quotes from the Taitt. Sam. VI.2.4. 2-3 as on ṚV I.61.7 and VIII.77.10).

There is no mention of the *durga* in the passages in ṚV, mentioned above. ṚV never mentions *durga*. Hence *durgāt āhartā and durge hantā* (occurring in Mait.Sam., Taitt. Sam. etc.) are later additions, or substitutions, for the *adri* or *giri* (mountain) at ṚV in these passages. There is no uniformity about the Emuṣa, who is named also as Vāma-muṣa and Vāma-moṣa. This later name is explained independently, without any mention of Emuṣa. The weapon is variously mentioned as 'a bunch of *darbha* grass' (Taitt. Sam. VI.2.4.3), 'arrow' (cf. *astā* at ṚV I.61.7, which indicates the arrow) or a bow (*bunda* at VIII.77.6) changed to cane-bow (Mait. Sam. III.8.3). The pattern from the Emuṣa myth, where the sacrifice is said to have been with the *asura*-s, away and hidden from the gods, is the same as from the Vāc myth where she is said to be with the *asura*-s. This indicates that Emuṣa, like the Asuras in such tales, was a mythical entity, like the 'Great *Asura*', but with inversion. Important gods are termed the 'Great Asura' (cf. ṚV III. 55 1-22 *mahad devānām asuratvam ekam;* also II.1.6. *rudro asuraḥ* said of Agni; I. 23.7 Varuṇa; V. 83.6 Parjanya and so on.) But later the meaning changed, Asura being against the gods. In the Ṛgvedic period it seems to have been a norm of bravery to control and surpass Emuṣa, who, though mentioned only once, was believed to control every thing. In this belief he was on par with the *varāha,* who is said to be smitten and defeated; but this is the goal for the gods to achieve. Hence, Rudra is the *varāha* of the sky (as noted above). So, Soma is *varāha* (IX.97.7). A glance at the occurrence of the word *varāha* and *emuṣa* in ṚV would show, that they are of a late origin (Books I, IX and X) and occur scantily (*varāha* seven times altogether and *emuṣa* only once). The only other book in which they occur together is VIII (77.10 *varāham emuṣam,* i.e. only once each). So there is no clear indication in ṚV of the *varāha* Emuṣa being definitely bad, or antagonistic to the gods, i.e. to the Vedic people. The passage where ṚV mentions Emuṣa simply says, that Viṣṇu, being urged by Indra brought a hundred buffaloes, the milk-cooked rice and also (Indra or Viṣṇu brought *Emuṣa),* the *varāha.* There is no mention of Emuṣa being killed, as it occurs in some later texts (like Mait. Sam.). In the same hymn one *gandharva* is said to have been shattered (VIII.77.5) by Indra in the regions that had no support (*abhi gandharvam atṛṇad abudhneṣu rajaḥsu*), and the *gandharva,* here, is undefined just like Emuṣa. The weapon of Indra in the exploit of shattering the *gandharva,* the mountains from which the cooked rice (*pakvam odanam*) and, impliedly, the riches of Emuṣa are brought, appears as *bunda* (Ib. v 6 and 11), which is the arrow, as it is associated with the *dhanus* (bow, Ib.11), as is clear from Yāska's authority (Nir.VI.32-33). The only other occurrence of *bunda* is at the same book (which is of the Bharadvājas) and in the context of Indra's exploit against Vṛtra (VIII.45.4). This would show that the *gandharva*, Vṛtra and Emuṣa are placed on the same footing. It is, hence, not convincing to take Emuṣa as a real person, an actual enemy of the gods who had evil designs about the Vedic people and their gods. That is why, he is not defined, nor has he a clear personality of his own; he is just a symbol of power that is seen as holding and hoarding the riches for the enemies of the gods (Vedic people), and, yet, seen in the same period (i.e. of the Brāhmaṇas; cf. Śat.Br. XIV.1.2.11) as the supreme god who is credited with the exploit of saving the earth from the clutches of a 'demon'— a myth well set in later years. In between these two phases of his nature he is portrayed as an enemy by the texts later than the Ṛgveda. In this middle period the original myth and a clear belief about Emuṣa were confused by the texts of that period, which say (Mait. Sam. VIII.3.3): (i) The sacrifice ran away from the gods (a common motif to suggest the importance of the sacrifice; likewise, Agni, Vāc and even sacrificial material);[36] (ii) gods seeking and searching the lost sacrifice; (iii) Viṣṇu, gaining importance as being the sacrifice itself, helping Indra (=gods); because, Indra, though the hero, is not identified with sacrifice; (iv) Indra, *durge hantā* (smasher in the inaccessible place; fortress) asks the *durgāt āhartā* (the bringer from the inaccessible place), who is sacrifice, spotted by Indra, but not yet Viṣṇu, to fetch the property of the Asuras beyond the twenty-one *puraḥ* (for the original *adri-giri,* 'mountains of ṚV), where stays Emuṣa; (v) Indra kills Emuṣa with the cane-bow (not corroborated by ṚV); (vi) Having poved himself to be the 'killer', Indra asks the sacrifice to prove himself to be the 'bringer'; (vii) (But) Viṣṇu brings the sacrifice; as he, indeed, is sacrifice. Here the Mait. Sam. says, that

ṚV VIII. 77.10 refers to this 'bringing'. Actually, the verse from ṚV does not speak of bringing back the lost sacrifice at all. The verses at ṚV immediately preceding this last verse have the consolidated imagery as follows: (i) Indra split the *gandharva* in the supportless void (mid-region; hence rain-imagery); (ii) Indra's arrow has 'a hundred feathers' (lightning ?); (iii) With it he fetches for the singers, men and women nourishment to eat (v 8 *stotṛbhyaḥ ... nṛbhyaḥ nāribhyaḥ attave*); (iv) All that *Viṣṇu* brought, being impelled by Indra, namely a hundred buffaloes, milk-cooked rice and Emuṣa the *varāha* (v 10). But, what about the lost sacrifice? This would indicate that the original from ṚV is used by the later text (may be after, or during, a period a thousand years. How to know? And, who knows?) for a different purpose, which is to extol the institution of sacrifice. The ṚV passages (verses) were chartered to give a required meaning. In this there happened a (con-)fusion of patterns: (i) Bringing the lost sacrifice; and (ii) Vanquishing the supreme power as a requirement for the hero. But, while the Ṛgveda speaks simply of bringing (subduing) Emuṣa, the Mait. Sam. adds that he was killed. This confusion is due to a wrong appropriation of the original myth. This is proved by the fact that the tradition even accepted Emuṣa, the boar, as the god who brought up the earth and stabilized 'her' for their sacrifice. He is even said to be the husband of the earth (Śat.Br.XIV.1.2.11). Emuṣa Varāha is for ever mentioned as having this unique status in the later Hindu myth and icons. This is, obviously, because he was never considered as an enemy, or even as real. Had it been so, one wonders how 'for eating' (*attave*, noted above) would suit him. The made necessary the shift, that he was killed! The fact is that he was mythical and was symbolic.

What has been said above would show that there is no sound ground to suppose that Emuṣa was, indeed, the Asura enemy of Indra. As there is no other mention of Emuṣa and the buffaloes together in ṚV, or later, there does not seem to be any reason for accepting that the buffaloes were (or buffalo, was) too conspicuously associated with the main god of the enemy of the Vedic people, also that "every trace has been wiped out by the Brāhmaṇa texts", suggesting "a deliberate discrimination against the buffalo by the conservative circles of the Vedic priesthood" (Parpola, p. 295). This opinion is, obviously, under the influence of ṚV VIII.77. 10, where Emuṣa, the *varāha*, is mentioned along with a hundred buffaloes. It is true that the sacrifice of a buffalo is not attested from the Vedic ritual texts (i.e. in the post-Vedic period). The reason seems to be its black colour and there was no necessity to support its non-acceptance as a sacrificial beast. Whether this be taken as a purposeful discrimination is, at the best, an open question. Now, about the prohibition for offering a horse to the goddess in a late Purāṇa text (Kālikā P.71. 46). Even if this prohibition is taken to be true it is not only for the horse. It is even for an elephant, a lion, a tiger and even a human being (*Ib*. not only *haya*, but *haya-hastinau* and 47 *siṁhavyāghranarān*), for fear of going to hell after death. But, this prohibition is for a *brāhmaṇa* (cf. *Ib. datvā brāhmaṇo narakam vrajet*), not for others. Likewise, *kṣatriya* and others were advised not to sacrifice to the goddess a black antelope (Ib.51). As a support for not sacrificing a horse to the goddess, Kane (and Parpola, who accepts him in toto cites a verse (from the Kālikā P.71.57-58), which is, in Kane's rendering, "as you hate a horse and as you carry Caṇḍikā...". The actual words are (addressed to the sacrificial buffalo): *yathā vāham bhavān dveṣṭi yathā vahasi caṇḍikām...*", where there seems to be a contrast, "you hate the *vāha*; (but) carry (*vahasi*) Caṇḍikā". This would suggest that the buffalo hates any other 'burden' (*vāha*)[37] except the goddess (and, of course, Yama). In any case, it is unclear if there *is* a polarization about the horse and the buffalo belonging to different deities belonging to people that are, or had been, inimical to each other, and that there really was discrimination between the victims on this account. On the contrary, there is evidence that the horse was not completely taboo as a victim to the goddess (noted by Parpola himself; p.289, where he refers to Kooij, Karel von, and his tr. of Kālikāpurāṇa). Further, if there was the so-called discrimination of the buffalo by the Vedic priests of the Brāmaṇa period on the point of the beast's being associated with the enemy's god, one wonders why it is not mentioned in the list of the "scape-goats", that were discarded in favour of the domesticated animals to be sacrificed. They were *kiṁpuruṣa, gaura, gavaya*, camel and the *śarabha* (Śat. Br. I. 2.3.9.; also VII.5.2. 32-37). If these "scapegoats", considered unfit for being offered by the Vedic people "appear to have been victims once offered by their rivals" (Parpola, p.280), what forbade them from making such a clear mention of the buffalo? The reply cannot be that, these "scapegoats" are wild animals and that the rivals of the Vedic people offered wild animals while the Vedic people offered the domesticated ones. There does not seem to be any connection between the buffalo not being attested as offered in the Brāhmaṇa texts and its being the beast of the enemy-god, as a reason for it. The reason could, as we have noted above, be in the colour, and the Vedic people avowedly had preference for the white or the tawny (symbolizing the sun and the fire respectively) colour. A question may be asked, "Why is it that the black antelope (*kṛṣṇamṛga*) was so sacred and his skin prescribed in rituals?" The answer is that this animal was not totally black. It had a combination of white and dark specks (or streaks) of hair; thereby it symbolized the day and the night (Taitt. Sam. VI.1.3.2) and also the sky and the earth. There was also a yellow or brownish streak or patches, which symbolized the mid-region (Śat. Br. III.2.1.3). Yet, the question remains: "Why is it that ṚV has references to the eating of the buffalo(es) by Indra, while the creature is totally absent in the Brāhmaṇa texts. The answer to this question lies in the difference in the nature of the Ṛgveda (and even the Atharvaveda) which is not a treatise on rituals, though verses from it are used at rituals unlike the later Saṁhitās and the Brāhmaṇa texts. Let us place together such references to the buffalo as indicate its being offered and Indra eating it.

All the references to the eating, or cooking, of the buffalo occur with Indra. No other god is associated with eating buffalo-flesh. Thus it is said, that three hundred buffaloes were cooked by the fire-god (Agni) for Indra and the latter is also said to have drunk three 'lakes' of the Soma-juice (V.29.7). He is also said to have eaten the flesh of the buffaloes (Ib.8). The context is the killing of Vṛtra. The god Pūṣan is said to have cooked a hundred buffaloes for Indra, and Viṣṇu prepared the intoxicating Soma-juice for him (VI.17.11); here also the context is of killing Vṛtra (cf. *vṛtrahaṇam madiram aṁśum*). He is said to have eaten a thousand buffaloes (VIII.12.8), and here it is said to be for increasing his vigour. In ṚV *vṛtrahatya* is symbolic for killing the enemies actually and for the gain of rain conceptually at certain places. But, when it comes to the cooking and eating of so many buffaloes, it could hardly refer to a regular sacrifice to Indra of all the buffaloes, even if he is said to fight Vṛtra. The probability is that this is suggestive of the real advance against an enemy, where the Indra-feast, as distinct from a sacrifice, was characterized by the killing and eating of the flesh of buffaloes.[38] The buffalo, as we have seen, was already a standard of comparison for important gods. As such, by sympathetic magic, its flesh was believed to invigorate the warriors prior to the set-off, or even after return with success. This is obviously, in view of an actual event. The ritual texts, like the Brāhmaṇas and later post-ṚV Saṁhitā texts, never deal with actual events; that is not their purpose, and even ṚV does not attest an offering of buffalo-flesh in the fire at any sacrifice. In the various sacrifices they deal with, there is a set pattern: Establishment of the fires, Agnihotra, half-monthly sacrifices (Full-moon and New-moon), the seasonal sacrifices (Cāturmāsyas), Paśubandha (Tying of the victim), Agniṣṭoma (which is the model for all Soma-sacrifices), Vājapeya, Rājasūya, Aśvamedha and even the Puruṣamedha. In this set there is absolutely no room for an actual battle-march. Though in the Vājapeya and the Rājasūya there are suggestive rites for the gain of cows and for showing the excellence of the royal sacrificer, they are only symbolic for the gain of supremacy; it is not an actual advance of an army. In the Horse-sacrifice, the horse is the symbol of the sun, or Prajāpati. Hence there is no occasion for the buffalo in the main sacrifice. Among other beasts also there was no propriety for it, in view of the invariantly black colour. Hence the question of deliberate discrimination against the buffalo does not arise. The Sūtra-texts follow the pattern of the Brāhmaṇa texts, and for the same reason there are no details of actual advance of an army; hence, there is no room for the buffalo there on the pattern of ṚV. Then dawns the early Kuṣāṇa period, which shows the idols of the Devī and the buffalo; but, there is nothing to show that they could be related to any military advance. When the early Purāṇas narrate the fight between the Devī and Mahiṣa, where the Devī is substituted for the god Skanda Kārttikeya, a subtle change is seen. Kārttikeya is commissioned to kill the Buffalo-demon in a regular battle, which reflects the same old motif: Indra goes to battle; buffaloes are killed; or buffaloes are captured for feast (cf. the ṚV Emuṣa-caputre and buffaloes won along with the milk-cooked *odana*). However, in the Kārttikeya myth there is no eating of the buffalo. With the Devī-Mahiṣa myths the old pattern changes. It is not only fight, as is the case with Kārttikeya; it is also the peculiar sexual element, together with the killing and eating of the buffalo. This latter element now gets prominence, though tradition associates the festival of 'nine nights' (*navarātra*) with military advance. However, the two have to be kept separate;[39] for, what has the military advance to do with the sexual expressions that are floated up at the festival of the Devī? The sexual element in the other Puranic accounts is subdued; it is restricted to the advances of Mahiṣa. But, in the Śabara-utsava of the comparatively later Kālikā P. and in the ritual and myth of the south Indian goddess Dayāmāva it is very prominent. This could not be explained as being a phase of devotion (*bhakti*) or as being a fossil of violent raids and 'pleasure' thereafter. Durgā has to be taken as the goddess of the *durga* (Parpola), the Pārvatī who is the daughter of the Himālaya mountain and the veritable earth-goddess, with whom various local goddesses got merged. She, with *her* Mahiṣa (buffalo) victim, formed a couple in the non-Vedic sphere, which is exactly like the Vedic Indrāṇī (earth)-Vṛṣākapi or Queen-horse couple, for the continued fructification of the earth as the first step and for general prosperity as the next, the male victim acting as the pseudo husband. Both, though of independent origin, got fused together, and have been important phases of the multifaced Hindu tradition. Though the chapter in the Virāṭaparvan which mentions Durgā (6.20[ab] *durgāt trāyase durge tat tvam Durgā smṛta janaiḥ*, 'You protect from inaccessible places, O Durgā; hence you are called Durgā by the people) is spurious and, hence, no proof of exclusive association of the goddess with the military advance, in the original nature of her worship, there seems to be no question about the association of Durgā with the mountains and the resorts therein. Durgā is mentioned in the ṚV-Khila (IV.2.12). However, the style of the expression *(Durgām Devīm śaraṇam aham pra-padye)* is post-Vedic. Here she is invoked for a multitude of things and favours, including protection in inaccessible places, from thieves, fire, evil constellations and planets, calamities involving enemies and war, by saying, "You are born in the Ṛgveda" (*Ib.*vv 5-12). This praise is said to be part of the hymn to Night (ṚV X.128). That she is said to be born in the Ṛgveda itself is a proof that she was a post-ṚV deity, and she is being adjusted in the Vedic pantheon. The Atharvaveda mentions Durgā in the hymn praising the *vaśā* (sterile cow) indicating that she is the deity, along with Earth, in the ritual for the *vaśā* (XII.4.23), also that she is the earth-goddess, which is her main aspect in the Puranic period. This is clear from her identification with Pārvatī, the daughter of the Himalaya mountain. In the Bṛhaddevatā, which is a sort of a ritual-commentary for the household rites (as against the Vedic, Śrauta, rites), Vāc is said to have become Durgā (II.77). This work is of about the fourth century B.C. and would suggest the mutual difference between

Vāc and Durgā. When the Taitt. Ār. praises Durgā in the Gayatrī *mantra* in the fashion of the famous Sāvitrī verse (ṚV III.62.10) it indicates that this goddess was ultimately given a status in the Vedic patheon. This was the period, roughly, of the fifth-fourth century B.C.[40], just prior to her depiction in the icons of the early Kuṣāṇa period. It may also be particularly noted that, these post-ṚV texts in the Vedic tradition do not mention the *mahiṣa*. The reason is clear. Though the essentially non-Vedic Goddess was incorporated in the Vedic tradition, the sacrifice of the buffalo was not. From slightly before the early Kuṣāṇa period, however, the fusion was complete.

References

1. Dates of individual Purāṇa texts are following P.V.Kane, *History of Dharmaśāstra*, Vol.V, Pt.2, pp.887-912.
2. Dange, *Encl.P.B.P.*, Vol.II, pp.710f; 721; see under "Gaurī", "Mahiṣāsuramardinī" and "Pārvatī"; W.D.O. 'Flaherty *Hindu Myths*, 1982(1975), Penguin, pp.238-49.
3. O'Flaherty, *op.cit.*, p.248.
4. Edith Hamilton, *Mythology*, p.372f; Richard Cavendish, (ed), *Legends of the World*, p.158.
5. In the part of Shri Lanka in the TV Series on the SAARC countries it was seen that buffaloes were yoked to the plough.
6. Gritli Von Mitterwallner, "The Kuṣāṇa Type of the Goddess Mahiṣāsuramardinī as compared to the Gupta and the Mediaeval Types", *German Scholars on India* Vol.II, Nachiketa Publications Ltd., Bombay, 1976, Figs. 1 and 2, pp.204 & 205.
7. Devendra Handa "Some Mediaeval Images of Mahiṣāsuramardinī", *Panjab University Research Bulletin* (Arts), Vol. XXII-1, Chandigarh, April, 1991, Fig.1
8. Cf. *gavhāḷī and mugāḷī* in Pt.I, ch. Three.
9. See Pt.I, pp.28f; and pp. 71ff.
10. Dange, *Encl.P.B.P.*, Vol. II, p.418; V, under "Tulasī", p.1482.

11. Cf. Śabarotsava in the north and the myth and ritual of Dayāmāva in the south, in India mentioned below in our discussion.

12. Mitterwallner, *op.cit.*, Fig.s 1 to 3.

13. A. Parpola, "The Metamorphoses of Mahiṣa Asura and Prajāpati" in *Ritual, State and History in South India* (Essays in Honour of J.C. Heesterman), (ed.), A.W. Van Den Hoek and others, E.J. Brill, Leiden, 1992, p.276.

14. Stephen Fuchs "The Baiga Understanding of the Universe", *URAM*, Vol. 1, No.3, Ontario, 1978, pp.163ff.

15. J.P. Murdock, *Our Primitive Contemporaries*, 18th ed., New York, 1957 (1934), p.33ff. The popularity of the water buffalo (*mahiṣa*) could be seen from such names as Māhiṣmatī (we have referred to above), the region called Mahiṣaka (Mb.Bhīṣmaparvan 9.59) and Mysore (in modern India) indicating its former form as Mahiṣapura (?). A popular village deity in Maharashtra is Mhasobā (*bā* is *buvā*, for respect in Marathi).

16. Stietencron, in Parpola, *op.cit.*, p.275.

17. Whitehead Henry, *Village Gods of South India*, Delhi, 1976 (1921), p.64 and at other pages.

18. *Ibid.*, p.52, 56, 66.

19. *Ibid.*, p.64f.

20. Dange, *Encl.P.B.P.*, Vol.IV, p.1406; also Bhaviṣya P. Brahmakhaṇḍa, 79-5-6.

21. Whitehead, *op.cit.*, p.84ff., 117 ff. This, and the stories that follow, have also been personally known by me in my long stay in south India.

22. *Ibid.*

23. P.V. Kane, *op.cit.*, p.185. Two articles on the two Durgā Hymns from the Mahābhārata have recently appeared in: *Modern Evaluation of the Mahābhārata* (Prof. R.K. Sharma Fel.Vol.), Nag Publishers, Delhi, 1995. One is by A.N. Jani and the other by U.N. Dhal (pp.113-15 and 127-31 respectively). These hymns occur, one each at the Virāṭaparvan and the Bhīṣmaparvan. However, they do not deal with the myth of

Mahiṣa and the Devī, nor do they mention the opinion of Kane.

24. Pupul Jaykar, *The Earth-Goddess*, Harper and Row, San Francisco, 1990 (earlier, Penguin Books India Ltd, 1989), pp.37-40.

25. *Ibid*., p.39. Comp. the case of the *devadāsī*, who is identified with Yellamma. p. 401ff; also p. 415, n. 40.

26. Goddesses on tiger in picture do occur in the eighteenth century A.D. and later; but they are not associated with the motif of Mahiṣāsura. The Silappatikāram (=Cilappatikāram), Old Tamil, mentions the goddess as standing on the back of the buffalo (which corresponds to the idols from the early Kuṣāṇa period and the early Purāṇas) and then on the lion (her regular portrayal). She is clad in a tiger-skin (Parpola, referring to V.R. Ramachandra Dikshitar's tr.: p.289). However, she is not associated with the tiger as her vehicle. Jai.Br. III.327, compares Vāc with a lioness, a tigress and a *śiṁśumārī;* but that does not prove much. The date of the Silappatikaram is 450 A.D.

27. Śat.Br. V.5.5.1-5; cf. Jai.Br. I.97-99.

28. The word *abhvam* is rendered by Eggeling (SBE 26, p.32) as "monster". Parpola accepts this meaning. However, the spirit of the myth told here does not go happily with it. Moreover, *abhva* has also a good meaning attached to it; cf. *abhva* of Agni at ṚV VI.4.3; also II.4.5.; *abhva* is something extraordinary' (*a*+√*bhū*: 'not a common Being'; cf. later *adbhutam*; also *ābhu* at 'ṚV X.129.3). This special birth is not restricted to the pairing of Vāc and Prajāpati. At Taitt. Sam. (VI.1.3.6) the female is Dakṣiṇā (sacrificial gift, anthropomorphosed) and the male is Sacrifice (Yajña). There Indra reflects. 'He who will be born from this union will be THIS'. What THIS (*idam*) is remains unclear. Keith renders it as 'This world' (Tr.); but, this is not quite convincing. The sense is 'This extraordinary one'. Indra wants to be THIS; hence he enters the womb of Dakṣiṇā.

29. See Ch. Eight, "Nṛsiṁha—Man-lion", pp. 275ff.

30. Cf. ṚV I.163.1 where the solar horse is said to have wings of a hawk and the 'arms' (fore-legs) of a deer. The Chinese dragon was a combination of a serpent, a stag, a fish, eagle and so on. His head was that of a camel. He had the horns of a stag, eyes of a demon, ears of a cow, neck of a snake;

Donald Mackenzie, *Myths of China and Japan*, p.46f. For metamorphosis, out of a number of instances, this for example: One party becomes a horse; then a dove; then a bead; then a worm, which is ultimately swallowed by the enemy who also succeeds after changing a number of forms; *Folk-lore and Legend Oriental*, London, 1889, p.45f.

31. The forms are the male and the female antelope; or Sky and Dawn in the case of the daughter (Ait.Br. III.35; Śat.Br. I.7.4.1) The Speech-Brahmā pair appears in the period of the later Purāṇas. In this period Speech came to be called Vāgīśvarī, taunted by Brahmā as a prostitute; see Dange, *Encl.P.B.P.*, Vol.II, p.202.

32. Dange, *Vedic Concept of 'Field' and the Divine Fructification*, Bombay Uni.Pbn., 1971, pp.68-82.

33. *Ibid* .; also Dange, *Sexual Symbolism from the Vedic Ritual*

34. Dange, *Encl. P.B.P.*, Vol.IV, p.1404; also Padma P.Uttara, 18. 73-86 for the myth.

35. Who the father and the mother are is not stated, in the verse. However, there can hardly be any doubt that they are Sky and Earth. For the pattern cf. ṚV I.164.3; -196.6; VI.51.5 etc., where the father and the mother are the sky and the earth.

36. Cf.Śat.Br. I.2.3.1. The motif is common. For Puranic instances see Dange, *Encl.P.B.P.*, Vol.II, p.522.

37. For *vāha* as 'burden' or 'carrier of burden' cf.Kau.Br. 27.1 *na vāhā-iva-abhimṛśe śūdrām*, spoken of Speech who is said to be a 'prostitute', *puṁścalī*; cf. Vāgīśvarī in n. 31 above. It will be interesting to note that at Chinsura (Hooghly Dist., India), the goddess Sarasvatī is worshipped by prostitutes. She is said to be the consort (not wife) of Kārttikeya, and is unmarried: see N.N. Bhattacharya, *Indian Mother Goddess*, Calcutta, 1971, p.39.

38. This would go well with the view that Indra was a human hero turned divine. See R.N. Dandekar, *Vedic Mythological Tracts,* Delhi, 1979, p.171 f.; earlier, L.D. Barnett had suggested, similarly, that "In faraway past, Indra was simply a hero. Very likely he was once a chieftain on earth. The story of his great deeds so fascinated the imagination of men that they raised him to the rank of chief god." L.D. Barnett, *Hindu Gods and*

Heroes, London, 1922, p.28. This is not a rare case. Other examples are Rāma of the Ikṣvāku family and Kṛṣṇa of the Vṛṣṇis. Alexander, the Great, made efforts for self-deification; see Peter Green, *Alexander of Macedon,* Uni. of California Press, Berkeley, Los Angeles, Oxford, 1991, pp.314, 318; he desired to be called a chosen son of Ahura Mazda, after defeating Darius. Olympia, his mother, had told him that he was begotten by a god on her, p.164. With the case of Indra who, unlike the Vedic gods in the Śrauta rituals, was offered buffaloes, we may compare the case of the pre-dynastic Egyptian king Zaru (Whose name means 'scorpion'). He impersonated Osiris and at the Sed festival, which was meant for the renewal of the king by sacrificing the old one and appointing a new one. He stopped this practice and cattle and captives were sacrificed in his honour. The buffaloes 'eaten' by Indra might he the ones captured from the enemies, or they were his speciality. For Zaru, see D. Mackenzie, *Egyptian Myth and Legend,* p.36.

39. Kane, *op.cit.*, p.187, where he discards the opinion of N.G. Banerjee in *Indian Historical Quarterly,* Vol.21, pp.227-31; Banerjee held, that Durgāpūjā was originally a military rite, mentioning Raghuvaṁṣa IV.24-25. According to Kane they were originally separate.

40. U.N. Dhal, "Relevance of the Hymns to Durgā in the Mahābhārata," *Modern Evaluation of the Mahābhārata* (Prof. R.K. Sharma Fel.Vol.), Nag Publishers, Delhi, 1995, p.131, may be compared on this point.

* The goddess at Koḍungallur (the former capital of Cochin, India), is said to be in her menses on the Bharaṇī constellation in kārttika (Oct.-Nov.) every year for three days. Only non-brahmin males are allowed to visit her at this period and pacify her with sexual expressions, one such being, "O Goddess! If I want to have union with you, how long and thick my *P.* should be !". Information from Dr. C.R. Swaminathan, Palghat.

Bibliography

Ali, Muzafer, 1973 (2nd Ed.; 1966) : *The Geography of the Purāṇas,* People's Publishing House, New Delhi.

Barnett, L.D., 1922: *Hindu Gods and Heroes*, London.

Berden, Frances, 1989: *The Aztecs*, Chelsea House Publishers, New York, Philadelphia.

Bodewitz, H.W. 1984: "What Did Indra do with the Yatis", *Amṛtadhārā*, (Dr.R.N.Dandekar Fel.Vol.), Ajanta Publications, Delhi. 7.

Brinton, Daniel, 1905: *Myths of the New World.*

Bhattacharya, N.N., 1971: *Indian Mother Goddess*, Calcutta.

Cassirer, E., 1955: *The Philosphy of Symbolic Forms*, New Haven.

Cavendish, Richard, (Ed.), 1994: *Legends of the World*, Barnas and Noble Books, New York.

Cox, G.W., 1870: *Mythology of the Aryan Nations.*

Dandekar, R.N., 1979: *Vedic Mythological Tracts,* Ajanta Publication, Delhi 7.

Dange, Sadashiv A., 1967: "Sasarparī and the Horse of Sudās", *Vishveshwaranand Indological Journal,* V-1, Hoshiarpur.

1969: *Legends in the Mahābhārata*, Motilal Banarsidass, Delhi 7.

1970: *Pastoral Symbolism from the Ṛgveda,* University of Poona, Pune.

1971: *Vedic Concept of 'Field' and the Divine Fructification,* University of Bombay

1979: *Sexual Symbolism from the Vedic Ritual,* Ajanta Publications, Delhi 7.

1980-81: "Religious suicide in the Vedic Period (?)", *Indologia Taurinensia* (Vols. VIII-IX), Dr. Ludwik Sternbach com. Vol., Institute di Indologia, Torino (Italy)

1982: *Vedic Myths in Social Perspective*, V.V.R.I. Press, Panjab University, Hoshiarpur.

1987: *Glimpses of Puranic Myth and Culture*, Ajanta Publications, Delhi 7.

1986-90: *Enclopaedia of Puranic Beliefs and Practices,* Vol.I-V, and Navrang Publishers, New Delhi 12.

1992: *Divine Hymns and Ancient Thought,* Vol.I *(Ṛgveda Hymns and Ancient Thought)*;

1995: Vol.II (*Ritual and the Quest for Truth*), Navrang Publishers, New Delhi 12.

Dange, Ms S.S., 1993: "Severed Head in Myth and Ritual" *Annals of the Bhandarkar Oriental Research Institute* (Amṛtamahotsava Volume), Vol.LXII-LXIII.for 1991-1992, Poona.

Darmestater, J., 1988 (1987): *Zend Avesta-Vendidad,* SBE, Vol.4, Motilal Banarsidass, Delhi 7

Davies, H.A., 1937 (1928): *An Outline History of the World*, Geoffrey Cumberlege, Oxford University Press, London

Deo, S.B., 1956: *History of Jain Monachism*, Deccan College, Poona.

Dhal, U.N., 1995:"Relevance of the Hymns of Durgā in the Mahābhārata", *Modern Evolution of the Mahābhārata* (Prof. R.K. Sharma Fel: Vol.), Nag Publications, Delhi.

Dharmadhikari, T.N., 1889: *Yajñāyudhāni*, Vaidika Samśodhana Maṇḍala, Pune.

Dhavalikar, M.K., 1982: "Kīrtimukha", Proceedings of the Seminar on *Symbolism in Temple Art and Architecture*, Anantacharya Institute of Indology, Bombay 5.

Dhere, R.C., 1973: *Śaktipīthāñcā Śodha* (Marathi), Moghe Prakashan, Kolhapur.

Eggeling, J., 1988 (1963-1988, Indian; 1882-1890, Clarendon Press), *Śatapatha Brāhmana* (Eng. Tr.), SBE Vol.s 12, 26, 41, 43, 44, Motilal Banarasidass, Delhi 7.

Elied, Miercia, 1951: *Myth and Reality* (Eng.Tr.), New York
1990: *Images and Symbols*, excerpted in "Observing Sacred Time", *Parabola*, Vol.XV, No.11, Spring (Feb.)

Faraday, Anna (No.yr.): *The Dream Game*, Harper and Row, New York.

Flowers, Betty Sue (Ed.), 1988: *The Power of Myth*, New York, London.

Frazer, J.G., 1918: *Folk-lore in the Old Testament*, Vols.I-III, Macmillan & Co., London.

1957: The Golden Bough (Abridged, Vols. I-II) Macmillan & Co., London.

Fuchs, Stephen, 1978: "The Baiga Understanding of Ultimate Reality and Meaning", *Ultimate Reality and Meaning*, Vol.1, No.3, Toronto.

Geldner, K.F., 1978 (1951): *Der Rigveda*, Harward Oriental Series (HOS), Vol.I-III + Index, Cambridge, Massachusetts.

Glucksmann, Miriam, 1974: *Structural Analysis in Contemporary Thought*, Routledge and Kegan Paul, London, Boston.

Goldman, R.P., "Mortal Man and the Immortal Woman", Journal of the Oriental Institute, Baroda, Vol.XVIII, No.4.

Gomme, G.L., 1908: *Folklore as an Historical Science*, London.

Gonda, J., 1954: *Aspects of Early Viṣṇuism*, Utrecht.
1961: "Ascetics and Courtesans", *Adyar Library Bulletin*, Vol. XXV, No.s 1-4.

Green, Peter, 1991: *Alexander of Macedon*, University of California Press, Berkeley, Los Angeles, Oxford.

Hamilton, Edith, 1942: *Mythology*, Brown and Co., Boston.

Hanson, Allan, 1983: "Dynamic Forms in Maori Concept of Ultimate Reality", *Ultimate Reality and Meaning*, Vol.6, No.3, Toronto.

Held, G.J., 1935: *The Mahābhārata*, London, Amsterdam.

Jain, Jyotindra, 1985 (Jan.): "Painted Myths of Creation", *India Magazine*, Vol. No.2, Delhi.

Jaykar, Pupul, 1990 (1989): *The Earth Goddess*, Harper and Row, San Francisco.

Joshi, Moreshwar-Shastri T. 1979; *Marāthawādyātila Śakti-dārśana* Igatpurī;

Kane, P.V., 1968-1977 (1930-1957): *History of Dharmaśāstra*, Vol.s I-V, Bhandarkar Oriental Institute, Poona.

1926: *Vyavahāramayūkha of Nīlakhaṇṭha*, Nirnayasagar Press, Bombay.

Kersenboom-story, Saskia, 1987: *Nityasumangalī-Devadāsī Tradition in South India*, Motilal B., Delhi 7.

Keith, A.B., 1989 (1925): *The Religion and Philosophy of the Veda and Upanishads*, Vol.s I-II, Reprint, Motilal Banarsidass, Delhi 7

1981 (1920): *Rigveda Brāhmaṇas*, Motilal B., Delhi 7.

1967 (1914) The Veda of the Black Yajurvada, *Taittirīya Samhitā*, Motilal B., Delhi 7

Kirk, G.S., 1970: *Myth*—Its Meaning and Functions in Ancient and other Cultures, Cambridge University Press.

1976 (1973): *The Nature of Greek Myths*, Penguin, Harmondssworth.

Lang, A. 1913(1887): *Myth, Ritual and Religion*, Vol.I, Longman's Green & Company, London.

1884: *Custom and Myth,* Vol.I Longman's Green & Company, London.

Lévi-Strauss, Claude, 1969: *Structural Anthropology,* (Eng. Tr., Clair Jacobson), Penguin, London.

1966: *Mythlogiques,* Vol.II, Paris.

1980 (1978): *Myth and Meaning,* Routledge & Kegan Paul, London, Hanley.

Mackenzie, Donald, (No year): *Myths of Babylonia and Assyria;*

Myths of China and Japan;

Myths of Crete and Pre-Hellenic Europe;

Myths of Pre-Columbian America;

Egyptian Myth and Legend,

Grasham Publishing Company, London.

Macdonell, A.A. and Keith, A.B. (Hindi rendering by Ram Kumar Rai): 1966 (1912): *Vedic Index of Names and Subjects,* Chaukhamba, Varanasi. (*Vedic Index*).

Malinowski, Bronislaw, 1926: *Myth in Primitive Psychology,* Kagen Paul T.T. and Co., London.

Mani, Vettam, 1975: *Puranic Encyclopaedia,* Motilal Banarsidass, Delhi.

Max Müller, F., 1907: *Chips from a German Workshop,* Vol.II (I-IV), Longmans Green and Co., London, Bombay, Calcutta.

Murdock, J.P., 1957 (1934): *Our Primitive Contemporaries,* Macmillan and Co., New York.

Nakamura, Hazime, 1992 (1975): *A Comparative History of Ideas,* Motilal Banarsidass, Delhi 7

Néve, Félix, (1847: *Esai sur le Mythe des Ribhavas)*

1985: G.V. Davane, Eng.tr., *An Essay on the Myth of the Ṛbhus,* Ajanta Publications, Delhi 7.

O'Flaherty, Wendy D., 1982 (1975): *Hindu Myths,* Penguin, Harmondsworth etc.

1981: *Sexual Metaphors and Animal Symbols in Indian Mythology*, Motilal Banarsidass, Delhi 7.

Olcott, W.B., 1914: *Sun Lore of All Ages*, New York.

Parpola, Asko, 1992: "The Metamorphoses of Mahiṣa Asura and Prajāpati" in, *Ritual, State and History in South India* (Essays in Honour of J.C. Heesterman), Eds.A.W.Van Den Hock and others, E.J. Brill, Leiden.

Prichard, J.B., 1955 (Ed.): *Ancient Near Eastern Texts Relating to the Old Testament* (ANET), Princeton.

Rundle Clark, R.T., 1959: *Myth and Symbol in Ancient Egypt*, Thames and Hudson, London.

Seler, E., 1904: *Mexican and Central American Antiquities*, Washington.

Seidenberg, A. 1959: "The Separation of the Sky and the Earth at Creation", *Folk-lore*, Vol.70, London.

Simpson, G.E., 1980: "Ideas about Ultimate Reality and Meaning in Haitian Vodum", *Ultimate Reality and Meaning*, Vol.3, No.3, Toronto.

Shastri, A.M. 1969: *India as seen in the Bṛhatsaṁhitā of Varāhamihira*, Motilal Banarsidass, Delhi 7.

Shroeder, L.V., 1908: *Mysterium und Mimus im Rigveda*, Leipzig.

Suziki, David and Kundston, Peter, :*Wisom of the Elders*, Banton Books, New York.

Velankar, H.D., 1965: "Viśvāmitra and Vasiṣṭha in the Ṛgveda", *Dr. Mirashi Felicitation Volume*, Nagpur.

Web, Clement C.J., 1937 (1910): *History of Philosophy*. Thornton Butterworth Ltd., London.

Whitehead, Henry, 1970 (1920): *The Village Gods of South India*, Delhi.

Index

(Figures in the bracket indicate numbers in the notes)